I0198437

Terror Flyers

TERROR FLYERS

THE LYNCHING OF AMERICAN AIRMEN IN NAZI GERMANY

Kevin T Hall

Indiana University Press

This book is a publication of

Indiana University Press
Office of Scholarly Publishing
Herman B Wells Library 350
1320 East 10th Street
Bloomington, Indiana 47405 USA

iupress.indiana.edu

© 2021 by Kevin T Hall
All rights reserved

No part of this book may be reproduced or utilized in any form or by any means, electronic or mechanical, including photocopying and recording, or by any information storage and retrieval system, without permission in writing from the publisher.

The paper used in this publication meets the minimum requirements of the American National Standard for Information Sciences—Permanence of Paper for Printed Library Materials, ANSI Z39.48–1992.

Manufactured in the United States of America

Library of Congress
Cataloging-in-Publication Data

Names: Hall, Kevin T., author.
Title: Terror flyers : the lynching of American airmen in Nazi Germany / Kevin T. Hall.
Description: Bloomington, Indiana : Indiana University Press, [2021] | Includes bibliographical references and index.
Identifiers: LCCN 2020007459 (print) | LCCN 2020007460 (ebook) | ISBN 9780253050151 (hardback) | ISBN 9780253050175 (paperback) | ISBN 9780253050168 (ebook)
Subjects: LCSH: World War, 1939-1945—Prisoners and prisons, German. | World War, 1939-1945—Atrocities—Germany. | Lynching—Germany—History—20th century. | United States. Army Air Forces—Airmen. | World War, 1939-1945—Aerial operations, American. | World War, 1939-1945—Campaigns—Germany. | Civilians in war—Germany.
Classification: LCC D804.G3 H35 2021 (print) | LCC D804.G3 (ebook) | DDC 940.54/724308913—dc23
LC record available at https://lccn.loc.gov/2020007459
LC ebook record available at https://lccn.loc.gov/2020007460

1 2 3 4 5 26 25 24 23 22 21

To Elizabeth, Lyn, and Lena, for your endless love,
encouragement, and inspiration.

Contents

Figures

Tables

Acknowledgments

I am indebted to numerous World War II veterans and their families, historians, archivists, journalists, and various institutions in the United States, Great Britain, and Germany, who offered generous support, advice, and encouragement for this book. I would like to express my deepest gratitude to Eric A. Johnson for his invaluable guidance, insight, and assistance throughout my academic career. I am extremely grateful to Lane Demas, Jörg Nagler, Paul Schulten, Gerhard L. Weinberg, and Richard F. Wetzell, who read the manuscript with great care and offered constructive suggestions and advice. I would like to thank Sean Scally and Felix Zuber, who reviewed several versions of the manuscript and were always willing to discuss key aspects. Finally, I would like to thank my family for their endless support.

Abbreviations

AA	Auswärtiges Amt; Foreign Ministry
Alte Kämpfer	lit., "old fighter"; refers to the members of the Nazi Party who joined before 1930
Auswertestelle West	Evaluation Center West
BDM	Bund Deutscher Mädel; League of German Girls
BdS	Befehlshaber der Sicherheitspolizei und des SD
Blockleiter	block leader (Nazi Party political rank)
DAF	Deutsche Arbeitsfront; German Labor Front
DPAA	Defense Prisoner of War/Missing in Action Accounting Agency
DPMO	US Department of Defense Department's Prisoner of War Missing Personnel Office
Dulag Luft	Durchgangslager der Luftwaffe; Transit Camp for Air Force Personnel
E&E Reports	Escape and Evasion Reports
Einsatzgruppen	lit., "task forces"; SS paramilitary groups responsible for mass killings
Gauleiter	regional leader (Nazi Party political rank)
Gestapo	Geheime Staatspolizei; Secret State Police
HJ	Hitlerjugend; Hitler Youth
IMT	International Military Tribunal
JAG Corps	Judge Advocate General's Corps
Jagdkommandos	Search and Pursuit Units
J-PAC	Joint POW/MIA Account Command

KdS	Kommandeure der Sicherheitspolizei und des SD
KIA	killed in action
Kindermörder	child murderers
Kreisleiter	county leader (Nazi Party political rank)
KriPo	Kriminalpolizei; Criminal Police
Landwacht	Rural Police
Luftwaffe	German Air Force
Lynchjustiz	Lynch Justice
MACR	Missing Air Crew Reports
Maquis	French Resistance
MIA	missing in action
Milice	Vichy French collaborators
MIS-X	Military Intelligence Service
Mitläuferfabrik	lit., "factory to produce followers"
NSDAP	Nationalsozialistische Deutsche Arbeitspartei; National Socialist German Workers' Party (Nazi Party)
NSKK	Nationalsozialistisches Kraftfahrkorps; National Socialist Motor Corps
NWCO	National War Crimes Office
OKL	Oberkommando der Luftwaffe; High Command of the Air Force
OKW	Oberkommando der Wehrmacht; High Command of the Armed Forces
OrPo	Ordnungspolizei; Order Police
Ortsgruppenleiter	group leader (Nazi Party political rank)
OSS	Office of Strategic Services
POW	prisoner of war

RAD	Reichsarbeitsdienst; Reich Labor Force
RAF	Royal Air Force
RSHA	Reichssicherheitshauptamt; Reich Main Security Office
SA	Sturmabteilungen; Storm Troopers
SD	Sicherheitsdienst; Security Service (of the SS)
Selbstjustiz	self-justice
SHAEF	Supreme Headquarters Allied Expedition Force
SiPo	Sicherheitspolizei; Security Police
SOE	Special Operations Executive
Sonderbehandlung	lit., "special treatment"; euphemism for mass murder used by Nazi functionaries and the SS
Sonderkommando	Special Unit of the SS
SS	Schutzstaffeln; lit., "protection squadron"
Stalag Luft	Stammlager der Luftwaffe; Prisoner of War Camp for Air Force Personnel
Terrorflieger	lit., "terror flyer" (also called: *Luftgangster* [gangsters of the sky] and *Kindermörder* [child murderers])
USAAF	United States Army Air Forces
Vergeltungswaffen	lit., "revenge weapons"
Volksgemeinschaft	lit., "people's community"
Volksjustiz	peoples' justice
Volkssturm	home guard
WCIT	War Crime Investigation Teams
Wehrkreis	military district

Terror Flyers

INTRODUCTION

Returning from a bombing mission over northern Germany on August 6, 1944, an American bomber crew bailed out over German territory after flak disabled their aircraft. Likely their first jump out of an airplane, the flyers were full of adrenaline and anxiety about the fate that awaited them. One flyer, believed to be Staff Sergeant Jack S. Patrick, landed safely in a field next to a highway near Lübeck-Siems, fourteen miles from the Baltic Sea, and German soldiers immediately captured him.[1] In addition to landing safely, being in the custody of soldiers must have contributed to an initial sense of relief, since rumors among airmen described German security forces, party officials, and especially civilians as being very hostile. Downed flyers who evaded capture and returned to England with the aid of resistance fighters, as well as prisoners of war (POWs) who had returned through medical exchanges, all bolstered these rumors with personal accounts of seeing flyers hanged from lampposts in bombed-out cities or from beams at train stations.[2]

Yet as the soldiers escorted the flyer along the highway toward the city of Lübeck, his sense of relief quickly turned to fear. Incensed by the aerial attacks, an angry mob (made up of several civilians, two SS soldiers, and the local *Blockleiter*) encircled him. Blockleiter Gotthard Parzyk, a low-level Nazi Party official responsible for neighborhood supervision, told the two soldiers guarding the flyer to "leave him to us so that we can have some sport with him."[3] After officials questioned Patrick about his nationality, the mob (including women) beat him mercilessly with farm tools, steel helmets, and anything they had at hand. The terrified flyer bled profusely as they ruthlessly directed blows at his head. The injuries quickly took their toll on him, and he collapsed from the pain and shock; however, the crowd did not stop even after they rendered him unconscious. They beat him until his face was unrecognizable and then dragged his lifeless body into a nearby cornfield, where members of the mob took turns shooting him. The perpetrators then threw his body in the trunk of a nearby vehicle and buried his remains in an unmarked grave. While the remaining crewmembers also received rough treatment, they survived their encounters with the German population and were eventually sent to a POW camp where they remained for the duration of the war.

A US postwar crime tribunal at Dachau tried twelve of the perpetrators in March and April 1947 for willfully, deliberately, and wrongfully encouraging and abetting in the killing of Patrick. Five civilians (Hans Ohrt, Willi Voight, Friedrich Lehmensick, Karl Neeb, and Hertha Stapelfeldt) and one SS soldier (Paul Doose) received sentences ranging from one to ten years; however, the Federal Republic of Germany released them all by 1952. Parzyk received a death sentence while two civilians (Otto Giese and Richard Hammer) and an SS soldier (Ernst Hachmeier) received life imprisonment, yet each of these men was paroled by the spring of 1954.[4]

On the same day as the incident in Lübeck, a B-17 crew parachuted from their damaged aircraft after flak knocked out several engines. They landed near Köthen—roughly forty miles northwest of Leipzig—and faced a similar mob of civilians, who were armed with "ropes, guns, pitchforks, [and] clubs. . . . [They] started knocking the crew around, and placed a rope in a tree, nearby, making preparations to lynch us," according to pilot First Lieutenant Jay J. Hatfield. Yet before they could be hanged, members of a flak battery arrived and prevented any further mistreatment. All but one of the airmen were eventually treated for their wounds and sent to a POW camp where they managed to survive the war; however, bombardier Second Lieutenant Edward Reichel was not so fortunate. He was allegedly denied medical treatment because he was Jewish, which resulted in his death.[5]

Such stories, though brutal and largely forgotten in popular memory, were not unique. From 1943 to 1945, instances of mob mentality, where German citizens sought revenge for personal and material losses, were abundant throughout Nazi Germany and its occupied territories, but the mistreatment of downed American airmen, identified as *Lynchjustiz* (lynch justice) by the Nazi regime, was most prominent in Nazi Germany.[6] While historians have focused mainly on a few cases involving the violence committed against airmen during World War II, the topic remains largely overlooked and the actual extent of the mistreatment is greatly underestimated.

The most infamous act of violence committed against American airmen in Germany occurred in Rüsselsheim on August 26, 1944, when German civilians and political officials ruthlessly beat eight airmen, six of whom were executed and two of whom managed to escape.[7] Known as the Rüsselsheim massacre, this event is most familiar because it was the first US postwar crime trial. In addition to setting a model for sentencing perpetrators in the proceeding trials, the prosecutors graphically depicted the brutality and hostility American flyers faced when confronted by German citizens. This quickly captivated media attention in the United States and throughout the world. The horror of violence against the young American flyers was shocking, especially to the family members, as newspaper articles released the names of the murdered airmen before the US War Department had notified their next of kin.[8]

According to military historian James J. Weingartner, "from the summer of 1943 until the end of the war, over 200 (and perhaps many more) downed American and British airmen may have been murdered by German civilians, military personnel, or police and party officials."[9] German historian Jörg Friedrich claimed that in the last year of the war alone "more than one hundred pilots were lynched."[10] However, historian Barbara Grimm's suggestion, based on German historian Ralf Blank's analysis, that roughly 350 downed Allied airmen experienced Lynchjustiz in Germany has become the standard used by historians.[11] Yet no significant research has verified or refuted this supposition. Despite using little archival evidence to support Blank and Grimm's claims, historians have repeatedly cited these estimates. While scholars have indicated the need to know more about the extent to which airmen were mistreated in Germany, none have attempted that assessment until now.[12]

Building on the lack of research on the topic, Austrian historian Georg Hoffmann is the latest to study the mistreatment of airmen during World War II, specifically American flyers shot down in Austria and Hungary. Hoffmann concluded that throughout Europe there were roughly 1,000 cases of Lynchjustiz (including both murders and assaults) committed against American airmen.[13] In fact, he determined that even more cases of mistreatment occurred in Austria and Hungary than in Germany (roughly 600, of which 130 resulted in death).[14] However, like previous historians, Hoffmann assumed that the historiographical standard of 350 cases was accurate. Despite this, his study is an improved attempt at analyzing these incidents. While the precise number of flyers who experienced Lynchjustiz is impossible to determine due to a lack of documentation, the need for a more accurate estimate, as well as a fuller historical analysis of the broader impact of these events on history, is apparent.

In determining the extent of popular violence committed against airmen, Hoffmann is the first to include the mistreated victims who survived. Furthermore, he is the first to analyze the perpetrators who carried out these acts of violence. Their backgrounds and social positions are key to understanding not only the phenomenon's origins but also how it persisted. Scholars have not attempted, however, to determine the extent of violence in Germany specifically or address the symbolic meaning and appropriateness of the term *lynching*, which was used heavily in the Nazi regime's propaganda. In fact, the majority of Lynchjustiz cases occurred in Germany not only because the largest number of airmen were shot down over German territory but also because propaganda and personal experiences with bombing and strafing raids greatly influenced the hostility of its populace. In addition, airmen shot down in Germany lacked aid and escape routes.[15]

Not simply a singularity within the pre–World War II boundaries of Germany, authorized mistreatment of downed airmen occurred throughout Europe, ranging from Italy to Denmark, France to Yugoslavia, and everywhere in between. A common feature of the mistreatment of downed airmen throughout Europe was the involvement of civilians, especially those who had repeatedly been exposed to aerial bombing attacks. Even downed German airmen faced the possibility of mistreatment. According to British historian Clive Emsley, "At least two British officers . . . were found guilty by courts martial and dismissed for assaulting captured German aircrew shot down over the south of England in 1940 and 1941."[16] However, there was a relatively limited number of downed German airmen in Britain and British officials did not condone the mistreatment of POWs—unlike the Nazi regime throughout occupied Europe. These two factors, therefore, resulted in a very low probability that Germans would be mistreated.

An additional aspect that historians have overlooked involves cases of downed airmen receiving *Sonderbehandlung*, the regime's euphemism for execution. In order to justify otherwise unlawful behavior, German officials often branded downed airmen as *Terrorflieger* (terror flyers), a classification that indicated the flyers allegedly fired at noncombat targets (primarily civilians) or were caught attempting to evade capture and were, therefore, considered spies or sabotage troops who could be executed with impunity. While bomber crews did target industrial and urban areas on a regular basis, the extent to which fighter pilots strafed trains, vehicles, and other targets of opportunity remains unknown. According to a Luftwaffe interrogation report, First Lieutenant James H. Weisel (who was shot down on May 21, 1944, near Bremen during a strafing mission) stated that such "'black sheep,' who strafed civilians and non-military targets, existed in every unit."[17]

Allied fighter aircraft equipped with cameras captured images during their attacks on targets, which military officials used to analyze the success of tactics and missions. However, if the airmen were shot down with their cameras and film intact, Luftwaffe and Gestapo officials (often interrogators and intelligence officers) could use this documentation to condemn enemy airmen as terrorists.[18] This could result in immediate death or imprisonment, torture, and subsequent internment in a concentration camp. For example, German officials sent nearly two hundred Allied airmen to Buchenwald in one transport alone from Fresnes Prison (located south of Paris, France) in September 1944. Within days, German officials attempted to send another group of Allied airmen from Saint Giles Prison in Brussels to an unidentified concentration camp in Germany. Belgian resistance fighters saved the flyers, however, along with the other political prisoners, by disabling the train. While the extent that other downed flyers were mistreated in a similar way remains uncertain, the dark figure of unknown cases is certainly substantial and calls into question the extent to which downed airmen were mistreated.

The 179 postwar crime trials analyzed in the following study identified 310 American airmen who were subjected to Lynchjustiz in Nazi Germany, of whom 220 were murdered. If the historiography is accurate in the fact that a similar number of British war crime trials investigated the mistreatment of a comparable number of downed British airmen, the occurrences of Lynchjustiz against downed British and American airmen in Germany conservatively exceeded 600.[19] However, the American and British war crime trials that investigated Lynchjustiz focused largely on the occupied areas of West Germany.

Accounting for the dark figure, along with the instances of Lynchjustiz that occurred in what became East Germany, it is likely that there were at least one thousand cases of Lynchjustiz committed against Allied airmen within Germany's postwar borders. However, hundreds of cases remain overlooked, especially those in Italy, France, Belgium, Luxembourg, the Netherlands, Denmark, Norway, and Poland. Preliminary research on violence against American airmen in the aforementioned nations concludes that Lynchjustiz occurred most often in France, Belgium, and the Netherlands. This is likely due to the increased number of airmen shot downed over these countries, the presence of German military and security forces, ardent collaborators, and civilians affected by the radicalized air war (tens of thousands of pro-Allied civilians died in bombings during the war). Taking into consideration Lynchjustiz committed against all Allied airmen throughout Germany and its occupied territory in World War II, three thousand cases of mistreatment is thus a conservative assessment.

Hoffmann's study on Lynchjustiz committed against American airmen in Austria and Hungary during World War II, thus far the most in-depth analysis, is a great help for this study of violence against American airmen in Germany. There are, however, divergences in our conclusions (possibly due to the different circumstances in each country during the war): for example, the perpetrators' roles as well as how the process of Lynchjustiz occurred. Hoffmann states that "*Lynchjustiz*, at its core, was not a result of a spontaneous act of violence in retaliation by the population for the air war; rather, the violence was a result of a corresponding initiation, control, and guidance by the Nazi regime."[20] However, this fails to consider spontaneous responses, most often exhibited by German civilians. The preliminary investigation into Lynchjustiz by German historian Klaus-Michael Mallmann is more indicative of violence against airmen in Germany and coincides with the results of the following study. Mallmann states: "*Lynchjustiz* culminated in a collective rampage. . . . It was a crime far outside the context of obedience to orders, in which hardly any individual can be distinguished incapable of self-determination. *Lynchjustiz* in the Third Reich cannot be considered as simply ordered from 'above.' Analogous to the extermination of the European Jews, this did not require central orders; the portrayal of the enemy and the invitation to participate in the murderous acts sufficed to trigger the catastrophe."[21]

Analysis of the violence perpetrated against American flyers in Germany has indicated that Lynchjustiz was approved by the Nazi regime, which used propaganda to incite the German population to partake in committing brutal atrocities against downed airmen. The regime withheld military and police protection for the flyers and threatened German citizens with severe punishment if they aided enemy flyers. In numerous instances, perpetrators denied airmen POW status or alleged that airmen attempted to escape in order to "justify" shooting them.

Various reasons caused each perpetrating group (civilians, police, security forces, party officials, military personnel, and state officials) to carry out Lynchjustiz. Civilians usually sought revenge for the losses they had experienced in the war, and their actions largely occurred in a group setting. According to trial data analyzed in this study, they were involved in 39 percent of the Lynchjustiz cases and were the overwhelming majority that took part in assaults, representing nearly 70 percent of perpetrators in such cases. Similarly, military personnel often took part because of war experiences but also out of camaraderie; however, they were least likely to participate in Lynchjustiz. Party officials, police, and security forces eagerly took part, allegedly as a way to protect the home front in a war that exceedingly blurred boundaries, as cities and ultimately the residents became targets in the air war. These three groups combined to participate in over 55 percent of all instances of Lynchjustiz that resulted in the death of an airman.[22] However, the significant role of civilians involved in killing downed American airmen (nearly 30 percent) should not be underestimated. The postwar trials sought to target predominantly Nazi officials, and a large number of perpetrators (especially civilians) went unpunished. For example, numerous cases revealed that alleged perpetrators were unable to be found or were believed to have fled to the eastern zone of occupation. Therefore, future research may reveal that civilians played an even larger role in Lynchjustiz than this study indicates.

Despite these facts, the Nazi regime did not initiate Lynchjustiz; rather, the violence was an initial response by the German public to avenge the devastation caused by the air war. It also signaled Germans' discontent regarding the Nazi regime's inability to deal with the burgeoning air war, as well as its inability to impede Allied advancement and fulfill its promises of success and retaliation. As could be expected, the regime's support and promotion of such violence greatly increased individuals' participation. As Hermann Göring affirmed in an interview with an American psychologist during the Nuremberg trials, "Naturally, the common people do not want war . . . but the people can always be brought to the bidding of the leaders. That is easy. All you have to do is tell them they are being attacked and denounce the pacifists for lack of patriotism and exposing the country to danger."[23] The fact that Germany experienced devastating bombing raids increased the likelihood of the regime garnering more support from the populace. As a common effect of aerial warfare, this was also exhibited in the bombing of Guernica in 1937, the bombing of Britain beginning in 1940, and in the numerous wars that followed World War II. While the Allied bombing effort expedited the defeat of the Nazis, it also helped facilitate Lynchjustiz. As Georg Hoffmann correctly asserted, "Nazi functionaries used *Lynchjustiz* as a method to counter the results of the air war, to strengthen society in the wake of the devastation, and finally to demonstrate and support the Nazi functionaries' own claim to power."[24] However, any notion that Lynchjustiz would not have happened if the regime did not condone and promote this violence is inaccurate. Roughly a year after the first known Lynchjustiz cases occurred (during the summer of 1943), the Nazis took advantage of the situation and attempted to harness the outrage of the German population by redirecting the anger explicitly toward downed airmen.

For the nations involved in World War II, previous war experiences uniquely influenced their boundaries of moral acceptability as well as physical and psychological possibility. World War I, for example, remained a constant reference point for military strategists, soldiers, and civilians. Members of the Nazi leadership, most of whom had personally experienced World War I, believed that the moral collapse of the home front—also known as the "stab in the back" myth—was the main cause for losing the Great War. Thus, they concluded that the home front would be the weakest and most vulnerable aspect of a future war. Similarly, beginning in the interwar period, American and British military strategists reasoned that air power would be the key element to winning future wars, as the new technology allowed for an even greater disruption of the home front—a radical expansion of the traditional blockade—and could hopefully prevent the heavy losses experienced in World War I.[25]

While the air war has become a significant characteristic of World War II being the foremost example of total war, aerial attacks on civilian populations were hardly new at the time.[26] Cities—and therefore civilian populations—were bombed from the air during World War I; for example, historian Christian Geinitz determined that some 740 Germans, almost all of them civilians, were killed in aerial bombing attacks.[27] Nevertheless, the degree of devastation in World War II, fostered by advancing technology and an increased intent to use the means to achieve the ends, was unparalleled.

Although noncombatants have historically been involved both directly and indirectly in wars, the division between civilians and soldiers emerged in popular understanding during World War I and "came to define twentieth-century warfare," according to historian Tammy Proctor.[28] While the term *civilian* has evolved to mean "a person protected from war or an innocent victim of war," Proctor demonstrates that the term also "assumes a particularly strong feminine connotation as it becomes a sort of shorthand for the phrase 'innocent women and children.'"[29] During World War II, this was of particular importance for Nazi propaganda, which argued that German women and children were being targeted by Allied air raids. While propaganda insisted that civilians were illegitimate targets, it "failed miserably in accurately capturing the multiple identities and experiences . . . that both soldiers and civilians (of both sexes) faced" in this total war.[30] The home front served as a vital counterpart to the battlefront, as soldiers needed a reason to fight and civilians supported the war effort by producing essential supplies. Thus, the German government closely monitored and controlled both fronts in a conflict that changed the dimensions and understandings of total warfare.

While the 1907 Hague Conventions prohibited the bombing of noncombatants, it did not prohibit the indiscriminate bombing of noncombatants in defended places.[31] At the start of World War II in 1939, the major European powers, including both Germany and Great Britain, agreed, at the request of US president Franklin Delano Roosevelt, not to bomb civilian targets. The bombing of cities far from the front during World War I, which was introduced by Germany (with Zeppelins and Gotha bombers), as well as Germany's participation in the bombing of Guernica in 1937 during the Spanish Civil War, significantly influenced national leaders. The Allies attempted to prevent Germany from repeating these efforts, but to no avail. Germany initiated World War II with the bombing of Wieluń, Poland, on the morning of September 1, 1939. Initially, the British began their air war against Germany by dropping leaflets, in an attempt to avoid civilian casualties; however, Germany's control spread throughout Europe due, in part, to its aerial warfare—for example, its attacks on Warsaw and Rotterdam in May 1940, the Blitz on London and the bombing of Coventry during 1940 and 1941, and the attacks on countless cities throughout the Soviet Union. Eventually, in 1944 and 1945, Germany used *Vergeltungswaffen* (V1 and V2 rockets) to attack cities, including London. Despite the earnest attempt by major western Allies to avoid civilian casualties at the outbreak of World War II, nations quickly ignored the agreement.

Despite Great Britain quickly responding in 1940, Allied bombing remained relatively limited at first. The first aerial attack on a German city during World War II came on May 10, 1940, when Freiburg was bombed on the same day the Wehrmacht invaded France. Ironically, it was the Luftwaffe, however, that dropped the bombs on their own city by mistake. Despite German authorities knowing this, they immediately blamed the Allies. In *Berlin Diary*, William L. Shirer noted in his entry on May 10: "Tonight the Germans claimed three Allied planes dropped bombs in the middle of Freiburg, killing twenty-four civilians. As a taste of what this phase of the war is going to be like, a German communique tonight says that 'from now on, every enemy bombing of German civilians will be answered by five times as many German planes bombing English and French cities.'"[32] Coincidentally, on the same day of the Freiburg bombing, Winston Churchill became prime minister of the United Kingdom. Hitler was quick to exploit the coincidence in dates. In a speech delivered on December 10, 1940, Hitler accused Churchill of commencing the bombing of German cities by attacking the civilian population of Freiburg on the very day he came to power.[33] Throughout the war, the Third Reich continually used Freiburg as proof of Allied aerial terrorism. For example, in 1943 the German Foreign Ministry issued a book entitled *Documents on England's Sole Guilt for the Bombing War against the Civilian Population*—which started with the bombing of Freiburg—in an attempt to garner international public opinion, especially among the neutral countries.[34]

The technological standards of the time and adverse weather conditions hindered the accuracy of aerial bombing and resulted in only one aircraft in five dropping its bombs within five miles of the designated target in late 1941. This was according to the Butt Report, which was a British assessment of the effectiveness of the British Royal Air Force (RAF).[35] With the United States joining the fight against Nazi Germany in 1942, the Allies focused on bombing strategic targets, primarily Germany's infrastructure, war economy, military sites (such as air bases), and even the civilian population itself. For the most part, these targets were deep in enemy territory, and aircrews shot down during such missions usually landed far from Allied lines, leaving them far more exposed to the wrath of the German population once they were on the ground.

Despite the well-known Norden bombsight used by the USAAF, which greatly increased the accuracy of aerial attacks, bombing nevertheless targeted cities and led to unwanted destruction and death, as strategic objectives were so closely related to urban and public areas. It remained difficult, if not impossible, to identify boundaries between the combat zone and the home front (and thus between combatants and noncombatants) because civilians played an indispensable role in the mobilization of society. Civilians, for example, supplied soldiers with weapons and other essential materials and provided a moral backing for the soldiers fighting at the front. The Allied nations accepted civilian deaths as a part of the process to prohibit the Nazi regime's attack on global safety. However, unlike the Nazi regime, the Allied nations never contemplated the explicit extermination of the enemy during the war. While the Allies generally rationalized the air war and its drastic effects as part of their moral duty to impede and destroy the growing threat to world order and humanity, the accuracy and efficacy remained less than favorable throughout the war and is still highly debated by scholars.[36]

Germany's devastating loss at Stalingrad in February 1942, its defeat in North Africa in May 1943, and the Allied invasion of Italy and France were turning points in the war—both strategically and psychologically—and facilitated the Allied advance across Europe. Not until the Casablanca Conference in 1943, however, was Hitler's uncompromising will to wage war met by the Allies' unequivocal response to seek victory at all costs with the Combined Bomber Offensive,[37] which targeted Germany's economic and industrial capability to wage war around-the-clock. Moreover, the failed attempt to assassinate Hitler on July 20, 1944, changed Hitler's attitude with regard to imposing total war. While Joseph Goebbels had promoted mobilizing German society for total war since 1942, Hitler and many others had avoided this; they feared that this would result in a collapse of the home front—as had occurred in World War I—and that this would result in not only Germany losing the war but also the destruction of the Aryan race. Nazi leadership imbued an even more radical sense of purpose following the attempt on Hitler's life. Goebbels was appointed plenipotentiary for total war measures, which resulted in the increased control over the German population to support the war effort. Increased responsibility for the defense of Germany fell to the various *Gauleiter* (regional Nazi Party leaders), who were, for example, involved in expressing the regime's desire to lynch downed enemy airmen. Yet despite the regime's attempt to keep the *Volksgemeinschaft* under control, it was never capable of exerting total control, as Jürgen Förster clarified.[38] The final step in mobilizing German society for total war was the establishment of the *Volkssturm* in September 1944. This fully incorporated the remainder of civilians (mostly young boys, old men, and women) in the war effort. By the summer of 1944, the Allies agreed that they needed to change not only the German government but also the attitude and outlook of the German people. City bombing was, therefore, viewed as a possible tactic to persuade Germans to stop fighting and setting the world on fire—a lesson, according to Allied leaders, they had not learned from World War I.

The lynching of American airmen reveals an overlooked aspect of this total war: namely, the explicit involvement and culpability of the German home front—whether security forces or soldiers, party officials or civilians, men or women—in committing violence against POWs. Given certain situational circumstances—for example, an environment of total war where violence was sanctioned by the regime and a society was in a perceived fight for survival—the German public tolerated and participated in the killing of downed aircrews. As historian Hew Strachan reasoned, perpetrators may need to be instructed by the state "to get over their initial revulsion, and they may still need the state's authority to rationalize their actions to themselves, but in the immediacy of killing other more basic impulses—including sadism—can come into play."[39] Given the intensity and totality of the war, especially in the final year, Lynchjustiz "could result as easily from a sense of panic and crisis as from any sense of collective cohesion," as historian Nicholas Stargardt clarified.[40]

Lynchjustiz blurred the parameters of war, representing an activity waged for (and in the name of) the regime out of political and strategic purposes as well as an endorsed, individual act of personal revenge by the German public. Downed American airmen offered the German home front—specifically civilians—an opportunity to actively confront the enemy, who they considered responsible for the air war. As the bombing raids increasingly disrupted the way of life for the German home front, it made the war more personal for the German public and it resulted in the possibility of more extreme reactions.[41] While this was a logical response in the minds of many individuals affected by the war, this violence "did not require Nazified zealots (though surely such were not lacking), [but] merely conscientious and politically obtuse soldiers [and civilians] to carry out the reprisals," as historian Jürgen Förster confirmed.[42] The bombing of cities inflicted great turmoil on all individuals, especially civilians, during the war, and wreaked angst, devastation, and death. Struggle for national survival and the desire to prevent the heavy losses of World War I provided the emotional foundation for the radicalization of war, which led to relaxed ethical limitations on violence.

This study of Lynchjustiz committed against downed American airmen relies heavily on the war crime records from the Dachau trials, which detailed how the events involving the lynching of airmen transpired, including witness and perpetrator testimonies and crucial profiles of the criminals. In addition, a sampling from the thousands of Escape and Evasion Reports (located with the postwar crime trial records at the National Archives and Records Administration in College Park, Maryland), particularly reports from airmen shot down in Germany, yield the experiences of airmen and feature descriptions of their interactions with civilians in their own words. Because the reports were written immediately upon the airmen's return to England, US military officials could pass on the up-to-date successful tactics that airmen described in these lengthy reports (some up to eight pages long) to aid airmen in the event they were shot down. Moreover, several rich images capturing the moment German citizens apprehended American airmen also exist and are included in this study. Beyond one small German village's publications recounting local experiences in World War II, these images are unknown and have rarely been published before, especially in the United States. Finally, satirical Nazi propaganda that vividly portrayed American flyers is another essential source for this study. For example, *Kladderadatsch* magazine, archived at the University of Heidelberg, offers unique, previously unpublished material to analyze how the Nazi regime portrayed American airmen to the German populace.

The main difficulty in analyzing Lynchjustiz is the lack of records that survived the war. While numerous copies of reports documenting lynchings were sent to several German government and military departments (such as the German Foreign Ministry, Luftwaffe, and Propaganda Ministry, as well as the RSHA and its subordinates), these documents, allegedly destroyed at the end of the war to cover up the atrocities, are nowhere to be found in German, American, or British archives. The lack of documents greatly hinders the ability to judge the dimensions of violence; nonetheless, postwar trial documents from over three hundred instances of Lynchjustiz committed against American airmen exist and indicate that the violence was unrestrained and widespread and involved all levels of society.

It is vital to understand how the violence committed against downed flyers occurred, as well as why German citizens reverted to such severe methods, as numerous cases involving the death of airmen remain unsolved. In fact, airmen's remains are still being uncovered today in

Germany and throughout the world.[43] Thus, this study incorporates Lynchjustiz within the broader milieu of the Nazi regime's war of atrocities as well as within the larger context of the air war and demonstrates that although the violence against airmen represented a minority of flyers—roughly one out of ten downed airmen were mistreated—it occurred far more often than previously acknowledged.

Chapter 1 assesses the various incidents downed American airmen faced. Examples include personal accounts of escape and evasion that detail the heroism of airmen (and their helpers), as they confronted daily dangers in their attempt to reach Allied lines. Depending on their location and the phase of the war, flyers were on the run for up to several months, often traveling over hundreds of miles. This chapter also investigates Nazi officials subjecting flyers to Sonderbehandlung. The best-known instance is the 168 Allied airmen sent to Buchenwald concentration camp in September 1944. Originally held as alleged spies in Fresnes Prison before they were sent to Buchenwald, these airmen experienced severe mistreatment. However, this was not the only instance of flyers experiencing Sonderbehandlung. Lastly, escape and evasion reports indicated that a few flyers received positive treatment from Germans, which is a significant occurrence that historians have also overlooked. Examples include German citizens treating airmen's wounds, giving them food and shelter, and even protecting them from lynch mobs. However, the motive behind these positive actions remains questioned, as these instances often occurred in the final months of the war when Allied troops were rapidly advancing through Germany and many Germans sought to avoid confrontations.

Chapter 2 analyzes the theme of Lynchjustiz in Nazi propaganda. The historiography of lynching suggests that the historical context of the United States was the primary source of inspiration for its use throughout the world.[44] The history of lynching in the United States offered the Nazi regime a unique opportunity to discredit America, particularly in describing the hypocrisy of lynching African Americans while at the same time promoting American democracy throughout the world. Nevertheless, the Nazis never denounced popular violence. Their propaganda used imagery to connect the concept of lynching with American flyers in an attempt to influence and escalate German citizens' response to the Allied air war.

Chapter 3 examines the history and escalation of Lynchjustiz in Germany. Given Nazi Germany's history of drawing on the US tradition and history of legalized and scientific racism—as demonstrated, for example, by legal historian James Q. Whitman's and German historian Stefan Kühl's respective studies—Lynchjustiz offered Nazi officials a way to fight Americans using "American justice."[45] In addition to describing the regime's pursuit to deny airmen POW status (and therefore disregard the legally required treatment), the determining factors of airmen being labeled Terrorflieger and the drastic consequences this had for them will be detailed. Furthermore, this violence revealed the desperation of the Nazis, and even the German public, due to the government's inability to counter or impede the devastation caused by the air war. Influenced by German civilians' spontaneous violence against downed enemy flyers, known to begin in the summer of 1943, the regime used the perilous situation to its advantage, condoning, promoting, and even ordering the mistreatment of downed airmen.[46]

Chapter 4 surveys the Lynchjustiz crimes, using the flyer trials as a guide for explanation and interpretation.[47] These proceedings were part of the Dachau trials, which the United States convened from 1945 to 1948. While these trials surely do not represent every instance of Lynchjustiz against American airmen, they offer a foundation for clarification. The trials focused mainly on convicting long-standing members of the Nazi Party—especially *Alte Kämpfer*—and, as a result, failed to bring countless perpetrators to justice. The analysis of these trials nevertheless allows for a better understanding of the extent of violence downed airmen experienced in Germany and throughout Europe. Furthermore, the results permit an increased awareness of the social milieu in Nazi Germany as well as an evaluation of the perpetrators involved in these horrific crimes.

Chapter 5 supplements the statistical analysis of the flyer trials by providing personalized narratives of twelve Lynchjustiz cases. The narratives are based on testimonies by witnesses, perpetrators, and occasionally even victims. Where possible, they are supported with Missing Air Crew Reports (MACRs), which often included accounts by other airmen who witnessed the circumstances surrounding the downing of their comrades. Moreover, photographs of victims and perpetrators are provided in an attempt to further the understanding of Lynchjustiz by illustrating the events that occurred and the individuals involved.

The final chapter addresses the rationalization of perpetrators who carried out Lynchjustiz. The methodology of various psychological studies from the 1960s and 1970s on perpetrators of the Holocaust—for example, psychologist Stanley Milgram's obedience studies and psychologist Philip Zimbardo's Stanford Prison Experiment on the psychological perception of power—is placed within the context of Lynchjustiz and used to analyze perpetrators' self-characterizations and their justifications specified at the war crime trials.[48] Three significant outside influences and motivations were the main defenses for perpetrators: obedience, endorsement by the regime, and the radicalization of war. While each of these stimuli could individually result in the mistreatment of American flyers, the combination of several, or even all, motives was often a factor in Lynchjustiz, which potentiated each other and increased the probability of German citizens killing airmen.

This study concludes that Lynchjustiz initially occurred as a spontaneous response to the devastation caused in a context of total war, with known cases beginning in the summer of 1943. The air war, compelled by the radicalization of Nazi atrocities, removed any form of security on the German home front. By the following summer, of 1944, the Nazi regime took advantage of German citizens' plight in enduring the overwhelming and ever more lethal air war that erased all physical and psychological boundaries. As a new element of total war, the regime sought to harness the outrage of the German population by condoning and permitting Lynchjustiz. This is best exemplified by Heinrich Himmler's order in August 1943 that the German police should not prevent the mistreatment of downed airmen by German civilians and Joseph Goebbels's May 1944 article in the *Völkischer Beobachter*, which publicly validated Lynchjustiz.[49] Moreover, a few days after Goebbels's article was published, Martin Bormann sent a secret circular to high-ranking Nazi Party officials—e.g., Gauleiter and *Kreisleiter*—that indicated German citizens would not be held legally accountable by the regime for their involvement in committing Lynchjustiz against downed airmen.[50] Representing a further attribute of this total war, the goal of the Nazi regime was to direct the angst and rage of the German public explicitly against the new enemy in their midst.

Notes

1. Analysis of trial records (Case No. 12-1307), witness statements, MACR reports, and captured German documents indicates that the identity of the flyer in this case is most likely Staff Sergeant Jack S. Patrick.

2. Review and Recommendations for Case No. 12-2370, Deputy Theater Judge Advocate's Office, War Crimes Branch, January 16, 1946, Records of the Office of the Judge Advocate General (Army), RG 153, Entry 143, Box 419,

National Archives at College Park, College Park, MD (here after NARA); See also: Case No. 12-1994, Deputy Theater Judge Advocate's Office, War Crimes Branch, RG 153, Entry 143, Box 403, NARA; Case No. 12-840, Deputy Theater Judge Advocate's Office, War Crimes Branch, RG 153, Entry 143, Box 324, NARA; Case No. 12-404, Deputy Theater Judge Advocate's Office, War Crimes Branch, RG 153, Entry 143, Box 264, NARA; "Citizens Menaced Hamburg Bombers," *New York Times*, October 22, 1943; "Germany Admits Fliers' Lynchings," *New York Times*, June 1, 1944.

3. Review and Recommendations for Case No. 12-1307, Deputy Theater Judge Advocate's Office, War Crimes Branch, RG 153, Entry 143; Box 350, NARA.

4. Review and Recommendations for Case No. 12-1307, Deputy Theater Judge Advocate's Office, War Crimes Branch, RG 153, Entry 143, Box 350, NARA.

5. According to a written account by First Lieutenant Jay J. Hatfield, which he wrote soon after being captured and concealed during his time spent in POW camps (MACR 7882 and 7892). No known perpetrator was ever tried or convicted for this incident. Missing Air Crew Reports (MACRs), 1942-1947, NARA, Record Group 92, Records of the Office of the Quartermaster General, https://catalog.archives.gov/id/91043082 (MACR 7882) and https://catalog.archives.gov/id/91043684 (MACR 7892), accessed March 6, 2016.

6. Throughout this study, the term *Lynchjustiz* will refer to the mistreatment (both assaults and killings) experienced by downed airmen in World War II. While lynching usually invokes the notion of being hanged, the majority of flyers were shot or beaten to death.

7. Sergeant Elmore L. Austin (Edinburg Falls, Vermont), Sergeant William A. Dumont (Berlin, New Hampshire), Second Lieutenant Norman J. Rogers Jr. (Rochester, New York), Second Lieutenant John N. Sekul (Bronx, New York), Field Officer Haigus Tufenkjian (Detroit, Michigan), Staff Sergeant Thomas D. Williams Jr. (Hazelton, Pennsylvania), Sergeant William A. Adams (Klingerstown, Pennsylvania), and Sergeant Sidney Eugene Brown (Gainesville, Florida). Adams and Brown managed to survive the brutal beatings. They escaped from the cemetery, where they were left on a cart to die. They evaded for four days before Nazi officials captured them. The two men spent the remainder of the war in a POW camp, Stalag Luft IV, in Tychowo, Poland.

8. Letter from the two surviving airmen from Rüsselsheim (William M. Adams and Sidney E. Brown) to Brigadier General C. Davidson, War Crimes Section, Seventh Army, Klingerstown, PA, and Gainsville, FL, August 1945, cited in Gregory A. Freeman, *The Last Mission of the Wham Bam Boys: Courage, Tragedy, and Justice in World War II* (New York: Palgrave Macmillan, 2011), 186.

9. James J. Weingartner, "Americans, Germans, and War Crimes: Converging Narratives from 'The Good War,'" *Journal of American History* 94, no. 4 (2008): 1170. See also Patrick Brode, *Casual Slaughters and Accidental Judgments: Canadian War Crimes Prosecutions, 1944–1948* (Toronto: University of Toronto Press, 1997), 116–56; Jörg Friedrich, *The Fire: The Bombing of Germany, 1940–1945*, trans. Allison Brown (New York: Columbia University Press, 2006), 433–34; Vasilis Vourkoutiotis, *Prisoners of War and the German High Command: The British and American Experience* (New York: Palgrave Macmillan, 2003), 188.

10. Friedrich, *Fire*, 433.

11. Barbara Grimm, "Lynchmorde an alliierten Fliegern im Zweiten Weltkrieg," in *Deutschland im Luftkrieg: Geschichte und Erinnerung*, ed. Dietmar Süß (Munich: R. Oldenbourg, 2007), 75; Ralf Blank, "Wartime Daily Life and the Air War on the Home Front," in *Germany and the Second World War*, ed. Jörg Echternkamp (Oxford: Oxford University Press, 2008), 466. This was first published in German as *Das Deutsche Reich und der Zweite Weltkrieg* (Deutsche Verlags-Anstalt: Munich, 2004); Richard J. Evans, *The Third Reich at War* (New York: Penguin Press, 2009), 465; Bas von Benda-Beckmann, *A German Catastrophe? German Historians and the Allied Bombings, 1945–2010* (Amsterdam: Amsterdam University Press, 2010), 328; Richard Overy, *The Bombing and the Bombed: Allied Air War over Europe, 1940–1945* (New York: Viking, 2013), 310.

12. Blank, "Wartime Daily Life and the Air War on the Home Front," 466; Grimm, "Lynchmorde an alliierten Fliegern im Zweiten Weltkrieg," 75; Evans, *Third Reich at War*, 465; Overy, *Bombing and the Bombed*, 310; Georg Hoffmann, *Fliegerlynchjustiz: Gewalt gegen abgeschossene alliierte Flugzeugbesatzungen 1943–1945* (Paderborn: Ferdinand Schöningh, 2015), 233, 383.

13. Hoffmann, *Fliegerlynchjustiz*, 383.

14. Ibid., 383.

15. For more information on the historiography of the Dachau trials, see Robert Sigel, *Im Interesse der Gerechtigkeit: Die Dachauer Kriegsverbrecherprozesse 1945–1948* (Frankfurt: Campus, 1992); Durwood Riedel, "The U.S. War Crimes Tribunals at the Former Dachau Concentration Camp: Lessons for Today," *Berkeley Journal of International Law* 24, no. 2 (2006): 554–609; Joshua M. Greene, *Justice at Dachau: The Trials of an American Prosecutor* (New York: Broadway Books, 2003); Ute Stiepani, "Die Dachauer Prozesse und ihre Bedeutung im Rahmen der Alliierten Strafverfolgung von NS-Verbrechen," in *Der Nationalsozialismus Vor Gericht: Die Alliierten Prozesse Gegen Kriegsverbrecher Und Soldaten 1943–1952*, ed. Gerd R. Ueberschaer (Frankfurt Am Main: Fischer, 1999), 227–35; Fern Overbey Hilton, *The Dachau Defendants: Life Stories from Testimony and Documents of the War Crimes Prosecutions* (Jefferson, NC: McFarland, 2004).

16. Clive Emsley, *Soldier, Sailor, Beggerman, Thief: Crime and the British Armed Services since 1914* (Oxford: Oxford University Press, 2013), 107. For more information, see records WO 71/1048 and WO 71/1061 at the British National Archives in London. See also Niall Ferguson, *The Pity of War: Explaining World War I* (New York: Basic Books, 1998), 372–85; Sean Longden, *To the Victor the Spoils: Soldiers' Lives from D-Day to VE-Day* (Gloucestershire, UK: Arris Books, 2004), chap. 14; Helmut Schnatz, "Lynchmorde an Fliegern," in *Kriegsverbrechen in Europa und im Nahen Osten im 20. Jahrhundert*, ed. Franz W. Seidler and Alfred M. de Zayas (Hamburg: E.S. Mittler & Sohn GmbH, 2002), 118–21.

17. Interrogation report on First Lieutenant James Harold Weisel (338th Fighter Squadron, 55th Fighter Group) and four other fighter pilots involved in the strafing attack of a train near Bremen on May 21, 1944, by Oberleutnant Maulbetsch (Fremde Luftwaffe West—Oberursel), June 3, 1944, Bundesarchiv Berlin-Lichterfelde: Generalstab der Luftwaffe/Luftwaffenführungsstab—RL 2-II/522.

18. First Lieutenant Norman Wesley Achen recalled that during his time confined at Dulag Luft in Oberursel, Luftwaffe interrogator Hanns Scharff told him, "We got the film out of your airplane and you have been accused of strafing civilians and shooting them. And if we can prove that, we are going to shoot you."

However, interrogators also used such tactics to intimidate flyers into giving up information (Norman Wesley Achen Collection, [AFC/2001/48504], Veterans History Project, American Folklife Center, Library of Congress).

19. Blank, "Wartime Daily Life and the Air War on the Home Front," 466; Ute, "Die Dachauer Prozesse und ihre Bedeutung im Rahmen der alliierten Strafverfolgung von NS-Verbrechen."

20. Hoffmann, *Fliegerlynchjustiz*, 365. The original German text states: "Die Fliegerlynchjustiz war im Kern nicht das Ergebnis einer spontanen Entladung von Gewalt seitens einer vom Bombenkrieg betroffenen Bevölkerung, sondern unterlag einer entsprechenden nationalsozialistischen Initiierung, Steuerung und Anleitung."

21. Klaus-Michael Mallmann, "'Volksjustiz gegen anglo-amerikanische Mörder': Die Massaker an westalliierten Fliegern und Fallschirmspringern 1944/45," in *NS-Gewaltherrschaft: Beiträge zur historischen Forschung und juristischen Aufarbeitung*, ed. Alfred Gottwaldt, Norbert Kampe, and Peter Klein (Berlin: Hentrich, 2005), 212–13. The original German text states: "Es handelte sich auch bei der Fliegerlynchjustiz um Verbrechen, die weitestgehend außerhalb des Kontextes von Befehl und Gehorsam zu sehen sind, bei denen kaum mehr zwischen Entscheidungsträgern und Handlangern zu unterscheiden ist. Lynchjustiz konnte auch im Dritten Reich nicht einfach von 'oben' angeordnet werden. Nicht das 'Du musst' regierte hier, sondern das 'Du darfst.' Analog zur Vernichtung der europäischen Juen bedurfte es dafür keines zentralen Befehls; es genügten das Feindbild und die Einladung zu mörderischer Aktivität, um die Katastrophe auszulösen."

22. See chapter 4 of this work.

23. G. M. Gilbert, *Nuremberg Diary* (Boston: De Capo Press, 1961), 279.

24. Hoffmann, *Fliegerlynchjustiz*, 365.

25. Roger Chickering and Stig Förster, "Are We There Yet? World War II and the Theory of Total War," in *A World at Total War: Global Conflict and the Politics of Destruction, 1937–1945*, ed. Roger Chickering, Stig Förster, and Bernd Greiner (Cambridge: Cambridge University Press, 2005), 12.

26. For example, see Chickering, Förster, and Greiner, *World at Total War*; Richard Overy, *The Air War: 1939–1945* (Washington, DC: Potomac Books, 2005); Friedrich, *Fire*; Overy, *Bombing and the Bombed*.

27. Christian Geinitz, "The First Air War against Noncombatants: Strategic Bombing of German Cities in World War I," in *Great War, Total War: Combat and Mobilization on the Western Front*, ed. Roger Chickering and Stig Förster (Cambridge: Cambridge University Press, 2000), 207–26.

28. Tammy M. Proctor, *Civilians in a World at War, 1914–1918* (New York: New York University Press, 2010), 3.

29. Ibid., 4.

30. Ibid., 5

31. International Committee of the Red Cross, "Treaties, States Parties and Commentaries—Convention IV: The Hague, October 18, 1907," https://ihl-databases.icrc.org/ihl/INTRO/195, accessed June 9, 2014.

32. William L. Shirer, *Berlin Diary: The Journal of a Foreign Correspondent, 1934–1941* (New York: RosettaBooks, 1968), May 10, 1940.

33. Hitler delivered a speech on December 10, 1940, to workers in a Berlin arms manufacturing plant.

34. Auswärtiges Amt, ed. *Dokumente über die Alleinschuld Englands am Bombenkrieg gegen die Zivilbevölkerung*, Auswärtiges Amt 1943 Nr. 8 (Berlin: Zentralverlag der NSDAP, 1943); Franz Eher, ed. *Englands Alleinschuld am Bombenterror*, Volksausgabe des 8. Amtlichen Deutschen Weissbuches (Berlin: Zentralverlag der NSDAP, 1943).

35. Charles Webster and Noble Frankland, *The Strategic Air Offensive against Germany*, vol. 4 (London: Naval and Military Press, 2006), 205–13.

36. For example, see Overy, *Bombing and the Bombed*; Friedrich, *Fire*; Overy, *Air War*; Stephan E. Ambrose, *The Wild Blue: The Men and Boys Who Flew the B-24s Over Germany, 1944–45* (New York: Simon and Schuster, 2001).

37. Jürgen Förster, "From 'Blitzkrieg' to 'Total War': Germany's War in Europe," in Chickering, Förster, and Greiner, *World at Total War*, 91.

38. Ibid., 93–94. For more information on Volksgemeinschaft, see Martin Broszat, "Zur Struktur der NS-Massenbewegung," *Vierteljahrshefte für Zeitgeschichte*, no. 1 (1983): 52–76; Andrew Stuart Bergerson, *Ordinary Germans in Extraordinary Times: The Nazi Revolution in Hildesheim* (Bloomington: Indiana University Press, 2004); David Welch, "Nazi Propaganda and the *Volksgemeinschaft*: Constructing a People's Community," *Journal of Contemporary History* 39, no. 2 (2004): 213–38; Dietmar Süß and Winfried Süß, *Das "Dritte Reich": Eine Einführung* (Munich: Pantheon, 2008); Frank Bajohr and Michael Weldt, eds., *Volksgemeinschaft: Neue Forschungen zur Gesellschaft des Nationalsozialismus* (Frankfurt: Fischer, 2009); Michael Wildt, "'Volksgemeinschaft': Eine Antwort auf Ian Kershaw," Zeithistorische Forschungen/Studies in Contemporary History, online edition, 8 (2011), https://zeithistorische-forschungen.de/1-2011/4756, accessed August 23, 2016; Detlef Schmiechen-Ackermann, *"Volksgemeinschaft": Mythos, wirkungsmächtige soziale Verheißung oder soziale Realität im "Dritten Reich"?* (Paderborn: Ferdinand Schöningh, 2012); Martina Steber and Bernhard Gotto, eds., *Visions of Community in Nazi Germany: Social Engineering and Private Lives* (Oxford: Oxford University Press, 2014); Nicholas Stargardt, "Legitimacy through War?" in *Beyond the Racial State: Rethinking Nazi Germany*, ed. Devin O. Pendas, Mark Roseman, and Richard F. Wetzell (Cambridge: Cambridge University Press, 2017), 402–30.

39. Hew Strachan, "Total War: The Conduct of War, 1939–1945," in Chickering, Förster, and Greiner, *World at Total War*, 47.

40. Stargardt, "Legitimacy through War?" 411.

41. As Hew Strachan declared, "The more personal the combat, the more brutal it seemed to become" (Strachan, "Total War: The Conduct of War, 1939–1945," 51).

42. Förster, "From 'Blitzkrieg' to 'Total War,'" 106.

43. For example, see "Remains of Pilot Shot Down during WWII to be Buried in N.Y.," CBS News, November 28, 2017, https://www.cbsnews.com/news/robert-mains-pilot-shot-down-wwii-remains-n-y-burial/; "Cleveland WWII Airman Receives Funeral in Willoughby," *News-Herald*, May 2, 2015, https://www.news-herald.com/news/ohio/cleveland-wwii-airman-receives-funeral-in-willoughby/article_68982449-1428-5329-8ba7-577a98993fab.html, accessed October 10, 2016; "Remains of Fallen WWII Airman Returned to Family for Burial," Stars and Stripes, August 23, 2012, https://www.stripes.com/news/europe/germany/remains-of-fallen-wwii-airman-returned-to-family-for-burial-1.186673; "WWII Army Aircrew Laid to Rest," Army News, October 26, 2011, https://www.army.mil/article/68064/wwii_army_aircrew_laid_to_rest, accessed October 10, 2016.

44. Manfred Berg and Simon Wendt, eds., *Globalizing Lynching History: Vigilantism and Extralegal Punishment from an International Perspective* (New York: Palgrove Macmillan, 2011); William D. Carrigan and Christopher Waldrep, eds., *Swift to Wrath: Lynching in Global Historical Perspective* (Charlottesville: University of Virginia Press, 2013); Robert W. Thurston, *Lynching: American Mob Murder in Global Perspective* (Farnham: Ashgate, 2011); W. Fitzhugh Brundage, *Lynching in the New South: Georgia and Virginia, 1880–1930* (Chicago: University of Illinois Press, 1993); Amy Louise Wood, *Lynching and Spectacle: Witnessing Racial Violence in America, 1890–1940* (Chapel Hill: University of North Carolina Press, 2009).

45. Stefan Kühl, *The Nazi Connection: Eugenics, American Racism, and German National Socialism* (New York: Oxford University Press, 1994); James Q. Whitman, *Hitler's American Model: The United States and the Making of Nazi Race Law* (Princeton, NJ: Princeton University Press, 2017).

46. For example, Heinrich Himmler ordered the police in August 1943 to not stop German civilians from mistreating downed enemy airmen. Roughly a year later, in May 1944, Joseph Goebbels began to publicly condone Lynchjustiz. For more information, see Heinrich Himmler memo from August 10, 1943, RG 549, Entry A1 2238, Microfilm T1021, Reel 10, Frame No. 771, NARA, https://catalog.archives.gov/id/40957462; Joseph Goebbels, "Ein Wort zum feindlichen Lufterror," *Völkischer Beobachter* (Munich), May 28, 1944.

47. The known and reviewed flyer trials were held at Dachau, Ludwigsburg, Ahrweiler, Munich, Darmstadt, Freising, and Heidelberg; however, over 75 percent of the cases were tried at Dachau.

48. Stanley Milgram, *Obedience to Authority: An Experimental View* (London: Tavistock Publications, 1974); Craig Haney, Curtis Banks, and Philip Zimbardo, "Interpersonal Dynamics in a Simulated Prison," *International Journal of Criminology and Penology* 1, no. 1 (1973): 69–97.

49. Himmler memo from August 10, 1943; Joseph Goebbels, "Ein Wort zum feindlichen Lufterror," *Völkischer Beobachter* (Munich), May 28, 1944. See Appendix A of this volume (figures A1.1 and A1.12) for the original texts and English translations.

50. Martin Bormann secret circular entitled "Volksjustiz against English-American Murderers," May 30, 1944, RG 549, Entry A1 2238, Microfilm T1021, Reel 10, Frame No. 764, NARA, https://catalog.archives.gov/id/40957462. See Appendix of this volume, figure A1.7, for the original text and English translation.

Chapter 1

Uninvited Guests

Experiences of Downed Airmen

American airmen during World War II had a dismal life expectancy. It was not a matter of if an airman was going to be shot down but when. Once downed, airmen faced an uncertain "reception committee," as Second Lieutenant Kenneth C. Reimer noted in a drawing he made as a POW in Stalag Luft I in Barth, Germany (fig. 1.1). According to military historian John C. McManus, "for every [ground combat] soldier killed in action, three or four others would be wounded; air combat was completely the opposite. For every man wounded, three were killed."[1] Based on the number of casualties per sortie (mission flown) in the European theater, the percentage of casualties (including killed, wounded, missing, and interned) steadily declined throughout the war from 24.0 percent in 1942 to 2.8 percent in 1945. The most significant drop in the casualty rate was from 19.0 percent in 1943 to 6.3 percent in 1944, after the Allied powers obtained air superiority over Europe. However, this stark decrease in the casualty rate is misleading. With the dramatic increase in sorties flown in 1944 (655,289), the number of casualties similarly increased to an extreme level (41,593) unmatched throughout the war (table 1.1).[2]

According to historian Donald L. Miller, "approximately 73 percent of the combat flyers who had arrived in England in the summer and fall of 1942 failed to complete their tour of duty. Fifty-seven percent were killed or missing in action, and another sixteen percent had either been seriously wounded, killed in crashes in England, or permanently grounded by a serious physical or mental disability."[3] A tour of duty in 1942 required flyers to complete twenty-five missions in order to return home. However, the introduction of the P-51 Mustang in late 1943,

A reception committee of the Third Reich
Was on hand to greet him
When he did alight . . .

Figure 1.1. Lieutenant Kenneth C. Reimer's depiction of a German "Reception Committee" from his comic written as a POW in Stalag Luft I, Barth, Germany, February 1945.
Source: http://www.b24.net/powStoriesLuft1toons.htm

Table 1.1. Casualty Rate per Sortie in European Theater

Year	Sorties	Killed	Wounded	Missing and Interned	Total Casualties	Casualty Percentage
1942	2,453	310	136	140	586	24%
1943	63,929	4,637	1,604	5,736	11,977	19%
1944	655,289	12,845	5,267	23,481	41,593	6.3%
1945	312,381	2,041	1,346	5,300	8,687	2.8%

Source: "Battle Casualties in European Theater" (table 36) and "Combat Sorties Flown, by Theater" (table 118), Army Air Forces Statistical Digest, World War II *(Washington, DC: Office of Statistical Control, December 1945). http://www.dtic.mil/dtic/tr/fulltext/u2/a542518.pdf.*

which was able to accompany and protect bombers for the duration of their mission, resulted in a decline in the loss of airmen, and thus tours increased to thirty-five missions by the summer of 1944. Even before airmen left the United States, they faced extreme risks, with over twenty thousand major accidents recorded during training throughout the war, resulting in the deaths of over five thousand US flyers; this, combined with the harsh reality faced overseas, indicates the real dangers of being an airman.[4]

Over thirty-five thousand American airmen were held as POWs in Germany, slightly less than one-third of American POWs in Europe.[5] Airmen's personal memoirs depict their missions over Europe and describe the adventure, danger, and vulnerability of air combat in World War II, as well as their experiences in POW camps. According to Major General Delmar Spivey (one of the senior POW officers during the war), "the life of a POW was . . . one of fear, apprehension, deprivations, danger, and frustration."[6] Nevertheless, death rates were respectively low in POW camps, with approximately five deaths per thousand prisoners.[7] Many scholars have examined the role of resistance fighters in France, Belgium, and the Netherlands in aiding downed flyers in their attempt to escape and evade during World War II.[8] To a certain extent, research has even reviewed the escape of POWs from camps in German-occupied territory, with the most well-known case being the Great Escape from Stalag Luft III in March 1944 (located today in Zagan, Poland). The eponymous movie from 1963, featuring Steve McQueen and James Garner (among other notable actors), immortalized the topic of American POWs in World War II, as did the 1950s classic *Stalag 17*.[9]

US Air Force major Laura C. Counts described the escape and evasion of downed airmen as a "new 'front' in the heart of the Axis."[10] By 1940, British airmen were already escaping and evading, and the United States soon followed this tactic, especially because it cost Germany important military resources. Although American flyers evading within Germany remains a relatively unknown aspect of the war, it is an important factor to consider to understand the various experiences downed airmen faced after parachuting from their damaged aircraft or following an emergency landing in enemy territory, especially since it resulted in personal contact between downed airmen and the location population. Therefore, this chapter will focus on airmen's escape and evasion tactics, the so-called Sonderbehandlung some experienced if they were caught, and to what extent flyers received assistance from German citizens.

Although there are few documented accounts of American airmen successfully evading capture in Germany (compared to numerous documented evasions in France, the Netherlands, and Belgium), these cases shed new light on how German society acted during World War II. Examples of Germans aiding flyers range from simply providing first aid to offering food and shelter. Regardless of the type of assistance offered, such behavior from helpers was punishable by prison sentences, either in a local jail or, in severe cases, a concentration camp.

Escape and Evasion

The legal difference between evading and escaping was quite important for a flyer's treatment. According to a manual issued in February 1944 from the Military Intelligence Service (MIS-X), a section of the US Department of War tasked with aiding captured servicemen, "a neutral country is obliged, under international law, to intern all evaders who reach its territory, while escapers must be repatriated as soon as practicable."[11] Therefore, flyers were advised to claim to be escaped POWs. The Geneva Convention of 1929 recognized the right of prisoners, regardless of nationality, to escape. By 1940, Allied doctrine evolved to expect downed airmen to escape and evade.[12] According to British military historians Michael R. D. Foot and J. M. Langley, "a fighting man remains a fighting man, whether in enemy hands or not, and his duty to continue fighting overrides everything else."[13] While the Germans, to a limited extent, recognized and honored the right of POWs to escape, they only did so with regard to western Allies and just until mid-1944 (prior to the Great Escape). Given the Nazi regime's deep-seated hatred of Slavic people and communists, as well as the fact that the Soviet government did not sign the Geneva Convention, Soviet POWs experienced atrocious treatment, including forced labor and extermination.

Estimates of the number of Allied airmen who evaded or escaped back to England during the war ranged between three thousand and five thousand; approximately half were Americans.[14] Counts estimated that nearly twenty-four hundred American servicemen escaped from behind enemy lines in Europe between November 1942 and October 1944.[15] In addition to the Allies achieving air superiority by 1944 and antiaircraft weaponry replacing enemy aircraft as the main cause of Allied aircraft losses (fig. 1.2), the Allied invasion of France on June 6, 1944, drastically increased the possibility of flyers successfully returning to Allied lines.[16]

According to Miller, the total number of United States airmen who escaped and evaded in Europe, regardless of success or duration, was around ten thousand.[17] Surprisingly, "up to 70% of American crewmen never received any escape and evasion training prior to their arrival in England. Their training consisted almost solely of a briefing (or two)," according to Counts's analysis of returned airmen's debriefing questionnaires. This escape and evasion training in England consisted mainly of lectures by experienced personnel who had successfully escaped and evaded.[18] By January 1945, POW escape attempts were no longer an obligation; the safety of the large number of Allied POWs in Germany was the new priority since the end of the war appeared to be inevitably close. Nevertheless, this did not stop airmen from attempting to regain their freedom. Even in the final months of the war, the dangers faced by flyers on the run did not wane. Armed citizens (whether civilians, police, security forces, party officials, or military personnel) were constantly on the lookout for enemy airmen.

An airman's ability to avoid being captured by German soldiers or occupation forces was hindered by many factors, including weather, geography, lack of proper clothing, cultural differences, and language. Downed airmen experienced a wide range of natural obstacles, such as mountains (e.g., the Alps and the Pyrenees) and waterways (the North Sea, the English Channel, and the Rhine River), that stood in their way to freedom. Flyers depended on aid from unknown people, yet the fear of landing in the hands of collaborators or being turned over to Germans was constant. Even if flyers were lucky enough to contact resistance

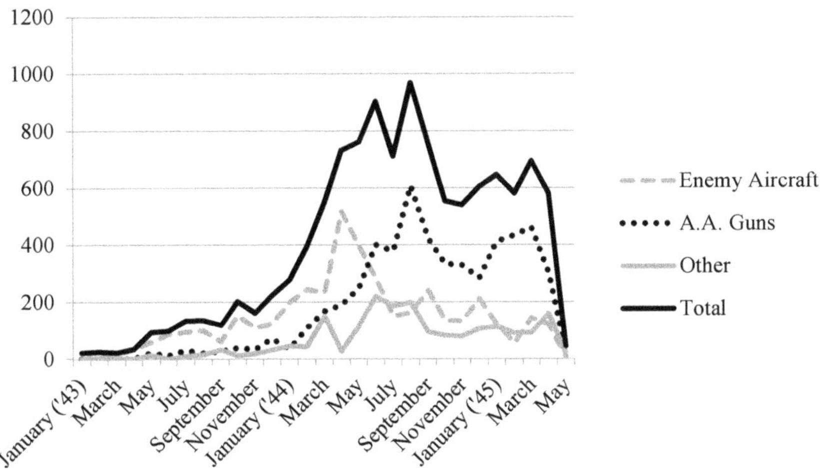

Figure 1.2. American Aircraft Losses by Cause in European Theater.
Source: "Airplane Losses on Combat Missions in European Theater" (table 159), Army Air Forces Statistical Digest *(Washington, DC: Office of Statistical Control, December 1945).*

and underground members, the danger of a German spy betraying them by posing as a potential helper was ever-present. Likewise, resistance and underground fighters faced the possibility of being betrayed by German spies disguised as downed Allied airmen.[19]

One particular spy, a Belgian named Jacques Desoubrie, was responsible for capturing many Allied airmen. He infiltrated the resistance network's Comet Line, which assisted airmen in their evasion from France to Spain and subsequent return to Britain. Desoubrie worked as an informant for the Gestapo and was responsible for capturing many of the 168 Allied airmen who were taken to Buchenwald in August 1944.[20] In addition to flyers, spies deceived over five hundred underground helpers during the war, many of whom were either executed or died in concentration camps.[21] In December 1949, France captured, tried, and executed Desoubrie as a collaborationist.

Clothing and language also presented serious problems for downed airmen. The inability to speak French, Dutch, or German—or even speaking the language with a heavy foreign accent—instantly identified an airman as being American or British. In addition, the inability to communicate effectively greatly exacerbated the uncertainty of knowing whom to trust. With regard to clothing, it was necessary to dispose of any insignias and easily identifiable flight suits immediately while retaining sufficient clothing to tolerate weather conditions. If airmen were able to contact the resistance (or at the very least encounter helpful civilians), they could receive civilian clothing, which aided them in blending in with the locals; however, if captured in such clothing, they also faced the risk of German forces accusing them of espionage. Such examples resulted in flyers being held as political prisoners, during which they were severely tortured and, in some cases, even executed. Legally, a court had to try the accused airmen; however, no evidence exists to indicate that any trials took place.[22]

While landing deep within German territory significantly decreased the chances of successfully evading capture due to a lack of resistance networks, downed flyers also faced uncertainty in the border regions of France, Luxembourg, Belgium, the Netherlands, Denmark, and Italy. Despite this, a deep-seated sentiment of nationalism in occupied countries often was positive for downed airmen, as nationalists sought to rebel against German occupation. This underground political opposition became a well-developed infrastructure. It was aided and supported by the British (MI9 and SOE) and the United States (OSS), and it provided opportunities for Jews to escape persecution as well as much-needed assistance for downed airmen.[23]

Switzerland, Sweden, Spain, Portugal, and Ireland were officially neutral during the war, which made reaching these countries the primary goal of every airman on the run or for pilots in need of an emergency landing site.[24] Nevertheless, flyers needed to exercise extreme caution, as these countries were the front lines of espionage warfare between the Allied and Axis powers. Reaching a neutral nation meant flyers were redesignated as internees and, according to international law, were not allowed to leave the neutral country, having entered during combat.[25]

Sweden was relatively flexible with the 1,400 Allied airmen it interned.[26] In late 1944, Sweden released 500 American airmen in exchange for nine interned B-17 bombers and four P-51 fighters.[27] Other nations exchanged airplanes for interned flyers as well. Turkey was a nonbelligerent nation during the war (until it declared war on Germany in February 1945) and interned 189 airmen.[28] However, in return for releasing the airmen, the United States gave Turkey six B-24 bombers for the Turkish air force.[29] Over 1,100 interned American airmen in Spain[30] and 135 in Portugal[31] were also released to the United States military; however, instead of simply giving away airplanes, the United States sold them to Spain and Portugal. Bombers were sold for $100,000 and fighters for $20,000. In total, Spain[32] bought five bombers and Portugal bought over twenty bombers and fighters.[33] Additionally, Ireland briefly interned over 250 American flyers before they were quietly returned to Allied military control.[34]

The Swiss, however, followed strict internment regulations. Though occasionally influenced by German political pressure, they generally released American internees following German approval. Over 1,700 United States airmen made it to Switzerland during the war. The majority of these men (1,516) had made emergency landings or had parachuted into the neutral territory.[35] Internees received relatively positive treatment in Switzerland. They were housed in hotels in Alpine villages, such as Wengen, Davos, and Adelboden. In some instances, airmen even had the opportunity to ski during the winter and go hiking in the Alps during the summer. Despite this positive treatment, the lack of food and severe boredom they suffered often made their experiences somewhat similar to those of their fellow flyers detained as POWs in Germany. Likewise, interned flyers in Switzerland attempted to escape in hopes of returning to England. There were 764 successful escapes out of a recorded 948 attempts.[36] However, camp and border guards caught at least 154 flyers attempting to escape and sent them to a special camp at Wauwilermoos, where their treatment pushed the limits of international law. These interned airmen in Switzerland were malnourished, medically neglected, and even tried by Swiss military tribunals for attempting to escape. According to historian Dwight S. Mears, "the average sentence was seventy-four days in prison, but the average time to complete the investigation and military tribunals was eighty-two days."[37] Only recently (in 2013) have these internees finally been acknowledged as POWs by the US government. During the war, many servicemen viewed these airmen as cowards who attempted to avoid combat.

According to Second Lieutenant Robert F. Rhodes, flyers also faced uncertain treatment in the tiny alpine principality of neutral Liechtenstein, located on the borders of Switzerland, Austria, and Germany. Rhodes, twenty-one years old at the time, was forced to land his fighter airplane in Liechtenstein due to flak damage on February 22, 1945, following an escort and strafing mission near Munich. He reported that

> the plane came down in the Rhine River which was very low at that time, and he waded to the east bank. There were a lot of people there. . . . Soon an official drove up in a car and asked Lt. Rhodes to accompany him to Schaan. . . . Lt. Rhodes said that he wanted to go across [the Rhine River into Switzerland] right away, and

> after some argument, they put him in a car, drove him across the bridge and handed him over to the Swiss guards. . . . Then Captain Rauch, a Swiss officer, arrived and [arrested Rhodes]. . . . [He said that] Liechtenstein was under partial German occupation, and that the people were in the habit of selling Allied military personnel to the Germans.[38]

While this is the only known reference of airmen in Liechtenstein being turned over to Germans for money, it was not a rare occurrence in Europe, especially in western European countries, whose citizens were often in need of money for food and supplies. The commander of the German military in France, for example, issued a public notice on March 25, 1943, in the *Pariser Zeitung* that "the French population is reminded that concealing or aiding enemy airmen or parachutists is punishable by death. . . . Persons giving information leading to [the] apprehension of enemy fliers or parachutists landing on French soil will be rewarded."[39]

The highest successful number of escapes and evasions occurred in France, the Netherlands, and Belgium because the populations of these countries were most likely to support the western Allies. If flyers were shot down in southern Germany, they faced three options. First, they could head west to France via Alsace in order to cross the Pyrenees Mountains into the tiny neutral principality of Andorra. From there, they would travel to Spain, where they could either fly or sail back to England. Second, flyers could travel south and cross into Switzerland. Or third, they could travel east across the Yugoslav frontier into the Balkans. If airmen were shot down in northern Germany, military officials advised them to head west to Belgium or the Netherlands, where they had a good chance of receiving support from resistance helpers. Occasionally military advisers instructed airmen to travel north, through Denmark, to Sweden as well. Moreover, airmen were advised to use the rivers and forests for safety and to guide them along their journey to meet up with the various escape lines in France, Belgium, and the Netherlands (figs. 1.3 and 1.4).

Generally, there were two ways that downed airmen could connect with resistance fighters and the escape lines. They could be immediately approached upon landing by members of the resistance or individuals who had acquaintances who were members. Often, the helpers sheltered and fed the airmen and continued passing them on to other members

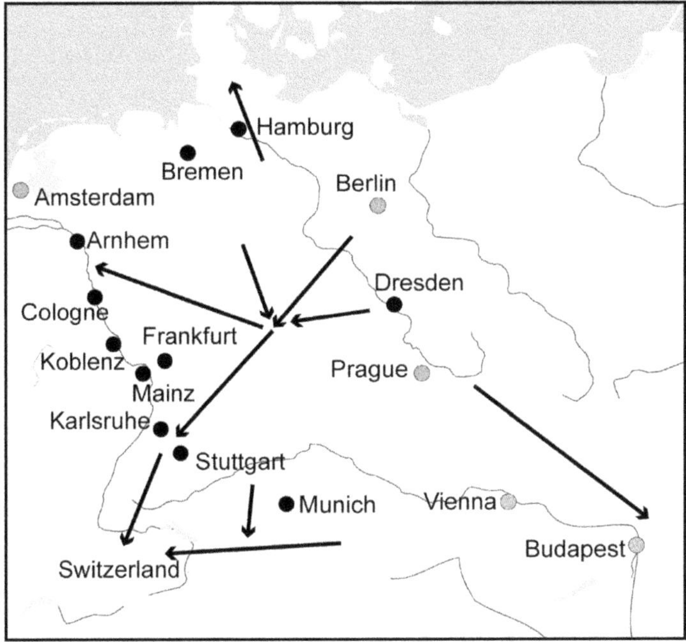

Figure 1.3. Escape and Evasion Map. The arrows indicate the direction in which downed airmen should travel in order to best evade capture. The map suggests that airmen utilize the forest system. *Escape and Evasion Map for Germany, undated, "Germany: Evasion," IRIS Number: 00224565 and 00229693 United States Air Force Historical Research Agency, Maxwell Air Force Base, Montgomery, Alabama.*

of the resistance, working their way along the escape lines. Airmen who did not immediately receive help from locals were forced to evade as best as possible and travel to neutral territory or to an area that offered the possibility of contacting resistance fighters. However, contacting resistance fighters meant that airmen had to approach local citizens and hope that they chose the right person to trust.[40]

The major escape routes included the Pat Line (also known as the O'Leary Line), which was based in Marseille, France; the Burgundy Line located in northwestern France; the Shelburne Line located in Brittany; the Comet Line, which shuttled downed airmen from Belgium to France; and the Dutch–Paris Line, which ferried airmen from the Netherlands to Paris (fig. 1.5).

Estimates regarding the number of flyers who escaped via each line vary. Aviation historian Graham Pitchfork concludes that over 600

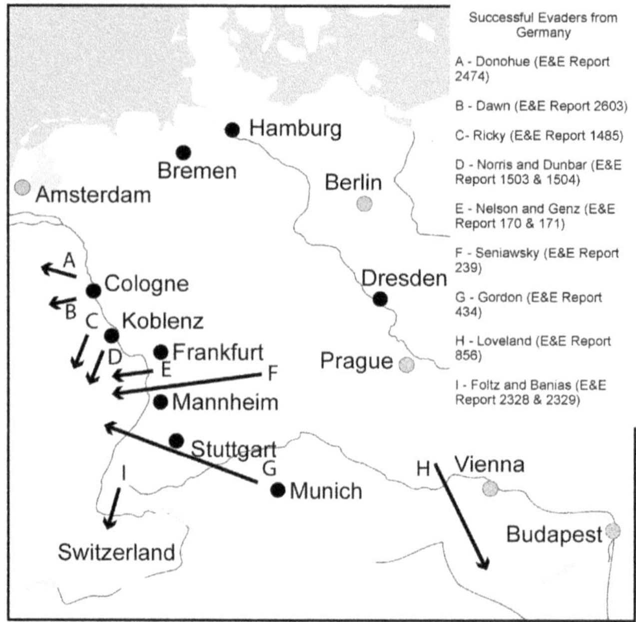

Figure 1.4. Map of Successful Escape and Evasions from Germany. The arrows indicate the routes followed by the nine successful airmen. The following escapes and evasions are depicted in this map: Line A: Second Lieutenant William W. Donohoe Jr. (from Long Island, New York), E&E #2474; Line B: First Lieutenant Robert L. Dawn (from San Francisco, California), E&E #2603; Line C: First Lieutenant Lowell L. Ricky (from Lincoln, Nebraska), E&E #1485; Line D: Sergeant Benjamin R. Morris (from Tarentum, Pennsylvania), E&E #1503, and Second Lieutenant D. E. Dunbar (from Atlanta, Georgia), E&E #1504; Line E: First Lieutenant Robert E. Nelson (from Gresham, Oregon), E&E #170 and Staff Sergeant Raymond A. Genz (McGrath, Minnesota), E&E #171; Line F: Staff Sergeant Peter Senlawsky (from Brooklyn, New York), E&E #239; Line G: Staff Sergeant Lee C. Gordon, E&E #434; Line H: Staff Sergeant Glenn Loveland (from Union City, Indiana), E&E #856; Line I: Second Lieutenant Bill B. Banias (from Kerman, California), E&E #2328, and Second Lieutenant Fred B. Foltz, (from Beverly Hills, California), E&E #2329. *Escape and Evasion Map for Germany, undated, "Germany: Evasion," IRIS Number: 00224565 and 00229693 United States Air Force Historical Research Agency, Maxwell Air Force Base, Montgomery, Alabama.*

individuals escaped via the Pat Line, with 100 helpers killed; over 800 via the Comet Line; over 100 via the Burgundy Line; over 350 via the Shelburne Line; and over 200 (and 1,000 Jews) via the Dutch–Paris Line, with 150 helpers arrested and several killed.[41] Additionally, an unknown number of airmen in France and Holland were rescued and flown back to England during numerous secret missions operated by the British (MI9 and SOE) and the United States (OSS).[42] Certainly, great

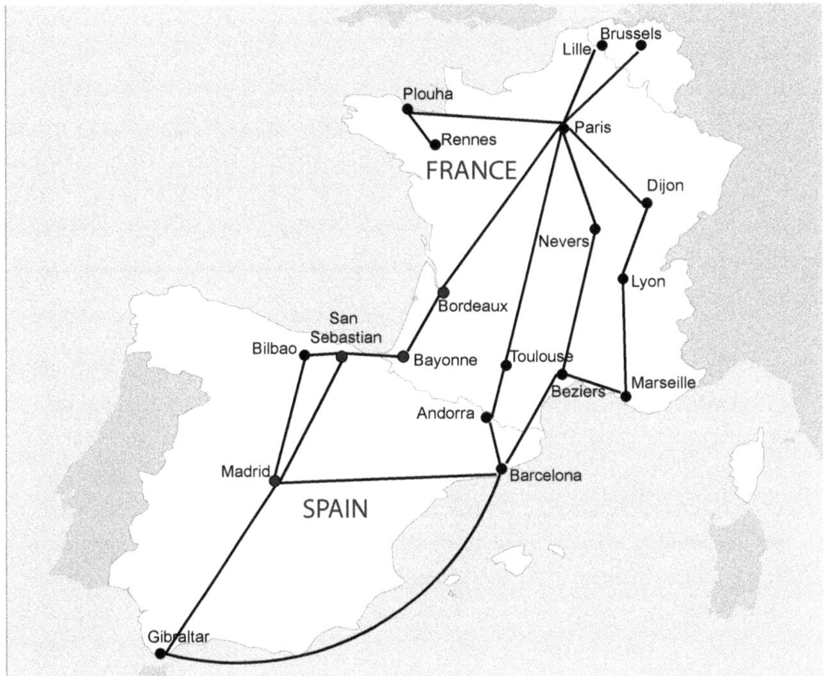

Figure 1.5. Major Escape Routes.

risk was involved in these missions. Anyone in German-occupied territory accused of aiding downed Allied airmen faced severe punishment from the German occupation forces. Experiences of airmen evading in Germany varied depending on their location and the phase of the war as well as the degree of devastation experienced by individuals in the area during the war.

While on a bombing mission attacking Schweinfurt on August 7, 1943, two US flyers (Captain Robert E. Nelson and Staff Sergeant Raymond A. Genz) experienced heavy flak near Aachen, Germany, damaging their B-17 bomber (nicknamed *King Malfunction II*). Eventually, this damage, along with subsequent damage inflicted by German fighters, forced the aircrew to bail out. As Nelson floated to the ground in his parachute, a German farmer shot at him but missed.[43] Once on the ground, Genz and Nelson met up and quickly fled the area. Over the next few days, the flyers avoided open territory when possible, heading initially west toward Luxembourg and Belgium and then south toward Switzerland. Supplementing their escape kit, they foraged for food, gathering berries, apples, and plums in woods as well as turnips and carrots in fields. Although farmworkers, a group of Hitler Youth members, German soldiers, and several civilians (including children) spotted the evading airmen on numerous occasions, even coming within mere feet at times, they experienced no problems. The Germans were either unsure what to make of the airmen or had other worries. As the flyers' report described,

> Late in the morning, we saw that the road was going to end or turn off in another direction. We were walking downhill about a quarter of a mile from the end of the road, talking to ourselves, when a man crossed in front of us. We saw then that our road led into a main highway. The man saw us at exactly the same moment we looked at him. We hesitated for a brief second but tried not to show excitement. We continued walking but more slowly. The man crossed from the right of the road to the other, stopped, and put down a small handbag he carried. Not until then did we realize he was a German soldier. We thought that he would move on, but soon it was obvious that he meant to wait for us. About 100 yards away we stopped and talked the situation over. We were about 200 feet from the nearest woods but did not want to run in case he was armed. He watched us, occasionally glancing up and down the highway as if looking for help. Once he pulled back his blouse and we were about to run thinking him armed but he lighted a cigarette. We decided then he was not armed and that since there were two of us we could take care of him if he tried to stop us. A train whistle sounded in the distance, and after looking at his watch, the soldier shrugged his shoulders, picked up the suitcase and walked away.[44]

An advantage of using woods as cover was the ability to start a fire to dry clothes and warm up. Since it was fall, the nights were cold and rainy, which was dangerous to the airmen's health. As the flyers found out, however, the downside of evading through woods was deer hunters. Nevertheless, even by avoiding open territory, it was impossible to avoid people completely. Nelson reported, "These scares forced us into using more caution but as we got more tired and desperate our carefulness would relax. . . . Many people saw us and glanced in our direction, but nothing unusual happened. We were getting bolder and did not care if civilians saw us."[45]

After arriving near Beaufort, Luxembourg, and traveling as far as they thought possible without substantial food, the airmen decided to approach a house, posing as Italian beggars, and ask for food. Their hunger and desperation, as well as knowing that they were no longer in Germany, led to an increasing boldness, and they approached more and more civilians. Approaching a house, Nelson described that,

> a young boy came out to meet us. We tried a few German words like "Brot" and "Essen," put our hands on our stomachs and pointed to our mouths. The boy called to his mother who leaned from an upstairs window and after he said something to her, she looked at us in a friendly manner. She seemed to be telling him to get us some food. While this was being done an old man came in the yard. He became quite excited and asked in German what nationality we were. He asked if we were flyers but we pretended not to understand. He was insistent and kept repeating "Amerikaner—Deutscher—Engländer?" Finally, we admitted we were Americans. We pulled out our maps and indicated that we would like to know our location. He pointed out that we were in Luxembourg and near Beaufort. We asked for more food, but he said it was too dangerous because of the Germans.
>
> We left after getting some bread and jam and worked through a wood until we struck open country. From the edge of the wood, we watched two men who were working near each other. We went up to the younger of the men and motioned we were hungry and then told him who we were. He said he was French and gave us a cigarette. We pulled out our maps again to learn from him, if we could, a more exact location of our position. We remembered that once we had been briefed to stay out of Luxembourg. While we were having a sign-language conversation with the Frenchman, the older man came over to see what was happening. As soon as he learned we were American airmen, he shook hands with us. Our morale went up when this happened, but we were still hungry. The old man, also a Frenchman, could give us nothing but apples, cigarettes, and directions. We left them feeling happier than at any other time since parachuting.
>
> Before the next village, we went up to a girl standing in a yard of a house and asked for food in our few German words. Although

she seemed to not want anything to do with us, she pointed to a shed. We went in and waited a few moments for her to bring bread and pieces of plum cake. We didn't tell her who we were but while we were eating we saw her leave the house on a bicycle. We left at once—running. . . .

We had walked about three miles before we met an old man alone and carrying a scythe. We stopped him and asked for food. He looked us over carefully but motioned us to follow him. We did because we understood that he was taking us to his brother who could speak English. He led us to a house and after we had waited outside a few moments the old man came out with a priest and an old woman. The woman was very unfriendly and, while the brother questioned us, acted as if she would like us to go away. The priest led us into a side building and while the old man went into the house for bread told us that as soon as we had food we must leave. We took the bread into the fields to eat while we were resting.

After starting out again we followed a road and passed three or four farm people. We approached one of them and asked for a cigarette. We showed our maps and asked the direction to Belgium. He told us that there were Germans in the next village. We followed a secondary road for three miles and came out on a hill which overlooked Edelburg. The town was spread over the small valley in front of us. We crawled into the brush to look over the situation. There was a main highway, a railroad and a river to cross. There was a barn near us and after dark we slept there.

At 0400 hours the next morning, we crossed through the town and valley without difficulty. At one crossroads we met a man carrying fishing tackle. Because he looked at us suspiciously, we approached him and asked for a cigarette. He gave us one and when we asked for the direction to Belgium and the location of German soldiers, he wanted to know if we were Americans. We nodded and he told us that a ten-minute walk along the road we were traveling would take us by a German camp. He pointed to a road that led up a hill and indicated that this road would be safer to follow. We had walked on a few yards when he called us back to give us his entire package of cigarettes. . . .

Instead of following a road we cut across the country but kept within sight of the road at all times. For three miles we struggled

> over fences and through fields and because we were exhausted and hungry we approached a farm which was surrounded by a concrete wall. While we were looking over the gate, a woman came out on the porch and saw us. She called in the house and four men came out to look at us. We spoke our few German words to indicate we were hungry and then said we were American flyers. They were scared and one of them came out to look up and down the road. A young boy who spoke English walked up to us and began asking us about our planes and how many days we had traveled. We told him our story and for five minutes the people talked among themselves. Then the boy said to follow him and took us to a wood about half-a-mile away.
>
> We waited for him to return. When he did he had food and water and was accompanied by several other people. One of them asked us how we could identify ourselves and we produced our dog-tags, wings, bars—in fact, everything we had. We saw one of the men riding off on a bicycle and asked where he was going. We were told not to worry—that he had gone off to get help for us. We felt that it was all right because we were in a position where we could run if the man brought back suspicious-looking people. While we were waiting, a complete shaving-kit and civilian clothes were brought to us. In the evening the man who had gone off on the bicycle returned with another man and from here our journey was arranged.[46]

Genz and Nelson eventually returned to England, with the aid of resistance fighters, on October 30, 1943. Their experiences depict a not uncommon situation and the challenges that confronted downed airmen. It took them approximately two and a half months (seventy-four days) to return to Allied lines, slightly more than the average number of days it took a downed flyer to return to England. Of the nearly four hundred successful escapes and evasions, it took airmen on average sixty-two days when shot down over France or the Benelux countries. Flyers who had evaded and escaped in Germany had the most success in the Rhineland region, due to its proximity to France and the Benelux countries as well as its relative proximity to Allied lines following the Normandy invasion. Even if captured, however, there were cases of flyers escaping numerous times. One airman, Staff Sergeant Glenn Loveland, was shot down on June 13, 1943, and immediately captured; however, he was able to escape on seven different occasions, for varying lengths of time, and finally returned to England on September 11, 1944.[47]

An Escape Intelligence Bulletin from November 1944 directed American airmen landing in Germany and Austria to "assume that the younger people are Nazis; when seeking help, rely on the older people, and when doing so 'play' on their sympathy."[48] Genz and Nelson demonstrated general success when it came to playing on sympathy for food and directions, especially after having evaded for over a month. Although their desperation and fatigue from evading increased significantly, this eventually worked in their favor and allowed them to connect with an escape line. The exhaustion and despair caused from being on the run for an extended period often resulted, however, in flyers being negligent, especially with regard to security, which could lead to capture.

The case of Genz and Nelson demonstrated that Catholic priests could be helpful, especially in France along the German border; at the very least, they offered the possibility of food. However, additional examples of successful evasions show that priests, aided by their connections throughout the area, could be of much more assistance. Forced to bail out following a mission to attack Berlin on March 6, 1944, during which their B-17 (42-40052) bomber received heavy flak damage, Sergeant Neal W. Person and Sergeant Bradley J. Standlee landed along the German-Dutch border. After immediately contacting the Dutch resistance, the flyers were taken to the first of three priests (located in Maastricht, Netherlands; Lüttich, Belgium; and Montbeliard, France) who aided them on their 350-mile journey to Switzerland. Finally returning to England on September 13, 1944, Person and Standlee had spent over six months (nearly two hundred days) on the run.[49] Person and Standlee were fortunate; in Germany, clergymen appear to have offered little assistance. In fact, two separate war crime tribunals found a priest and a deacon guilty of aiding and abetting in Lynchjustiz.[50]

Ordinary citizens in France, the Netherlands, and Belgium were vital to the evasion efforts of airmen and their survival. These helpers took an extreme risk, putting not only their own lives in danger but also the lives of their family and friends. As in the case of First Lieutenant Meyles A. Sheppard—a navigator of the B-17 (42-31040) nicknamed *Duffy's Tavern*, shot down near Prüm, Germany, on January 29, 1944—chance also played a considerable role in flyers' success. After evading for five days, making his way west into Luxembourg, Sheppard described:

> I was beginning to get hungry and at dusk I approached a house. A woman came to the door and I said, "Je suis aviateur americain. Pouvez-vous m'aider?" Although excited, she did not seem unfriendly, so I waited to see what happened. She returned with her husband and another man. They talked to me and when they learned that I was hungry, brought me food and drink. They told me to wait and went to get the village priest and a priest who spoke English. The latter questioned me carefully to discover who I was. He seemed satisfied with my dog tags as identification. He told me that the people whom I had approached were friendly but that they had relatives who had been sent to concentration camps in Germany for helping Allied airmen. They would try to get me clothing and shelter me for the night, but I would have to move on before dawn. He told me that the neighbors on both sides were pro-German, so I realized how lucky I was to have hit this house.[51]

Foreign workers (e.g., French, Belgian, Dutch, Russian, and Polish) were a possible source of aid for flyers as well. In Germany, foreign workers were most likely to sympathize with Allied airmen as the evasion of Second Lieutenant Stanley C. Krzywicki revealed. During an intense air battle on March 16, 1945, between four P-47 fighters and twenty German fighters, Krzywicki's plane was hit, and he was forced to bail out near Kirn, Germany. After avoiding the pursuit of Germans, he met two Russian workers who gave him food and hid him in a barn for four days. On March 20, 1945, Krzywicki emerged from the barn to find the US Eleventh Armored Division advancing through the town. Shortly thereafter, he was able to return to England.[52]

In eastern Europe, primarily in the Balkans, downed airmen had another way of returning to Allied military control—namely, rescue operations. The most well-known mission that rescued airmen from behind enemy lines was Operation Halyard, during the summer and fall of 1944. The OSS rescued over 500 servicemen, including over 400 flyers, after they bailed out over Serbia and German-occupied Yugoslavia.[53] By October 1, 1944, the United States military had rescued 2,694 Allied flyers from the Balkans (the majority in Yugoslavia).[54] By the end of the war, the number of Allied airmen rescued (mostly Americans), exceeded 4,000.

During the summer of 1944, however, Germans became more prone to reprisals against evading servicemen, resulting in training instructions advising airmen to keep their weapons, equipment, and uniforms unless they were compelled to dispose of them. Previously throughout the war, airmen were strongly advised to either avoid bringing their service pistols on missions or to immediately dispose of them upon landing to avoid any misinterpretations of being a threat by the agitated, and often hostile, German captors.

Sonderbehandlung

Sonderbehandlung was one of the most severe ways downed airmen could be mistreated. This was a typical tactic used by the SD and the Gestapo. There were no limits to how severe they would mistreat their victims. Torture tactics included, for example, thumb and shin screws, waterboarding, electrocution, and severe beatings, which usually culminated in execution or imprisonment in a concentration camp. While Nazi officials determined that airmen who targeted German civilians would be considered Terrorflieger and should receive Sonderbehandlung, flyers did not necessarily have to meet the established criteria to be mistreated. German citizens often considered airmen to be terrorists merely because of their association with the Allied air forces and, therefore, sought revenge as a way to suppress the enemy, as well as retaliation for the personal losses they experienced.

A typical example was the murder of Second Lieutenant Arthur M. Scott in Ailingen, Germany, on July 20, 1944. Following a bombing attack on Friedrichshafen, Scott parachuted from his disabled B-24, nicknamed "Hairless Joe," and landed near Ailingen—two miles from where the bombing attack occurred. The *Ortsgruppenleiter* immediately took Scott into custody and confined him in the local jail. The following day, on orders from the Kreisleiter to kill the alleged "gangster," the Ortsgruppenleiter, along with an SS soldier, took the flyer to the outskirts of town, where he was murdered.[55]

Instances of airmen hunted down by a so-called *Jagdkommando* (search and pursuit unit) also occurred. Similar to the notorious *Einsatzgruppen* that liquidated Jews in eastern Europe, the Jagdkommando were ruthless, hunting downed Allied flyers in Germany and killing them without mercy. An example from the postwar crime trials revealed that

> following a bombing attack on the interior of Germany, September 12, 1944, a disabled American bomber made an emergency landing near Ruppertshütten (45 miles East of Frankfurt am Main). . . . A Jagdkommando was dispatched from Würzburg

> consisting of eleven men, four from the criminal police, two from the Gestapo, four regular uniformed police, and the driver. Upon arrival at the plane, the detail found a gendarmerie and from 80 to 100 people from the village standing by. . . . All four flyers were collected and taken into the woods by members of the Jagdkommando party and shot to death.[56]

Perpetrators buried the four American airmen (First Lieutenant Edward J. Lower, First Lieutenant Roman H. Newman, Second Lieutenant Harvey Dater, and Sergeant Robert E. Kuhn) in the local cemetery at Ruppertshütten. Following the war, the only member of the Jagdkommando brought to justice was the leader, who attempted to reason that he had acted on orders and that the flyers had allegedly attempted to escape. The prosecution, however, clearly proved that the airmen had surrendered and that the execution was premeditated. The man convicted was a thirty-nine-year-old member of the KriPo who had belonged to the Nazi Party since 1937. However, for reasons unclear in the trial documents, he received only one year in prison.

Instances of airmen treated as spies revealed that the majority of flyers wore civilian clothing (after having evaded with the help of escape lines) and had occasionally lost or thrown away their dog tags. Jewish airmen in particular often removed their dog tags, which revealed their religion for burial purposes, to avoid additional danger. The most well-known example of Sonderbehandlung was the 168 airmen (81 American, 47 British, 29 Canadians, 9 Australians, and 2 New Zealanders) sent to Buchenwald. Shot down during the first half of 1944 in France, Belgium, and the Netherlands, the airmen evaded for several days, and in some cases even months, before their capture. German agents—for example, Jacques Desoubrie—who had infiltrated the resistance groups in France and the Benelux countries betrayed the airmen to local Gestapo officers.

German officials held the flyers, believed to be spies, at Fresnes Prison (located south of Paris) for up to two months. Conditions were horrific and prisoners faced brutal torture and interrogations. Describing his experience in Fresnes, First Lieutenant Joseph F. Moser wrote, "It was dark and mercifully cooler in the tiny cell. The door slammed and locked behind me. I was alone. My eyes adjusted to the dim light, and I could see a concrete bed on one wall, covered with a dirty and very thin straw mattress. There was no toilet, only a hole in the floor and a small concrete sink."[57]

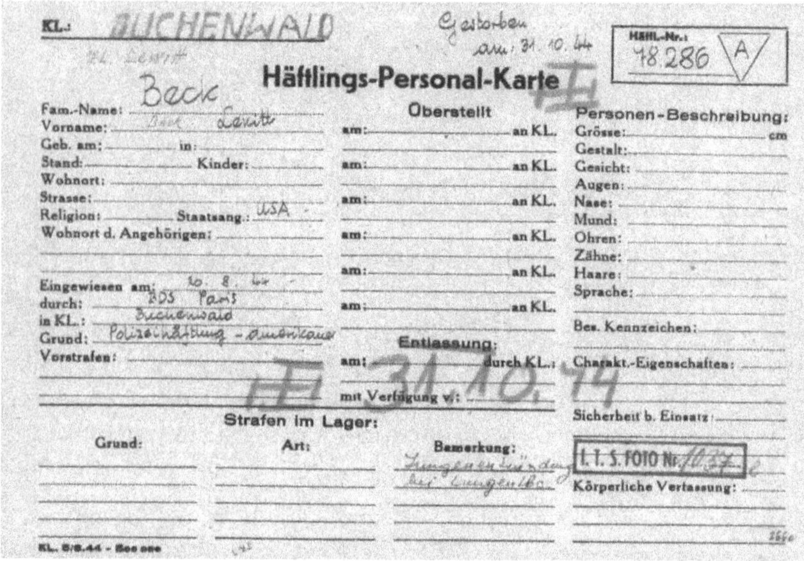
KL.: BUCHENWALD

Gestorben am: 31. 10. 44

Häftl.-Nr.: 78286 A

Häftlings-Personal-Karte

Fam.-Name: Beck
Vorname: Levitt
Geb. am: in:
Stand: Kinder:
Wohnort:
Strasse:
Religion: Staatsang.: USA
Wohnort d. Angehörigen:

Eingewiesen am: 10. 8. 44
durch: BdS Paris
in KL.: Buchenwald
Grund: Polizeihäftling – amerikaner
Vorstrafen:

Überstellt
am: an KL.
am: an KL.
am: an KL.
am: an KL.
am: an KL.
am: an KL.

Entlassung:
am: 31.10.44 durch KL.:
mit Verfügung v.:

Personen-Beschreibung:
Grösse: cm
Gestalt:
Gesicht:
Augen:
Nase:
Mund:
Ohren:
Zähne:
Haare:
Sprache:
Bes. Kennzeichen:
Charakt.-Eigenschaften:
Sicherheit b. Einsatz:
I.T.S. FOTO Nr. 1037
Körperliche Verfassung:

Strafen im Lager:

Grund:	Art:	Bemerkung:

KL. 8/8.44 - Bee ose

Figure 1.6. Prisoner Identification Card for First Lieutenant Levitt Clinton Beck Jr. He died in Buchenwald due to mistreatment and illness. For more information on Levitt C. Beck, see Levitt Beck, *Fighter Pilot. Buchenwald Prisoner Identification Card, Levitt C. Beck, 1944, 1.1.5.3/ 5497776/ International Tracing Service (ITS) Digital Archive, Arolsen Archives, International Center on Nazi Persecution.*

With the airmen designated as *Polizeihäftlinge* (police prisoners) on their prisoner identification cards (fig. 1.6), prison officials forced them into cattle cars and sent them to Buchenwald on August 15, 1944, along with over twenty-three hundred French men and women who had been held as political prisoners at Fresnes.[58] Four days later, the Allies liberated Paris. Due to overcrowding in the boxcars, many prisoners stood for the entire five-day trip. Although it is quite clear that these airmen were legally POWs attempting to evade capture, their reclassification meant that German officials considered the airmen criminals involved in acts of sabotage or connected to the resistance. This misidentification sent them on a doomed trip to Buchenwald (fig. 1.7).

Article 30 of the 1907 Hague Regulations granted all suspected spies the right to a trial. While the airmen generally wore civilian clothes upon capture and were connected to the resistance, even if it was legitimately in an attempt to evade capture, it was logical for the Germans to inquire about their status. Even if airmen were suspected of espionage, the horrific treatment they received and the lack of trials the Germans employed clearly fall within the realm of war crimes.

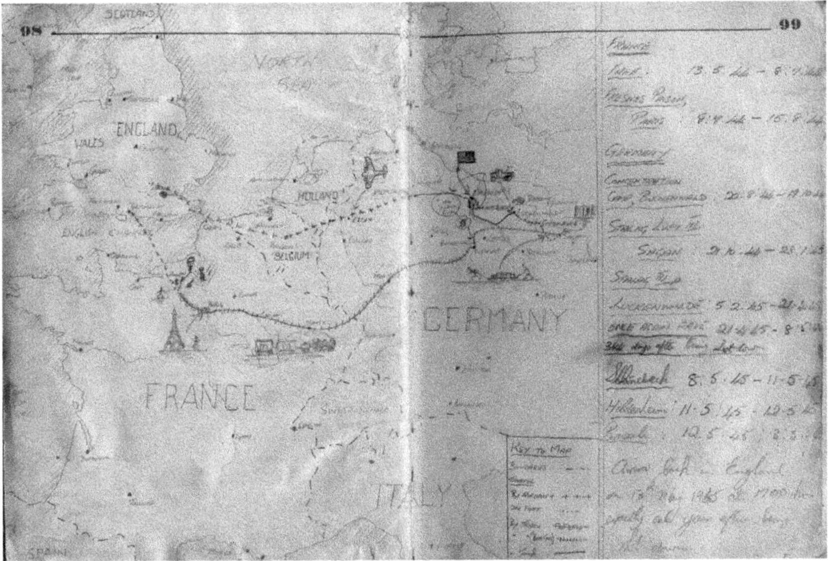

Figure 1.7. Map recording the route Allied airmen took to Buchenwald (Field Officer James A. Stewart, RAF pilot). *Page from James A. Stewart's diary. On display in the museum at Buchenwald.*

While in Buchenwald, guards treated the airmen the same as other prisoners. Upon arrival, the flyers had their heads shaved and received the usual prisoner uniform. The airmen slept outside in an area known as the Little Camp for two weeks. According to Moser, "At first it was very hot and the evenings were cool and comfortable, but as we headed into September, the night chill nearly overcame the increasing pain in our stomachs. We wondered if we were expected to spend the cold winter sleeping outside with no cover, only a thick blanket between three of us."[59] Although camp officials did not use the airmen as forced labor, they did force the flyers to salvage materiel from the German Armament Works factory following an Allied bombing attack shortly after their arrival. The factory was located next to the camp and used prisoners from Buchenwald as forced laborers.

While on an inspection of the bomb damage at the German Armament Works factory, Luftwaffe colonel Hannes Trautloft observed that Allied airmen were wrongfully held in the camp. Disturbed that fellow airmen, regardless of nationality, were kept in such deplorable conditions, Trautloft had 156 flyers transferred to Stalag Luft III on October 19, 1944. The remaining 10 flyers were sent to the POW camp over the following weeks; however, two airmen (US pilot First Lieutenant Levitt C. Beck and British flyer Philip Derek Hemmens) died from illness while in Buchenwald. After over two months of experiencing the hell of the concentration camp, the airmen were finally treated as POWs and brought one step closer to making their way home. It was not until 1997, however, that the United States government officially recognized that these airmen were prisoners in Buchenwald.[60]

This was not the only instance of airmen being mistreated in this manner, however. German officials held at least forty-one airmen (twenty-eight American, ten British, one Australian, one Canadian, and one New Zealander) as spies at Saint-Gilles Prison in Brussels between July 1944 and September 2, 1944. While a few had evaded between November and December 1943, the majority were shot down in Belgium between April and July 1944. Similar to the airmen sent to Fresnes, these pilots were shot down in France near the Belgian border as well as in the Netherlands, but while they evaded, with the help of the resistance (and often aided by Catholic priests), German spies betrayed them after promising to take them to Switzerland. Instead, the spies drove the flyers directly to the front door of the Gestapo headquarters in Brussels and, shortly thereafter, confined them in Saint-Gilles Prison.

Saint-Gilles was the Belgian version of Fresnes. Conditions were horrible. According to First Lieutenant William G. Rychman, "I was put in a dark cell about 6' wide by 4' deep with a high ceiling and no light except for three small holes in the door. A bucket served for a toilet. There were no blankets. For five days I received no water."[61] This was a typical experience. Airmen were often put in solitary confinement in darkened cells and beaten and threatened with execution if they did not answer questions. The interrogations often occurred at the local Gestapo headquarters by a Luftwaffe interrogation officer. Although no known lethal violence occurred against Allied airmen, one flyer recalled an interrogator pulling out the teeth of a Belgian man after he did not answer questions as well as several women who were severely beaten after they did not name additional resistance fighters.[62] Some Germans took out personal vendettas on captured airmen; for example, a German interrogator accused Staff Sergeant James M. Wagner and his fellow flyers "of having killed his wife in a bombing."[63]

Similar to what occurred at Fresnes, the airmen, along with over twelve hundred additional prisoners held at Saint-Gilles, were loaded into boxcars on September 2, 1944, destined for an unknown German concentration camp.[64] This occurred just one day before the liberation of Brussels on September 3, 1944. However, Belgian resistance fighters sabotaged the locomotive and train tracks, prohibiting the train from traveling farther than Schaerbeek, a few miles northwest of Brussels. The airmen eventually escaped and the majority finally reached Allied lines within a day. Numerous airmen reported, however, that they were not the only aviators to have been held at Saint-Gilles; these additional flyers had been sent to German camps a week prior.[65]

Airmen also frequently faced immediate execution upon capture. One such case detailed a *Sonderkommando* (special unit of the SS) that executed Sergeant Robert W. Zercher (USAAF) and Flight Sergeant Kenneth Ingram (RAF). Postwar investigations determined that the Dutch underground in Apeldoorn had hidden both flyers. Ingram was shot down in June 1944 near Emst, Holland, and Zercher was shot down in August 1944 near Laren, Holland. After the airmen were discovered when an informer tipped off local Gestapo agents, officials arrested them on September 30, 1944. A few days later, on October 2, 1944, the chief of the SD in Holland ordered the execution of both airmen and six Dutch helpers. Afterward, a witness stated, "the bodies were exposed in the streets of Apeldoorn with the label 'terrorists' around their necks."[66]

Another brutal case involved the killing of an injured American flyer by lethal injection administered by a German Luftwaffe doctor in Marquise, France, in May 1944. Following the death of the flyer, the doctor decapitated the airman's body and then boiled, skinned, and soaked the skull in hydrogen peroxide. After keeping the skull on his desk for a few weeks, he sent it home to his wife in Germany as a "souvenir," according to the doctor's deposition. Put on trial after the war, the war crime tribunal sentenced the man to ten years' imprisonment.[67]

The two hundred recorded instances of airmen held and mistreated as spies and criminals in France and Belgium, as well as cases of airmen executed upon capture, calls into question how many more flyers faced similar experiences. Different headquarters of the BdS were located in Paris, Brussels, The Hague, Metz, and Strasbourg. In addition, subordinate departments, of the KdS were located in cities throughout France—for example, in Marseille, Bordeaux, Lyon, Nancy, St. Quentin, and Orleans. Furthermore, the BdS had offices throughout the rest of Europe, in Prague, Krakow, Budapest, Verona, Trieste, Belgrade, Kiev, Riga, Oslo, and Copenhagen (fig. 1.8). The cases of airmen held in Paris (Fresnes) and Brussels (Saint-Gilles) are unlikely to have been

Figure 1.8. Locations of BdS (dark circles) and KdS (light circles). *"Das Netz der Gestapo," Haus der Geschichte, Baden-Württemberg, http://www.geschichtsort-hotel-silber.de/das-netz-der-gestapo/europa/bds-fuer-die-operationszonen-alpenvorland-und-adriatisches-kuestenland-in-triest/.*

isolated occurrences given the extensive network of the BdS and the fact that one of their primary tasks was to eliminate spies and Terrorflieger. Flyers certainly experienced a greater extent of mistreatment throughout Europe than previously believed.

While being considered a spy meant certain mistreatment and likely death for flyers, one case from May 25, 1944, revealed the beneficial aspects of the reverse situation—a spy being considered a downed airman. During a secret OSS mission to aid *Maquis* (French resistance fighters) in their effort to sabotage and disrupt the German war effort, Major Cyrus E. Manierre and Sergeant L. T. Durocher parachuted into occupied France near Beaurepaire, thirty-five miles south of Lyon. The OSS agents were successful in aiding the Maquis until August 5, 1944, when the *Milice*—a political paramilitary organization of the Vichy regime that fought against the French resistance—captured Manierre. The

Milice turned him over to the Gestapo in Lyon, where he suffered intense interrogations and beatings for being a suspected spy. However, a fortunate turn of events resulted in his reclassification as an airman POW. After nearly a week in the hands of the Gestapo, French resistance fighters attacked the Gestapo headquarters and killed the Gestapo officers. Manierre was able to convince German soldiers, who had found him in a prison cell, that he was actually a downed flyer and that he received civilian clothing by the Maquis in an attempt to evade to Spain. Over two weeks passed before German military officials sent him on a fifteen-day train ride to the Luftwaffe interrogation center (Dulag Luft) in Oberursel, Germany. There, he was also able to convince the Luftwaffe interrogators that he was indeed an airman, and he was accordingly sent to Stalag Luft I, where he remained until he was liberated on April 30, 1945.[68] All western Allied airmen shot down in Europe, regardless of their location, were supposed to be brought to Dulag Luft for interrogation and then be imprisoned in POW camps. However, even if flyers were lucky enough to make it to Dulag Luft, the possibility of mistreatment and the risk of being accused of acts of terrorism or sabotage, which could still result in Sonderbehandlung, remained.[69]

Positive Treatment by Germans

Although the previous examples describe the mistreatment of flyers at the hands of Germans, there are a few examples of Germans treating airmen favorably. These include providing food, shelter, first aid, and even life-saving support; however, the motives behind such actions remain uncertain. The examples speak, nevertheless, to the difficulty involved in trying to understand the zeitgeist in Germany during the war. Regardless of the manner of assistance, such behavior had the potential of leading to incarcerations either in a local jail or, in the most severe cases, a concentration camp.

Following the crash of an American bomber in November 1944 near Bawinkel, Germany (located in the southern Emsland region of Lower Saxony), local farmers arrived at the crash site, where they found ten airmen—six wounded and four dead. A local man, Hermann Kessen, who had spent years in the United States and spoke fluent English, was able to talk to the downed airmen and helped immobilize the wounded flyers' broken arms and legs. A local firefighter, Heinrich Brinker, arrived afterward with his vehicle and helped transport the wounded airmen to the local hospital. Upon notification of the situation, the

Kreisleiter immediately stated that not only was it not permitted to help the survivors of the plane crash but also it would be best to shoot the prisoners. Although the shootings did not occur, the Gestapo took the six airmen for interrogation, and the Kreisleiter demanded Brinker inform him who had spoken English with the downed airmen, which he refused. Later that evening, however, the Gestapo arrested Brinker and subsequently interrogated and tortured him over a forty-five-day period.[70] Brinker exhibited true moral courage, standing up to local Nazis, not only aiding the downed airmen, but also protecting the identity of his fellow townsman, which saved Kessen's life.

A similar episode of helping American aviators occurred on October 14, 1944, between the villages of Würselen and Verlautenheide (near Aachen). During his forty-fifth mission, Second Lieutenant William W. Donohoe Jr. was tasked with supporting ground troops, as well as strafing nearby targets of opportunity. However, after receiving flak damage, he was forced to land his P-47 fighter plane. Upon landing, he reported his position and situation to his wingman before his airplane was fully engulfed in flames. Donohoe then immediately sought a hiding place in a nearby field. Once the sun set, he became very cold and hungry and decided to break into a nearby abandoned barn—or so he thought. As he crossed the courtyard of the farm, a man appeared and spotted him with his flashlight. Trying in vain to hide in a dark corner, Donohue knew he was caught. Unsure of what would happen next, he stood up, lit a cigarette, and simply said to the farmer: "American." To his great surprise, the farmer began to smile and replied: "Kamerad."

The farmer welcomed the flyer into his house, where his daughter and wife brought him some milk and bread. Donohoe was surprised that, except for the absence of salt, pepper, and other spices, nothing seemed to be lacking in the kitchen. There was plenty of simple country food, such as butter, milk, potatoes, and meat. Seeing how cold and wet he was, the farmer's wife took some of his clothes to dry. Still astonished by this German family's friendly reception, Donohoe sat at the kitchen table with hesitation. The arrival of the farmer's son a short time later only increased Donohoe's nervousness. He found out that the son was around thirty years old and had been wounded in the war, as had the father in World War I, having lost an arm. Acutely aware of being the "enemy" in the presence of a family who had experienced the tragedies of both world wars, Donohoe remained cautious for any sign of impending mistreatment and, if necessary, the possibility of a quick escape. However, to his great surprise and even greater relief, based on what he could understand from the family's discussion and their demeanor, the family appeared to be fed up with the war. Moreover, they seemed equally surprised that Donohoe was a decent human and not a brute, as American flyers were constantly depicted in German media. Sitting around the kitchen table, they noticed Donohoe's rosary and after showing him their own rosary beads tensions instantly eased.

Sleeping hidden in the haystack, Donohoe stayed in the farm's barn for four nights. The family told Donohoe to remain hidden during the day in case anyone came to the house. In addition to continually bringing him lunch, each night they invited him back into the farmhouse for dinner. However, Donohoe could also hear and see German troops moving all around the farm. Knowing the front was only a few miles away, he hoped to stay with the German family, who offered the best option for safety, until the US military arrived.

The flyer's presence at the farm remained an open secret; each night, neighbors would come to visit. In particular, two young girls in their early twenties enjoyed stopping by regularly to joke and laugh with the American. For Donohoe, it seemed like he was being shown off to the locals as a curiosity, and he was surprised that none of them were afraid of the Gestapo finding out that they were treating an enemy flyer so well. Although, unknown to Donohoe and other downed airmen at the time, the likelihood of receiving positive treatment by Germans was highest at the end of the war, as Allied troops increasingly occupied territory throughout Europe. If Germany was to lose the war, the German public faced an uncertain future, particularly in regard to their treatment at the hands of the Allies. Therefore, while some citizens responded by committing violence against downed airmen, others offered aid and assistance in hopes of improving their complicated situation.

On October 18, at around six in the morning, the family's son advised Donohoe to hide in the barn, as soldiers were closing in. Only a few hours later, he heard a commotion outside, and the son came running, shouting "Kamerad!" Fortunately for Donohoe, US soldiers had arrived at the farm.[71] Yet unexpectedly, the situation remained very tense, as the soldiers suspected Donohoe to be a German sniper hiding in the barn. Despite desperately trying to convince his brothers-in-arms that he was indeed a downed American pilot, it was to no avail. Eventually, Donohoe was marched back to the US command post with twenty-six German POWs, their hands raised above their heads. On the way there, however, Donohoe was able to point out his crashed airplane in a field a few hundred yards away, and he finally convinced the

US soldiers of his story. Later that day, he was sent by jeep to a town in Holland, where he was questioned and required to write an Escape and Evasion Report describing his encounter with the German family.[72]

Such positive treatment of downed flyers by Germans has rarely been documented. In fact, only one postwar trial referenced an instance of Germans helping downed airmen. This case involved Captain Everett S. Lindley, who was shot down on April 15, 1945, near Mühldorf, Germany—fifty miles east of Munich. According to court records, members of the *Volkssturm* immediately captured Lindley and took him to a nearby village, where several civilians beat him. After several minutes, two members of the SA, one of whom was the mayor and a member of the Nazi Party since 1931, took custody of Lindley and drove him into the countryside. Lindley became uneasy about what the two men had planned. Seeing the mayor pull a gun and shoot, Lindley immediately

> jumped a ditch but tried to surrender again by facing his assailants and raising his hands. They fired at him again and one bullet hit him in the left shoulder. He then turned and ran a zigzag course while both accused pursued and fired many times. The flyer turned and attempted to surrender the second time but when the firing at him continued, fled again. . . . The flyer took up a position on a small bridge near a farmhouse. By this time a group of people came out of the house. . . . From the group came an elderly white-haired man, a Luftwaffe pilot and a Wehrmacht Sergeant who indicated that the flyer should surrender to them and that they would protect him. He did not do so until the old man prevented the fire from a *Volkssturm* rifleman who approached from the flyer's rear. The sergeant dressed the wound while the old man kept the others away. . . . The Luftwaffe pilot and the sergeant delivered the American to nearby Mettenheim Air Field as a prisoner of war.[73]

Chance and timing had an enormous influence on airmen's experiences. As First Lieutenant Ira Weinstein described after he landed on March 6, 1944, between Kassel and Göttingen, "I got rid of my 'chute and ran up in the hills and I hid under some trees. . . . I saw my pilot (1st Lt. Myron H. Donald) come down in the valley. . . . Soon some farmers came along and they pitchforked him to death. When night came along, I went down and got his dog tags, and they had stripped him of everything but his underpants." Weinstein continued to evade capture for over a week until he came upon the town of Nentershausen. He recalled, "There must have been twenty churches in the town. So I thought, 'If I am going to get a fair shake, it will be in a place where they had so many churches.'"[74] As he walked into town, a boy approached him and asked if he was one of the Americans flyers. Shocked by the boy's fluency in English and anxious about facing a death similar to that of his crewmember, Weinstein acknowledged that he was an American flyer. After taking Weinstein into custody, the boy walked him to the mayor's house. Along the way, the boy admitted that he had gone to school in Milwaukee, Wisconsin, before the war. The mayor's wife fed Weinstein and told him, "If I turn you over to the military in this town [the SS troops], they will shoot you on sight. If you stay here, I will call the Air Force . . . and they will take care of you." A few hours later, members of the Luftwaffe arrived and took Weinstein prisoner; he spent the remainder of the war in a POW camp.[75]

As countless examples exhibit, German civilians rarely feared the downed airmen they encountered. For example, a postwar crime trial depicted how Sergeant Ferdinand E. Flach, shot down near Hattenrod on September 27, 1944, was discovered hiding in the woods by a young woman carrying an infant: "She took him into custody, conducted him to town and turned him over" to the mayor. While Flach's initial encounter with the German woman was fortunate, his luck quickly ran out, and he was murdered, along with at least one other crewmember (Sergeant Lee R. Huffman), a few hours later. After the war, the perpetrators argued that the flyers had attempted to escape; however, the US war crime tribunal sentenced the murderers (a leader of a Hitler Youth Camp and a civilian member of the fire brigade) to death and eight years' imprisonment, respectively.[76]

Women were particularly interested in flyers because they sought their silk parachutes. The material was highly desired during the war, as supplies and goods were limited. As Second Lieutenant Paul Kaufman recalled, after bailing out after a bombing mission over Germany, "on the way down, I saw a lot of farmers running toward me. . . . Farmers came after me and then I heard a couple of shots. . . . Then I noticed the women were running after me screaming. They wanted my parachute."[77] This was not unique to Germany; examples in other European countries, including Great Britain, were numerous.[78]

Rare photos (figs. 1.9–1.12) of captured American airmen in German villages depict civilian's interest and curiosity; many desired to see the enemy whom they had heard so much about in the news and

Figure 1.9. Staff Sergeant Ernest Lacross (waist gunner) captured in Heckendalheim (Willy Mohr). *Klaus Zimmer, "Die Fliegende Festung 'Solid Sender' des amerikanischen Piloten Merlin Chardi abgestuerzt am 25. Februar 1944 bei Alschbach" in* Saarpfalz-Blätter für Geschichte und Volkskunde, *1999/3, 26–29.*

Figure 1.10. B-17 (42–97218) *Toonerville Trolley* with German Family near Bubach on April 24, 1944. Cherry tree stuck in the middle of the left wing. Grandmother, mother, and children. (Dr. Gernot Spengler). *Photo was taken by Ludwig Spengler while home on leave from Italy. See also photo in Klaus Zimmer and Edward D. McKenzie, "Die Fliegende Festung bei Bubach im Ostertal abgestuerzt am 24. April 1944" in* Westricher Heimatblaetter Kusel, *Heft 4/1995.*

Figure 1.11 Technical Sergeant George C. Michie (top turret) B-17 (42–31611) captured near Dillingen on May 11, 1944 (Hella Kuntz). *Taken by Luftwaffe Oberleutnant Herbert Kuntz on May 11, 1944 in Diefflen (Dillingen). See also Stefan Reuter, "Operation No. 351—Der 11. Mai 1944: Die Fliegende Festung des amerikanischen Piloten Marion Holbrook" in Armin Jost and Stefan Reuter, eds.,* Dillingen im Zweiten Weltkrieg: Eine Dokumentation der Dillinger Geschichtswerkstatt *(Dillingen, Germany: Geschichtswerkstatt, 2002), S. 31–55.*

Figure 1.12. Most likely Staff Sergeant William T. Collins captured in Drohne on February 24, 1944. Collins, along with Staff Sergeant Delbert Cress and Staff Sergeant William H. Bower, was one of the only crew members to survive after his B-24 nicknamed *Dusty Demons* (42–64440) was attacked by a German fighter aircraft. All three flyers were captured in Drohne, Germany, on February 24, 1944. Photo taken by Heinz Reiningen. *Courtesy of Lieselotte Meyer-Reiningen.*

propaganda. While many were surprised to see that the airmen were not beastly savages, as they were so often portrayed, the close contact presented civilians with a person whom they could hold accountable for the death and destruction of the war.[79]

While the majority of downed airmen held in POW camps were treated relatively humanely and more according to international laws, growing evidence suggests that a significant number of flyers were not so fortunate.[80] Allied airmen, in particular, were viewed as the enemy who had brought the war to the German home front and escalated the devastation to new extremes. Germans' personal experiences in the war, the influence these had on their attitude toward the Nazi regime, their previous familiarity with the United States and Great Britain, their religious and moral principles, and the phase of the war, as well as chance and timing, were all influential in the treatment of downed aviators. The possibility of airmen receiving aid and assistance from the German public was unlikely but possible. Such occurrences were most likely to transpire during the final months of the war. As the Allies were quickly overrunning Germany and Allied victory became evident, individuals sought to positively influence their uncertain future in an Allied-occupied Europe.

Notes

1. John C. McManus, *Deadly Sky: The American Combat Airmen in World War II* (New York: Nal Caliber, 2016), 209.
2. "Battle Casualties in European Theater" (table 36) and "Combat Sorties Flown, By Theater" (table 118), *Army Air Forces Statistical Digest, World War II* (Washington, DC: Office of Statistical Control, December 1945), http://www.dtic.mil/dtic/tr/fulltext/u2/a542518.pdf.
3. Donald L. Miller, *Masters of the Air: America's Bomber Boys Who Fought the Air War against Nazi Germany* (New York: Simon & Schuster, 2006), 143.
4. "Battle and Nonbattle Deaths—Continental U.S.," *Army Battle Casualties and Nonbattle Deaths in World War II—Final Report: December 7, 1941–December 31, 1946*, Statistical and Accounting Branch Office of the Adjutant General, 1950, 102, https://archive.org/details/ArmyBattleCasualtiesAndNonbattleDeathsInWorldWarIi Pt1Of4.
5. "Battle Casualties in Air Corps, by place, type and disposition," *Army Battle Casualties and Nonbattle Deaths in World War II*, 78.
6. Stan Sommers, *The European Story* (Marshfield, WI: American Ex-Prisoners of War, Inc., July 1980), 1; Mitchell G. Bard, *Forgotten Victims: The Abandonment of Americans in Hitler's Camps* (Oxford: Westview Press, 1994), 35.
7. Miller, *Masters of the Air*, 400.
8. For example, see Herman Bodson, *Downed Allied Airmen and Evasion of Capture: The Role of Local Resistance Networks in World War II* (London: McFarland and Company,

2005); Aidan Crawley, *Escape from Germany, 1939–1945: Methods of Escape Used by RAF Airmen during World War II* (London: Stationery Office, 2001); Betty Gatewood and Jean Belkham, *Kriegie 7956: A World War II Bombardier's Pursuit of Freedom* (Shippensburg, PA: Burd Street Press, 2001); Kenneth W. Simmons, *Kriegie* (New York: Thomas Nelson & Sons, 1960); Sherri Greene Ottis, *Silent Heroes: Downed Airmen and the French Underground* (Lexington: University of Kentucky Press, 2001); Peter Eisner, *The Freedom Line* (New York: Harper Collins, 2004); Graham Pitchfork, *Shot Down and on the Run: The RCAF and Commonwealth Aircrews Who Got Home from behind Enemy Lines 1940–1945* (Toronto: Dundurn Group, 2003); Bruch H. Wolk, *Jewish Aviators in World War II: Personal Narratives of American Men and Women* (Jefferson, NC: McFarland, 2016); Jerome W. Sheridan, *Airmen in the Belgian Resistance: Gerald E. Sorensen and the Transatlantic Alliance* (Jefferson, NC: McFarland, 2014); McManus, *Deadly Sky*; Alexander Jefferson and Lewis H. Carlson, *Red Tail Captured, Red Tail Free: The Memoirs of a Tuskegee Airman and POW* (New York: Fordham University Press, 2005); David A. Foy, *For You the War Is Over: American Prisoners of War in Nazi Germany* (New York: Stein and Day, 1984).

9. *The Great Escape*, directed by John Sturges (USA: Mirisch Company, 1963). Although the original plan was for several hundred POWs to escape through tunnels, only seventy-six were able to get out before a guard spotted the men escaping. Three men were successful in escaping; two traveled to Sweden and one eventually reached the British consulate in Spain. Within a few days, the remaining escapees were captured, fifty of whom were executed by members of the SS and Gestapo on orders from Hitler. The 1953 film *Stalag 17* was based on Donald Bevan and Edmund Trzcinski's Broadway play, which was based on their personal experiences as POWs in Stalag 17B near Krems, Austria.

10. Major Laura C. Counts, "Were They Prepared? Escape and Evasion in Western Europe, 1942–1944" (thesis, Air Command and Staff College, 1986), 1.

11. "Evasion in Europe," Military Intelligence Service (MIS-X) Manual on Escape, Evasion, and Survival (Washington, DC: War Department, February 1944), 3. https://wwiinetherlandsescapelines.files.wordpress.com/2012/08/evasion-in-europe-part-of-mis-x-manual.pdf.

12. Since World War II, United States strategy and doctrine involving POWs as well as escape and evasion have evolved with the times, varying with the experiences gained from wars up to the present.

13. Michael R. D. Foot and J. M. Langley, *MI-9: Escape and Evasion, 1939–1945* (Boston: Little, Brown and Company, 1979), 15.

14. Wolk, *Jewish Aviators in World War II*, 137.

15. Major Laura C. Counts, "Were They Prepared?", 31. See also: "PW&X Escape and Evasion Report Summary," memorandum, London, October 22, 1944.

16. "Airplane Losses on Combat Missions in European Theater" (table 159), *Army Air Forces Statistical Digest, World War II* (Washington, DC: Office of Statistical Control, December 1945), http://www.dtic.mil/dtic/tr/fulltext/u2/a542518.pdf.

17. Miller, *Masters of the Air*, 398.

18. Counts, "Were They Prepared?," 26, 33.

19. For an example of German spies disguised as Allied airmen who betrayed a resistance group, see Airey Neave, *Little Cyclone* (London: Bitback Publishing, 1954), 62–74.

20. Levitt Clinton Beck Jr., *Fighter Pilot* (Los Angeles: Wetzel Publishing Company, 1946); Sherri Greene Ottis, *Silent Heroes: Downed Airmen and the French Underground* (Lexington: University of Kentucky Press, 2001), 141–45.

21. Pitchfork, *Shot Down and on the Run*, 4.

22. "Evasion in Europe," 4.

23. Military Intelligence Section 9 (MI9) supported resistance networks. Special Operations Executive (SOE) conducted espionage, sabotage, and reconnaissance. The Office of Strategic Services (OSS) coordinated espionage and other activities behind enemy lines.

24. Spain eventually changed its status to "nonbelligerent" following the fall of France in 1940. Turkey was also a nonbelligerent country until it declared war on Germany in February 1945.

25. "Evasion in Europe," 4.

26. Stephan Tanner, *Refuge from the Reich: American Airmen and Switzerland during World War II* (New York: Sarpedon, 2000), 335; Bo Widfeldt and Rolph Wegmann, *Making for Sweden: The United States Army Air Force, The Story of Allied Airmen Who Took Sanctuary in Neutral Sweden* (Walton-on-Thames, UK: Air Research Publications, 1998).

27. Dwight S. Mears, "Interned or Imprisoned?: The Successes and Failures of International Law in the Treatment of American Internees in Switzerland, 1943–45" (dissertation, University of North Carolina–Chapel Hill, 2012), 26–29.

28. See Confidential and Secret Incoming and Outgoing Messages 1942–1945, NARA, RG 319, E57, Turkey Box 635, 636, and RG 319, E47C, G2 Project Decimal File 1941–1945, Turkey Box 1032. For additional reference, see Mears, "Interned or Imprisoned," 40.

29. Memo from Major Robert Brown, Assistant Military Attaché for Air in Turkey, to Military Attaché in Turkey, "Force landed Aircraft," dated November 23, 1943, MID 383.01, Top Secret Incoming and Outgoing Cables 1942–1945, Switzerland, NARA, RG 319, E58, Turkey Box 41. For additional reference, see Mears, "Interned or Imprisoned," 42.

30. See Raymond L. Proctor, *Agony of a Neutral: Spanish-German Wartime Relations and the "Blue Division"* (Moscow: Idaho Research Foundation, 1974), 276; Carlton J. H. Hayes, *Wartime Mission in Spain, 1942–1945* (New York: Macmillan Company, 1945), 103. Analysis of War Department records indicates that Spain interned approximately 170–200 United States airmen. See Confidential and Secret Incoming and Outgoing Messages 1942–1945, NARA, RG 319, E57, Spain Box 594–601. For additional reference, see Mears, "Interned or Imprisoned," 32.

31. See "General Status USAAF Aircraft in Portugal," dated August 15, 1944, NARA, RG 319, E47C, Army Intelligence Project Decimal File 1941–1945, Portugal Box 964; Carlos Guerreiro, *Aterrem em Portugal: Aviadores e aviões* beligerantes em Portugal na II Guerra Mundial (Lisbon: Pedra da Lua, 2008), 222–92. For additional reference, see Mears, "Interned or Imprisoned," 37.

32. See memo from Chief, Foreign Branch, Collection Unit, Military Intelligence Division, to U.S. Military Attaché in Spain, "Force landed Aircraft," November 23, 1943, NARA, RG 319, E47C, Army Intelligence Project Decimal File 1941–1945, Spain Box 1008; telegram from U.S. Military Attaché in Spain to G-2, U.S. War Department, October 13, 1943, No. 431; telegram from G-2, U.S. War Department to U.S. Military Attaché in Spain, February 28, 1944, No. 555, Confidential and Secret Incoming and Outgoing Messages 1942–1945, RG 319, E57, Spain Box 598, NARA; telegram from U.S. Military Attaché in Spain to G-2, U.S. War Department, October 11, 1943, No. 372, Confidential and Secret Incoming and Outgoing Messages 1942–1945, RG 319, E57, Spain Box 595, NARA; telegram from General Arnold to U.S. Military Attaché in Spain, June

27, 1944, No. WAR 56671, Confidential and Secret Incoming and Outgoing Messages 1942–1945, RG 319, E57, Spain Box 599, NARA. For additional reference, see Mears, "Interned or Imprisoned," 34.

33. See memo from Chief, Foreign Branch, Collection Unit, I.G. to Liaison Officer, Department of State, "Proposed purchase by Portuguese Government of a Force landed B-17 Plane," April 28, 1943, RG 319, E47C, G2 Project Decimal File 1941–45, Turkey Box 1600, NARA; "General Status USAAF Aircraft in Portugal," August 15, 1944, RG 319, E47C, Army Intelligence Project Decimal File 1941–1945, Portugal Box 964, NARA. For additional reference, see Mears, "Interned or Imprisoned," 40.

34. T. Ryle Dwyer, *Guests of the State: The Story of Allied and Axis Servicemen Interned in Ireland during World War II* (Dingle, County Kerry, Ireland: Brandon Book Publishers, 1994).

35. Tanner, *Refuge from the Reich*, 335.

36. Ibid., 18, 248.

37. Mears, "Interned or Imprisoned," 77, 126.

38. Escape and Evasion Report Number 2844, Second Lieutenant Robert F. Rhodes, March 9, 1945, RG 498, Entry 133, Box 51, NARA, https://catalog.archives.gov/id/5557455.

39. *Pariser Zeitung*, March 25, 1943, in "Evasion in Europe," 11.

40. For more information, see Philip D. Caine, *Aircraft Down: Evading Capture in WWII Europe* (Washington, DC: Brassey's, 1997).

41. Pitchfork, *Shot Down and on the Run*, 55–96.

42. For more information, see Ben Macintyre, *Rogue Heroes: The History of the SAS, Britain's Secret Special Forces Unit That Sabotaged the Nazis and Changed the Nature of War* (New York: Crown, 2016), 239–44.

43. For similar cases of airmen shot and killed while in their parachutes, see the following: Summary Report, Security and Intelligence Section, Fort Sheridan, September 22, 1945, RG 153, Entry 143, Box 147, NARA; Statement of Facts, Judge Advocates Office—War Crimes Group—US European Theater, War Crimes Case No. 11-496, October 7, 1946, RG 153, Entry 143, Box 152, NARA; War Crimes Deposition, October 3, 1945, War Crimes Case No. 12-2253, RG 153, Entry 143, Box 415, NARA.

44. Escape and Evasion Report Number 170, First Lieutenant Robert E. Nelson, October 30, 1944, RG 498, Entry 133, Box 520, NARA, https://catalog.archives.gov/id/5554811.

45. Ibid.

46. Ibid.

47. Escape and Evasion Report Number 856, Staff Sergeant Glenn Loveland, September 11, 1944, RG 498, Entry 133, Box 22, NARA, https://catalog.archives.gov/id/5555497.

48. "Escape Intelligence Bulletin Number 4," November 13, 1944, from the Fifteenth Air Force Headquarters, Maxwell AFB, Montgomery, AL.

49. Escape and Evasion Report Number 2057, Sergeant Neal W. Persons, September 13, 1944, RG 498, Entry 133, Box 39, NARA, https://catalog.archives.gov/id/5556687.

50. Review and Recommendations for Case No. 12-1292, RG 153, Entry 143, Box 349, NARA; Review and Recommendations for Case No. 12-2064, RG 153, Entry 143, Box 408, NARA.

51. Escape and Evasion Report Number 734, First Lieutenant Meyles A. Sheppard, June 11, 1944, RG 498, Entry 133, Box 19, NARA, https://catalog.archives.gov/id/5555374.

52. Escape and Evasion Report Number 2886, Second Lieutenant Stanley C. Krzywicki, March 22, 1945, RG 498, Entry 133, Box 52, NARA, https://catalog.archives.gov/id/5557493.

53. Gregory A. Freeman, *The Forgotten 500: The Untold Story of the Men Who Risked All for the Greatest Rescue Mission in World War II* (New York: NAL Caliber, 2007); Edi Šelhaus, *Evasion and Repatriation: Slovene Partisans and Rescued American Airmen in World War II* (Manhattan: Sunflower University Press, 1993); William Matthew Leary, *Fueling the Fires of Resistance: Army Air Forces Special Operations in the Balkans* (Washington, DC: US Air Force History and Museums Program, 1995).

54. "Special Operations: AAF Aid to European Resistance Movements, 1943–1945," U.S. Air Force Historical Study No. 121. Air Historical Office Headquarters, Army Air Forces, June 1947, 133–34.

55. Review and Recommendations for Case No. 12-931, RG 153, Entry 143, Box 329, NARA.

56. Review and Recommendations for Case No. 12-1034, RG 153, Entry 143, Box 333, NARA.

57. Joseph Moser, *A Fighter Pilot in Buchenwald* (Bellingham: Edens Veil Media, 2009), 34.

58. Ibid., 40.

59. Ibid., 90.

60. "Recognizing and Commending American Airmen Held as Political Prisoners at the Buchenwald Concentration Camp during World War II for Their Service, Bravery, and Fortitude," H. Con. Res. 95, 105th Congress (1997–1998), https://www.congress.gov/bill/105th-congress/house-concurrent-resolution/95/text, accessed February 20, 2017.

61. Escape and Evasion Report Number 1591, First Lieutenant William G. Ryckman, September 7, 1944, RG 498, Entry 133, Box 32, NARA, https://catalog.archives.gov/id/5556221.

62. Escape and Evasion Report Number 2143, Staff Sergeant Royce F. McGillvary, September 14, 1944, RG 498, Entry 133, Box 40, NARA, https://catalog.archives.gov/id/5556773.

63. Escape and Evasion Report Number 1870, Staff Sergeant James M. Wagner, September 9, 1944, RG 498, Entry 133, Box 36, NARA, https://catalog.archives.gov/id/5556500.

64. See Appendix E for list of known airmen. See also: "The Ghost Train," World War Two Escape and Evasion, http://www.conscript-heroes.com/escapelines/EEIE-Articles/Art-17-Ghost-Train.htm, accessed April 4, 2016.

65. Escape and Evasion Report Number 1861, Staff Sergeant Donald H. Swanson, September 10, 1944, RG 498, Entry 133, Box 36, NARA, https://catalog.archives.gov/id/5556491.

66. Letter to Lieutenant Colonel I. Davidson, AAG Liaison (British), War Crimes Branch, USFET, March 20, 1946, RG 153, Entry 143, Box 512, NARA.

67. Deputy Theater Judge Advocate's Office, War Crimes Branch Case No. 11-773, (United Nations War Crimes Commission Case Number 412), April 24, 1947, RG 153, Entry 143, Box 152, NARA.

68. "Major Cyrus E. Manierre," World War II—Prisoners of War—Stalag Luft I, http://www.merkki.com/manierrecyrus.htm, accessed March 28, 2016.

69. For more information on Dulag Luft, see Stefan Geck, *Dulag Luft/Auswertestelle West: Vernehmungslager der Luftwaffe für westalliierte Kriegsgefangene im Zweiten Weltkrieg* (Frankfurt am Main: Peter Lang, 2008); Raymond F. Toliver, *The Interrogator: The Story of Hanns Joachim Scharff, Master Interrogator of the Luftwaffe* (New York: Schiffer Publishing, 1997); Philip M. Flammer, "Dulag Luft: The Third Reich's Prison Camp for Airmen," *Aerospace Historian* 19, no. 2 (1972): 58–65.

70. Hermann Kessen, "In 45 Tagen Gestapo-Haft den Freund nicht verraten," *Lingener Tagespost*, November 2, 2015.

71. The soldiers were members of I Company, Third Battalion, Thirtieth Infantry, Thirtieth Division.

72. Escape and Evasion Report Number 2474, Second Lieutenant William W. Donohoe Jr., October 20, 1944, RG 498, Entry 133, Box 45, NARA, https://catalog.archives.gov/id/5557090.

73. Review and Recommendations for Case No. 12-581, RG 153, Entry 143, Box 289, NARA.

74. Despite the number of churches, six months later, on September 27, 1944, five American airmen were murdered in Nentershausen by a local SS soldier and three civilians.

75. Wolk, *Jewish Aviators in World War II*, 105.

76. Review and Recommendations for Case No. 12-472, RG 153, Entry 143, Box 274, NARA.

77. Wolk, *Jewish Aviators in World War II*, 108.

78. For example, a newspaper article described how "a band of women confronted a downed German airman with pitchforks to steal his silk parachute to make knickers." See "The Women Who Stole Downed German Airman's Silk Parachute to Make Knickerbockers," *The Telegraph*, January 10, 2013.

79. These images are extremely rare, as the Nazi regime prohibited taking photos of POWs. If caught, the individuals faced being put in jail. The airmen in these photos experienced quite favorable treatment from their captors and managed to survive the war.

80. For more information, see Clare Makepeace, *Captives of War: British Prisoners of War in Europe in the Second World War* (Cambridge: University of Cambridge Press, 2017); "Battle Casualties in Air Corps, by Place, Type and Disposition," *Army Battle Casualties and Nonbattle Deaths in World War II*, 78.

Chapter 2

American "Terror Flyers" in German Propaganda

With the aid of propaganda to consolidate power by integrating, mobilizing, and motivating German citizens, the Nazi regime created an environment in which illegal and immoral actions could not only occur but also thrive and be consciously carried out with zeal and resoluteness. The regime used both positive and negative elements of propaganda, depending on the desired psychological effect, in response to the developing situations on all fronts.[1] The air war was a key theme, especially after 1943, when American participation increased and the Combined Bomber Offensive resulted in around-the-clock air raids against Germany.

The Nazi regime described Lynchjustiz as an appropriate way to treat the so-called Terrorflieger, *Luftgangster*, and *Kindermörder* (fig. 2.1). The violence worked in accordance with the regime's desires to combat the enemy and offered a potentially rewarding opportunity for propaganda—namely, an attempt to solidify the obedience of the German population and thus to harden the Volksgemeinschaft. Nazi officials took advantage of the situation and used the precarious state of the German populace—experiencing daily bombing and strafing raids—in an attempt to combat the Allied air war. In fact, according to SD reports, many Germans began questioning the regime by 1943 due to the failure on the eastern front, the threat of the Allies opening a second front in western Europe, the rapidly increasing devastation of the Combined Bomber Offensive, and the unfulfilled promises of Vergeltungswaffen.[2]

From the German perspective, American airmen represented not only the key symbol of American savagery and immorality but also the

Roosevelts Tiefflieger gegen Frauen und Kinder
US
Murder Inc.
Nord-Amerikaner? — Mord-Amerikaner!

Figure 2.1. "Roosevelt's strafers against women and children. North American?—Murder American!" *"Roosevelts Tiefflieger gegen Frauen und Kinder,"* Völkischer Beobachter *(Berlin), June 14, 1944.*

source of destruction and devastation in Germany. Caricatures from satirical magazines (e.g., *Kladderadatsch*, *Lustige Blätter*, *Fliegende Blätter*, and *Simplicissimus*) offered a variety of images underutilized by historians. *Kladderadatsch*, the largest and most well-known political satire magazine in Germany, often focused on attacking the viciousness of Allied war tactics. When discussing the overall topic of the air war in Europe, Nazi Party magazines (e.g., *Das Schwarze Korps* of the SS) and newspapers (e.g., *Das Reich* and the *Völkischer Beobachter*) focused mainly on updating readers on the alleged results from the most recent bombing or strafing raids, often exaggerating the number of enemy aircraft shot down. Many other articles, however (often published following the Allied invasion on

June 6, 1944), focused on preserving the cohesiveness of the German public and rallying them to combat the enemy. Satirical magazines on the other hand focused more on the identity and characteristics of airmen and consistently used images and caricatures to convey directly the regime's desired message.

In 1942, propaganda focused on introducing the new enemy—the "true American"—to German society and often attempted to convey the uncivilized characteristics of American society. A subtheme found throughout the war was the history of lynching African Americans in the United States. In particular, German propaganda emphasized the immoral culture and the impure racial makeup of the United States.

By 1943, flyers, in particular, had become the main focal point of anti-American propaganda; airmen were thus the prime representatives of the enemy. Attempting to demonstrate the coarse nature of American society, propaganda stressed that the US government specifically recruited criminals to be airmen. Propaganda often portrayed airmen as mercenaries who received cash bonuses for directing their attacks on "soft targets" (e.g., women, children, and hospitals). Additional targets of American flyers were allegedly sites of cultural and historical significance. These were supposedly unfamiliar and insignificant to the allegedly ignorant Americans because the United States had neither a significant history nor cultural value, especially in comparison to Europe. Images of African American airmen also greatly increased over time, attempting to further signal American impurity and its inferiority to Germany.

Finally, as the air war reached a climax in 1944 and Germany experienced drastic losses on the eastern front, as well as the Normandy invasion in the summer of 1944, the general theme in propaganda focused on increasing morale on the German home front for ultimate survival. This meant incriminating the Allies' motives in the most radical and crass manner. The air war allegedly intensified through a new crusade, with Allied airmen blessed by and fighting under the auspices of both the Church of England and Judaism. A connection to Bolshevism was also made, which conveyed a link between the western Allies and the alleged Jewish-Bolshevik-plutocratic conspiracy to dominate the world. More specifically, the tone of this Jewish-Bolshevik conspiracy aimed at robbing Europe of its culture, wealth, and history by bombing and pillaging European cities. The Nazi regime used this propaganda theme especially during the Allied bombardment of Italy.

1942

Two years of fighting had already been underway when the United States entered World War II at the end of 1941. Large-scale bombing of cities and urban areas such as Warsaw, Rotterdam, the Ruhr region, Berlin, London, and Coventry, as well as Germany's Blitzkrieg warfare that devastated France and the Benelux countries, generally ended in favor of Nazi Germany. Nevertheless, the radicalization of warfare continued to grow. The mood of the war gradually shifted in favor of the Allies, however, once the United States entered the war, bolstered by its vast resources (i.e., its workforce, soldiers, and industries). Although Nazi propaganda occasionally included the United States before 1942—describing President Roosevelt, for example, as a cunning gangster—it mostly focused on the alleged incompetence of the British RAF and Prime Minister Winston Churchill due to the ongoing air war between Britain and Germany.

Nazi propaganda built on the primary concerns of the German public throughout the war. For example, beginning in 1940 the alleged mistreatment and murder of downed German airmen by French soldiers and civilians in France caused "widespread outrage" throughout Germany.[3] The regime, specifically Hermann Göring, assured revenge. However, Göring's infamous quote days before the outbreak of World War II, that "no enemy bomber can reach the Ruhr. If one reaches the Ruhr, my name is not Göring. You can call me Meyer—Hermann Meyer," became a point of sharp embarrassment to the Luftwaffe as the war progressed.[4] This quote was something the Nazi propaganda campaign continually had to counter.

Despite this, the German public longed for the "great satisfaction" of revenge, especially since they believed enemy POWs were often treated "too friendly."[5] The issue of Germans, especially women, treating POWs favorably—talking to them, giving them food, and even in extreme situations having sexual relations with them—became a great concern. Despite an increased threat of punishment for "shameful behavior" with foreigners, instances of sexual relations with foreigners had increased by the end of 1942.[6] Additional alarm existed after reports that African French POWs and white French POWs received the same treatment as German soldiers. This development "countered the propaganda" image of Africans being an inferior race, and therefore, many Germans questioned this treatment.[7] However, the lack of well-publicized revenge against the alleged wrongs committed against the German

MARSCHALL MC. ARTHUR: „Bester Manilahanf, Mr. Roosevelt!"

Figure 2.2. "The best abaca fibers, Mr. Roosevelt!" Kladderadatsch, *January 25, 1942, Page 13. http://digi.ub.uni-heidelberg.de/diglit/kla1942/0062.*

soldiers—and even against civilians by this point, with the beginning of the air war and the bombing of cities—resulted in "anxiety" and "restlessness" among the German public.[8] Furthermore, a gradual shift in the mind-set of German citizens from "we will win" to "we must win" began in 1942, which pointed to a radicalization of the war.[9]

Das Schicksal von drei geschlagenen sowjetrussischen Generälen kam in dem alten Volkslied zum Ausdruck: „Es fuhren drei Burschen wohl über den Don, die holde Frau Wirtin wartete schon."

Figure 2.3. "The fate of three defeated Soviet Generals was described in the old folktale: *Three fellows rowed a boat across the Don River and the sweet hostess was already waiting.*" Kladderadatsch, *January 4, 1942, Page 7. http://digi.ub.uni-heidelberg.de/diglit/kla1942/0008.*

Throughout 1942, anti-American propaganda attempted to explain the relatively unknown history and culture of the United States to the German public to create a basis for future propaganda. According to SD reports, the average German knew little about American ideology or politics; thus, "North America was not only spatially distant for the average German, but also psychologically."[10]

Initially, caricatures used the symbol of a noose (symbolically connected to lynching) to represent the justice offered by the Soviet state political police agency of the interwar period and a potential way to combat the growing Anglo-American problem (figs. 2.2 and 2.3). These images also attempted to indicate a sense of similarity between American and Russian mentality and morality, at least concerning a proper treatment of these similar enemies. In addition, the noose represented an uncivilized and antiquated means of justice similar in style to that associated with frontier justice in the United States. Both nations were perceived as untamed (with regard to the environment as well as the people) and had wild frontiers.

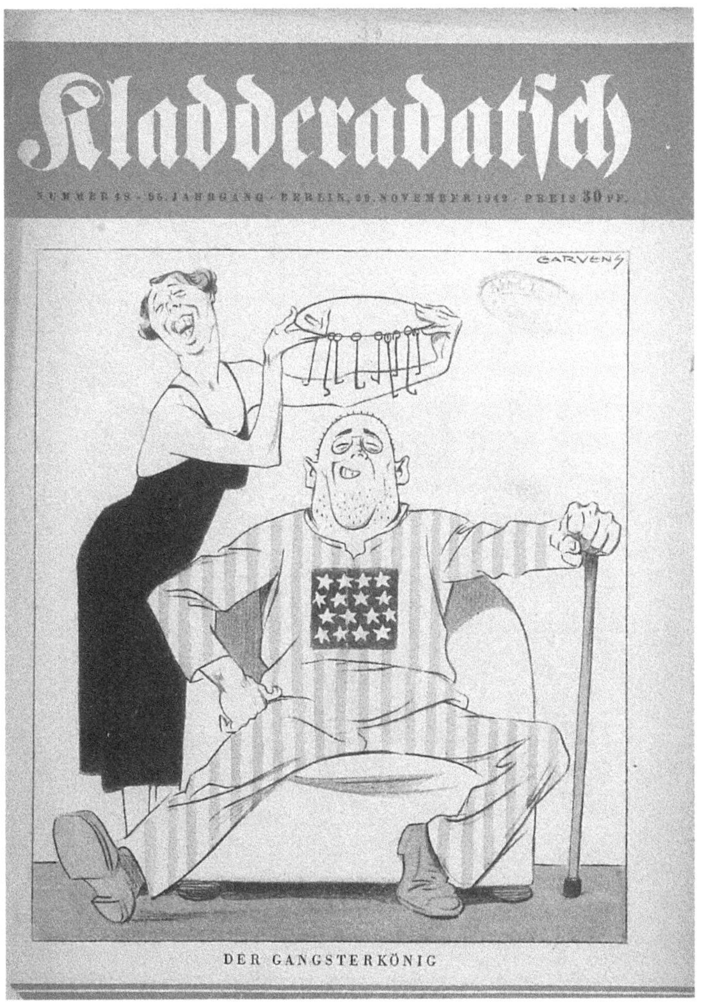

Figure 2.4. President Roosevelt being crowned by his wife, Eleanor, as the "King of the Gangsters." Kladderadatsch, *November 19, 1942, cover page, http://digi.ub.uni-heidelberg.de/diglit/kla1942/0753.*

Building on these alleged cultural characteristics of the new American enemy, German propaganda viewed President Roosevelt as the principal representative of American society and was often portrayed as conspiring with criminals, gangsters, and kidnappers—a theme that recurred throughout the war (figs. 2.4 and 2.5). This notion of Americans

Figure 2.5. President Roosevelt, saying, "Soldiers of America! Al Capone, the greatest gangster of all time, my Chief of Staff, is watching over you!" Kladderadatsch, *March 15, 1942, page 15, http://digi.ub.uni-heidelberg.de/diglit/kla1942/0176.*

as gangsters built on the established portrayal of British POWs as mercenaries in World War I as well as the widely popular American gangster movies of the 1930s, portrayals well remembered by the majority of Germans during the 1940s. The representation of British mercenaries during World War I had led to rather extensive civilian violence against

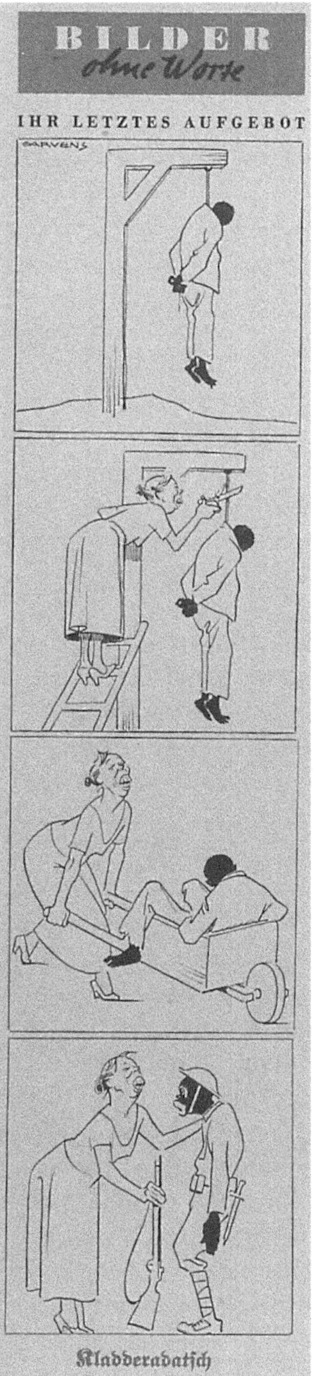

Above, Figure 2.6. "The 'American Century': My grandfather was lynched—my father was lynched—how about if I send 10,000 of you to your death?!" Kladderadatsch, *March 8, 1942, page 2, http://digi.ub.uni-heidelberg.de/diglit/kla 1942/0147.*

Left, Figure 2.7. "Her last contingent." Eleanor Roosevelt (representing America) portrayed saving an African American man from being lynched and sending him off to war to fight for the United States. Kladderadatsch, *March 15, 1942, page 3, http://digi.ub.uni-heidelberg.de/diglit/kla 1942/0164.*

POWs, similar to the violence perpetrated against downed airmen in World War II.

A final theme introduced to degrade Americans further focused on the supposedly troubled and debauched history of the United States, particularly on its impure race and culture. Specifically propagated were the typical use and abuse of African Americans (e.g., lynching) and the hypocrisy of calling on the subjugated race to fight in the name of democracy (figs. 2.6 and 2.7). In addition, propaganda images portrayed "Roosevelt's interventionist policy"—the supporting of the British war effort—and his increasing divergence from the "war-resistant American public," which implied that America had to rely on African Americans to fight the war.[11]

Nazi propaganda attempted to enlighten the German public on the alleged inadequacies of capitalism and democracy, such as the indifference toward racial, societal, and cultural morals and principles. The need to use African Americans as soldiers implied that white American men were either unwilling or unable to fight. Moreover, the propaganda suggested that using African Americans would result in the United States military being of little threat to Germany's ultimate triumph in the war and would lead to the downfall of America as a whole. Such images sought to calm concerns among the German populace about the United States entering the war, conveying that the Americans had no chance of defeating a superior Germany, and maintain a cohesive national community.

1943

The portrayal of airmen as gangsters and criminals became the common propagandistic depiction of western Allies, particularly of the United States, beginning in 1943. This was due to the intensification of the Allied air war, especially the Combined Bomber Offensive against mainland Europe, which started in June 1943. Propaganda alleged that Jews, Bolsheviks, and plutocratic propensities influenced and motivated the increased devastation of the air raids, which killed German women and children and destroyed European culture. Hypocrisy, immorality, and corruption described the characteristics of airmen as well. Furthermore, the negative portrayal of airmen became the focus of anti-American propaganda in hopes that this would overshadow the increasing military failures on the eastern front, especially after the German defeat at Stalingrad. According to historian Aristotle A. Kallis, by 1943 the

Figure 2.8. "USA Niggers are hoisted to the sky." Das Schwarze Korps, *July 15, 1943, page 2.*

"denigration of the USA as the destroyer of European civilization and a land without heart became a highly popular subject of Nazi propaganda."[12] The immoral aspect of the Allies' tactics in the air war also came progressively to the forefront in Nazi propaganda.[13]

Throughout 1943, Nazi propaganda persistently criticized the United States for the immoral air war it was waging as well as for being

Figure 2.9. "Bearer of good news from the USA: 'Hey boy, come with me! When you fly with us, you can shoot white women and children!'" Lustige Blätter, *no. 43, 1943, http://research.calvin.edu/german-propaganda-archive/index.htm.*

racially impure and morally wanting, a society that allegedly relied on undesirables (e.g., prisoners, mercenaries, and African Americans). Kallis also describes how "the U.S. was depicted as the land of the most devastating experiment in racial miscegenation, resulting in a people without identity, biological quality and spiritual unity"[14] (figs. 2.8–2.10).

„Unser eifrigster Flugschüler! Sollte wegen Tötung einer Weißen gelyncht werden
und konnte im letzten Moment noch gerettet werden."

Figure 2.10. "Our enthusiastic student pilot! He was supposed to be lynched for killing a white person, but was able to be saved at the last minute." Lustige Blätter, *no. 43, 1943, http://research.calvin.edu/german-propaganda-archive/index.htm.*

Propaganda images portrayed African Americans as good enough to fight in the name of democracy but not adequate to obtain such freedom in the United States. Furthermore, propaganda depicted the United States as supporting and even promoting the targeting of German women and children. German publications likened such hypocritical acts to the long history of alleged wrongdoings of African Americans against

Figure 2.11. "Racial-Lecture in Detroit (U.S.A.)—'Damn Niggers! When the Roosevelts talk about racial equality, that is with regard to Europe, but never for the U.S.A!'" Kladderadatsch, *July 11, 1943, http://digi.ub.uni-heidelberg.de/diglit/kla1943/0392.*

white women and children, building on a stereotypical justification for lynching African Americans.

The Nazis were quick to capitalize on incidents of racial and national divide in the United States—for example, the Detroit race riot in 1943. Despite the increased roles of African Americans during the

GARVENS
VOR DEM START
„Was hast du nun für ein Gefühl, wenn du Bomben auf Frauen und Kinder wirfst?"
„Das kommt auf die Höhe der Geldprämie an."

Figure 2.12. "How do you feel when you bomb women and children? It depends on the amount of the cash bonus." Kladderadatsch, *May 30, 1943, page 6, http://digi.ub.uni-heidelberg.de/diglit/kla1943/0317.*

war, racial equality was far from reality. The regime attempted to depict the inferiority of American culture and society by illustrating American men as wild and murderous, killing even women and children (fig. 2.11). The wicked anger and infliction of violence were supposed to remind the German public of the lack of moral rationality that divided

American culture and society. The German use of the English word *nigger* (figs. 2.8, 2.11, and 2.26) was also quite telling; the English word *Negro* was already used in the German language (*Neger*) yet the introduction of the English pejorative was adopted by Nazi propaganda to convey American bigotry and the unlikelihood of success in the war.

The degraded characteristics of Americans were actively portrayed, depicting American airmen as mercenaries who fought in any manner necessary to win the war, including attacking women, children, and nonmilitary targets (such as hospitals) for a cash bonus (fig. 2.12). In addition, while Americans were continuously portrayed as criminals, American airmen were singled out for this archetype (fig. 2.13). This was due to the increasing devastation of the air war throughout Germany, especially in urban areas, but also in rural areas where communities feared strafing raids.

According to SD reports, the air war reached drastic dimensions in 1943 with fear that the devastation and destruction, centered mainly in western Europe, could quickly spread to every corner of the greater German Reich.[15] Even in the Alpine region, known to Germans as the "air raid bunker of Germany," fears of aerial attacks were pervasive by mid-1943.[16] The German public's longing for revenge against enemy air raids resulted in uncertainty about Germany's ability to deter such attacks after the continued inability of the Nazi regime to follow through on their promises for vengeance. The hatred for Allied airmen reached a point where "drastic methods"[17] were considered a possible defense against the increasingly devastating air war, following reports that Japan executed downed American airmen in 1942 and 1943.[18] In fact, as historian Gary Anderson described, "the killing of downed airmen in Japan was well-known and acted as an example to follow."[19] However, the German public was also hesitant about such direct violence due to the uncertain treatment of German POWs held by the Allies. The air war had evolved to such a degree that the German population realized it could not bear the terror for an extended period; many citizens had reached their "psychological limit."[20]

The Casablanca Conference in 1943, which resulted in the Allies demanding Germany's unconditional surrender, undoubtedly aided Nazi propaganda by "presenting the Allies' uncompromising stance as both a ploy to 'annihilate' the Reich and to advance the 'Jewish-Bolshevik' goal of world domination," thus giving credence to previous Nazi propaganda and aiding "integration inside the Reich."[21] Nevertheless, SD reports show that by late 1943 and early 1944, German citizens were

Figure 2.13. "How many years did you get for arson? I've been promoted to Lieutenant in the Air Corps." Kladderadatsch, *July 18, 1943, page 11, http://digi.ub.uni-heidelberg.de/diglit/kla 1943/0404.*

growing skeptical of the regime's pledged Vergeltungswaffen to seek vengeance against the Allied air raids.[22] The attacks on downed airmen were not only a direct reaction of anger to the bombing and strafing raids but also an indirect response to the regime's inability to prevent or hinder the devastating effects of the air war. An August 1943 propaganda image

BRITEN-TERROR
„Unfair von den deutschen Fliegern, uns abzuschießen, wo wir nicht gegen sie
sondern nur gegen die Zivilbevölkerung kämpfen . ."

Figure 2.14. "It is unfair of the German airmen to shoot us down since we are not fighting against them but only against the civilian population." Kladderadatsch, *May 30, 1943, page 2, http://digi.ub.uni-heidelberg.de/diglit/kla1943/0311.*

maintained that Allied airmen were fighting against civilians as opposed to soldiers, indicating that there could be no sanctuary for downed airmen (fig. 2.14). Even Joseph Goebbels described this similar intensification of propaganda in a speech at a Nazi Party rally at the Berlin *Sportpalast* two months earlier, stating, "We know that against British-US

Figure 2.15. "USA—Gangster of the Sky call themselves 'Murder Club.'" *"USA—Luftgangster nennen sich selbst 'Mordverein,'"* Völkischerbeobachter *(Berlin), December 20, 1943.*

bombing terror there is only one effective remedy: counter-terror. Today there is but one thought in the minds of the whole of the German people: To repay the enemy in his own kind. . . . One day the hour of retribution will come."[23]

In November 1943, a downed American airman gave the Nazi regime an additional option for their anti-American propaganda. Second Lieutenant Kenneth Daniel Williams, bombardier, was shot down during a mission to bomb Bremen on November 26, 1943. He was captured wearing his bomber jacket that featured the ill-advised name of his bomber: *Murder Inc.*[24] A photo of Williams in his bomber jacket (fig. 2.15) was widely published in Germany, with articles describing how "the murder characteristic of the Anglo-American terror attacks on the German civilian population no longer needed additional proof or explanation."[25] In addition, one article described the "despicable" American airmen, with their "underworld conviction . . . murder and pillage because they are too cowardly to fight honorably."[26] Historians have assumed Williams was the reason why propaganda portrayed American flyers as gangsters and murderers; however, earlier propaganda images prove these depictions were already common years before.

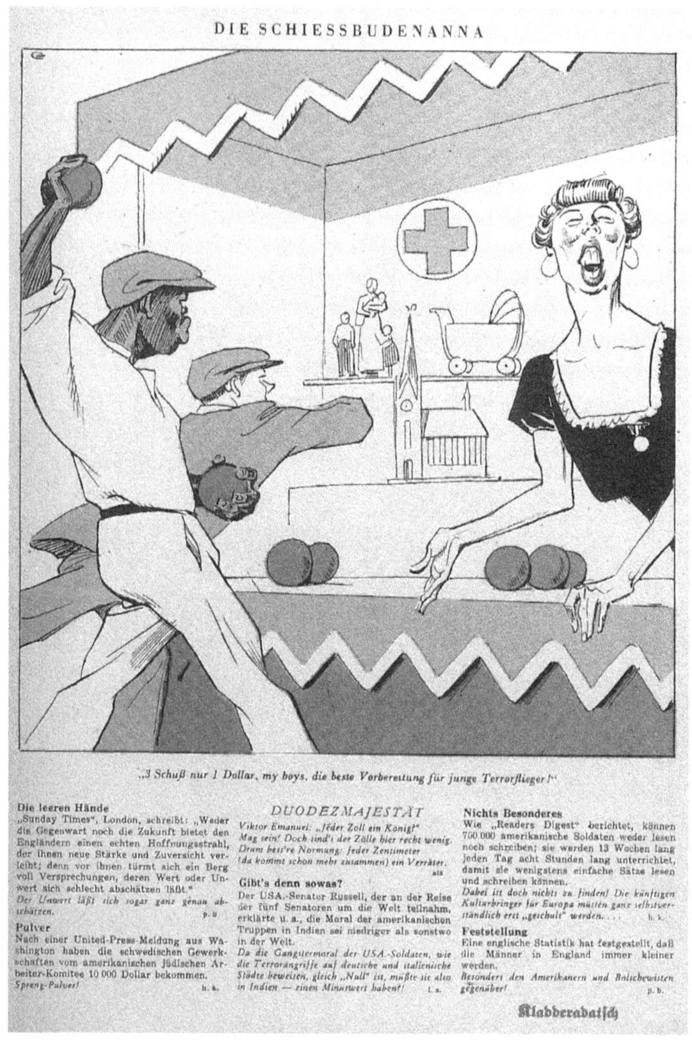

DIE SCHIESSBUDENANNA

„3 Schuß nur 1 Dollar, my boys, die beste Vorbereitung für junge Terrorflieger!“

Die leeren Hände
„Sunday Times“, London, schreibt: „Weder die Gegenwart noch die Zukunft bietet den Engländern einen echten Hoffnungsstrahl, der ihnen neue Stärke und Zuversicht verleiht; denn vor ihnen türmt sich ein Berg voll Versprechungen, deren Wert oder Unwert sich schlecht abschätzen läßt.“
Der Unwert läßt sich sogar ganz genau abschätzen. p. b.

Pulver
Nach einer United-Press-Meldung aus Washington haben die schwedischen Gewerkschaften vom amerikanischen jüdischen Arbeiter-Komitee 10 000 Dollar bekommen.
Spreng-Pulver! h. a.

DUODEZMAJESTÄT
Viktor Emanuel: „Jeder Zoll ein König!“
Mag sein! Doch sind's der Zölle hier recht wenig.
Drum bess're Normung: Jeder Zentimeter
(da kommt schon mehr zusammen) ein Verräter.
als

Gibt's denn sowas?
Der USA.-Senator Russell, der an der Reise der fünf Senatoren um die Welt teilnahm, erklärte u. a., die Moral der amerikanischen Truppen in Indien sei niedriger als sonstwo in der Welt.
Da die Gangstermoral der USA.-Soldaten, wie die Terrorangriffe auf deutsche und italienische Städte beweisen, gleich „Null“ ist, müßte sie also in Indien — einen Minuswert haben! l. s.

Nichts Besonderes
Wie „Readers Digest“ berichtet, können 750 000 amerikanische Soldaten weder lesen noch schreiben; sie werden 13 Wochen lang jeden Tag acht Stunden lang unterrichtet, damit sie wenigstens einfache Sätze lesen und schreiben können.
Dabei ist doch nichts zu finden! Die künftigen Kulturbringer für Europa müssen ganz selbstverständlich erst „geschult“ werden. . . . h. k.

Feststellung
Eine englische Statistik hat festgestellt, daß die Männer in England immer kleiner werden.
Besonders den Amerikanern und Bolschewisten gegenüber! p. b.

Kladderadatsch

Figure 2.16. At the "Shooting Stand," Eleanor Roosevelt states, "3 throws for just 1 dollar, my boys. The best training for young terror flyers!" Kladderadatsch, *November 28, 1943, http://digi.ub.uni-heidelberg.de/diglit/kla1943/0625.*

Nazi publications introduced the morality of bombing, juxtaposing the indiscriminate area bombing of the Allies to German restraint with civilian targets, thus allowing the Nazis to claim "the moral high ground, presenting the Reich's war as an allegedly noble enterprise geared towards rescuing 'European civilization.'"[27] Some images depict

Figure 2.17. "So boys—pay attention. All of the churches and national sanctuaries are marked in red on the map." Kladderadatsch, *August 15, 1943, page 2, http://digi.ub.uni-heidelberg.de/diglit/kla1943/0443*

churches and national sanctuaries specifically targeted and emphasized the sinister actions of the Allied air war (figs. 2.16–2.18).

Furthermore, Nazi propaganda introduced a new religious theme by the end of 1943, in a further attempt to connect Jewish collusion with Allied authorities. Images emphasized the Christian (Church of

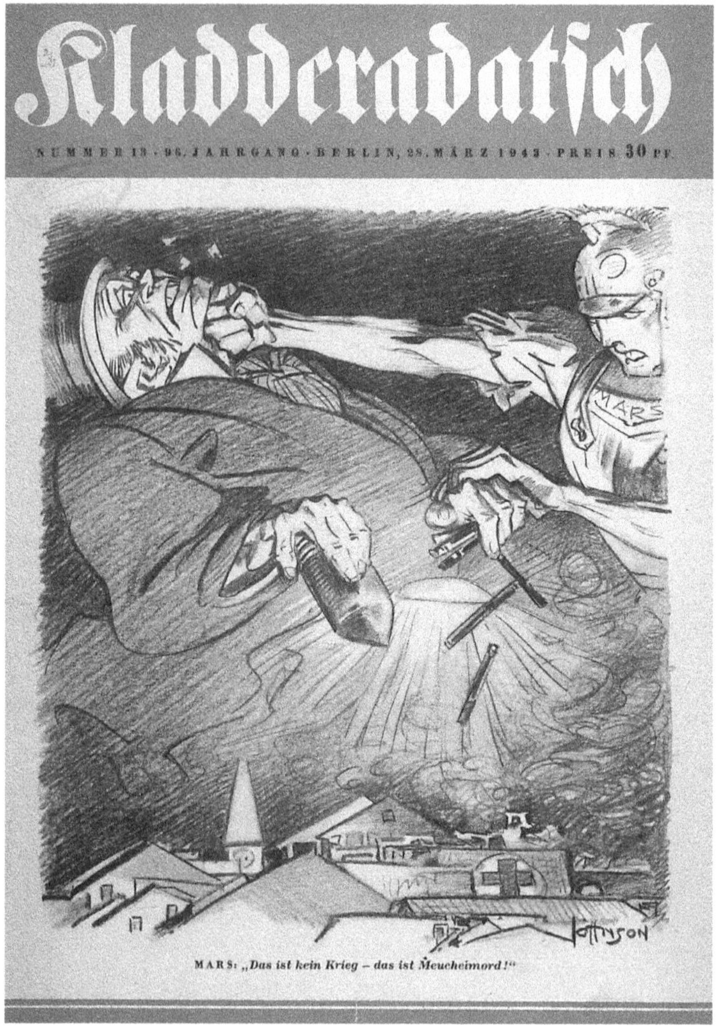

Figure 2.18. "Mars: 'That is not war—that is insidious murder!'" Kladderadatsch, *March 28, 1943, http://digi.ub.uni-heidelberg.de/diglit/kla1943/0193.*

England) and Jewish blessing for the Allied air war. Goebbels specifically ordered propaganda to focus on the attack on Cologne, especially on the Cologne Cathedral, insisting that "people who have never been able to establish their own culture or adapt to the culture of others now want to destroy German culture" (fig. 2.19).[28] The allusion that "Jewish world domination [was] on the tips of U.S. bayonets" became a more

Figure 2.19. "Onward, Christian Soldiers!" Kladderadatsch, *July 18, 1943, http://digi.ub.uni-heidelberg.de/diglit/kla1943/0393.*

widely propagated theme (fig. 2.20).[29] By the end of 1943, however, propaganda ultimately caused fear among the German public. Not only did Germans face the harsh reality that they were losing the war, but they also feared that their families, especially their children, might suffer a sad and terrible fate.[30]

DAS GEBET DES RABBI DER R.A.F.
Der Großrabbiner der R.A.F. im Nahen Osten, Isidor Borodie, segnete auf einem afrikanischen Flugplatz Gruppen von englischen Bombern ein.
Lindlaf
„Ist das nun ein englischer oder ein Moskauer Segen?“ – „Mensch, das ist doch dasselbe!“
Kladderadatsch

Figure 2.20. "The prayer of the R.A.F's Rabbi"—"Now is this an English or Russian blessing?"—"Man, that is the same thing!" Kladderadatsch, *September 26, 1943, http://digi.ub.uni-heidelberg.de/diglit/kla1943/0517.*

1944

The height of the air war against Nazi Germany came in 1944, with the most sorties flown against Germany, the most bombs dropped, and the highest number of airmen shot down. Simultaneously, this coincided with the climax of popular violence against downed airmen.

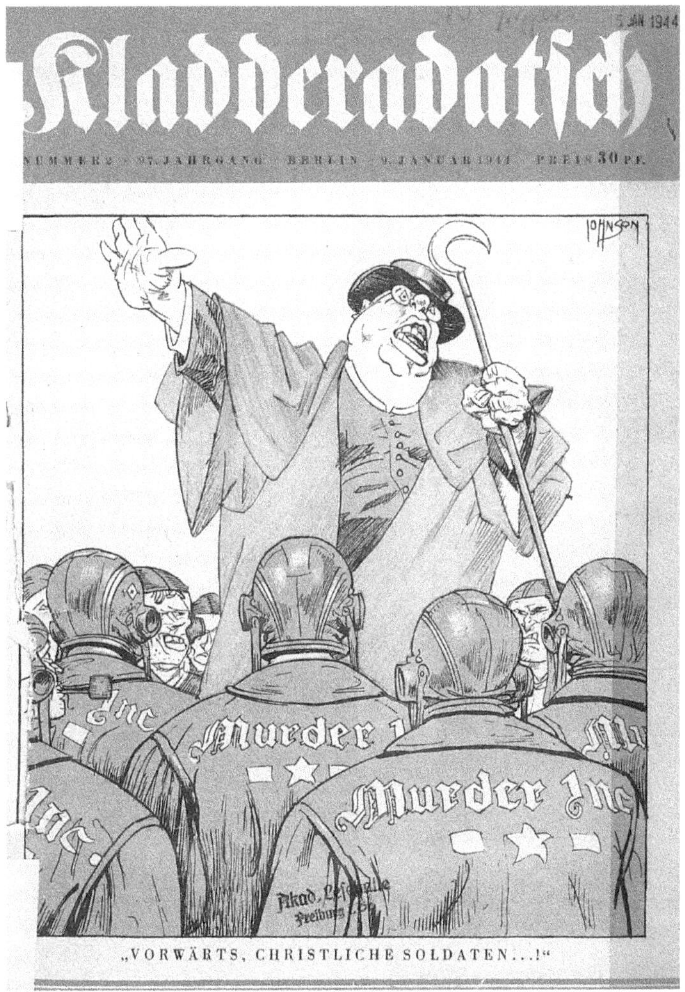

Figure 2.21. "Onwards, Christian Soldiers . . .!" Kladderadatsch, *January 9, 1944, cover page, http://digi.ub.uni-heidelberg.de/diglit/kla1944/0013.*

Goebbels's article in the *Völkischer Beobachter* from May 28, 1944, which was translated and printed throughout the world on the same day, encouraged and invited German civilians to seek revenge against downed airmen. He stated:

> Only with the help of armed forces is it possible to secure the lives of downed enemy flyers from attacks by the public. Otherwise

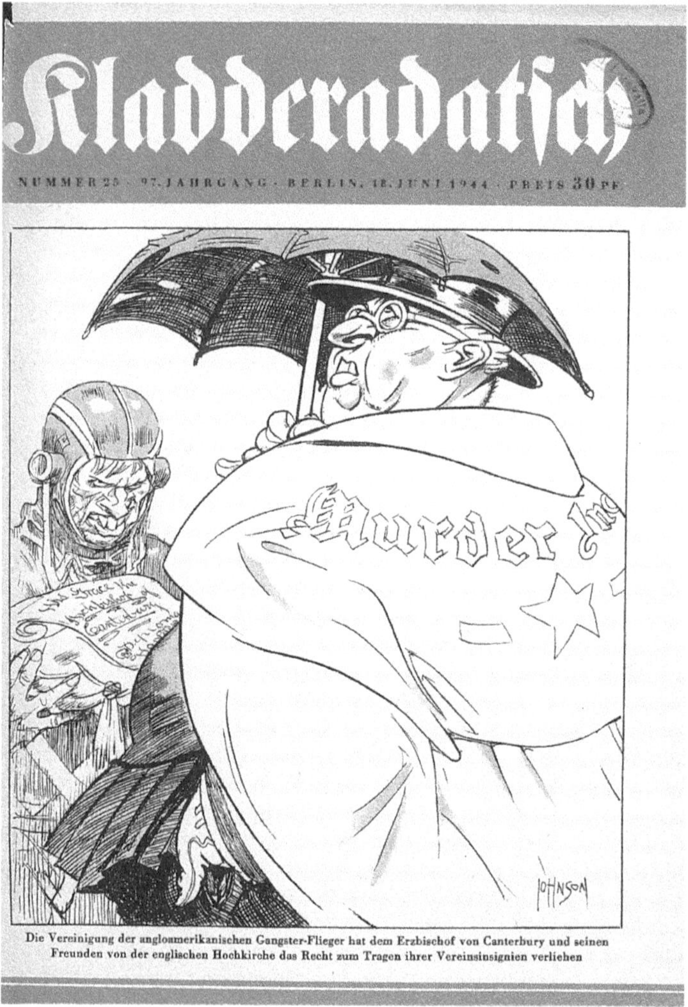

Figure 2.22. "The organization of the Anglo-American Gangster-Flyers received permission from the Archbishop of Canterbury and his friends from the Church of England to wear their insignia." Kladderadatsch, *June 18, 1944, cover page, http://digi.ub. Uni-heidelberg.de/diglit/kla1944/0285.*

these men would be killed by the sorely tried population. Who is right here? The murderers who, after their cowardly crimes, still expect humane treatment from their victims, or the victims who want to defend themselves on the principle of "an eye for an eye and a tooth for a tooth." This question is not difficult to answer.

Figure 2.23. "Satan's Holding a Parade" Kladderadatsch, *January 9, 1944, page 90–91, http://digi.ub.uni-heidelberg.de/diglit/kla1944/0090.*

> In any case, it cannot be expected that we demand German soldiers to protect child murderers, against rage-stricken parents who resort to self-defense after having lost their most precious possessions through the brutal cynicism of the enemy.[31]

Furthermore, the air war in propaganda became a symbolic representation of a new crusade, in which the Allied airmen were sent to war under the auspices of the Church of England—represented particularly in the images of the Archbishop of Canterbury William Temple, who received criticism for being "not only non-pacifist but anti-pacifist."[32] The increasingly negative depiction of flyers was evident in their hardened and hostile facial expressions. Particularly interesting was a January 4, 1944, depiction of the archbishop of Canterbury (fig. 2.21). The archbishop is at center, holding a staff adorned with either a crescent moon or a sickle. The former represented innocence, purity, and chastity and implied that the Allied airmen would be redeemed for their otherwise sinful actions.[33] The latter represented a symbol of communism in an attempt to remind the German population of the indivisibility of Anglo-American airmen with the Jewish-Bolshevik terror (see also fig. 2.23).

Figure 2.24. "The Final Days of Pompeii" Kladderadatsch, *May 7, 1944, page 2, http://digi.ub.uni-heidelberg.de/diglit/kla1944/0215.*

The Nazis also harshly depicted the fall of Rome on June 4, 1944, mere days before the Allied invasion of France. Images featured Jews scavenging through the remaining artifacts and national treasures after the bombing of Pompeii (fig. 2.24). Defeated Italian men were depicted as being forced to transport massive, priceless statues; all the while,

„Wir kommen als Befreier zu euch – habt Vertrauen in eure Zukunft!"

Figure 2.25. "We come to you as liberators—have faith in your future!" Kladderadatsch, *February 8, 1944, page 6, http://digi.ub.uni-heidelberg.de/diglit/kla1944/0067.*

an African American pilot (depicted as a member of *Murder Inc.*) oversaw the devastation that he inflicted. The German public often discussed the destruction in Italy caused by Allied air raids. According to SD reports, even citizens of occupied western nations viewed this as a "cultural disgrace."[34]

The depictions of American airmen used the concepts of race and lynching more drastically in 1944. However, propaganda portrayed the idea of lynching always as a form of an alleged American justice and implied that Americans largely deserved it. Nevertheless, descriptions and caricatures rarely portrayed Germans mistreating downed flyers. Nazi propaganda depicted future "American justice" for Europeans in the form of gallows; this again indicated that German society was morally elevated above the United States (figs. 2.25 and 2.26). A "self-serving

Figure 2.26. "From the land of lynchers"; "We Niggers sure are lucky that no Americans live here." Das Schwarze Korps, *February 24, 1944, page 2, http://research.calvin.edu/german-propaganda-archive/index.htm.*

bias" (*Semmelweis Reflex*), which confirmed negative behavior against downed airmen in order to help create an environment that rejected any evidence contrary to the established paradigm, was often expressed in Nazi propaganda against American airmen.[35]

Building on previous stereotypes used to describe the immorality and hypocrisy of the United States, an April 1944 image in *Kladderadatsch*

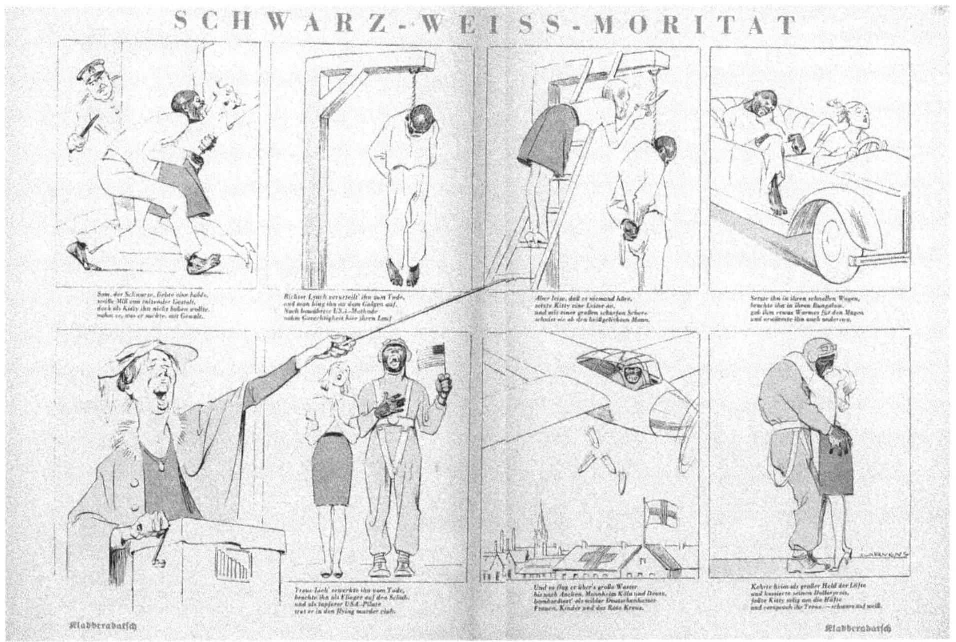

Figure 2.27. Eleanor Roosevelt presenting this "Black-White *Moritat*." Kladderadatsch, *April 16, 1944, page 5–6, http://digi.ub.uni-heidelberg.de/diglit/kla1944/0186.*

depicted a "black and white *Moritat*" (fig. 2.27).[36] The images as a whole represented a story that described the immoral actions of African Americans raping white women, the lynching of African Americans, the bombing of civilians and hospitals, and principally the inability to follow racial segregation.

Focusing on the second scene, the magazine reported, "Judge Lynch sentenced him to death and hanged him from the gallows according to the USA-method of justice." After being saved by Kitty (the white woman, whom he allegedly raped), the sixth scene stated that "he became a member of the 'flying murder club.'" The seventh scene described how "he flew over the big ocean to Aachen, Mannheim, Cologne, and Deutz and bombed women, children, and the Red Cross as a wild German-hater." The final image stated that "he returned home as a great hero of the sky and received his cash bonus. He ecstatically grabbed Kitty by the hips and promised her fidelity—in black and white."[37] These statements were a cynical attempt to attack the American disregard for and immorality of racial integration.[38]

Public Knowledge of Violence against Airmen

The lynching of flyers was widely known in both Germany and the United States during the war, though knowledge of the extent was uncertain, especially in the United States. Images of Terrorflieger were also widely known throughout German society and sought to arouse popular anger against Allied airmen; however, propaganda articles and speeches directly incited the German public to exercise Lynchjustiz. The widely publicized mistreatment of American airmen in Japan greatly influenced Germany's policy of dealing with airmen designated as Terrorflieger. A Nazi announcement in the spring of 1943 indicated that "the German people approve the Japanese precedent of executing airmen who deliberately bomb non-military objectives as the proper answer to the form of aerial warfare which the British and Americans have made their standard pattern in the belief that this will wear down the Axis home front."[39]

In the United States, both the public and government knew about the lynching and mistreatment of flyers as early as 1943. At least thirty *New York Times* articles, from 1943 to 1950, reported on the execution of airmen. In April and May 1943, articles focused on "Axis Reprisals on Flyers" in Italy as well as on the German appeal for "American and British airmen [to] be executed—Tokyo fashion."[40] The reprisal killings committed against downed American airmen of the Doolittle Raid by the Japanese for killing Japanese civilians were especially well-known following President Roosevelt's public disclosure on April 21, 1943—nearly a year to the day of the Doolittle Raid on Tokyo.[41] Newspapers around the world reported on the anger of the American public for the "inhuman, uncivilized, bestial, and brutal" behavior.[42] By the fall of 1943, the United States feared that Germany and Italy would follow the Japanese precedent of executing downed airmen (the Enemy Airmen's Act),[43] as government officials from Germany and Italy publicly supported Japan's law that legally established and expected mistreatment of Terrorflieger.[44] At the end of October 1943, the United States government lifted the censorship on stories brought back by repatriated flyers, permitting airmen to disclose their experiences in prison camps and encounters with Germans. By the end of that year, the threat of reprisal killings in Nazi Germany was clear. Staff Sergeant Benjamin Spring from Denver, Colorado, was interviewed for a *New York Times* article in October 1943 and stated that "enraged German civilians tried to mob American flyers shot down near Hamburg . . . and that they had heard reliably that two Americans were lynched."[45] Technical Sergeant Norman C. Goodwin of Bradford, Massachusetts, recalled "civilians shooting at airmen as they parachuted from their wrecked planes," while Staff Sergeant Milton Williams of Omaha, Nebraska, remembered being "surrounded by a dozen angry Germans when he landed. Several of them had guns and threatened to shoot me. . . . But I was saved by a member of the Luftwaffe."[46] These mistreatments came as a great shock to the Allies, especially for citizens reading such accounts with their loved ones fighting in the midst of the war. The Allies feared "that the threatened German reprisals, if carried out, are certain to result in a complete nullification of the rights of soldiers under international law."[47]

Following the translation and publication of Goebbels's May 1944 article in newspapers throughout the world, which invited civilians to attack downed airmen, British news reports described that German radio broadcasts pursued an "increasingly hysterical propaganda campaign against American and British air attacks."[48] SS leader Heinrich Himmler's order in 1943 regarding the treatment of downed airmen was also published in the *New York Times* in July 1944. The article noted that Himmler was instructing the SS to kill British and American airmen in a manner "that will suggest they have been shot while resisting arrest."[49] In addition, an article in the *Jewish Criterion* (Pittsburgh, Pennsylvania) from January 1944 reported that the impending "trials of captured American airmen, mostly Jews, on charges of bombing German cities, will take place in Hamburg."[50] While no evidence exists that such trials took place, this was likely an attempt by Germany to disguise the murders of airmen as justified punishment, which paralleled Japan's actions against the Doolittle raiders.

As to the response of either the German or United States governments regarding such appalling allegations, the German government naturally denied any wrongdoing, with Admiral Karl Dönitz stating that any airmen killed "died in an attempt to escape."[51] The US government, on the other hand, remained relatively silent on the matter, stating only that they had "no official data on the killing of U.S. Flyers."[52] However, newspapers continually published articles about new instances of airmen who were mistreated. For example, the well-known murders of fifty Allied airmen POWs who escaped from Stalag Luft III in March 1944 received considerable attention in newspapers in the United States and throughout the world for the rest of the year.

The reaction by the American public to the overall mistreatment of airmen was multifaceted, although there was more of a call for increased action against Nazi Germany. A letter to the editor of the *New York Times* from July 20, 1944, stated that a "united declaration of ruthlessness is urged to curb atrocities"; this "eye for an eye" approach is unfortunately similar to that used in Goebbels's article to incite and condone reprisal killings by German civilians.[53] Though on December 1, 1944, an article in the *San Antonio Register* urged the realization of the

> bitter irony that the Japanese . . . had an excellent illustration of the American way of lynching last week . . . [in Parkville, Tennessee]. A 17-year-old boy, accused of a heinous crime, was summarily riddled with bullets by a mob that dragged the youth through the streets. Then other Negroes were forced to march by the mangled, grotesquely heaped body as 'an example' of what might happen to them. . . . The world can eye that brutal lynching in Tennessee with no less concern than the lynching of American fighting men in Japan. Each is equally atrocious and in violation of all laws of a civilized world.[54]

While this article solely connected the lynching of airmen in Japan, it is also related to instances of lynching in Germany. Goebbels attempted to rationalize and justify the violence against the alleged criminals and sought to deter Allied flyers from terrorizing and attacking German citizens, especially women and children, which was shockingly similar to the motivations of lynching African Americans in the United States. In fact, the nation's largest black newspaper, the *Chicago Defender*, observed in 1944 that Goebbels "studiously copied the exact language of American apologists for lynching."[55]

The Influence and Effectiveness of Propaganda

In the context of the air war in World War II, the Nazi regime could not prevent the devastating bombing and strafing raids and, therefore, could not protect its citizens, allowing and even promoting members of the populous to take matters into their own hands against what they viewed as unjust crimes. According to political scientist Daniel Goldstein, "Lynchings are collective expressions of rage and despair in a context of total vulnerability, not only to crime but to the ravages of a political-economic order."[56] Popular justice against downed airmen was an example of citizens' agency within the regime, where direct involvement and mere spectating resulted in varying degrees of complicity. Perpetrators were involved in order to seek revenge for their losses but also to protect their nation. This was a way for the government to regain confidence in their citizens, reaffirming their control over the German public from within by attacking the enemy in their midst. In addition, this established an excuse for the public's actions taken against downed airmen for the foreign community in hopes of diverting accountability from the Nazi command to the masses.

While Hoffmann emphasized that "most lynchings of Allied airmen were not perpetrated in the heat of the moment," and such descriptions were simply "*ex-post* propaganda of the Nazi Party," this tends to reduce the civilians' immediate emotional responses and to some extent their agency and accountability.[57] Nevertheless, Hoffmann correctly asserted that the "situation was deliberately intensified by certain individuals . . . not only major figures in the local Nazi Party but also deeply rooted in their local 'community.'"[58]

On the one hand, the Nazis directed propaganda to a domestic audience by permitting private vengeance. The regime focused on convincing the German society of the justice of lynching American flyers and then hypocritically using this violence for societal control. In addition, propaganda solicited the German public to carry out such actions. This was, however, only after the popular violence began from below within the population, as had occurred in World War I. The government then saw the opportunity to use this phenomenon to its advantage. Furthermore, the regime ordered security forces (drawn mainly from the SS) to disguise themselves as civilians in order to incite a civilian mob response.[59]

On the other hand, the foreign audience was just as significant to the regime's propaganda. The regime attempted to show the public response to the Allied air campaign, thus attempting to identify the Allies as the perpetrators and the Germans as the victims to justify the means to an end. While popular violence was historically widespread throughout the United States, Germany downplayed any condemnation of civilian violence against airmen as American hypocrisy. In addition, propaganda attempted to demoralize the American airmen. Overall, it became a premeditated attempt for the Nazi regime to distance itself from direct culpability.

Similar incidents of Germans mistreating Allied POWs occurred in both world wars. According to Heather Jones, "Civilian violence against prisoners and the media response to it set a significant precedent, whereby an image of transgressive violence against the enemy was established in a way that legitimized further violent radicalized civilian responses in retaliation."[60] A common theme of national mobilization, through "mass conscription, the popular press and the growth of nationalism, triggered a powerful individual response, be it fear or euphoria."[61] In turn, this caused a type of "socially 'constructive' aggression," facilitated through the voyeuristic imagery of propaganda, in order "to popularize and culturally teach the new mark of 'otherness' of the enemy, a means of redefining the new wartime boundaries."[62] Likewise, this hostility toward POWs sent a powerful message to enemy nations that such violence was "popularly sanctioned and had public approval."[63]

Nazi propaganda did indeed influence the treatment of downed airmen by the German population; however, the degree of influence is difficult to determine. The most obvious and direct correlation is with Goebbels's article in the *Völkischer Beobachter* from May 1944, which justified and permitted the German populace to deal with downed flyers as they deemed fit. Goebbels described that it was

> only possible with the aid of arms to secure the lives of enemy pilots shot down . . . for they would otherwise be killed by the sorely tried population. . . . The victims will defend themselves according to the principle of an eye for an eye, a tooth for a tooth! . . . We can find ways and means to defend ourselves against these criminals. We owe this to our people who bravely defend their lives in a proper manner, and therefore in no way deserve to be declared fair game for enemy man-hunters.[64]

Figure 2.28 notes the increased number of airmen known to have been mistreated (based on the postwar crime trials) in Germany during the

Facing top, Figure 2.28. Known Mistreatment of Downed American Airmen in Germany in 1944. Based on quantitative analysis of the flyer trials (see chap. 4).

Facing middle, Figure 2.29. Tons of Bombs Dropped by the United States in the European Theater in 1944. *Source: "Airborne and Effective Sorties Flown in ETO" (table 140),* Army Air Forces Statistical Digest, World War II.

Facing bottom, Figure 2.30. Number of American Airmen Shot Down in the European Theater (excluding wounded who were evacuated) in 1944. *Source: "Battle Casualties in European Theater by Casualty Type" (table 36),* Army Air Forces Statistical Digest, World War II.

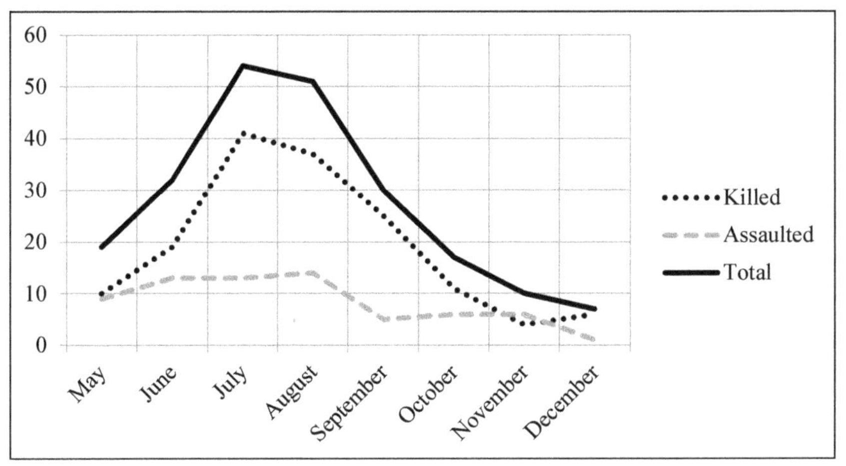
60
50
40
30
20
10
0
May
June
July
August
September
October
November
December
Killed
Assaulted
Total

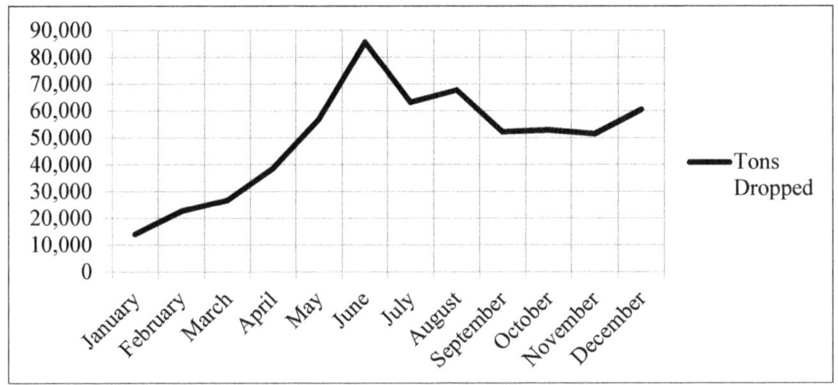
90,000
80,000
70,000
60,000
50,000
40,000
30,000
20,000
10,000
0
January
February
March
April
May
June
July
August
September
October
November
December
Tons Dropped

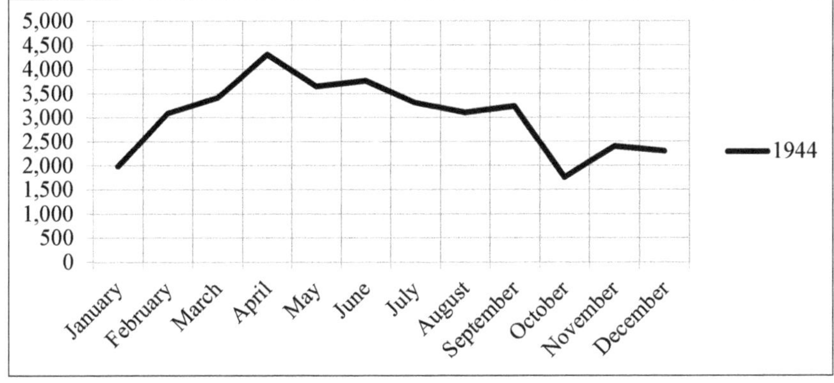
5,000
4,500
4,000
3,500
3,000
2,500
2,000
1,500
1,000
500
0
January
February
March
April
May
June
July
August
September
October
November
December
1944

months following Goebbels's article.[65] The increase in violence immediately followed his public call for the German populace to take action against downed airmen. Nevertheless, despite the increasing Allied bombardment of Germany, analysis of the flyer trials indicated that Lynchjustiz gradually decreased after a few months. The likelihood that the postwar crime trials uncovered every instance of Lynchjustiz is low, and therefore, it is certain that more instances of violence against downed airmen occurred, especially prior to Goebbels's article and at the end of 1944. In the months following the Normandy invasion on June 6, 1944, Allied bombardment of Germany also drastically increased (fig. 2.29), resulting in a consistent number of airmen shot down (fig. 2.30) and, therefore, a steady contact between downed airmen and the German population.[66]

Although this increase in violence against downed airmen cannot be dismissed as mere coincidence, it also cannot be definitively concluded that Goebbels's articles and speeches, or Nazi propaganda in general, were the sole influences. Nevertheless, the timely increase in the mistreatment of flyers was most likely to result in death throughout 1944. As Gary Anderson described, "without the explicit encouragement and 'orders' in Nazi newspapers and Nazi-elites which legitimized the killing of airmen[,] the instances of *Lynchjustiz* would have been substantially less."[67] Lynchjustiz represented a state-sponsored, summary justice fostered by radicalized propaganda that helped facilitate the regime's "state-sanctioned murder of defenseless enemies."[68]

Notes

1. Aristotle A. Kallis, *Nazi Propaganda and the Second World War* (New York: Palgrave Macmillan, 2005), 6.

2. "Wide circles of the population, indicate a certain reduction in trust in the leadership." Source of English translation: Jeremy Noakes, ed., *Nazism, 1919–1945*, vol. 4, *The German Home Front in World War II* (Exeter, UK: University of Exeter Press, 1998), 550–51. Source of original German text: Bericht an die Parteikanzlei vom 29. November 1943, reprinted in Heinz Boberach, ed., *Meldungen aus dem Reich: Die geheimen Lageberichte des sicherheitsdienstes der SS 1938–1945*, vol. 15 (Herrsching: Pawlak, 1984), 6064–66.

3. Boberach, *Meldungen aus Dem Reich*, May 30, 1944, 71–72.

4. See, Nicholas Fleming, *August 1939: The Last Days of Peace* (London: Davies, 1979), 171.

5. Boberach, Meldungen aus dem Reich, June 10, 1940, 75.

6. Ibid., October 12, 1942, 309–10.

7. Ibid., June 10, 1940, 75.
8. Ibid., June 10, 1940, 76–77.
9. Ibid., October 12, 1942, 313.
10. Ibid., February 7, 1944, 483–84.
11. Kallis, *Nazi Propaganda*, 75–76.
12. Ibid., 86.
13. Joseph Goebbels diary entry, June 30, 1943, in *Nationalsozialismus, Holocaust, Widerstand und Exil 1933–1945*, Online-Datenbank, De Gruyter, http://db.saur.de/DGO/basicFullCitationView.jsf?documentId=TJG-5807.
14. Kallis, *Nazi Propaganda*, 76.
15. Meldungen aus den SD-Abschnittsbereichen from July 2, 1943, in *Nationalsozialismus, Holocaust, Widerstand und Exil 1933–1945*.
16. Meldungen aus dem Reich (Nr. 379), April 29, 1943, in *Nationalsozialismus, Holocaust, Widerstand und Exil 1933–1945*.
17. Ibid.
18. Boberach, *Meldungen aus dem Reich*, February 7, 1944, 481–82.
19. Gary Anderson, "Lynchjustiz gegen alliierte Piloten: Drei Fälle aus dem Bodenseeraum 1944/45," in *Opfer des Unrechts: Stigmatisierung, Verfolgung und Vernichtung von Gegnern durch die NS-Gewaltherrschaft an Fallbeispielen aus Oberschwaben*, ed. Edwin Ernst Weber (Stuttgart: Jan Thorbeck, 2009), 276. Original German text: "Das Töten von abgesprungenen Piloten über Japan war in Deutschland gut bekannt und wirkte als Vorbild."
20. Meldungen aus den SD-Abschnittsbereichen from July 2, 1943, in *Nationalsozialismus, Holocaust, Widerstand und Exil 1933–1945*.
21. Kallis, *Nazi Propaganda*, 173.
22. SD-Berichte zu Inlandsfragen from August 12, 1943 (Rote Serie: Kulturelle Gebiete), in *Nationalsozialismus, Holocaust, Widerstand und Exil 1933–1945*.
23. *Völkischer Beobachter*, June 6, 1943, reprinted in Helmut Heiber, ed., *Goebbels Reden 1932–1945* (Bindlach: Grondom, 1991), 225–28; source of English translation: Noakes, *Nazism, 1919–1945*, 500.
24. Popularized by United States news media beginning in the 1930s, the term *Murder Inc.* was often used to describe gangsters, organized crime, and the mafia. Such media attention gave the Nazi regime additional sources for anti-American propaganda, similar to the way lynchings in the United States had been used during World War I and interwar period to fuel German portrayals of America.
25. "USA—Luftgangster nennen sich selbst 'Mordverein,'" *Völkischerbeobachter*, December 20, 1943.
26. Ibid.
27. Kallis, *Nazi Propaganda*, 87.
28. Report from Goebbels, "Propagandistische Auswertung des Angriffs auf Köln," June 30, 1943, BA: NS 18 alt/744, in *Nationalsozialismus, Holocaust, Widerstand und Exil 1933–1945*. Original German text: "Die Tendenz müsse sein, dass Menschen, die nie einer eigenen Kulturschüpfung fühig gewesen wären, Völker, die von der Kultur anderer glebet hätten, jetzt die deutsche Kultur zerstören."
29. "Jüdische Weltherrschaft auf den Spitzen der USA-Bajonette," *Völkischer Beobachter*, August 10, 1943.
30. SD-Berichte zu Inlandsfragen from August 12, 1943 (Rote Serie: Kulturelle Gebiete), in *Nationalsozialismus, Holocaust, Widerstand und Exil 1933–1945*.

31. "Goebbels Invites Attacks on Fliers," *New York Times*, May 28, 1944; Joseph Goebbels, "Ein Wort zum feindlichen Luftterror," *Völkischer Beobachter* (Munich), May 28, 1944. See Appendix A (fig. A1.11) for the original text.

32. W. Temple papers 51, Temple to Hobhouse, March 26, 1944; also Melanie Barber, "Tales of the Unexpected: Glimpses of Friends in the Archives of Lambeth Palace," *Journal of the Friends Historical Society* 61, no. 2: 87–123.

33. D. L. Galbreath and Léon Jéquier, *Lehrbuch der Heraldik* (Frankfurt am Main: Krüger, 1977), 91–101.

34. The original German text: "Diese Massnahme der Amerikaner sei auch von frankophilen Lothringern stark verurteilt und al seine Kultureschande bezeichnet worden," Boberach, *Meldungen aus dem Reich*, (SD-Gruppenstab Metz, June 9, 1943 [Meldungen aus Lothringen], 11.6.1943).

35. Karthik Narayanaswami, "Analysis of Nazi Propaganda: A Behavioral Study," https://blogs.harvard.edu/karthik/files/2011/04/HIST-1572-Analysis-of-Nazi-Propaganda-KNarayanaswami.pdf, accessed October 10, 2015.

36. A *Moritat* represents a direct medium of communication, often in the form of a dark and dismal story in order to teach the public to follow the moral lesson exemplified by the protagonist.

37. *Kladderadatsch*, April 16, 1944, page 5–6, http://digi.ub.uni-heidelberg.de/diglit/ kla1944/0186, accessed October 10, 2015.

38. In the German language, the term "in black and white" (*Schwarz auf Weiß*) is a pun to represent reliability and confirmation.

39. "Axis Barbarity May Extend," *Examiner* (Launceston, Australia), April 27, 1943.

40. "Flyers' Execution Urged: Rome Newspapers Call for Death Penalty for Our Bombers," *New York Times*, April 30, 1943; "Axis Reprisals on Flyers Are Demanded by Gayda," *New York Times*, May 4, 1943; "Nation's Anger Rises at Jap Murders," *Daily Illini* (Urbana-Champaign), April 23, 1943; "Angry Germans Lynch American Bombing Fliers," *Daily Sun* (San Bernardino), October 22, 1943; "Death Facing Allied Airmen in Nazi Hands," *Daily Banner* (Greencastle, IN), December 24, 1943; "Believed Executed by Japs" *Breckenridge (TX) American*, April 23, 1943; "Japanese Appeal to America to Stop Tokio Raids," *Queensland Times* (Ipswich, Australia), April 30, 1943.

41. "U.S. Flyers Executed," *Virginia Monocle*, May 14, 1943.

42. Ibid.; "Jap Murders of U.S. Airmen Horrifies United Nations; Americans Angry," *Army News* (Darwin, Australia), April 23, 1943; "Natives Betray Allied Airmen, Nurses to Japs," *San Bernardino Sun*, May 16, 1943; "Churchill Vows R.A.F. to Help Avenge Murder," *San Bernardino Sun*, April 24, 1943; "World News at a Glance," *Daily Illini*, April 23, 1943; "Bombers to Blast Japan Near Future," *Madera (TX) Tribune*, April 23, 1943; "Revenge Pledged for Executed Fliers: Barbaric Japs Murder Captive Tokyo Raiders," *San Bernardino Sun*, April 22, 1943; "Jap Murder of U.S. Airmen Horrifies United Nations; Americans Angry," *Army News* (Darwin, Australia), April 23, 1943; "Reprisals Urged Against Japs: Murder of Airmen Angers American Public," *The Mercury* (Hobart, Australia), July 17, 1944.

43. This law was established on August 13, 1942, and was largely an ex post facto attempt to condemn enemy airmen who allegedly attacked noncombat targets.

44. "German, Italy May Follow Jap Precedent in Executing Fliers," *San Bernardino Sun*, April 25, 1943; "R.A.F. Will Help to Avenge Murdered U.S. Pilots,"

Advocate (Burnie, Australia), April 26, 1943; "Allied Airmen Attacked Civilians in Italy," *Western Mail* (Perth, Australia), May 6, 1943.

45. "Citizens Menaced Hamburg Bombers," *New York Times*, October 22, 1943.

46. "Germans Stone Yanks," *Madera Tribune*, October 28, 1943; "Mobs Enraged Nazis Threatened Yank Airmen," *Brooklyn Daily Eagle*, October 21, 1943; "Flier Tells How Yanks Lynched," *Mexia (TX) Weekly Herold*, October 22, 1943; "Urge Lynchings of Jewish Flyers," *Jewish Criterion* (Pittsburgh), June 6, 1944; "Nazis Wild Outburst on Airmen," *Army News* (Darwin, Australia), June 4, 1944; "Dr. Goebbels Incites to Murder," *Palestine Post*, May 29, 1944; "Goebbels on 'Murder' by Allied Airmen," *The Times* (London), May 27, 1944.

47. "Revenge Pledged for Executed Fliers: Barbaric Japs Murder Captive Tokyo Raiders," *San Bernardino Sun*, April 22, 1943; "Nazis Threaten Reprisal Trials on American and British Flyers," *New York Times*, December 23, 1943.

48. Daniel T. Brighamb, "Goebbels Invites Attacks on Flyers," *New York Times*, May 27, 1944; "Five Yank Airmen Lynched by Nazis," *Breckenridge (TX) American*, May 30, 1944; "Huns Lynch Yank Airman," *Madera (TX) Tribune*, May 31, 1944; "Flyers Reported Lynched in Reich," *New York Times*, May 31, 1944.

49. "Prussian Killings Pressed by Nazis: Himmler Also Reported to Have Ordered Slaying of Allied Flyers Downed in Reich," *New York Times*, July 27, 1944.

50. "Jews Head List of U.S. Fliers Facing Nazi Trials," *Jewish Criterion* (Pittsburgh), January 7, 1944.

51. "Nazis Rebuff Eden on Slain Captives," *New York Times*, July 23, 1944.

52. "Stimson Is Silent on Nazi 'Lynchings,'" *New York Times*, June 2, 1944.

53. "Reprisal on Enemy Sought," *New York Times*, July 20, 1944.

54. "Lynchers at Work in Tennessee and Japan," *San Antonio Register*, December 1, 1944.

55. "People and Places," *Chicago Defender*, June 10, 1944.

56. Daniel M. Goldstein, "Flexible Justice: Neoliberal Violence and 'Self-Help' Security in Bolivia," in *Global Vigilantes*, ed. David Pratten and Atreyee Sen (London: Hurst Publishers, 2005), 242; see also Berg and Wendt, *Globalizing Lynching History*, 8.

57. Georg Hoffmann, "The Lynching of Airmen at Graz 1945: War Crimes Committed against Allied Airmen in the Context of Violence Control and Post-War-Trials," in *From the Industrial Revolution to World War II in Easter Central Europe*, ed. Marija Wakounig and Karl Ruzicic-Kessler (Münster: LIT, 2011), 224.

58. Ibid.

59. Office of Strategic Services (OSS) Research & Analysis Report (R & A) No. 1113.65, June 24, 1944, RG 153, Entry 143, Box 235, Case 12-239-4, NARA.

60. Heather Jones, *Violence against Prisoners of War in the First World War* (Cambridge: Cambridge University Press, 2011), 37.

61. Ibid., 39.

62. Ibid.

63. Ibid., 68.

64. Joseph Goebbels, "Ein Wort zum feindlichen Luftterror," *Völkischer Beobachter (Munich)*, May 28, 1944. See Appendix A (fig. A1.12) for the original text.

65. Based on quantitative analysis of the flyer trials (see chapter 4 of this volume).

66. "Airborne and Effective Sorties Flown in ETO" (table 140) and "Battle Casualties in European Theater by Casualty Type" (table 36), *Army Air Forces*

Statistical Digest, World War II (Washington, DC: Office of Statistical Control, December 1945), http://www.dtic.mil/dtic/tr/fulltext/u2/a542518.pdf.

67. Anderson, "Lynchjustiz gegen alliierte Piloten," 289. Original German text: "ohne die ausdrücklichen Ermutigungen und 'Befehle' in NS-Zeitungen und durch Nazi-Größen . . . die die Tötung von Piloten legitimiert haben . . . die Fälle von Lynchjustiz wesentlich weniger Zahlreich gewesen wären."

68. Ibid., 289.

Chapter 3

The History and Escalation of Lynchjustiz in Germany

The term *Lynchjustiz* is used to describe the violence perpetrated against downed airmen during World War II; however, questions remain about how this form of violence accurately fits within the broader frame of extrajudicial action. The limited historiography on this subject suggests that lynching in the United States was the primary source of inspiration for its use throughout the world.[1] Lynching in the United States offered the Nazi regime a unique opportunity to discredit the American hypocrisy of lynching African Americans while at the same time promoting American democracy throughout the world. During World War II, accusations expanded to include how the United States used African Americans to help fight for freedom, despite their ill-treatment throughout American history. Nevertheless, Nazi propaganda never denounced popular violence per se. Rather it used imagery to connect the concept of lynching directly with American airmen in an attempt to reinforce a civilian response.

Despite lynching being a well-known and widespread phenomenon, it is particularly difficult to determine a universal definition. Likening it to terms such as *Holocaust* and *genocide*, German historians Manfred Berg and Simon Wendt have described lynching as an "extralegal punishment, usually entailing death or severe physical harm, perpetrated by groups claiming to represent the will of the larger community" to keep perceived crimes in check.[2] Although historically lynching is a global occurrence, racial crimes against African Americans in the United States throughout the nineteenth and twentieth centuries have stigmatized the term.

Using the historiography of lynching in the United States and adapting it to the conditions in Nazi Germany, it is clear that this form of violence was, as Berg and Wendt reasoned, also a "communal self-defense against alleged crimes unchecked by the state."[3] Although perpetrators could claim to represent the will of the larger community, they could also act out of private vengeance without fear of penalty by the state.[4] This violence was crucial to a "system of terror" that operated in an attempt to keep control over German society, as well as to combat the otherwise unstoppable and escalating air war.[5] Nevertheless, the phenomenon was due to a "rapid deterioration of societal and political stability."[6] Community approval and complicity were expressed either in "popular acclaim for the mob's actions or in the failure of law officers either to prevent lynchings or to prosecute lynchers."[7] The regime allowed and urged citizens to actively get involved in the violence, which exhibited "collective expressions of rage and despair in a context of total vulnerability, not only to crime but to the ravages of a political-economic order," which, according to political scientist Daniel Goldstein, is indicative of lynching.[8]

Pre–World War II

Historians William D. Carrigan and Christopher Waldrep determined that the term *lynching* was included in the German language (*Lynchjustiz* or *Lynchmord*) as early as 1900.[9] However, various German magazines from the nineteenth century, as well as a German etymological dictionary, demonstrate that the German press occasionally used the term as early as the mid-1800s to describe lynchings in the United States, often sarcastically condoning such violence, as well as to report occasional lynchings, or at least attempts thereof, in Germany.[10]

By the early 1900s, German newspapers directly connected American lynching to violence in Germany. A *New York Times* reporter in Germany wrote an article titled, "Stories of American Lynchings Inspire Assaults on Negros in German Capital."[11] The article noted that two hundred black men, most of them American, reported incidents of attacks, beating, and stone-throwing: "These occurrences are ascribed to the lynching news which the New York correspondents of German papers are particularly fond of cabling, the impression being produced . . . that this is the proper way to treat negroes [*sic*]."[12]

During World War I, the German press used the 1918 lynching of Robert Prager, a German immigrant in the United States, "to give the impression that lynching Germans is indulged in as a daily sport in America."[13] Furthermore, newspapers reported that "lynch law belongs to the approved rites of 'culture' in the United States" and "the most horrible scenes of human bestiality which can be recorded . . . are quite natural for the Yankee."[14] In an attempt to counter this portrayal of an unjust and hypocritical America, President Woodrow Wilson accused Germany of "reprisals" and "Hun bestiality," redirecting attention away from lynching in the United States and toward Germany, which had "disregarded the sacred obligations of law and made lynchers of her armies. Lynchers emulate her disgraceful example."[15] This statement was in response to the atrocities committed against thousands of Belgian and French civilians by German soldiers during World War I.[16]

Violence against POWs in Europe, particularly British prisoners in Germany, was also widespread in World War I, mainly due to the German view of British soldiers as mercenaries. Heather Jones describes how this phenomenon of civilian violence committed against prisoners "emerged from below within local populations, rather than being orchestrated from above by the authorities." Such actions were a "spontaneous reaction" and "notably vicious,"[17] where, for the crowd, "prisoners served as a metonym for the war onto which they could project their frustrations, their anguish and show solidarity." In fact, prisoners experienced violent behavior by German women, which they found as "a particularly shocking transgression of gender norms." Ultimately, the media response to such violence "both reflected and distorted the reality of prisoners' experiences," she notes. "Representations of real acts of violence by civilians against prisoners fueled further violent behavior against captives, creating nascent 'cycles of violence'; later in the war, these representation-based cycles would spiral into full-scale cycles of violent military reprisals against prisoners." World War I "marked a new era in the complex relationship between prisoners of war, violence and the media," creating a foundation for Germans to draw on and carry out nearly identical violence against downed Allied airmen in World War II.[18] In August 1944, for example, the *Westdeutscher Beobachter* attempted to describe the history of enemy aerial terror attacks committed against German civilians in both world wars.[19]

Two specific events marked the influence of lynching in Germany by the interwar period. Despite the inability of the US Congress to pass an anti-lynching bill, the National Association for the Advancement of Colored People looked globally, reaching to Germany, in its attempt to gather international support. Family members of lynching victims, like

Ida Wright, whose two sons were part of the highly publicized Scottsboro Nine and were sentenced to death in Alabama for attacking white girls, traveled to Germany as part of the Communists' "Red Aid" "to arouse the public to protest against the executions."[20] Wright also sought the cooperation of German intellectuals on behalf of the Scottsboro victims.[21] Although citizens did not lynch the alleged criminals, a fact that locals were quite proud of, the incident nevertheless helped bring additional international attention to the issues surrounding lynching. Over three hundred German intellectuals (including Thomas Mann) formed *The Committee for Saving the Scottsboro Victims* to condemn lynching, writing a letter directly to President Herbert Hoover and Governor B. M. Miller of Alabama in an attempt to gain a pardon for the eight young men, seven of whom faced the death penalty.[22] Communist organizations also reported on the "Fight for Doomed Negroes" in the United States in order to "save the victims of judicial murder" and as a way to gain followers and international support.[23]

In 1919, the murders of Rosa Luxemburg and Karl Liebknecht in Germany were a widely publicized example of violence reported as lynching in Europe. Cofounders of the Spartacus League and the Communist Party of Germany, the two revolutionists took part in the January Uprising, a struggle for power in Germany between the Social Democratic Party and Communist Party. After the suppression of the revolt, a right-wing paramilitary militia known as the Freikorps captured, tortured, and executed them. Newspapers in Germany and the United States covered the incident in articles with titles like "Lynchings Shock People of Berlin" that described how the events "characterize . . . lynching worthy of the wildest West."[24]

During the 1920s, the Inter-Allied Rhineland High Commission, created by the Treaty of Versailles to oversee the occupation of the Rhineland, deeply angered the German population. The *New York Times* even reported that "there is much talk about lynch law, which, in view of the spirit kindled among the German people by the latest French measures must be taken as serious. According to these rumors, German secret societies will send desperate members to the Rheinish [*sic*] provinces to make short work of any person aiding the French authorities."[25] Lynching, at least from a German viewpoint, thus had a history of association with right-wing justice against enemies of the political left (e.g., Bolsheviks) and social outsiders (e.g., alleged criminals).

By the 1930s, the *New York Times* was reporting that lynching in the United States was connected to a form of justice exhibited by Hitler.

An October 31, 1933, story stated that "the protest here (in the United States) against anti-Semitism in Germany would be more effective . . . if lynchings were curbed in this country."[26] Furthermore, religious groups in the United States, such as the Methodist Church, argued that "the condoning by the authorities of violence against radicals by lawless bands, their participation in it, was an accomplishment of the rise to power of fascism in Italy, in Germany and Japan."[27] They went on to question: "What are the religious people who know that violence is wrong-doing to do about this?"[28]

Following the 1933 *Reichstag* fire, newspapers reported persistent "fears of a lynching by Nazi extremists . . . notably General Göring's threat of vengeance."[29] The political unrest was not isolated to Germany, however. In 1934, a group of over one hundred Austrian Nazis assassinated Austrian chancellor Engelbert Dollfuss in a failed coup attempt. The imprisoned Austrian Nazis faced both civilians and *Heimwehr* troops who wanted to lynch those responsible for assassinating Dollfuss.[30] The propagation of "race hatred in the U.S.," similar to the rhetoric used by Germany during World War I, continued in the mid-1930s as the German press viewed it as an "unwritten law in America" and maintained that a "civilized Central European is likely to be molested for exchanging a few friendly words with a Negro."[31] By 1939, the German press even used the term *lynching* to describe the treatment of two concentration camp inmates who, while attempting to escape, attacked an SS sentry.[32] Ultimately, before World War II, lynching was already portrayed in the German press as an extrajudicial action that evolved from an improper and unjust behavior, as witnessed in the United States, into a form of vindicated retribution, including a viable option for dealing with groups that posed a threat to the state.

Of course, the Nazi regime also looked to the history and tradition of the United States (e.g., legalized racism, immigration laws, and the eugenics movement) for general inspiration, especially in the wake of the Great Depression. As German historian Stefan Kühl demonstrates in his comparative study on the relationship between national eugenics movements and various forms of state control, there was an active exchange between American eugenicists and German hygienists until the late 1930s.[33] Moreover, legal historian James Q. Whitman has described that although the Nazis "derided the liberal and democratic commitments of American society . . . when it came to immigration, second-class citizenship, and miscegenation, America was indeed 'the classic example' of a country with highly developed, and harsh, race law in the early 1930s, and Nazi lawyers made repeated reference to American models and precedents in the drafting process that led up to the Nuremberg Laws and continued in their subsequent interpretation and application."[34] While the Nazis could draw on the history of second-class citizenship in the United States to deal with the "Jewish Question" in Europe, America's conquest of the West, where Native Americans suffered massacres and marginalization, was also a model for Hitler's pursuit of *Lebensraum* in eastern Europe.[35] Although Whitman noted "the Nuremberg Laws were intended to institute official state persecution in order to displace street-level lynchings . . . [and] the United States by contrast remained faithful to lynch justice," the Nazi regime condoned and promoted Lynchjustiz against downed airmen due to the radicalization of war by the end of 1943.[36] Indicative of this radicalization, civilian involvement in mistreating and killing flyers was startlingly abundant, with civilians representing over one-third of known perpetrators.[37]

While the Nazis "admired the racial hierarchy and exclusion they found in the United States, . . . they denounced the *unruliness* of lynching," according to historian S. Johnathan Wiesen.[38] Nazis believed that lynchings represented an aspect of a failed state, where extralegal violence was permitted by a government otherwise unwilling to impede such spectacles. During the 1930s, the Nazis sought to prevent such public acts of violence, as it could undermine the regime's authority and the role of citizens within the Volksgemeinschaft.[39] With the Nazis establishing a strictly regulated racial state, the notion of an unsystematic lynch mob and its lawlessness was quite unsettling. For the Nazis, lynchings exposed the "dangerous combination of vigilantism and hyper-individualism."[40] According to Wiesen, lynching provided the Nazis with "easy ammunition against the United States at a time when Americans were criticizing Hitler's racism. . . . The regime hoped that by exposing American hypocrisy on matters of race, the German public would dismiss similar charges against National Socialism, place them in a wider global context, or at least sympathize with the Nazi regime's calls for a more institutionalized racism."[41]

Although similar to instances of lynching in the United States, where public officials, security groups, and civilians all participated in lynchings, a January 1938 article in the *Völkischer Beobachter* attempted to argue that in contrast to how Americans deal with African Americans, "we Germans [handle Jews] in a humane way. We do not beat them to death but instead lock them up only after an orderly court hearing and even feed them for years at the cost of the state."[42] The Nazis viewed their mob violence as efficient, state-sanctioned, and a "respectable racism," as German historian Claudia Koonz described, whereas in the US violence was haphazard and inconsistent.[43] Ultimately, violence had to be rational rather than emotional.[44] Although racism in the United States, particularly during the twentieth century, was decentralized and did not necessarily inspire industrialized mass murder, as is symbolic of the Nazi regime, lynching was a clear concept that influenced Nazi Germany, particularly as the war drastically radicalized, as a means to combat downed airmen. Similar to what Nazis condemned in the 1930s as "America's racial dysfunction,"[45] lynching "served as an outlet for pent-up frustrations and as a site of immediate remedy" for dealing with downed airmen and the air war.[46]

Nazi propaganda depicted the hypocrisy of the United States, which took pride in its society as a model that embodied freedom and independence despite having numerous groups of second-class citizens and relying on these groups to fight for, and in the name of, freedom. In a sarcastic response to the United States' negative reaction to the anti-Jewish pogrom of November 1938, Goebbels asserted in *Völkischer Beobachter* on January 21, 1939, that "the American press takes particular pleasure in criticizing Germany on grounds of humanitarianism, civilization, human rights, and culture. It has every right to do so. Its humanity is shown in most vivid form by lynchings. . . . And its culture exists only because it is always borrowing from the older European nations."[47] Moreover, Nazis also criticized and puzzled over the United States public denial of discrimination but the unapologetic sanction of systemic racism.[48] The comparison between Nazi Germany and the United States is by no means an attempt to align the policies of these two nations. As Whitman described, "Unlike American segregation laws, which simply applied the principle of 'separate but equal,' German laws were part of a program of extermination."[49] Yet the growing historiography indicates that the history of the United States was a large influence for the Nazi regime in the 1930s.[50]

World War II

During World War II, the Nazis fully embraced the concept of lynching, and support for such violence gradually increased throughout the war. The number of lynchings in Germany increased in direct proportion to the increase in Allied sorties flown over Germany, which

Figure 3.1. "Triumphal Procession of the U.S. Civilization." Kladderadatsch, *November 1, 1942, http://digi.ub.uni-heidelberg.de/diglit/kla1942/0696.*

resulted in mounting devastation. While the history of the United States was fairly well known by the Nazi elite, the regime published a series of newspaper columns in *Völkischer Beobachter* titled, for example, "What Is English about Americanism?" beginning in the spring of 1944. The series, along with propaganda images (figs. 3.1 and 3.2), informed the public about the hypocritical history and questionable culture of the United States.[51] By that summer, ex post facto propaganda depicted the appropriateness of Lynchjustiz against downed airmen since Americans used this form of violence to punish their own criminals in the United States.

Regarding the development of Germany permitting violence against downed airmen, historians cite two main documents that established justification for Lynchjustiz. The first was Goebbels's *Völkischer Beobachter* article from May 28, 1944, and the second was Nazi Party secretary Martin Bormann's letter sent to *Reichsleiter*, Gauleiter, *Verbändeführer*, and Kreisleiter on May 30, 1944. As Goebbels wrote:

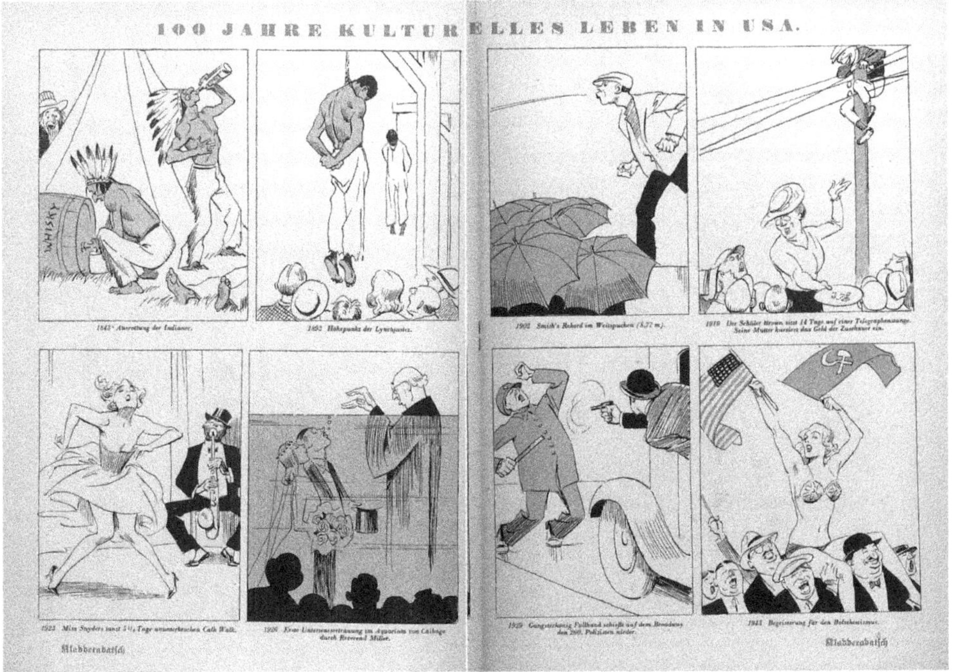

Figure 3.2. "100 Years of Cultural Life in the U.S.A." Kladderadatsch, *April 18, 1943, http://digi.ub.uni-heidelberg.de/diglit/kla1943/0242.*

> It is only possible to protect the lives of downed enemy pilots with the use of armed forces, as they would otherwise be killed by the afflicted population. Who is right here? The murderers who, after their cowardly misdeeds, still expect humane treatment on the part of the victims or the victims who want to defend themselves according to the principle of an eye for an eye and a tooth for a tooth. This question is not difficult to answer. In any case, it would be intolerable to use German soldiers to protect child murderers from the rage-stricken parents who resort to self-defense after having just lost their most precious possessions through the brutal cynicism of the enemy.[52]

Bormann's letter took Goebbels's article a step further, acknowledging that the German population had already lynched downed airmen repeatedly. Bormann wrote that

> In recent weeks, English and North American airmen have repeatedly shot at children playing, women and children working in the fields, peasants working on farms, wagons on the road, etc. during low-level strafing attacks. This is the most awful way to murder defenseless civilians—especially women and children. It has often occurred that downed crewmembers of such aircraft were immediately arrested and lynched on the spot by the outraged population. Police and criminal prosecution of the people involved were omitted.[53]

Bormann's letter was distributed throughout the Nazi Party chain of command—for example *Reichleister*, Gauleiter, and Kreisleiter; however, he requested that Ortsgruppenleiter be notified verbally. The effect and interpretation of this letter can be seen in an order issued by Albert Hoffman—Gauleiter and national defense commissioner of the Gau Westphalia South—to Kreisleiter and Volkssturm officials on February 25, 1945. The order reads as follows:

> Any fighter-bomber pilots shot down are on principle not to be protected against the indignation of the people. I expect from all police offices that they will refuse to lend their protection to these gangster types. Authorities acting in contradiction to the popular sentiment will be taken to account by me. All police and gendarmerie officials are to be informed immediately about this.[54]

However, despite the order to destroy correspondence pertaining to Lynchjustiz, a few documents remain that discuss the treatment of downed flyers as early as March 13, 1940, and the development of Lynchjustiz, which peaked in 1944. An order written by Deputy Führer Rudolf Hess on March 13, 1940, described how civilians should react and behave toward downed enemy airplanes and airmen in German territory. Hess wrote that the "enemy airplane must be secured immediately . . . that the airman should be captured or rendered harmless . . . that they should prevent the destruction of any material (including the airplane) . . . and finally that they should report the incident to the nearest military or Gendarmerie post."[55] This set the foundation for the future mistreatment of Allied airmen.

Hitler's Commando Order of October 18, 1942, stated that "from now on, all enemy soldiers . . . in battle or attempting to escape are to be killed to the last man regardless of whether they are seamen, airmen, or paratroopers. Secret agents and saboteurs . . . are to be given over to the SD."[56] This set the precedence for the verbal order to "exterminate terror and sabotage troops."[57] In another pre-1944 document describing the development of Lynchjustiz, a short August 10, 1943, memo by Heinrich Himmler instructed that "it is not the job of the police to interfere between the German folk and downed English and American terror flyers."[58] In a meeting on May 16, 1944, Göring proposed on-the-spot executions of such downed airmen.[59] Accordingly, these five documents show the escalation of Lynchjustiz into authorized vigilantism by 1944. Lynchjustiz began as a decentralized form of popular justice by German citizens in an attempt to seek revenge for the devastation caused by the air war, but by the end of 1943, it had become a state-sponsored form of seeking justice and combatting the enemy.

Throughout June 1944, the process of finalizing the classification of a Terrorflieger took place at a meeting with representatives from the Reich Foreign Ministry, SS, OKL, OKW, and the commandant of Dulag Luft. In addition, these officials established the desired treatment for Terrorflieger as well as how to implement the topic in propaganda (both domestically and internationally). After an initial meeting on June 6, 1944, which coincided, though likely unintentionally, with the Allied invasion of Normandy, German officials decided that "*Lynchjustiz* would have to be considered as the rule."[60] The specifics were set by June 14, 1944, with Reich Foreign Ministry agreeing to them by June 20, 1944, despite its "obvious objections founded on international law."[61] Influenced by Japan's Enemy Airmen's Act (from August 13, 1942), which allowed airmen to be sentenced to death for attacking civilians and nonmilitary targets, Germany established four criteria that constituted acts of terror for which airmen could be executed.[62] These included:

1. Attacking civilians, individuals as well as crowds;
2. Firing at German shot-down aircrews parachuting in the air;
3. Attacking passenger trains in the public service;
4. Attacking military hospitals, civilian hospitals, and hospital trains, which are clearly marked with the Red Cross.[63]

This document was distributed by the OKW to the OKL, the Reich Foreign Ministry, and the chiefs of the SiPo and SD. These four acts of terrorism were used as an attempt to justify Sonderbehandlung after airmen were held as POWs, for example at Dulag Luft. Additionally, these criteria were to be used as justification when cases of Lynchjustiz were published, although no evidence indicates that specific cases were publicly circulated. Yet analysis of Lynchjustiz committed against American airmen indicates that participation in these alleged acts of terror were not required to result in mistreatment. The mere association with the enemy and being aviators was often enough justification for perpetrators to murder airmen.

Regardless of accuracy, Goebbels sought to publicize lynchings for propaganda purposes.[64] He noted that local German police authorities were to report all attacks to the RSHA in Berlin, "giving details as to place, time and number of dead and wounded. This central agency would have to forward this report . . . to the Reich Foreign Ministry for exploitation."[65] Furthermore, a June 24, 1944, secret bulletin from the senior SS and political Führer West Göhrum informed local political leaders that in cases involving retaliation by the folk, if the downed airmen took any action against them, for example, defending themselves or attacking back, they were to "immediately intervene with a firearm."[66] In addition, "if the leader of a state or local office (police chief, district council, mayor) or a commander or leader of the *Ordnungspolizei* (OrPo) decides that an immediate execution of a foreigner without a trial is needed, it is allowed . . . in cases of immediate danger."[67]

A problem, however, that the Reich Foreign Ministry had to solve was the redesignation of POWs in order to "legally" impose Sonderbehandlung. In accordance with international rules of law, "when an enemy airman has been captured by the armed forces or by the police and has been delivered to the air corps reception camp at Oberursel, he thereby has already acquired the legal status of a prisoner of war."[68] Since the procedure for Sonderbehandlung by the SD nearly always meant certain death, officials maintained that

> an emergency solution would be to prevent suspected airmen from ever attaining a legal prisoner of war status; that is, that immediately upon seizure they be told that they are regarded not as prisoners of war, but as criminals, and that they will be delivered not to . . . a prisoner of war camp, but to the authorities . . . for the prosecution of criminal acts. . . . If interrogations during those proceedings should reveal circumstances which show that *Sonderbehandlung* is not applicable to the particular case, then the

> airmen concerned might . . . be subsequently transferred to the legal status of prisoners of war by being sent to the reception camp at Oberursel. Naturally even this expedient would not prevent Germany from being accused of violating existing treaties, nor would it necessarily be a safeguard against reprisal measures . . . against German prisoners of war. But at least this expedient would make it possible to follow a clear line, thus relieving us of the necessity of openly renouncing the present agreements, or, upon publication of each individual case, using excuses which no one will believe.[69]

Additionally, the OKL ultimately was responsible for downed Allied airmen. Upon capture, the nearest airfield headquarters was responsible for security of the crash site and collection of the airmen and information, along with gathering any personal property. This information was vital, as it allowed the Luftwaffe to salvage the aircraft in an attempt to gain insight into Allied technology as well as compile a thorough database on downed flyers that interrogators used at Dulag Luft. However, as First Lieutenant Maulbehre of the Luftwaffe wrote in a diary entry from October 2, 1944, Göring agreed to the orders by the OKW that in cases where downed airmen were lynched by the population, the action of soldiers "may be issued by the Luftwaffe as an order of the OKW but *not* as an order of the OKL."[70]

Captured airmen from all over Germany and occupied territories were brought to Dulag Luft, also known as Auswertestelle West, for interrogation, in order to gain information relating to troop numbers and locations, as well as targets of aerial missions and aeronautical technology.[71] Although the camp was under the jurisdiction of the Luftwaffe, the Gestapo was also actively involved in the interrogation of airmen. According to historian Philip M. Flammer, twenty-nine thousand POWs went through Dulag Luft in 1944 alone, necessitating between sixty and sixty-five interrogators.[72] According to the Karlsruhe Study, completed by Major General Andreas L. Nielsen, a general order was

> issued by the OKW, specifying that all airmen flying enemy planes who had been shot down were to be brought immediately to Oberursel without any prior interrogation [as] . . . occasionally, when prisoners were captured by a forward combat element . . . "interrogation" degenerated into a sociable conversation that

> was spiced by intoxicating beverages, so that the prisoners were often completely spoiled by the time they reached the proper interrogation authorities.[73]

According to historian Charles Rollings, "rumors of what they [the airmen] would expect at *Dulag Luft* ranged from kid-glove treatment—drinks at the local inn, lavish dinner parties, prostitutes, and skiing trips in the Taunus Mountains—to brutal beatings and unendurable torture. The truth was less dramatic but just as sinister."[74] Repatriated airmen reported "beat treatment" in 1944:

> A frequent interrogation device is the threat to regard a prisoner as a saboteur who faces the death penalty unless he talks. . . . [The] approach is friendly, and military questions are inserted at intervals during the casual conversation. When the prisoner refuses to give information the interrogator reels off accurate information on field, group, squadron, target, crews and previous training with dates. The effect of this is frequently shocking. . . . Another device for identification of units is the request that Allied flyers attempt to identify bodies of other Allied flyers.[75]

The interrogations were carried out by special officers at all hours of the day and night. For airmen who refused to talk, interrogators threatened to hand them over to the Gestapo. Flyers experienced increased heat in their 10' x 4' solitary cells, erasing the possibility of comfort or sleep.[76] Often officials at Oberursel employed so-called stool pigeons in order to obtain information. These were specially trained German soldiers who belonged to an organization called Adverse. The USAAF reported in an Intelligence Bulletin on November 22, 1944, that Adverse was a cover name for a section of the Abwehr Defense Agency. They were trained to "speak English with an American accent and have lived in the United States."[77] By the end of 1944, due to the increase in airmen sent through Dulag Luft, the use of both stool pigeons and overly friendly behavior were largely ended "in favor of fairly rough treatment, uncomfortable conditions, and threats," according to a special escape bulletin.[78]

A camp in Wetzlar, sixty kilometers north of Oberursel, functioned as a transit facility that allowed for the processing of POWs after their interrogations at Dulag Luft. From there, German officials transferred flyers to POW camps throughout Germany and Austria. However, if the airmen made it to Oberursel they were not safe from experiencing the same fate of their fellow flyers killed by the rampant mob mentality. Despite legally being POWs, airmen could be considered Terrorflieger by Germans, which meant that they had allegedly committed one of the four acts agreed on at the end of June 1944. In such cases, the SD took responsibility for the airmen, subjecting them to Sonderbehandlung, which meant certain death. The lack of any known documents, however, results in an inability to determine the extent to which this occurred. By the fall of 1944, First Lieutenant Erich Killinger, the commandant of Oberursel, "and his interrogators had come under increasing criticism from the Gestapo for 'Anglophile tendencies, defeatism, and transgression of Service rules.'" This resulted in the SS "demanding punishment of the defenders and attempting to take over the interrogation center."[79] According to British journalist Charles Rollings, the Gestapo had Killinger taken to court on charges of fraternization and defeatism. Although a German tribunal acquitted Killinger, he was relieved of his command at Dulag Luft.[80]

Following the war, the British Military Court in Wuppertal charged Killinger and four other Luftwaffe officers with the mistreatment of POWs at or near Oberursel between November 1, 1941, and April 15, 1945.[81] Killinger and two other men were sentenced to five years each while the other two were found not guilty. Whether the downed airmen were actually treated favorably at Oberursel, as is described throughout the historiography, is difficult to determine, yet it is true that the Luftwaffe generally treated downed flyers more favorably than other Nazi organizations due to their understanding of an airman's duties and their desire to receive positive treatment if they were shot down.[82]

Jurisdictional issues caused confusion among German military forces and frustration among the police forces. Such irritation was evident in a memo from the head of the SiPo and SD in Rhein/Westmark to the Gestapo, KriPo, and SD within the region in October 1944: "The Wehrmacht often prevents the suitable procedure by the [German] population against the downed *Terrorflieger* by arresting and guarding them. In the future, all related cases are to be immediately and thoroughly documented and reported, detailing the individuals and the incidents."[83] This struggle between individual Wehrmacht soldiers and the SiPo, civilians, and the OKW lasted throughout much of the war. A December 1944 order from Lieutenant General Schmidt reiterated this issue referring again to Goebbels's newspaper article from May and stating that

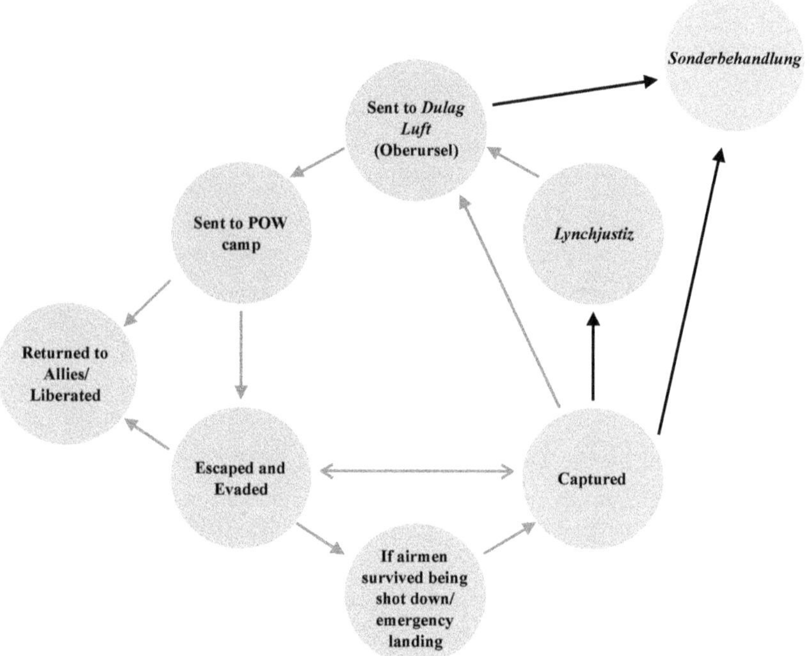

Figure 3.3. The Process of Treating Downed Airmen (black arrows represent mistreatment and possible death). *Created by author.*

> recently, it has happened that soldiers have actively protected Anglo-American terror flyers from the civilian population, thus causing justified resentment. You will take immediate steps to ensure by oral instruction of all subordinate units and authorities that soldiers do not oppose the civilian population in *such* [emphasis in original] cases by demanding that the enemy flyers be handed over to them as prisoners, and by protecting, and thus ostensibly siding with, the enemy *Terrorflieger*.[84]

This order, along with the relevant subsequent correspondence, was ordered to be destroyed after they were "brought to the cognizance of the divisional commanders, the commanders of the airport areas, the commander of the Antiaircraft Groups, [and] of the Luftgau Forces. . . . Instructions concerning this order will be given to all levels down to the regimental commanders and airfield commanders; as far as is practicable in the local conditions this will be done orally."[85]

This verbal transmission of orders was likely responsible for the confusion regarding the treatment of airmen. Although personal beliefs and moral reasoning are sure to have played a role in any positive treatment of flyers, any widespread extent of positive treatment by society was doubtful. Meek and rife obedience to the political and policing orders, not to mention the overshadowing desire and fulfillment of retribution for the constant and often prolonged exposure to war at their doorsteps, were the emotions that contributed to German citizens' extensive reprisals against downed airmen. Propaganda, however, was the engine of consumption and action for German society; it was powered by and influenced incidences involving Terrorflieger. Nevertheless, the people's justice against downed airmen preceded Goebbels's propaganda by over a year, both directly influencing each other. Human agency, in particular regarding German civilians and their role in facilitating Lynchjustiz, nevertheless deserves further recognition. As social scientist and historian Eric A. Johnson has described, "The implementation and effectiveness depended on the voluntary choices and local actions of individual German citizens."[86] Furthermore, the political influence was especially widespread regarding the police forces. According to Johnson, most Gestapo officers were "career Nazis first . . . and policeman second [while] most of the rank-and-file officers were . . . career police officers before they joined either the Nazi Party or the SS."[87] Regardless of whether a police officer had had an extensive career with the police force, they "were men who may have been attracted to violence but believed in law and order. The problem was that they were willing to enforce and carry out whatever laws and orders they were given, no matter how criminal."[88] Specifically in terms of "rural towns and villages across Nazi Germany . . . political policing was carried out under control of the regular police department, which in turn was under the control of the local mayor's office."[89]

Notes

1. Berg and Wendt, *Globalizing Lynching History*; Carrigan and Waldrep, *Swift to Wrath*; Thurston, *Lynching*; Brundage, *Lynching in the New South*; Wood, *Lynching and Spectacle*.
2. Berg and Wendt, *Globalizing Lynching History*, 5.
3. Ibid., 3.
4. Ibid., 5.
5. Robert W. Thurston, "Lynching and Legitimacy: Toward a Global Description of Mob Murder," in Berg and Wendt, *Globalizing Lynching History*, 70.

6. Ibid., 70.

7. Brundage, *Lynching in the New South*, 18.

8. Goldstein, "Flexible Justice," 242. See also Berg and Wendt, *Globalizing Lynching History*, 8.

9. Carrigan and Waldrep, *Swift to Wrath*, 5.

10. *Kladderadatsch*, Number 1, January 3, 1858, http://digi.ub.uni-heidelberg.de/diglit/kla1858/0001, accessed November 5, 2015; Gerhard Köbler, "Deutsches Etymologisches Wörterbuch," *Deutsches Etymologisches Wörterbuch*, 1995, http://www.koeblergerhard.de/der/DERL.pdf, accessed February 23, 2017; *Kladderadatsch*, Berlin January 1848-May 1944, http://digi.ub.uni-heidelberg.de/diglit/kla, accessed November 8, 2015.

11. "Color Line in Berlin," *New York Times*, October 4, 1908.

12. Ibid.

13. "Germans Magnify Lynchings Here," *New York Times*, September 9, 1918; "Germany Protests Prager Lynching," *New York Times*, June 13, 1918; "Bitter at Attacks on Germans Here," *New York Times*, June 17, 1918; "Probe Lynching of Illinois German," *Los Angeles Herald*, April 18, 1918.

14. "Germans Magnify Lynchings Here," *New York Times*, September 9, 1918.

15. "President Demands That Lynchings End," *New York Times*, July 27, 1918.

16. John Horne and Alan Kramer, *German Atrocities, 1914: A History of Denial* (New Haven, CT: Yale University Press, 2001); Alan Kramer, *Dynamic of Destruction: Culture and Mass Killings in the First World War* (Oxford: Oxford University Press, 2007).

17. Jones, *Violence against Prisoners of War in the First World War*, 42, 47.

18. Ibid., 67–68, 59, 37–38.

19. "Feindlicher Luftterror schon seit 1914," *Westdeutscher Beobachter* (Eupen), August 24, 1944.

20. "Appeals in Germany in Scottsboro Case," *New York Times*, May 11, 1932.

21. Ibid.

22. "Ask Pardon for 8 Negroes," *New York Times*, March 27, 1932.

23. "Fight for Doomed Negroes," *New York Times*, June 1, 1931.

24. "Lynchings Shock People of Berlin," *New York Times*, January 20, 1919.

25. "Germans Threaten Rhine Lynchings," *New York Times*, February 8, 1923.

26. "Hitlerism Likened to Lynch Law Here," *New York Times*, October 31, 1933. See also Fumiko Sakashita, "Lynching across the Pacific" in Carrigan and Waldrep, *Swift to Wrath*, 198–207.

27. "Methodists Find Liberty Ebbing," *New York Times*, January 20, 1936.

28. Ibid.

29. "British Gratified at Verdict on Fire," *New York Times*, December 24, 1933.

30. "All of Rebels Prisoners," *New York Times*, July 26, 1934.

31. "German Press Cites Race Hatred in U.S.," *New York Times*, August 30, 1935.

32. "Nazi Guards 'Lynch' Two for Attempting to Escape," *New York Times*, December 11, 1939.

33. Kühl, *Nazi Connection*, xvii.

34. Whitman, *Hitler's American Model*, 6, 12–13.

35. The Nazis even researched the discrimination against Aborigines in Australia. For more information, see Jens-Uwe Guettel, *German Expansionism, Imperial Liberalism, and the United States, 1776–1945* (Cambridge: Cambridge University Press, 2012); Carroll P. Kakel III, *The American West and the Nazi East: A Comparative and*

Interpretive Perspective (New York: Palgrave Macmillan, 2011); Bundesarchiv Berlin R4902, file 3859 titled "Rassenfragen in Australien."

36. Whitman, *Hitler's American Model*, 144.

37. This is based on the quantitative analysis of the flyer trials in chapter 4.

38. S. Johnathan Wiesen, "American Lynching in the Nazi Imagination: Race and Extra-Legal Violence in 1930s Germany," *German History* 36, no. 1 (2017): 39.

39. Ibid., 40.

40. Ibid., 49.

41. Ibid., 43. Goebbels even commissioned the propaganda ministry to create "anti-American" reports, which detailed racial tensions and Jim Crow legislation in the United States. For example, see Bundesarchiv Berlin R901 (Presse- und Nachrichtenabteilung, Auswärtiges Amt), file 59692 ("USA 2—Neger"); Bundesarchiv Berlin R55 (Propaganda Ministry), file 24843 (Handakten Dr. Karl Mergele, 1938–1941).

42. "Verfeinerte Demokratie = Lynchjustiz?," *Völkischer Beobachter*, January 12, 1938; see also Wiesen, "American Lynching in the Nazi Imagination," 46.

43. Claudia Koonz, *The Nazi Conscience* (Cambridge, MA: Harvard University Press, 2003), 190; see also Wiesen, "American Lynching in the Nazi Imagination," 47.

44. Wiesen, "American Lynching in the Nazi Imagination," 47.

45. Ibid., 49; see also Heinrich Krieger, *Dass Rassenrecht in den Vereinigten Staaten* (Berlin: Juncker and Dünnhaupt, 1936).

46. Ibid., 48.

47. Joseph Goebbels, "Was will eigentlich Amerika," *Völkischer Beobachter*, January 21, 1939.

48. For example, see "Europe and Amerika: Fehlerquellen im Aufbau des amerikanischen Volkstums," Schulungs-Unterlage Nr. 18 (Der Reichsorganisationsleitung der NSDAP, Hauptschulungsamt, 1942), http://research.calvin.edu/german-propaganda-archive/hsa02.htm, accessed March 20, 2017; "Amerika als Zerrbild europäischr Lebensordnung," Schulungs-Unterlage Nr. 19 (Der Reichsorganisationsleitung der NSDAP, Hauptschulungsamt, 1942), http://research.calvin.edu/german-propaganda-archive/hsa01.htm, accessed March 20, 2017; A.E. Johann, *Das Land ohne Herz: Eine Rise ins unbekannte Amerika* (Berlin: Deutscher, 1942); "Die Gefahr des Amerikanismus," *Das Schwarze Korps*, March 14, 1944.

49. Whitman, *Hitler's American Model*, 13.

50. See Daniel Rodger, *Atlantic Crossings: Social Politics in a Progressive Age* (Cambridge, MA: Harvard University Press, 1998); Victoria de Grazia, *Irresistible Empire: America's Advance through Twentieth-Century Europe* (Cambridge, MA: Harvard University Press, 2005); Ira Katznelson, *When Affirmative Action Was White: An Untold History of Racial Inequality in Twentieth-Century America* (New York: Norton, 2005); Wolfgang Schivelbach, *Three New Deals: Reflections on Roosevelt's America, Mussolini's Italy, and Hitler's Germany, 1933–1939*, trans. Jefferson Chase (New York: Metropolitan, 2006); Victoria Nourse, *In Reckless Hands:* Skinner v. Oklahoma *and the Near Triumph of American Eugenics* (New York: Norton, 2008); Stephan H. Norwood, *The Third Reich in the Ivory Tower* (New York: Cambridge University Press, 2009); David Bernstein, *Rehabilitating Lochner: Defending Individual Rights against Progressive Reform* (Chicago: University of Chicago Press, 2011); Kakel, *American West and the Nazi East*; David Ellwood, *The Shock of American: Europe and the Challenge of the Century* (New York: Oxford University Press,

2012); Adam Tooze, *The Deluge: The Great War, American, and the Remaking of the Global Order* (New York: Penguin, 2014); David Scott Fitzgerald and David Cook-Martin, *Culling the Masses: The Democratic Origins of Racist Immigration Policy in the Americas* (Cambridge, MA: Harvard University Press, 2014); Thomas C. Leonard, *Illiberal Reformers: Race, Eugenics, and American Economics in the Progressive Era* (Princeton, NJ: Princeton University Press, 2016); Whitman, *Hitler's American Model.*

51. Edmund Fürholzer, "Was ist englisch am Amerikanismus?," *Völkischer Beobachter* (Berlin), April 14–16, 1944. See also Dr. Th. Böttiger, "Die Spinnen Roosevelts," *Völkischer Beobachter* (Berlin), May 12–13, 1944; "Von Washington bis Roosevelt: Geschichte der USA im Spiegel ihrer Briefmarken," *Völkischer Beobachter* (Berlin), May 19, 1944.

52. Joseph Goebbels, "Ein Wort zum feindlichen Lufterror," *Völkischer Beobachter* (Berlin), May 28, 1944; "Ein Wort zum feindlichen Luftterror," *Völkischer Beobachter* (Vienna), May 28, 1944; "Ein Wort zum feindlichen Luftterror," *Völkischer Beobachter* (Munich), May 28, 1944; "Goebbels Invites Attacks on Fliers," *New York Times*, May 28, 1944; "Ein Wort zum feindlichen Luftterror," *Kölnische Zeitung*, May 28, 1944;"Kindermörder sind keine Soldaten," *Westdeutscher Beobachter* (Aachen), May 30, 1944. See also, "The Terror Flyer Order" in *Trials of War Criminals before the Nuremberg Military Tribunals under Control Council Law No.10, Volume XI* (United States Government Printing Office: Washington, 1960), 166–69. See Appendix A (fig. A1.12) for the original German text.

53. Martin Bormann, "Volksjustiz gegen anglo-amerikanische Mörder," letter to Reichsleiter, Gauleiter, Verbändeführer, and Kreisleiter. August 30, 1944, RG 549, Entry, A1 2238, Microfilm T1021, Reel 10, Frame No. 764, NARA, https://catalog.archives.gov/id/40957462. See Appendix A (fig. A1.7) for the original German text.

54. Order from Albert Hoffman, Gauleiter and National Defense Commissioner for the Gau Westphalia South, to Nazi Party county leaders (Kreisleiter) and Volkssturm officials, February 25, 1945, in *Trial of the Major War Criminals before the International Military Tribunal: Nuremberg, 14 November 1945–1 October 1946, Volume XX* (Nuremberg, 1948), 54, https://www.loc.gov/rr/frd/Military_Law/NT_major-war-criminals.html, accessed March 6, 2015.

55. Rudolf Hess, "Belehrung der Zivilbevölkerung über sachgemässes Verhalten bei Landungen feindlicher Flugzeuge oder Fallschirmabspringer auf deutschem Reichsgebiet," Order to Reichsleiter, Gauleiter, Reichsorganisationsleitung, Reichspropagandaleitung, Reichsstudentenführung, SS-Gruppenführer Heydrich, March 13, 1940, RG 549, Entry A1 2238, Micorfilm T1021, Reel 10, Frame No. 783, NARA, https://catalog.archives.gov/id/40957462. The original German text states: "Jedes feindliche Flugzeug, das auf deutschem Boden landet, ist sofort unter wirksamen Schutz zu stellen. . . . Die Flieger sind sofort festzunehmen und vor allem ist ein Wiederstart, sowie die Zerstörung doer Verbrennung des Flugzeugs oder seines Inhalts zu verhindern. . . . Ebenso sollen feindliche Fallschirmjäger sofort festgenommen oder unschädlich gemacht werden. Der nächste Militär- oder Gendarmerieposten ist sofort zu benachrichtigen."

56. Adolf Hitler, Commando Order, October 18, 1942. The original German text states: "Von jetz ab sind alle . . . Gegner . . . im Kampf oder auf der Flucht bis auf den letzten Mann niederzumachen. Es ist dabei ganz gleich, ob sie zu ihren Aktionen durch Schiffe und Flugzeuge angelandet werden oder mittels Fallschirmen abspringen . . . Agenten, Saboteurs, usw. . . . sind sie dem SD zu

übergeben" (RG 549, Entry, A1 2238, Microfilm T1021, Reel 10, Frame No. 775-777, NARA, https://catalog.archives.gov/id/40957462).

57. Wagner, letter attached to the forwarded Hitler Decree from October 18, 1942. The original German text states: "Anliegend wird ein Erlass des Führers über die Vernichtung von Terror- und Sabotagetruppe übersandt" (RG 549, Entry A1 2238, Microfilm T1021, Reel 10, Frame No. 774, NARA, https://catalog.archives.gov/id/40957462).

58. Heinrich Himmler memo from August 10, 1943. The original German text states: "Es ist nicht Aufgabe die Polizei, sich in Auseinandersetzungen zwischen deutschen Volksgenossen und abgesprungenen englischen und amerikanischen Terrorfliegern einzumischen" (RG 549, Entry A1 2238, Microfilm T1021, Reel 10, Frame No. 771, NARA, https://catalog.archives.gov/id/40957462. The original German text states: "Es ist nicht Aufgabe der Polizei, sich in Auseinandersetzungen zwischen deutschen Volksgenossen und abgesprungenen englischen und amerikanischen Terrorfliegern einzumischen." See Appendix A (fig. A1.1) for the original document.

59. Hermann Göring, "Jägerbesprechung beim Reichsmarshall," May 16, 1944, RG 549, Entry A1 2238, Microfilm T1020, Reel 10, Frame No. 487–495, NARA, https://catalog.archives.gov/id/40957462).

60. "Behandlung der feindlichen Terrorflieger," from Deputy Leader of the Armed Forces Operations Staff (Stellv. Chef WFSt.), June 6, 1944, RG 549, Entry A1 2238, Microfilm T1021, Reel 10, Frame No. 760–763, NARA, https://catalog.archives.gov/id/40957462). The original German text states: "Die Lynchjustiz würde als die Regel zu gelten haben."

61. Ambassador Ritter, "Draft of Letter from the Foreign Office to Chief OKW concerning Treatment of Enemy Terror Flyers," to Chief of the High Command of the Armed Forces, Salzburg from June 20, 1944, *Trials of War Criminals before the Nuernberg Military Tribunals under Control Council Law No. 10*, Vol. 11 (Washington, DC: United States Government Printing Office, 1960), 175–77.

62. For more information regarding Japan's Enemy Airmen's Act, see *Judgement of the International Military Tribunal for the Far East, Chapter VIII* (1948), http://www.loc.gov/rr/frd/Military_Law/pdf/Judgment-IMTFE-Vol-II-PartB-Chapter-VIII.pdf, accessed March 6, 2015; Philip R. Piccigallo, *The Japanese on Trial: Allied War Crimes Operations in the East, 1945–1951* (Austin: University of Texas Press, 1979); James D. Morrow, *Order within Anarchy: The Laws of War as an International Institution* (Cambridge: Cambridge University Press, 2014); Jeanne Guillemin, *Hidden Atrocities: Japanese Germ Warfare and American Obstruction of Justice at the Tokyo Trial* (New York: Columbia University Press, 2017).

63. "Behandlung der feindl. Terrorflieger," letter from Oberkommando der Wehrmacht (OKW/Armed Forces Operations Staff) to Oberbefehlshaber der Luftwaffe (Commander in Chief Air Force) Concerning Treatment of Enemy "Terror" Flyers, June 14, 1944, *Trials of War Criminals before the Nuernberg Military Tribunals*, 170–71. See also RG 549, Entry A1 2238, Microfilm T1021, Reel 10, Frame No. 454–455, NARA, https://catalog.archives.gov/id/40957462.

64. Unfortunately, the validity and extent of the Germans' claims of Allied strafing is unknown.

65. Ritter, "Draft of Letter," *Trials of War Criminals before the Nuernberg Military Tribunals*, 175–77.

66. Bulletin from Senior SS and Political Fuehrer West Göhrum, "Volksjustiz an plündernden Ausländern und abgesprungenen feindlichen Fliegern und Erschiessen dieser durch Ordnungspolizei," from June 24, 1944, RG 549, Entry A1 2238, Microfilm T1021, Reel 13, Frame No. 872–873, NARA, https://catalog.archives.gov/id/40957462. The original German text states: "Gehen abgesprungene feindliche Besatzungsmitglieder gegen die Bevölkerung vor, so ist sofort mit der Schusswaffe einzugreifen."

67. Ibid.

68. Ibid.

69. Ritter, "Draft of Letter," *Trials of War Criminals before the Nuernberg Military Tribunals*, 175–77.

70. War Diary by First Lieutenant Maulbehre, Operations Staff—Foreign Air Forces West, Concerning Conduct of Soldiers in Cases of Lynchings of Allied Airmen by the Population from October 2, 1944, *Trials of War Criminals before the Nuernberg Military Tribunals*, 178–79.

71. For a complete study on Dulag Luft/Auswertestelle West see, Geck, *Dulag Luft/Auswertestelle West*. There was also an Auswertestelle Ost (Evaluation Center East) that dealt with downed airmen from the Soviet Union.

72. Flammer, "Dulag Luft: The Third Reich's Prison Camp for Airmen," 58.

73. Major General Andreas L. Nielsen, "The Collection and Evaluation of Intelligence for the German Air Force High Command: Karlsruhe Study," (Air Force College, 1955), Maxwell Air Force Base (AFB), Montgomery, Alabama (Al).

74. Charles Rollings, *After the Battle: Dulag Luft*, No. 106, (London: Battle of Britain International Ltd, 1999), 4.

75. Escape Intelligence Report—Escape Information Series A-13, "Late Information on Dulag Luft," June 21, 1944, from the Fifteenth Air Force Headquarters, Maxwell AFB, Montgomery, AL.

76. Flammer, "Dulag Luft," 60.

77. Escape Intelligence Bulletin, November 22, 1944, Fifteenth Air Force Headquarters, Maxwell AFB, Montgomery, AL.

78. Special Escape Bulletin No. 16a, Fifteenth Air Force Headquarters, Maxwell AFB, Montgomery, AL.

79. Rollings, "Dulag Luft," 25.

80. Ibid.

81. "Law-Reports of Trials of War Criminals, The United Nations War Crimes Commission, Volume III, London," HMSO, 1948, http://www.phdn.org/archives/www.ess.uwe.ac.uk/WCC/killinger.htm, accessed August 23 2016.

82. It is stated in the Special Escape Bulletin No. 16a that "the threats [by the interrogators] are never carried out" (Fifteenth Air Force Headquarters. Maxwell AFB, Montgomery, AL); in the article by Flammer, he states that "the camp administration could not be accused of mistreating the prisoners to a great degree" ("Dulag Luft," 61); see also Toliver, *Interrogator*.

83. "Verhalten der Wehrmacht gegenüber abgesprungenen Terrorfliegern" (Conduct of the Wehrmacht relating to downed terror flyers), letter from Leader of the SiPo and SD in Rhein/Westmark to the Gestapo, KriPo., and SD in Frankfurt a.M., Koblenz, Darmstadt, Saarbrücken, and Metz, from October 6, 1944, RG 549, Entry A1 2238, Microfilm T1021, Reel 10, Frame No. 790, NARA, https://catalog.archives.gov/id/40957462.

84. Order by Lieutenant General Schmidt (Anti-Aircraft Artillery), transmitting order of Chief OKW of July 9, 1944, concerning oral instructions to be given to soldiers not to protect enemy terror flyers from the German populace, sent to Divisional Commanders, Commanders of airport areas, Commander of Antiaircraft Groups in the area, and Luftgau Forces, from December 11, 1944, *Trials of War Criminals before the Nuernberg Military Tribunals*, 179–80.

85. Ibid.

86. Eric A. Johnson, *Nazi Terror: The Gestapo, Jews, and Ordinary Germans* (New York: Basic Books, 2000), 27.

87. Ibid., 77–78.

88. Ibid., 69.

89. Ibid., 65.

Chapter 4

Analysis of the Flyer Trials

> The crimes of which these persons were convicted were brutal, vicious, and unfeeling, and while American sympathy may be aroused at the prospect of hanging women and old men, it must always be remembered that halfway measures will never impress upon the people of Germany that their actions have been unlawful and degenerate. The deterrent effect of punishment must be great enough to prevent forever crimes that are an abomination in the eyes of men and blasphemy in the sight of God.
>
> Colonel C. Robert Bard, JAGD (1945)[1]

The postwar crime trials, especially those conducted at Nuremberg and Jerusalem, are known for prosecuting high-ranking Nazi officials, and highlighting the Holocaust and Nazi crimes against humanity. However, the "lesser" war crime trials (e.g., the Dachau trials [1945–48], the Hamburg-Ravensbruck trials [1946–1948], and the Wuppertal trials in 1946) were very significant as well; these not only assist in understanding how and why events occurred under the Nazi regime but also allow for a closer evaluation of the "ordinary" Germans involved in war crimes.[2] Although often overshadowed by the International Military Tribunal of the Major War Criminals held in Nuremberg, these "lesser" war crime trials focused on specific issues and prosecuted lower-ranking war criminals and civilians. In addition, these hearings were directed by single nations. For example, the US government administered trials throughout its occupied sectors of West Germany and Austria (though mostly held in Dachau) and focused on war crimes committed against American military personnel and civilians throughout Germany and its formerly occupied territories. Similarly, the British government administered trials—for example, in Hamburg and Wuppertal—that focused largely on crimes committed against British forces. The same appropriation of powers was administered by France and the Netherlands as well.

Focusing on the US cases, the Dachau trials consisted of over four hundred hearings that prosecuted over fifteen hundred "lesser" war criminals, with American airmen representing the largest group of victims (nearly 40 percent). The remaining trials dealt with crimes against Americans and Europeans at various concentration camps (e.g., Mauthausen, Flossenburg, Buchenwald, Mühldorf, and Dora-Nordhausen), the Malmedy Massacre (the execution of eighty-four POWs during the Battle of the Bulge), and the Skorzeny trial, which dealt with German soldiers wearing US military uniforms during a false flag operation.

Concentrating specifically on the flyer trials—held in numerous locations, although mainly at Dachau—the following study offers quantitative and qualitative analyses to better understand these relatively unknown proceedings. The accused perpetrators involved in the killings (their ages, careers, motivations, and political positions), as well as how the atrocities were committed and how many downed airmen were involved, will be examined in detail. Furthermore, the process of sentencing perpetrators will be reviewed.[3] These trials provide an attempt to discern the identity of war criminals, as well as the attitudes of the German population toward downed American flyers. Although the flyer trials surely do not describe every instance pertaining to the lynching of downed airmen, they represent the largest known collection of documents pertaining to this topic. Therefore, they provide a valuable opportunity to establish a basis for understanding the details and extent of these atrocities, as well as offering a comparison for future studies to build on.

The proceedings involving the mistreatment of downed airmen were fairly elaborate; each lasted on average three days. The cases brought to trial included quite extensive judicial sources.[4] Often, investigative files, transcripts of court proceedings, detailed depositions, appeals for clemency, and justifications for verdicts elaborately described the crimes that occurred against airmen. Autopsy reports were also included when the victims' bodies were discovered. However, airmen were not identified in numerous cases due to the lack of remains or the poor condition of their bodies.[5] This resulted in the standard evidence for conviction relying, out of necessity, largely on witness testimonies, which often included hearsay. Thus, for this research, it was imperative to critically analyze not only the defense statements but also the witness testimonies for their reliability to determine how and why these events unfolded.

A vast amount of evidence exists to demonstrate the applicability of the term *lynching* to the violence perpetrated against downed American airmen during World War II. Nevertheless, a difficulty remains in separating ordered, and often premeditated, murders from sanctioned (though often impulsive and voluntary) acts of murder. Adding to the difficulty was the increased nationalism and wartime atmosphere that created indistinct societal boundaries between civilian and government roles, where civilians could commit acts on the wishes of the state and where state representatives could be considered as being in a civilian role (e.g., soldiers home on leave were occasionally involved in the violence against downed airmen). Looking at lynching in the United States, similar difficulty exists in determining the status of perpetrators; for example, a member of the KKK—a paramilitary group—could also act in the role of a public official (such as a police officer or mayor). Despite this, the incidents involving the mistreatment of downed American airmen represent a state-sanctioned summary justice carried out by all levels of society and fostered by radicalized propaganda.[6]

Overview of the US Trials against "Lesser" War Criminals

The war crime investigations were complicated by a lack of qualified personnel and resources, the inability to locate alleged perpetrators and witnesses, the unwillingness of Germans to cooperate with investigators, and increasing pressure from the American public and other Allied nations to swiftly bring war criminals to justice. Beginning as early as August 1944, army group commanders were instructed by the Supreme Headquarters Allied Expedition Force (SHAEF), commanded by General Dwight D. Eisenhower, to report alleged war crimes committed against American nationals. The commanders were expected to create a detailed list, which included the location, date, and brief description of the incident, as well as possible perpetrators, victims, and witnesses. Commanders were not tasked, however, with actually investigating or gathering any additional evidence.

While the primary goal during the war was to defeat the enemy, collecting any information about possible war crimes would aid in the future prosecution of criminals. Reports quickly exceeded military and government officials' expectations, as the scale and extent of Nazi atrocities were drastically underestimated. It became clear that only the most malicious crimes could proceed to trial. During the war, no trials were held out of fear that reprisals would be committed against American POWs; several years could therefore pass before a case was brought to trial. Even once a trial was finished, the official review and approval of the sentences lasted an average of fifteen weeks due to the volume of cases.[7] This greatly impeded the process of bringing the criminals to justice (and certainly not in a swift manner), as well as hindered prosecutors' ability to grasp the extent and frequency of Lynchjustiz.

As American troops advanced throughout Europe, beginning in the summer of 1944, the increased number of atrocities became evident with the discovery of massacres (e.g., the Malmedy Massacre) and eventually concentration camps. However, instances of Lynchjustiz were far more difficult to uncover, as perpetrators and witnesses repeatedly refused to discuss such crimes and physical evidence often had long disappeared. In spite of this difficulty, it became increasingly evident that the crimes were not just "committed by the German military forces in the battlefield" but rather that "more crimes [were] committed by German civilian[s] . . . over a long period of time," according to Lieutenant Colonel Joseph C. Breckenridge (chief of the Twelfth Army Group War Crimes Office).[8] The mounting extent of war crimes not only forced investigators to look beyond the battlefields for atrocities but also required that the US military broaden the meaning of what designated a war crime, leading General Omar Bradley to expand the definition to violence committed against "persons or property, which outrage[s] common justice or involve[s] moral turpitude, [or violence] committed in connection with military operations or occupation with or without orders or sanctions of governments or commanders."[9] Thus, investigators primarily sought individuals who ordered or directed crimes "without regard to . . . the capacity in which they acted."[10] By March 1945, the Judge Advocate General (JAG) Corps could foresee the pending issues of the investigations and trials. Regarding the mistreatment downed airmen in particular, First Lieutenant Norman A. Stoll reported,

> The actual evidence in these cases is very nebulous. There is no doubt that the incidents occurred, but the problem of identifying

> the "trigger men" is practically an impossible one in most cases. Although I think we should not overlook these cases, I am not hopeful about finding the actual perpetrators except through the fortuitous circumstances of evidence turning up in particular cases incidental to AMG [Allied Military Government] control. . . . Despite the practical difficulties in individual cases, there will be strong pressure for justice in these cases. Lack of convictions against the trigger men will make prosecution of higher-ups all the more imperative.[11]

Immediately after the war, the United States established the NWCO in Washington, DC, which, along with JAG, was responsible for investigating and trying all war crimes committed against American nationals and any crimes that occurred within the US zone of occupation. Trials were permitted by the fall of 1945; however, understaffed investigating teams were tasked with not only uncovering new crimes but also assisting prosecutors in preparing their cases for trial. The investigations were also hindered by political pressure, as Americans demanded swift retribution after crimes committed against American nationals became more public. Prompt results were therefore insisted on; the quickest and easiest way to achieve them was to focus on members of Nazi organizations, such as the Nazi Party, SS, SD, and the Gestapo, which the charter of the IMT deemed illegal in the fall of 1945.[12]

Further impeding the investigations was the lack of qualified personnel. Few had professional training, and numerous claims circulated among the German public about the use of improper interrogation methods. Although no such evidence corroborated these claims, the US Army did investigate the accusations. This further hindered the abilities of investigators to uncover atrocities, however, as witnesses were even less likely to collaborate with the occupiers. While many of the men recruited to be investigators were refugees who had left Europe before the outbreak of war in 1939 and were allegedly fluent in German, comparison of the German interviews and witness statements to the English translations indicate numerous inaccuracies in content.[13] Moreover, analysis of the investigation documents indicates that the investigators (and even the entire system of war crime proceedings) never fully comprehended the "basic structure of the Third Reich, let alone the mechanisms of its policies."[14]

Despite the surrender of Germany on May 7, 1945, the war crime investigation teams suffered a major loss of personnel in the aftermath

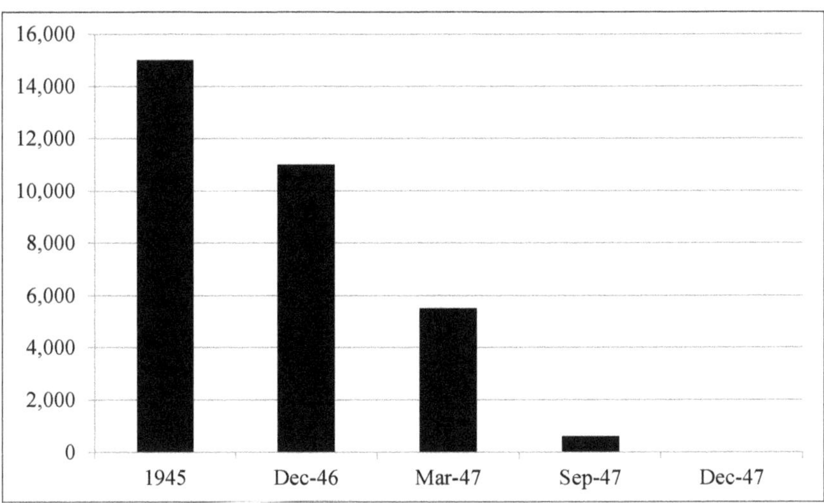

Figure 4.1. Suspects in American Custody. Based on report by the Deputy Judge Advocate, General Administration, NARA, RG, 549, Entry 290, Box 13, p. 13; see also Yavnai, "Military Justice," 127.

of the Axis defeat in Europe, as the War Department redeployed many soldiers to the Pacific theater or back to the United States. Nevertheless, the investigations focused on three main tasks: to prosecute the perpetrators of mass atrocities and violence committed against American nationals, interview American POWs for possible information regarding crimes, and screen war crimes enclosures that detained suspected criminals—the most well known of which was located at the former Dachau concentration camp. At the end of 1945, the US Army held over fifteen thousand individuals who were suspected of war crimes or arrested for membership in Nazi organizations. However, the investigations that involved these individuals were quickly processed, and thousands were extradited to other occupied zones to stand trial for crimes committed in their respective zone or against their citizens. By September 1947, just a few months before the conclusion of the US war crime trials, the number of individuals detained had diminished to six hundred, and by December, there were no war crime suspects in American custody (fig. 4.1).

The task of carrying out these investigations was left to the Third Army stationed at Dachau and the Seventh Army posted near Ludwigsburg. There were nineteen WCIT responsible for completing these goals within the US zone of occupation; however, three WCIT were sent to Le Havre, Cherbourg, and Antwerp to question American POWs before they left the Continent for the United States. This quickly became a daunting task, as the sheer volume of POWs (some ninety thousand Americans) held in Europe during the war overwhelmed the drastically understaffed and inexperienced personnel. A report by the NWCO indicated, however, that little useful information was obtained about war crimes.[15]

By the end of 1946, it had largely been determined what crimes committed against American nationals would be brought to trial, as pressure to prosecute the accused and reduce the number of suspects in American custody increased. Thus, given the circumstances that hindered the investigations and trials, it is no surprise that so few instances of Lynchjustiz were discovered. Targeting members of illegal organizations, and especially the Alte Kämpfer, allowed investigators to fulfill the United States' goals of punishing individuals who violated laws of war, reeducating Germans about the atrocities of the Nazi regime, and supporting the denazification and democratization process of Germany. The average number of trials gradually increased from three a month in 1945 to four in 1946; however, the greatest increase occurred in 1947, when there was an average of seven flyer trials per month (figs. 4.2 and 4.3).

The flyer trials were held throughout the US zone of occupation, depending on location of the crime and availability of courts, assigned army personnel, accused, witnesses, and even audiences. Throughout the first year after the war, the majority of the trials were held at either Dachau or Ludwigsburg, as these were the two locations of the WCIT headquarters. By mid-1946, however, all war crime investigations and trials were taken over by the 7708 War Crimes Group, which relocated the remaining trials to Dachau. In order to get through the cases scheduled for trial as quickly as possible, the United States consolidated the 848 cases that involved all "lesser" war criminals into 460 trials—these became known as the "Dachau trials." It was thus possible to have over seventy defendants combined in one trial. Ultimately, the United States' goals of occupation shifted from punishing Germans for war crimes to enabling a self-sustaining economy and the growth of a democratic political system, which had a direct impact on the war crime trials. As a result, the 7708 War Crimes Group was officially disbanded in July 1947. Open cases were handed over to West German officials in order to alleviate the insurmountable task of finding, investigating, and

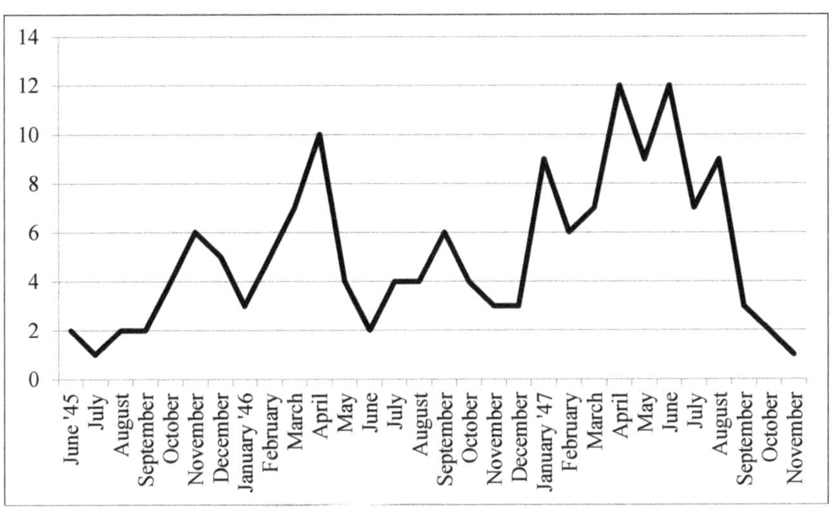

Figure 4.2. Flyer Trials Held by Month. *Source: Deputy Theater Judge Advocate's Office, War Crimes Branch, January 16, 1946, NARA, RG 153, Entry 143, Box 155–510.*

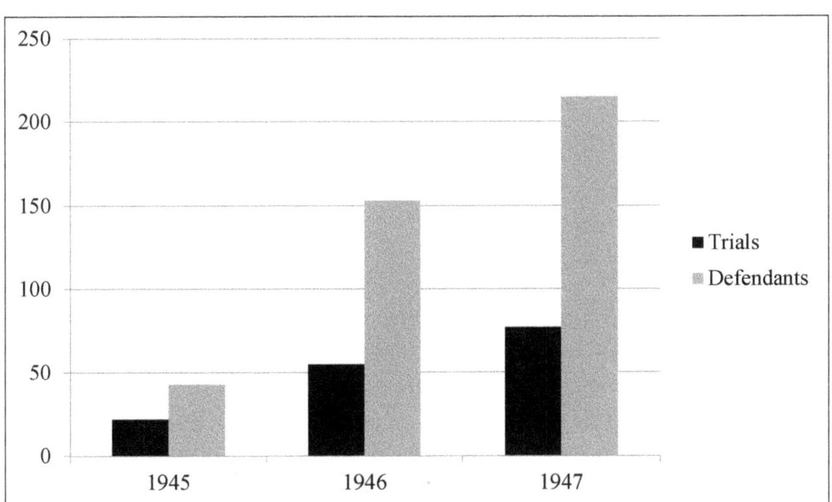

Figure 4.3. Number of Flyer Trials and Defendants by Year. *Source: Deputy Theater Judge Advocate's Office, War Crimes Branch, January 16, 1946, NARA, RG 153, Entry 143, Box 155–510.*

trying accused perpetrators of war crimes; however, the West German government rarely prosecuted perpetrators and the majority of those convicted by the American military courts were released from prison by the mid-1950s. As historian Lisa Yavnai noted, "The release of convicted war criminals became a bargaining chip in the negotiations between the United States and Federal Republic of Germany over the latter's integration into Western defense plans."[16] However, the release of war criminals not only hindered the German public from accepting responsibility for the crimes of the Nazi regime but also impeded the understanding and discourse of Lynchjustiz committed against American airmen.

Despite their attempts to shed light on the "lesser" war criminals of World War II, the Dachau trials as a whole did little to advance the understanding of the "Final Solution" or Lynchjustiz committed against downed airmen. This missed opportunity could have aided in educating the German public, and even the world, about the atrocities committed against Allied POWs, which could have furthered the historical narrative—for example, by placing Lynchjustiz within the broader aspect of Nazi atrocities. However, after the fall of 1946, the likelihood of uncovering additional crimes committed against American airmen became remote as the United States faced the looming Cold War (with the Soviet blockade of West Berlin beginning in 1948 and the Korean War beginning in 1950); Germany also sought to quickly move on from its Nazi past.

The Flyer Trials

Analyzing 179 flyer trials held between 1945 and 1948 regarding airmen mistreated in Germany reveals that 490 perpetrators were charged with "deliberately and wrongfully encourag[ing], aid[ing], abet[ting], and participat[ing] in committing assaults upon (or killing of) a surrendered prisoner of war." [17] The victims included 310 American airmen, 71 percent of whom were killed.[18] In numerous cases, airmen's bodies were never identified—or, at least, not until recently with the ability to test DNA—which indicates the extent that Nazi officials took to cover up these known crimes. This made it often necessary for the prosecutors to rely on circumstantial evidence in postwar trials and to include witness testimonies that were based on hearsay evidence. Additionally, local Germans were rather uncooperative in the criminal investigations after

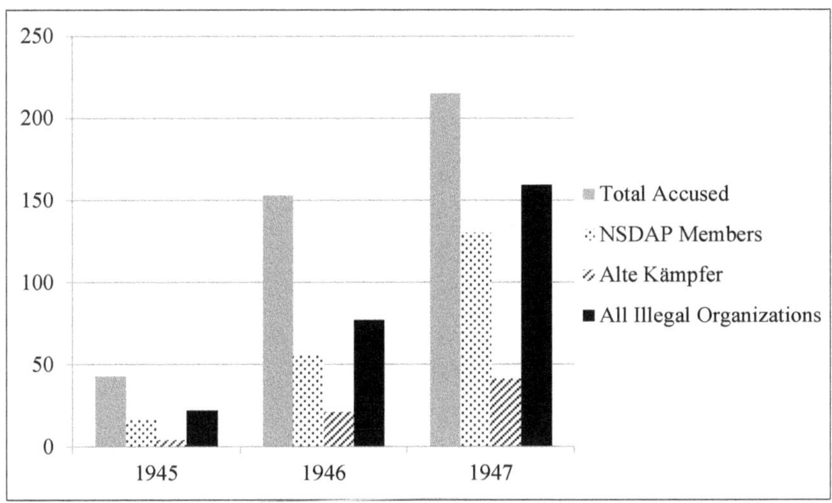

Figure 4.4. Perpetrators Tried by Year Who Were Members of Illegal Organizations. *Source: Deputy Theater Judge Advocate's Office, War Crimes Branch, January 16, 1946, NARA, RG 153, Entry 143, Box 155–510.*

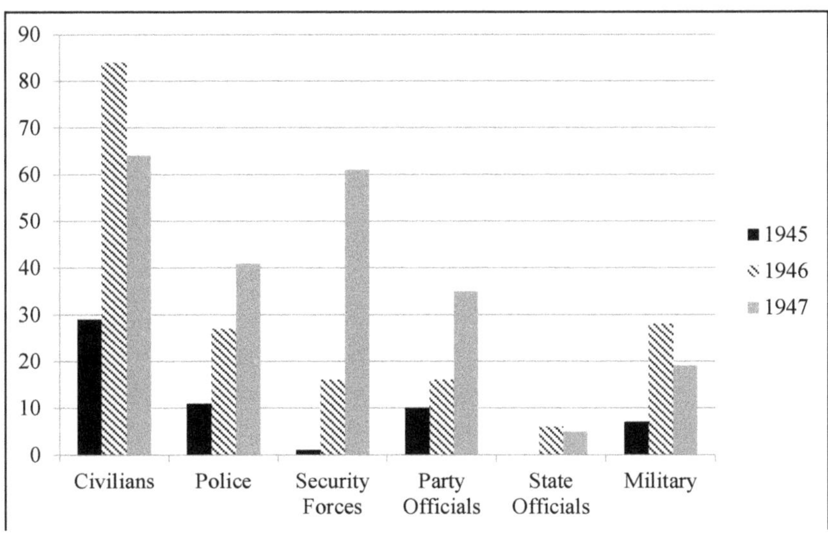

Figure 4.5. Trials Arraigned against Perpetrator Groups by Year. *Source: Deputy Theater Judge Advocate's Office, War Crimes Branch, January 16, 1946, NARA, RG 153, Entry 143, Box 155–510.*

Table 4.1. Information Pertaining to Tried Perpetrators

Total number of perpetrators	490
Average age of perpetrators (during trials)	45 years old
Known NSDAP members	50%
Range of years when perpetrators joined the NSDAP	1922–43
Known NSDAP membership prior to 1933	61%
Known NSDAP membership prior to 1939	91%
Percentage of known Alte Kämpfer among perpetrators	30.5%

Source: Deputy Theater Judge Advocate's Office, War Crimes Branch, January 16, 1946, Records of the Office of the Judge Advocate General (Army), RG 153, Entry 143, Box 155–510, National Archives at College Park, College Park, MD.

the war, and this hindered determining the identity and nationality of the flyers and the perpetrators. Ultimately, it thwarted the possibility of uncovering additional cases.

At first glance, this suggests that the courts sought to swiftly punish perpetrators who were long-standing members of the Nazi Party. This correlated with the large percentage of perpetrators tried in 1945 and 1946 who were members of the Nazi Party (50 percent). By 1947, this percentage increased to nearly 74 percent, as the pressure grew to bring criminals to justice for crimes committed against American nationals, as well as to bring the trials to a close (figs. 4.4 and 4.5). Furthermore, 61 percent of the accused had been members of the Nazi Party before 1933 (table 4.1), which clearly indicates the war crime trials pursued the so-called Alte Kämpfer.[19]

According to historian Michael Kater, in 1933 German membership in the Nazi Party accounted for less than 2 percent of the total population (with nearly 850,000 members). By 1939, party membership had risen to nearly 5 million and comprised roughly 7.25 percent of the total population.[20] However, the Alte Kämpfer represented at least 30.5 percent of the accused in the postwar crime trials. Thus, these perpetrators on trial represented a very small segment of the overall German population. Although it appears that the Alte Kämpfer were actively involved in ordering and personally carrying out Lynchjustiz, countless perpetrators, especially civilians, were not brought to justice for their participation in the violence. After the war, the difficulty in finding perpetrators persisted, as many disappeared into hiding or individuals refused to reveal known instances of Lynchjustiz.

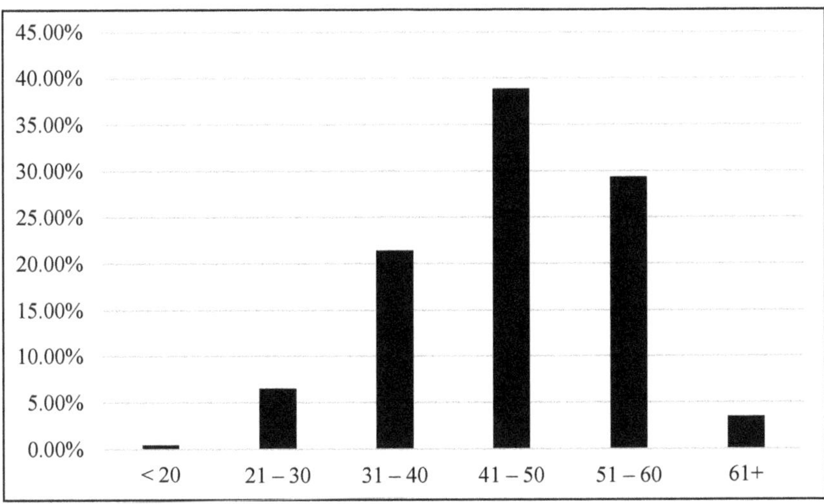

Figure 4.6. Breakdown of Perpetrators by Age. *Source: Deputy Theater Judge Advocate's Office, War Crimes Branch, January 16, 1946, NARA, RG 153, Entry 143, Box 155–510.*

At the time of the trials, perpetrators' ages ranged between nineteen and seventy-two-years, with the average age being forty-five (fig. 4.6). Accordingly, the perpetrators were often ardent supporters of the regime who had joined the Nazi Party before Hitler had come to power. In the atrocities committed against downed airmen, eight women (less than 2 percent of all known perpetrators) were tried, although the number of undocumented women (and even men) involved was undoubtedly higher. Numerous trials, along with personal accounts from aviators, recounted the increased brutality suffered at the hands of civilian crowds. Witnesses reported that these mobs could include hundreds of individuals and often consisted of a large number of women.[21]

Georg Hoffmann categorized perpetrators as instigators, who promoted and condoned the lynching of airmen, or followers who were often provoked by the "bystander effect."[22] This follows, however, the designated categories of the denazification process, which, according to German historian Lutz Niethammer, resulted in creating a *Mitlaüferfabrik*, literally a "factory to produce followers."[23] Using these categories results in focusing blame on a small group of Nazi elites. It is more beneficial to categorize the perpetrators into six main groups (civilians, police, security forces, party officials, military personnel, and state officials) that represent the broader German society.[24]

Each group had unique motives that influenced their actions. As seen in figure 4.7, civilians represented the largest number of perpetrators tried with 39 percent.[25] Closer examination indicates that they overwhelmingly represented the number of assaults committed against downed airmen with nearly 70 percent (fig. 4.8).

The civilians acted primarily out of rage and distress as a direct response to the devastating bombing and strafing raids, an emotional situation that party officials used to their advantage, inciting the public to seek revenge.[26] The second-largest group was the police (e.g., KriPo, OrPo, Gendarmerie, and rural and auxiliary police forces), which represented 17.25 percent of perpetrators. Individuals of this group were often acting on orders from party officials and security force members. Members of security forces, which consisted of SS, SD, and Gestapo, represented 16.81 percent of perpetrators; however, the greatest disparity between involvement in killings and assaults within a single group existed with the security forces. This group was far more likely to resort to killing downed airmen. Party officials (e.g., Kreisleiter and Ortsgruppenleiter), who represented 13.14 percent of perpetrators, were most likely to be indoctrinated and radicalized by the Nazi regime. Party officials and members of security forces were prosecuted mainly for passing on orders to mistreat and kill downed airmen, although their active participation in carrying out the violence was common. Military personnel and state officials (e.g., nonparty government officials) represented the smallest groups of perpetrators with 11.63 percent and 2.15 percent, respectively. This corresponds to the widespread belief among the United States military during the war, and reiterated by downed flyers in postwar interviews, that the military, particularly the Luftwaffe, offered the best option for safety.[27] A sense of camaraderie existed between the Luftwaffe and Allied airmen. Nevertheless, soldiers who mistreated and killed downed airmen (most likely to occur when soldiers were home on leave) often did so out of revenge for lost family members or out of fear of retaliation for not following orders. Overall, Nazi Party members were represented in every group and were most likely to be found guilty of direct involvement in killing downed American aviators. Nevertheless, the significant role of civilians involved in killings (27.94 percent) should not be underestimated.[28]

While the mistreatment of downed flyers was committed throughout Europe, with airmen shot down in nearly every European country, the violence was not unique to American flyers. Although the overwhelming majority of aviators were shot down over Germany (fig. 4.9), flyers were

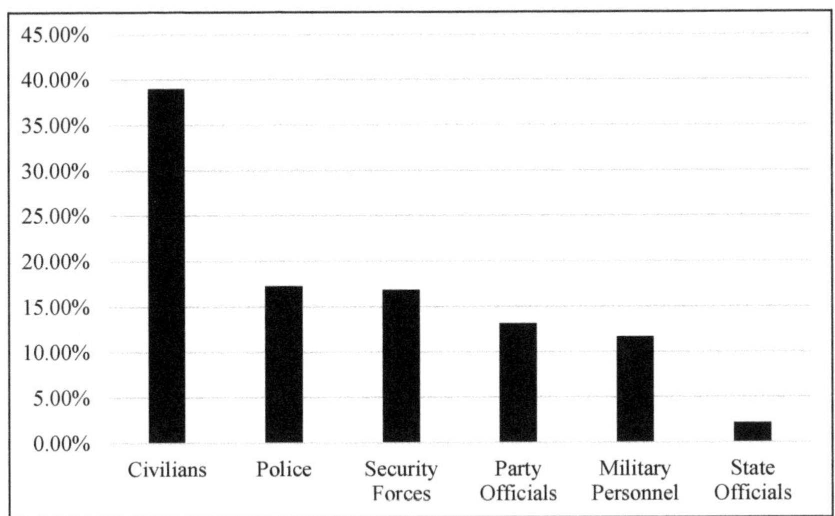

Figure 4.7. Groups Tried for Their Involvement in Lynchjustiz (by percent). Examples of civilian perpetrators include farmers, teachers, students, shoemakers, chemists, butchers, bakers, innkeepers, merchants, salesmen, musicians, carpenters, plumbers, machinists, mechanics, painters, attorneys, businessmen, and housewives (RG No. 242/388, Roll No. 10, Frame No.12 792, NARA). *Source: Deputy Theater Judge Advocate's Office, War Crimes Branch, January 16, 1946, RG 153, Entry 143, Box 155–510, NARA.*

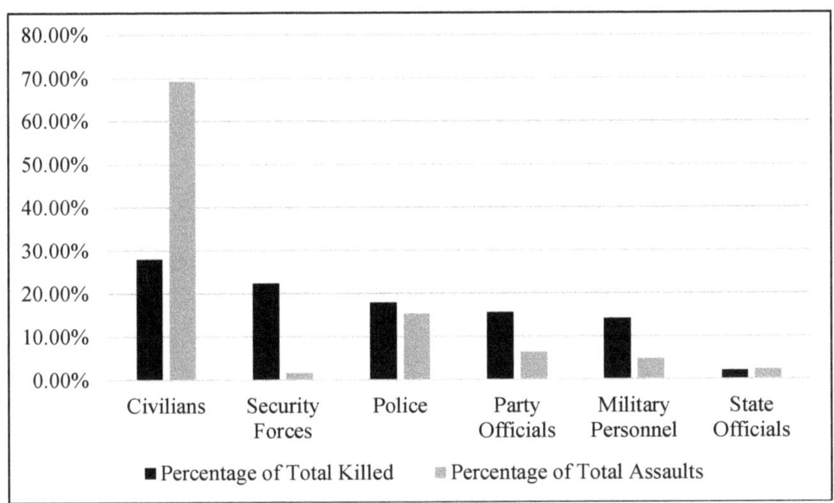

Figure 4.8. Groups Involved in Lynchjustiz (by percentage of killings and assaults). *Source: Deputy Theater Judge Advocate's Office, War Crimes Branch, January 16, 1946, RG 153; Entry 143; Box 155–510, NARA.*

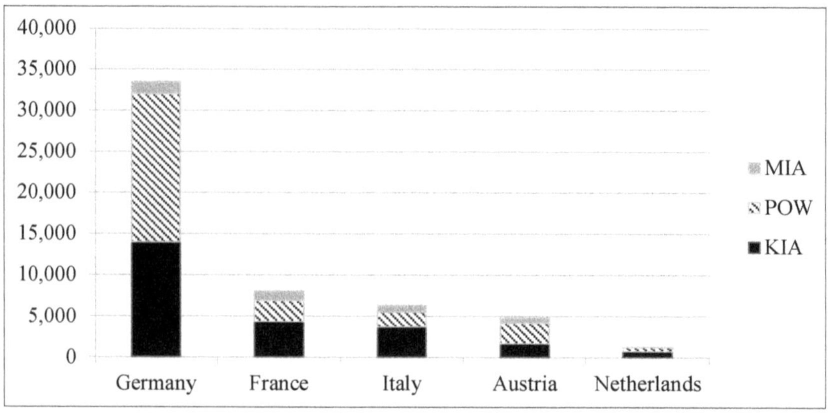

Figure 4.9. Top Five Countries in Europe Where American Airmen Were Shot Down. *Source: Army Battle Casualties and Nonbattle Deaths in World War II—Final Report: December 7, 1941–December 31, 1946 Statistical and Accounting Branch Office of the Adjutant General, 1950.*

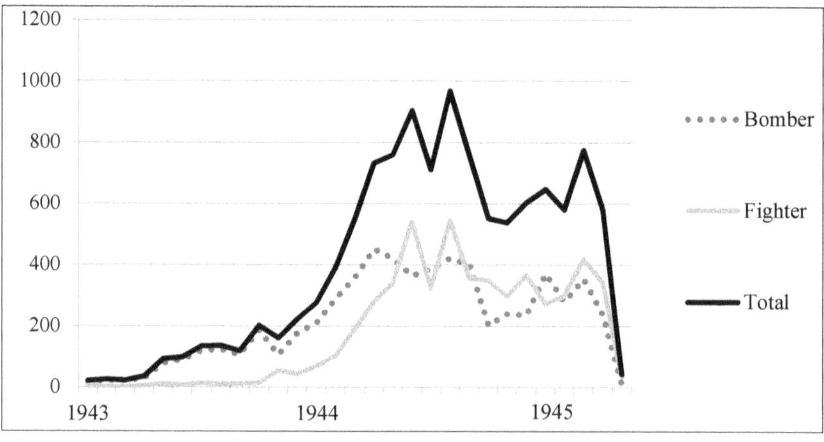

Figure 4.10. American Airplanes Lost in the European Theater. *Source:* Army Air Forces Statistical Digest, World War II, *Office of Statistical Control–December 1945, Battle Casualties in European Theater by Casualty Type, Table 159.*

frequently brought from other countries to Germany (if they were not initially killed) in order to be interrogated at Dulag Luft.

Before May and June 1944, assaults committed against downed flyers consistently outnumbered instances of homicide. In fact, from August 1943 until May 1944, assaults consistently increased. The level of both killings and assaults reached a climax between July and August

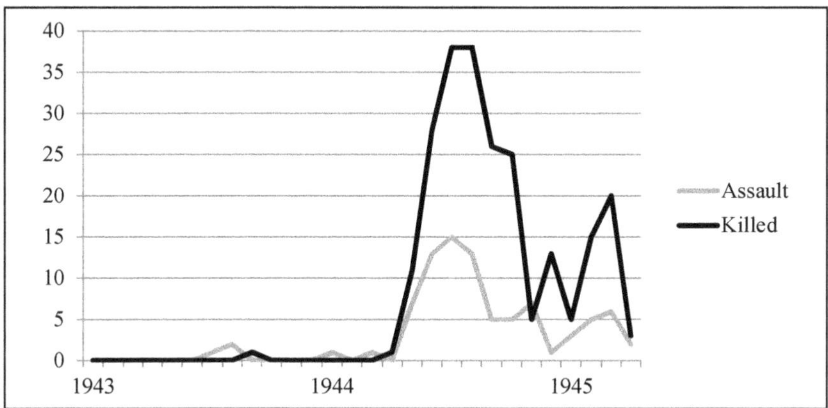

Figure 4.11. Lynchjustiz Committed against Downed Airmen in Germany. *Source: Deputy Theater Judge Advocate's Office, War Crimes Branch, January 16, 1946, RG 153, Entry 143, Box 155–510, NARA.*

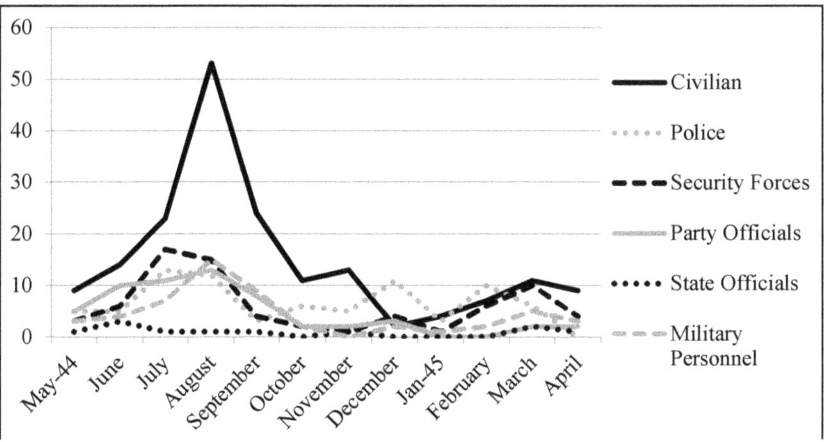

Figure 4.12. Groups Involved in Lynchjustiz. *Source: Deputy Theater Judge Advocate's Office, War Crimes Branch, January 16, 1946, RG 153, Entry 143, Box 155–510, NARA.*

1944. Unsurprisingly, this rise in violence was connected to the increase in Allied bombing raids at this time (figs. 4.10 and 4.11).

In particular, the drastic increase in the participation of civilians in mistreating downed airmen (fig. 4.12) following Goebbels's article from May 1944 is quite telling. It indicated, arguably, the initial effectiveness of Nazi propaganda (especially with regard to civilians), as well as the extreme degree of radicalization in the war. In addition, a secondary surge in violence occurred in March 1945—mostly by civilians and security forces. This was mainly due to the final call by the Nazi regime to fight to the death.

The most widely known incident that involved reprisal killings of downed flyers was the Rüsselsheim massacre.[29] American prosecutors charged eleven German civilians with beating eight downed aviators (six of whom died from their injuries) on August 26, 1944.[30] After parachuting and landing near Osnabrück, these eight flyers were captured and taken to Dulag Luft for interrogation (nearly two hundred miles away). However, before they reached Oberursel, two German military guards marched the flyers through the town of Rüsselsheim between 9:00 a.m. and 10:00 a.m. With the citizens "still in an excited condition" following the "longest and most destructive" bombing raid they experienced during the war, a crowd quickly began to gather around the airmen.[31] Slurs and insults quickly led to demands for reprisal by civilians, including women, who shouted, "Beat them to pieces!" "Beat them to death!" "They are the ones, they are the ones who were here last night! They are the terrorizers of last night! Kill the dogs!"[32]

According to the prosecution's report, the flyers were bleeding after being struck countless times by rocks, shovels, hammers, and other foreign objects. "Perpetrators badly beat one flyer such that by the time the group neared the end of the Taunusstrasse . . . a piece of stone was sticking in his skull."[33] After continuing down various streets in downtown Rüsselsheim in an attempt to avoid the deadly onslaught, the flyers struggled to seek refuge. Eventually, their walk was reduced to a crawl and continued to slow until they huddled together on the ground for protection. The propaganda chief of Rüsselsheim administered the final blows, for those who were still alive, with shots to the head. After the flyers' roughly two hours of constant torture and beatings, Hitler Youth members removed their bodies, some still showing signs of life, to the local cemetery, where they were buried later that afternoon. Perpetrators gave no forethought about what might happen if these bodies were identified—each airman still wore his uniform and dog tags. While two men received fifteen-year imprisonments and the nine remaining perpetrators, including two women, were sentenced to death, only five men were actually executed. The remaining offenders were paroled by January 1954, after serving roughly eight and a half years.

Similar to the incident in Rüsselsheim, where several American flyers were mercilessly beaten to death, an incident occurred on the

German island of Borkum, located in the North Sea. This case involved a group of captured flyers being marched through a gauntlet of terror and resulted in the death of seven American flyers on August 4, 1944. The bomber crew was initially interrogated by the flak battalion, which was then ordered to march the airmen to the airport. This was standard protocol since the Luftwaffe had jurisdiction over downed airmen; however, instead of being marched directly to the airport, the crew was purposely sent through a densely populated part of town. It was predetermined to "expose the unarmed prisoners to assaults by civilians," following Goebbels's decree ordering police not to interfere with civilians attacking downed airmen.[34] As the group was marched down one of the town's main streets, a group of eighty to one hundred men belonging to the RAD "formed two lines . . . through which the flyers had to march. . . . The RAD men shouted and beat the flyers with spades . . . and kicked them . . . the guards did not interfere."[35] Afterward, the airmen faced a ruthless crowd of civilians incited by the town mayor and Ortsgruppenleiter, Jan Akkermann. Eventually, after being paraded through the streets and experiencing severe beatings, a German soldier shot each airman in the back of the head in front of the sports field.[36] Fifteen men were tried, resulting in five receiving death sentences; one, life imprisonment; and nine, prison sentences ranging from two to twenty-five years.[37] The mayor and three members of the flak battalion were executed by the end of 1948, but the remaining perpetrators were paroled by 1952.

Race and Religion

Although just being an American flyer was more than enough justification for German reprisals, race, ethnicity, and religion also played a role in the treatment of downed airmen. Throughout the flyer trials, these aspects were particularly mentioned as a further justification for killing airmen. While only a few cases involved such reasoning for mistreating downed flyers, this seems extremely disproportionate to the overall number of airmen mistreated, and it is expected to increase with future research.

On July 20, 1944, for example, two flyers parachuted safely and were captured by the police in Moosinning. The Kreisleiter Anton Schosser demanded that the police deliver the airmen to the local party headquarters; however, this was initially refused for unknown reasons. After a heated discussion with the Luftwaffe commander of the local airfield, Schosser's demands were fulfilled, at least partially; he received one flyer, allegedly an African American for interrogation.[38] Here, the power and influence of the party officials became evident. Immediately after leaving the police station with the airman, the perpetrators escorted the flyer to the edge of town and executed him.[39] Of the four men tried, only Schosser received death by hanging and was executed; the other men were acquitted for lack of evidence. An example of how race was used to portray American airmen can be seen in figure 4.13.

Ethnicity and religion, particularly if a flyer was Jewish, was also an essential determining factor in airmen's treatment. Cases are known of POWs who were taken to concentration camps (e.g., Berga) because they were presumed to be Jewish.[40] An example of this from the flyer trials took place near Hausen, Germany, where several flyers were shot down on November 21, 1944. Ortsgruppenleiter Wilhelm Heene, along with a member of the RAD, Wilhelm Matthaei, immediately set out to find the downed airmen: "an hour later they came to the tavern and washed their bloody hands." After showing off their newly acquired loot (e.g., a compass, patches, and a watch) stolen from the airman, they stated to a woman that "we have killed an American flyer. He was a Jew."[41]

In a separate incident, numerous bombers were shot down during a raid on the city Hanau in the late morning of February 17, 1945. Four American airmen (Technical Sergeant Charles Bernard Goldstein, Staff Sergeant Warren George Hammond, and one unknown) landed near the harbor of Hanau. They were taken into custody by civilians and turned over to the local police. The airmen were held in separate rooms until later in the afternoon when Adolf Weger and Karl Neuber (Gestapo officials) and Julius Schulze of the KriPo interrogated the flyers in the presence of the police director (Fehrle).[42] When Fehrle discovered that Goldstein was Jewish, he "flew into a rage, cursing and shouting." The interrogation quickly became very abusive, and Fehrle threatened to shoot the flyers, pointing his pistol at them and constantly crying out, "Gangsters! Murderers!" Sometime later, a doctor arrived to check on one of the airmen. He had been told that a wounded American flyer needed medical attention at the police station. The doctor suggested that the injured airman be sent to a military hospital since he was a POW, but Fehrle objected furiously and stated that Allied flyers were no longer to be delivered to the Wehrmacht; they were to be retained by the police to be executed. He then reminded Weger that the airmen were to be considered not soldiers but rather murderers and as such he would either have to shoot them himself or have someone kill them. Weger

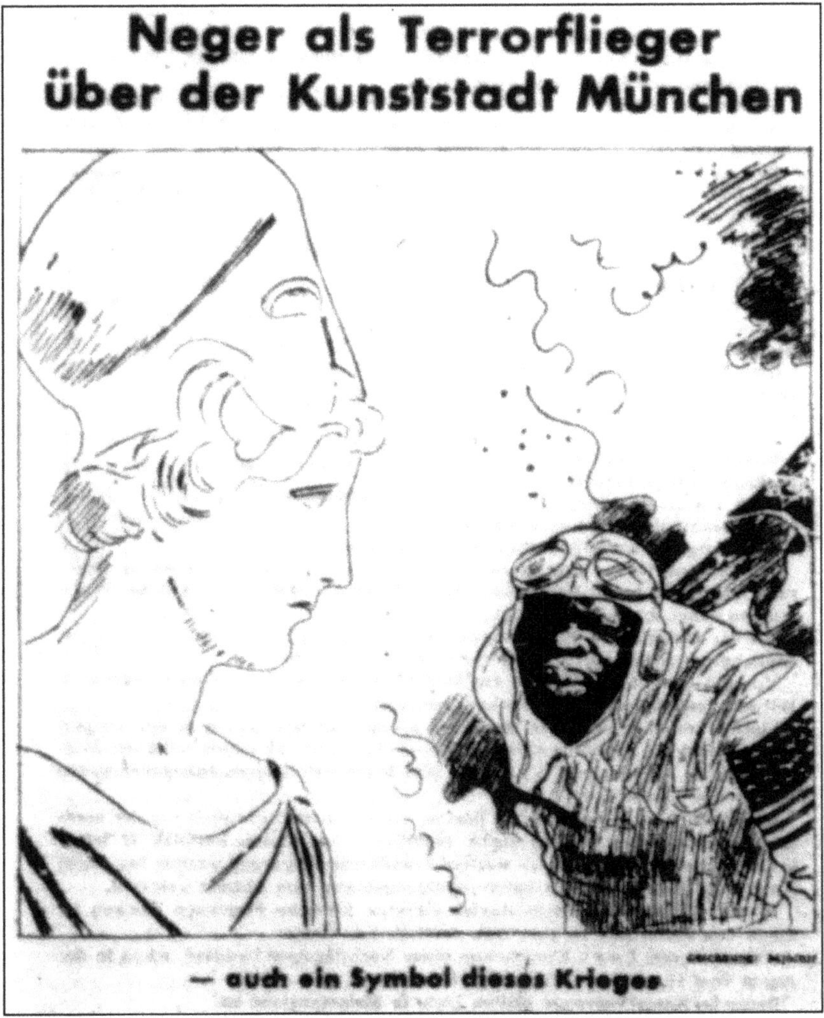

Figure 4.13. "Negro terror flyers over the art-city of Munich—also a symbol of this war." *"Neger als Terrorflieger über der Kunststadt München,"* Völkischer Beobachter *(Berlin), June 19, 1944.*

immediately passed on the instructions to Neuber and Schulze, who took the flyers one at a time into the courtyard behind the police headquarters, where they executed the POWs. The bodies were then loaded into a vehicle and transported to a crashed bomber near the harbor and put with the remains of seven other flyers who had allegedly died in the crash. The next morning, all ten bodies were removed from the

Figure 4.14. Locations of known Lynchjustiz cases based on war crimes trials (each point could include several victims).

wreckage and buried in the local cemetery. It was then reported that all ten bodies had been found in the wreckage and had died as a result of the crash.[43]

While the mistreatment of downed airmen was widespread, the majority of tried incidents occurred in western and central Germany, as seen in figure 4.14. The western Allies had an advantage in investigating within these regions since they were under American and British occupation after the war. In addition, these regions also experienced the most flight traffic during the air war. Regardless of where the targets were within Germany (the largest targeted region being the Ruhr), the Eighth Air Force (based in England) flew mostly over the western and northwestern regions while the Fifteenth Air Force (based in Italy) flew mainly over the southern, southwestern, and even southeastern regions.

Trial Sentencing

Although disconcerting, the swift punishment of criminals by the Allied war crime trials between 1945 and 1948, and by German authorities thereafter, was due to two main reasons. One was the mercilessly troubled relationship between the United States and the Soviet Union after the war, which resulted in the US government becoming less focused on punishing Germans. The second reason was the desire of the newly formed Federal Republic of Germany, after it was founded in 1949, to begin to move on from its Nazi past.[44]

The largest percentage of sentences resulted in death by hanging with 27 percent of perpetrators tried (fig. 4.15). The number of convicted perpetrators who were executed nearly doubled each year from 1945 to 1947 (figs. 4.16 and 4.17). However, US military review boards reduced a significant number of sentences and even overturned convictions due

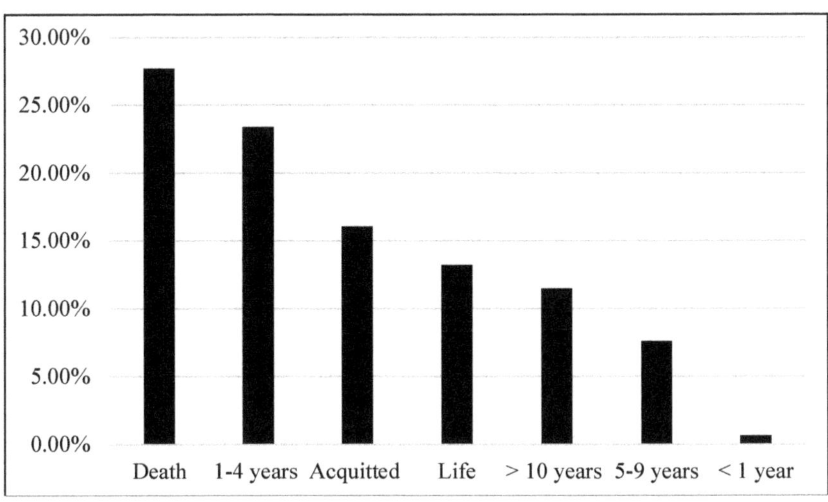

Figure 4.15. Distribution of Sentences (by percent). *Source: Deputy Theater Judge Advocate's Office, War Crimes Branch, January 16, 1946, RG 153, Entry 143, Box 155–510, NARA.*

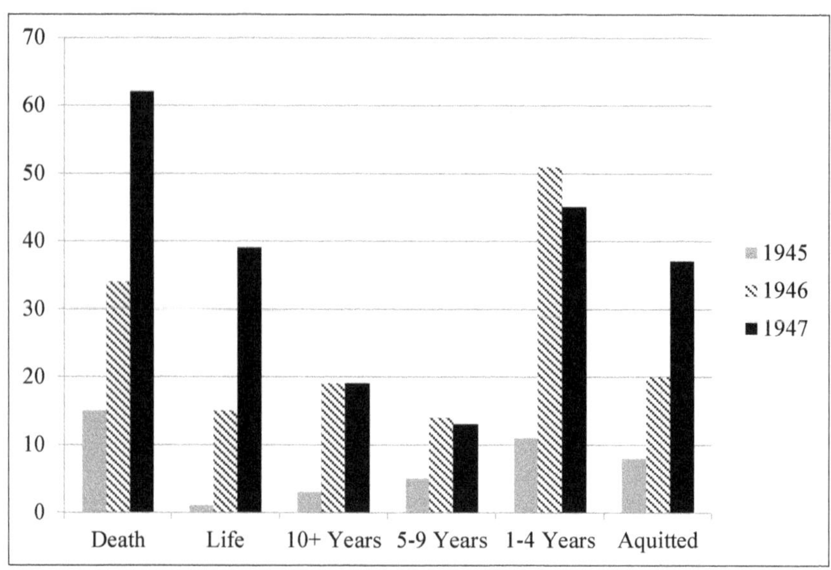

Figure 4.16. Overall Sentences by Year. *Source: Deputy Theater Judge Advocate's Office, War Crimes Branch, January 16, 1946, RG 153, Entry 143, Box 155–510, NARA.*

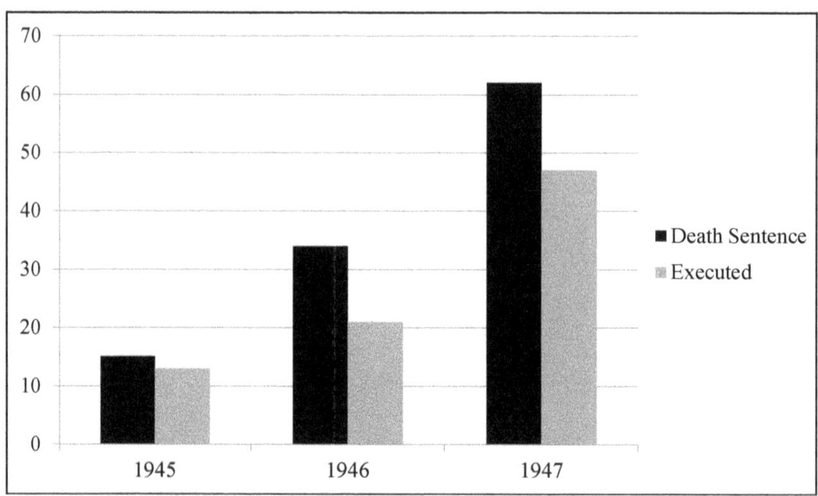

Figure 4.17. Number of Death Sentences by Year. *Source: Deputy Theater Judge Advocate's Office, War Crimes Branch, January 16, 1946, RG 153, Entry 143, Box 155–510, NARA.*

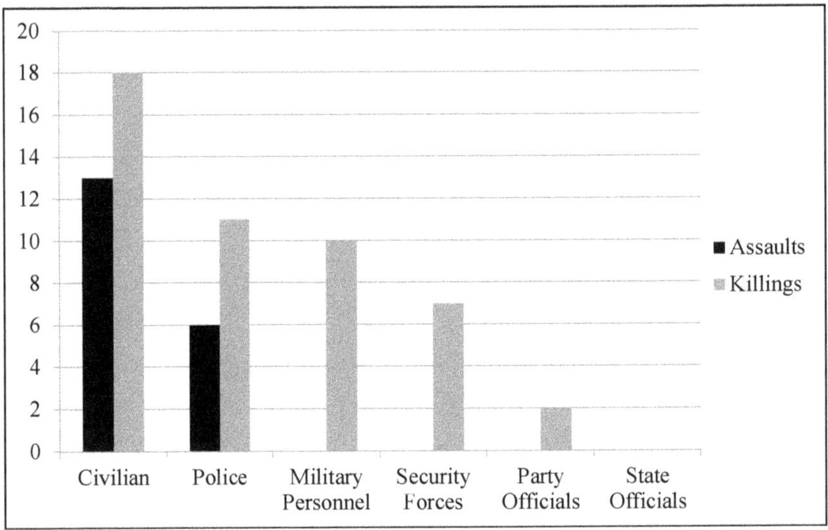

Figure 4.18. Number of Perpetrators Acquitted by Group. *Source: Deputy Theater Judge Advocate's Office, War Crimes Branch, January 16, 1946, RG 153, Entry 143, Box 155–510, NARA.*

to insufficient evidence. Once the Federal Republic of Germany was established, it pardoned an even greater number of convicted criminals. As a result, the average criminal served roughly seven years in prison. This includes over 25 percent of perpetrators who were sentenced to death.[45] Moreover, as many accused were interned in camps immediately following the war, convicted perpetrators were able to deduct their time served in the camps from their sentences. Numerous convicted perpetrators were therefore released following their convictions. By 1955, the Federal Republic of Germany had paroled the majority of war criminals due, in part, to various pressure groups throughout the United States and Germany.[46] In total, nearly 20 percent of perpetrators were acquitted mainly because of lack of evidence (fig. 4.18). Keep in mind that the number of people put on trial was still only a fraction of the number who were actually involved in the violence.

Civilians primarily argued that the trauma they experienced from the bombing and strafing raids, along with the relentless Nazi propaganda, influenced their acts of spontaneous revenge against downed airmen. The violence perpetrated by party officials and security forces was far more likely to be premeditated. The most common defense among the remaining groups was the notion that they were following orders and, had they not done so, would have faced being sent to prison or death. Ironically, however, Goebbels argued in 1944 that "it is not provided in any military law that a soldier in the case of a despicable crime is exempt from punishment because he blames his superior, especially if the orders of the latter are in evident contradiction to all human morality and every international usage of warfare."[47] The police as well as the Gendarmerie and Volkssturm, in particular, claimed this defense, repeatedly stating they "were under the jurisdiction of the SS" and, therefore, had to obey orders.[48]

A further development that came out of the witness statements of the flyer trials was the forging of documents after downed airmen were killed in order to justify and conceal the true actions. German perpetrators often reported that airmen were allegedly shot while attempting to escape. Whether the Reich Foreign Ministry meant this strictly for propaganda purposes in case news of the numerous killings became public or if this was some warped justification to perpetrators' personally questionable morals is not exactly clear. It is likely, however, that both reasons played a role. Their actions were often premeditated and knowingly deceitful. The overwhelming majority of cases detailed that airmen were shot while attempting to escape, which leads to a concern regarding the accuracy of the statistics relating to the number of mistreated airmen during the war.

The analysis of the war crimes trials, USAAF mission statistics, and the existing historiography indicates that there are more cases of violence against downed airmen still to be uncovered. German historian Ralf Blank set the historiographical standard, stating 350[49] Anglo-American flyers were mistreated in Germany during the war.[50] Yet this is far too few given the fact that there were more than 85,000 casualties in Europe among American flyers (over 38,000 in Germany alone)—of which over 32,000 were KIA and nearly 36,000 were interned as POWs, according to a US military statistical report from 1950.[51] As of July 2019, the Defense POW/MIA Accounting Agency (DPAA), which is an agency within the US Department of Defense tasked with recovering missing personnel from past wars, reported that 72,686 American servicemen from World War II were still considered missing. Over 20,000 of these men represent flyers, including nearly 800 lost in Germany.[52] Although the extent that Lynchjustiz was committed against these aviators remains uncertain, the possibility is overwhelming.[53] Moreover, the likelihood is high that some airmen considered KIA also experienced Lynchjustiz.

Hoffmann concludes that in Austria and Hungary there were roughly 600 mistreated American airmen, which included 130 killed.[54] He estimates the total number of cases in Europe to be roughly 1,000,[55] an estimate that also seems too low. Compared to Austria, there were roughly seven times as many airmen downed in Germany. This statistic, as well as the fact that there was a longer air war in Germany (Austria was only consistently targeted after mid-1944), indicates there would have been more airmen mistreated in Germany.

Additional instances of violence and mistreatment that went untried is certain. In fact, referencing the index of American war crime trials reveals that the US military opened nearly three hundred additional investigations, which included over four hundred airmen mistreated in Germany. Due to the lack of evidence and insufficient participation of witnesses, as well as the inability to apprehend the accused, the US military was forced to close the cases. Of the nearly four thousand war crime cases opened for investigation, over three thousand were closed, according to historian Lisa Yavnai.[56] The percentage of these investigations that contained crimes against airmen is uncertain; however, the dark figure of crime is certainly high, especially since the Sonderbehandlung of downed airmen has mostly been forgotten and ignored.[57] Adding the known cases of airmen imprisoned and mistreated, for example in Fresnes Prison (south of Paris) and Saint-Gilles Prison (Brussels), to the number of airmen revealed in the flyer trials, along with Hoffmann's results on Austria and Hungary, results in over eleven hundred known American airmen mistreated as alleged Terrorflieger. Considering instances of Lynchjustiz and Sonderbehandlung committed against all Allied airmen throughout Europe results in a conservative estimate of three thousand cases of mistreatment (roughly one out of every ten downed Allied airman).

In comparison to the 489 "lesser" war crimes trials held by the United States, which tried 1,672 perpetrators (of which 1,416 were convicted), the French convicted over 2,000 German perpetrators and the Soviets convicted 13,198 (of 14,820 accused).[58] By 1950, the West German courts convicted 5,228[59] people, of which only 228 were for capital offenses.[60] Although this number represents roughly as many convictions as the United States, British, and French military tribunals sentenced, very few German trials prosecuted cases of severe brutality and often only administered light sentences; many convicted perpetrators were fined instead of imprisoned. By the 1990s, German courts had sentenced only 6,487 perpetrators.[61] The relatively small number of convictions and lack of punishment for perpetrators in postwar crime trials is similar to the results of the German denazification tribunals. Of the roughly 3.6 million people determined to have belonged to the Nazi Party or a Nazi organization, only roughly 9,500 were sentenced to prison, of which only 300 remained incarcerated by 1949.[62]

The German public viewed the war crime trials as illegal and regarded the "convicted war criminals as 'prisoners of war,'" according to Yavnai.[63] The German public even argued that "the convicted war criminals had not violated existing German law during the war and therefore their convictions were ex-post facto in nature."[64] Furthermore, German criminal law required that defendants know the illegality of their alleged acts; yet, as Holocaust historian Rebecca Wittmann explains, "this led, in Nazi trials, to a perverse result: the more a defendant claimed that he believed in and identified with the Nazi worldview, the less likely he was to be convicted. In turn, . . . the more remorse he showed, the more likely he was to be convicted."[65] According to German historian Norbert Frei, the mind-set during the Adenauer administration was "an increasing prevalent theory limiting the blame for Nazi crimes to the narrow band of top Nazi leaders."[66] The issues surrounding the coming to terms with the Nazi past continued throughout the history of Germany and still linger today.[67]

Despite the widespread direct and indirect involvement of German society in the war crimes, Francis Biddle and Geoffrey Lawrence (American and British judges at the Nuremberg trials) remained opposed to a "blanket-guilt theory." This was common among postwar trials.[68] Although the fact that many sentenced perpetrators received reduced or commuted sentences, the end goal, as stated by Colonel C. Robert Bard (US war crime tribunal judge), of "the deterrent effect of punishment . . . great enough to prevent forever crimes that are an abomination in the eyes of men and blasphemy in the sight of God" did, to an extent, materialize.[69]

Although the flyer trials do not describe every instance of downed American airmen being mistreated, they represent the largest known collection of documents pertaining to this topic. Therefore, they provide a critical opportunity to establish a foundation for understanding the details and extent of these atrocities and this will hopefully lead to future studies. The fundamental knowledge gained from the numerous "lesser" war crimes trials further emphasizes the "absence of 'normal' human decency, humanity, compassion, and conscience . . . through the Nazi period."[70]

While a minority of airmen were subjected to Lynchjustiz, analyzing this violence helps better understand the social milieu within Nazi Germany and the interaction between the German public and downed flyers. German civilians played an unsettlingly significant role in the mistreatment of downed aviators and shared similar responsibility with police, party officials, and security forces. The calculated development of this state-sponsored vigilantism allowed emotions and outside influences to direct individuals' actions. As German historian Klaus-Michael Mallmann describes, "The mass shootings of paratroopers, the lynching of aircrews, as well as the massacre of American POWs by the *Leibstandarte SS Adolf Hitler* at Malmedy on December 17, 1944, show the Western Allies were also victims of the German war of extermination."[71]

Notes

1. The closing comment given by Colonel C. Robert Bard, Judge Advocate General's Department (JAGD), in the review of the Russelsheim Massacre trial held in Darmstadt, Germany, by the Seventh United States Army on July 25, 1945, Review and Recommendations for Case No. 12-1497, RG 153, Entry 143, Box 361, NARA.
2. The term *lesser war crime trials*, in accordance to the Moscow Declaration, distinguished the accused perpetrators from the high-profile war criminals at the International Military Tribunal held in Nuremberg. In no way does it refer to the severity of their accused crimes committed.
3. Though reviewed flyer trials were held at Dachau, Ludwigsburg, Ahrweiler, Munich, Darmstadt, Freising, and Heidelberg, over 75 percent of the cases were tried at Dachau.
4. More cases were opened but never tried than were actually brought to trial due to lack of evidence.
5. At the very least, investigators were often able to identify the remains as American or British by analyzing the clothing, rings, and the contents of their pockets. For example, one case relied on a Wrigley's chewing gum wrapper, discovered in the pants pocket of a flyer, to identify his remains as American. For more information, see Case No. 12-1982, Records of US Army Europe, War Crimes Branch, General Administration, and War Crimes Case Files, 1947-1958, RG 549, Entry 290, Box 175, NARA.
6. Perpetrators involved in mistreating downed American airmen were from all levels of society and included, for example, representatives from the various police organizations (SiPo, KriPo, OrPo, Rural Police, and Gendarmerie); Security Forces such as SS, SD, and Gestapo; party officials (e.g., Ortsgruppenleiter, Kreisleiter, and Blockleiter); state officials (e.g., nonparty community officials); civilians from various backgrounds (for example farmers, teachers, students, butchers, bakers, musicians, mechanics, attorneys, and even housewives); and military personnel (usually members of the army or flak battalions).
7. This is based on analysis of the flyer trials.

8. Breckenridge to Judge Advocate, 12th Army Group, April 5, 1945, War Crimes Branch, General Administration, RG 549, Entry 290, Box 1, NARA; see also Elisabeth M. Yavnai, "Military Justice: The U.S. Army War Crimes Trials in Germany, 1944–1947," in *Atrocities on Trial: Historical Perspectives on the Politics of Prosecuting War Crimes*, ed. Patricia Heberer and Jürgen Matthäus (Lincoln: University of Nebraska Press, 2008), 99.

9. Thomas to Commanding Generals, April 30, 1945, War Crimes Branch, General Administration, RG 549, Entry 290, Box 1, NARA; see also Yavnai, "Military Justice," 100.

10. Thomas to Commanding Generals, April 30, 1945, War Crimes Branch, General Administration, RG 549, Entry 290, Box 1, NARA.

11. Memorandum from First Lieutenant Norman A. Stoll, Deputy Theater Judge Advocate's Office, to Colonel Purvis, March 30, 1945, RG 153, Entry 143, Box 178, Case No. 12-214, NARA.

12. Control Council Law No. 10, "Punishment of Persons Guilty of War Crimes, Crimes against Peace, and Crimes against Humanity," December 20, 1945, reprinted in *XV Trials of War Criminals before the Nuremberg Military Tribunals under Control Council Law No. 10*, (Washington, DC: Government Printing Office, 1950), 23–28, https://www.loc.gov/rr/frd/Military_Law/pdf/NT_war-criminals_Vol-XV.pdf.

13. Tom Bower, *Blind Eye to Murder: Britain, America, and the Purging of Nazi Germany—A Pledge Betrayed* (New York: Harper Collins, 1981), 134–36; Yavnai, "Military Justice," 107.

14. Yavnai, "Military Justice," 206.

15. Report of the Deputy Judge Advocate, War Crimes Branch, General Administration, RG 549, Entry 290, Box 13, pg. 37, NARA; see also Yavnai, "Military Justice," 106.

16. Yavnai, "Military Justice," 235.

17. Deputy Theater Judge Advocate's Office, War Crimes Branch, January 16, 1946, Records of the Office of the Judge Advocate General (Army), RG 153, Entry 143, Box 155–510, NARA.

18. Nearly 23 percent of all airmen in the flyer trials were identified by their rank. Over 53 percent of the known American airmen were officers, and over 46 percent were enlisted men. Furthermore, at least 60 percent of all airmen were identified as bomber crewmembers. The majority of whom (over 70 percent) were killed through Lynchjustiz.

19. Deputy Theater Judge Advocate's Office, War Crimes Branch, January 16, 1946, Records of the Office of the Judge Advocate General (Army), RG 153, Entry 143, Box 155–510, NARA.

20. Michael H. Kater, *The Nazi Party: A Social Profile of Members and Leaders, 1919–1945* (Cambridge, MA: Harvard University Press, 1983), 262. According to 1933 and 1939 census records, the population went from around 65 million to roughly 69 million. In 1939, the Greater German Reich had a total population of roughly 79 million. Accounting for this additional population results in Nazi Party membership comprising roughly 6.33 percent of the total population of the Greater German Reich.

21. According to trial data, over 52 percent of the known perpetrators represented the working class (with occupations such as farmers, butchers, bakers,

carpenters, and mechanics) and over 44 percent embodied the lower-middle class (which, for example, included administration officials, police, merchants, teachers, and electricians).

22. Hoffmann, *Fliegerlynchjustiz*, 324. See also Victoria J. Barnett, *Bystanders: Conscience and Complicity during the Holocaust* (London: Praeger, 1999), 28.

23. Lutz Niethammer, *Die Mitlaüferfabrik: Die Entnazifizierung am Beispiel Bayerns* (Berlin: J. H. W. Dietz, 1982); David Cohen, "Transitional Justice in Divided Germany After 1945," in *Retribution and Reparation in the Transition to Democracy*, ed. Jon Elster (Cambridge: Cambridge University Press, 2006), 59–88.

24. It can be difficult to categorize perpetrators due to indistinct social boundaries in Nazi Germany (e.g., party officials could embody a state official—an Ortsgruppenleiter could also be a mayor). Lisa Yavnai's noteworthy dissertation and subsequent article about the Dachau trials categorizes perpetrators as civilians, Nazi officials, and military; however, the separation of military and security forces is very important given the increased radicalization of the security organizations (Yavnai, "Military Justice," 49–74).

25. Examples of civilian perpetrators include farmers, teachers, students, shoemakers, chemists, butchers, bakers, innkeepers, merchants, salesmen, musicians, carpenters, plumbers, machinists, mechanics, painters, attorneys, businessmen, and housewives.

26. In this study, members of the Volkssturm are included in the category of civilians since members were largely young boys, old men, and even women. Moreover, the Volkssturm was considered a national militia, which served mostly as a last line of defense and often given the task (by party officials and security forces) of rounding up downed airmen. The Volkssturm often blurred the boundaries between security forces and civilians, although members were largely civilians before Hitler assembled the Volkssturm in October 1944. Also, SA members have been characterized as civilians in this study. While members of this group also blurred the roles between security forces and civilians, they most often acted in the role of civilians. Moreover, they were not considered a criminal organization under the IMT. The members that represent Security Forces (SS, SD, and Gestapo) were, however, clearly defined by the IMT as criminal organizations. For more information, see Armin Nolzen, "The NSDAP, the War, and German Society," in *Germany and the Second World War*, vol. IX/I, ed. Jörg Echternkamp (New York: Oxford University Press, 2008), 188–200; Franz W. Seidler, *Deutscher Volkssturm: Das letzte Aufgebot, 1944/45* (Munich: Herbig, 1989); Kerstin Siebenborn, *Der Volkssturm im Süden Hamburgs, 1944/45* (Hamburg: Verein für Hamburgische Geschichte, 1988).

27. For more information, see the Veterans History Project, https://www.loc.gov/vets/.

28. For half of the civilians, it remained unknown if they had been members of the Nazi Party. However, of the remaining civilians, 75 percent were confirmed to have been party members, most of whom had joined before 1939.

29. Günter Neliba, *Lynchjustiz an amerikanischen Kriegsgefangenen in der Opelstadt Rüsselsheim (1944): Rekonstruktion einer der ersten Kriegsverbrecher-Prozesse in Deutschland nach Prozessakten (1945–1947)* (Frankfurt: Brandes and Apsel, 2000); Augusto Nigro, *Wolfsangel: A German City on Trial 1945–48* (Washington, D.C.: Brassey's, 2000); Freeman, *Last Mission of the Wham Bam Boys*.

30. Review and Recommendations for Case No. 12-1497, Darmstadt by the Deputy Theater Judge Advocate's Office—War Crimes Branch, August 23, 1945, RG 153, Entry 143, Box 361, NARA.

31. Ibid.

32. Ibid.

33. Ibid.

34. Ibid.

35. Ibid.

36. Today, the communities of Borkum and Rüsselsheim have acknowledged the atrocious and immoral wrongdoings, erecting permanent memorials to the murdered flyers.

37. Review and Recommendations for Case No. 12-489, Ludwigsburg by the Deputy Theater Judge Advocate's Office—War Crimes Branch, August 1, 1947, RG 153, Entry 143, Box 284, NARA.

38. There were over nine hundred African American pilots who fought during World War II, of whom sixty-six were killed in combat and at least thirty-two were held as prisoners of war. For reference, see Jefferson and Carlson, *Red Tail Captured, Red Tail Free*, xxi.

39. Review and Recommendations for Case No. 12-1149-1, Dachau by the Deputy Theater Judge Advocate's Office—War Crimes Branch, December 1, 1945, RG 153, Entry 143, Box 345, NARA.

40. Daniel B. Drooz, *American Prisoners of War in German Death, Concentration, and Slave Labor Camps* (Toronto: Edwin Mellen Press, 2004); Flint Whitlock, *Given Up for Dead* (New York: Basic Books, 2009); Wolk, *Jewish Aviators in World War II.*

41. Review and Recommendations for Case No. 12-1086, Dachau by the Deputy Theater Judge Advocate's Office—War Crimes Branch, December 1, 1945, RG 153; Entry 143, Box 345, NARA.

42. First name is unknown.

43. Review and Recommendations for Case No. 12-926, Ludwigsburg by the Deputy Theater Judge Advocate's Office—War Crimes Branch, November 29–December 8, 1945, RG 153; Entry 143, Box 330, NARA.

44. Yavnai, "Military Justice," 56.

45. The Federal Republic of Germany passed the *Straffreiheitsgesetz* in 1949 and 1954, which, granted amnesty to Nazi criminals, although it was not directed primarily at freeing them. For more information see: "Straffreiheitsgesetz 1954," Bundestageblatt, Bonn, July 17, 1954, http://www.bgbl.de/xaver/bgbl/start.xav?startbk=Bundesanzeiger_BGBl&jumpTo=bgbl154021.pdf.

46. Yavnai, "Military Justice," 65.

47. Joseph Goebbels, "Ein Wort zum feindlichen Luftterror," *Völkischer Beobachter* (Berlin), May 28, 1944; See also, "The Terror Flyer Order" in *Trials of War Criminals before the Nuernberg Military Tribunals*, 166–69.

48. Review and Recommendations for Case No. 12-1247, Dachau by the Deputy Theater Judge Advocate's Office—War Crimes Branch, April 1947, RG 153, Entry 143, Box 348, NARA.

49. Blank, "Wartime Daily Life and the Air War on the Home Front," 466. This was first published in German as *Das Deutsche Reich und der Zweite Weltkrieg* (Deutsche Verlags-Anstalt: Munich, 2004); Grimm, "Lynchmorde an alliierten Fliegern im Zweiten Weltkrieg," 75; Evans, *Third Reich at War*, 465; Overy, *Bombing and the Bombed*, 310; Hoffmann, *Fliegerlynchjustiz*.

50. In fact, Blank even states that the roughly 350 Anglo-American airmen is "equivalent to about 1 percent of those who ended up as prisoners of war in Germany" (466). That equates to roughly 35,000 Anglo-American airmen that were POWs in Germany; however, there were 35,621 American airmen POWs alone in Germany. For reference, see *Army Air Force Statistical Digest, World War II*, (Washington, DC: Office of Statistical Control, December 1945), table 35, Archives Branch, Maxwell Air Force Base, Montgomery, AL.

51. "Battle Casualties in Air Corps by Place, Type, and Disposition," *Army Battle Casualties and Nonbattle Deaths in World War II*, 76.

52. DPAA, Service Personnel Not Recovered Following WWII for the United States Army Air Forces, July 26, 2019, https://www.dpaa.mil/Portals/85/Documents/WWIIAccounting/united_states_army_air_forces.html. Established in 2015, the DPAA is the result of a merger of the Defense Prisoner of War/Missing Personnel Office (DPMO) and the Joint POW/MIA Account Command (JPAC).

53. Carol Schultz Vento, "The Missing in Action (MIA) of World War II," Defense Military Network, May 28, 2012, https://www.defensemedianetwork.com/stories/the-missing-in-action-mia-of-world-war-ii/.

54. Hoffmann, *Fliegerlynchjustiz*, 233, 383.

55. Ibid., 383.

56. Yavnai, "Military Justice," 55.

57. The 168 Allied airmen sent to Buchenwald concentration camp in the fall of 1944 are the best-known examples.

58. Cohen, "Transitional Justice," 66–67.

59. Dick de Mildt, *In the Name of the People: Perpetrators of Genocide in the Reflection of their Post-War Prosecution in West Germany: The "Euthanasia" and "Aktion Reinhard" Trial Cases* (The Hague: Martinus Nijhoff, 1996), 20; Cohen, "Transitional Justice," 84–86.

60. Cohen, "Transitional Justice," 84–86; de Mildt, *In the Name of the People*, 22.

61. Cohen, "Transitional Justice," 84–86; Adalbert Rückerl, *NS-Verbrechen vor Gericht: Versuch einer Vergangenheitsbewältigung* (Heidelberg: Müller Juristischer, 1982), 121–23.

62. Raul Hilberg, *The Destruction of the European Jew* (New York: Holmes and Meier, 1985), 1085; Cohen, "Transitional Justice," 75.

63. Yavnai, "Military Justice," 66.

64. Ibid., 66.

65. Rebecca Wittmann, "Tainted Law: The West German Judiciary and the Prosecution of Nazi War Criminals," in Heberer and Matthäus, *Atrocities on Trial*, 216.

66. Norbert Frei, *Adenauer's Germany and the Nazi Past: The Politics of Amnesty and Integration* (New York: Columbia University Press, 2002), 304.

67. According to Rebecca Wittmann, "while over 100,000 Nazis were investigated and 6,000 tried in the post-war period, over 125,000 communists were investigated and 6,500 tried" ("Tainted Law," 224). This was a major complaint, for example by the Red Army Faction members (also known as the Baader-Meinhof Gang), who claimed during the infamous Stammheim trial that "they were judged more harshly than Nazi defendants . . . at the time because of their knowledge of the illegality of the acts and their goal to commit crimes against the state" (ibid., 224).

68. "Nazi Leader Corps Splits Crime Court," *New York Times*, December 18, 1945.

69. This is the closing comment by C. Robert Bard, colonel JAGD, in the review of the Russelsheim Massacre trial held in Darmstadt, Germany, by the Seventh United States Army on July 25, 1945 (Review and Recommendations for Case No. 12-1497, RG 153, Entry 143, Box 361, NARA).

70. Lorie Charlesworth, "Forgotten Justice: Forgetting Law's History and Victims' Justice in British 'Minor' War Crime Trials in Germany 1945–8," *Amicus Curiae*, no. 74 (2008): 2–10.

71. Klaus-Michael Mallmann, "Nationalsozialistische Gewaltverbrechen Im Deutschen Reich" in *NS-Gewaltherrschaft: Beiträge Zur Historischen Forschung Und Juristischen Aufarbeitung*, Vol. 11, ed. Alfred Gottwaldt, Norbert Kampe, and Peter Klein (Berlin: Hentrich, 2005), 211–12. The original German text states: "Wie die Massenerschießungen von Fallschirmspringern, die Lynchmorde an Flugzeugbesatzungen, aber auch das Massaker an amerikanischen Kriegsgefangenen durch die 'Leibstandte Adolf Hitler' der Waffen-SS bei Malmedy am 17. Dezember 1944 zeigen, wurden nunmehr zunehmend auch west-alliierte Soldaten Opfer des deutschen Vernichtungskrieges."

Chapter 5

Lynchjustiz Narratives

While the statistical analysis of the flyer trials provides new and important findings regarding the mistreatment of downed American airmen, the power and impact of personal narratives offers an essential perspective on Lynchjustiz. Narratives of these cases are based on postwar trial testimonies by witnesses, perpetrators, and occasionally victims, as well as Missing Air Crew Reports (MACR), which often include statements by fellow airmen who witnessed the circumstances surrounding the downing of an aircraft.

Twelve Lynchjustiz cases were chosen to provide an overall example of the mistreatment that American airmen faced and how the violence transpired. As far as the evidence offered, cases spanned the majority of the war, occurred throughout Germany, were carried out by all six perpetrator groups, and involved both assaults and killings. Although the majority of known incidents were located throughout the western zones of occupation, there were occasional investigations and trials held in the eastern occupied zone that focused on the mistreatment of western Allied flyers. However, due to the escalating Cold War and bureaucratic shortcomings, it was difficult to identify, locate, and extradite alleged perpetrators.

Frank's Nightmare (August 17, 1943)[1]

One of the first known instances of Lynchjustiz committed against an American flyer in Germany occurred on August 17, 1943, near the village of Schleiden—located roughly forty-five miles west of Bonn, along the German/Belgian border. Named *Frank's Nightmare*, the B-17

Figure 5.1. Second Lieutenant Eugene D. Cook, pilot of *Frank's Nightmare* (42–5437). *Courtesy of Eugene D. Cook's family via Bill Cosgrove.*

was heavily damaged by flak during a bombing raid over Schweinfurt. According to Lieutenant Robert E. Nichols (a crewmember of another bomber in the formation), the disabled aircraft "snapped up out of formation and fell into a tight spin." Only one flyer (Second Lieutenant Eugene D. Cook) was seen bailing out of the aircraft (fig. 5.1). The remaining nine airmen died when the aircraft crashed near Hergarten—located twelve miles south of Düren.[2]

While he was surely worried about the fate of his fellow crewmembers, Cook must have been relieved to have escaped the damaged aircraft as well as anxious about what he would experience once he landed. Meanwhile, on the ground, German soldiers and civilians were watching the damaged bomber as it crashed near a wooded area; however, their interest quickly turned to Cook, as he landed in the nearby woods. Cook was lucky to not be shot while helplessly dangling in his parachute, which witness statements throughout the flyer trials confirmed occurred regularly.

A local police officer, August Klaebe, picked up a German soldier, who was home on furlough, and they quickly drove to the crash site to assist with securing the plane wreckage and searching for any enemy flyers. As the two walked along a road through the woods, they were surprised to see Cook cross the road in front of them. Klaebe immediately shouted in German, "Come out! I won't harm you!" He then shouted in broken English, "Come on, come on," which he allegedly remembered from his experiences in the First World War. Yet they received no response. After waiting a few minutes, Klaebe and the soldier separated and walked in the direction Cook was heading. In an interview after the war, Cook recalled that as soon as he landed, "I disposed of my parachute [and] about five minutes afterward two German soldiers, each on a motorcycle, approached me. There were also quite a few German civilians around so I had no chance to get away."[3]

After searching for several minutes, Police Chief Paul Foerster summoned Klaebe to come out of the woods. Standing on the side of the road, they discussed where the flyer might be hiding. To their surprise, Cook appeared moments later, wearing his unmistakable flight suit. He was standing on the edge of the woods on the opposite side of the road, several hundred feet away from the two police officers. Foerster immediately said, "There he is! Shoot!" Startled, Cook instinctively turned away and raised his hands, as he saw Klaebe aim a pistol at him. Klaebe fired at Cook, who instantly fell to the ground.[4]

Believing that the flyer was dead, Foerster urged Klaebe to follow him to the crash site, where the bomber was on fire; however, Klaebe first walked over to see the flyer. By the time he approached Cook, a soldier and a civilian had heard the shot and came to investigate. They were standing over Cook's body, as Klaebe approached. He noticed that Cook was wounded but still alive. He ordered the soldier to guard the wounded prisoner and to stop the first passing car and take him to a doctor.

Klaebe then walked a short distance to the wreckage and took over control of the crash site. Four bodies were discovered in the burned wreckage and were removed on Klaebe's orders. They were then placed in coffins and eventually buried in the village cemetery. A local farmer who helped recover the flyers' remains was caught stealing a ring off the hand of one of the bodies, and allegedly Klaebe put him in jail. While Klaebe was at the crash site, Cook was taken to a hospital in Bad Münstereifel (located fifteen miles to the east), where he spent nearly two months recovering from the gunshot wound and the surgery to remove the bullet (which required three blood transfusions). He was eventually transferred to a POW camp and survived the war.

At the postwar trial in April 1947, Klaebe testified that he ordered the soldier to guard Cook so that he would not "be beaten or robbed" by civilians. He also claimed that he shot Cook not because of Foerster's order but rather because he "thought the flyer was escaping" and "the police regulations . . . required a policeman to shoot to prevent an escape."[5] Although the court agreed that Klaebe did willfully and wrongfully assault an unarmed prisoner of war, it acknowledged that he "did all toward the care of the wounded man [that could] have been reasonably expected of him." Such a statement is astounding and rare when compared to other flyer trials. However, this was one of the final postwar trials conducted by the United States and evidence and witnesses were difficult to find—especially given the extended timespan (four years) between the shooting and the trial. Nevertheless, the victim survived to give his account of the event, which was helpful and uncommon in the postwar trials. Ultimately, the court credited Klaebe with giving the four members of the crew a proper burial and determined that he "acted entirely without malice." Because of this, he was sentenced to eight years in prison; however, in June 1947, a review board reduced the sentence to three years (commencing on May 26, 1946). He was subsequently released in May 1949.[6]

Schierstein (March 10, 1944)[7]

On March 10, 1944, five unknown American flyers, who were guarded by members of the Luftwaffe, were waiting at the train station in Schierstein to take a bus to the nearby city of Wiesbaden. The airmen were supposed to travel to Dulag Luft—located just thirty miles to the northwest. However, the short journey was anything but easy.

As the bus arrived, the driver refused to allow the enemy prisoners aboard. A crowd of civilians waiting to board the bus quickly became restless and agitated. A man in the crowd pushed one of the flyers out of the way in an attempt to board the bus. Allegedly a civilian, Hans Pohl, saw one of the flyers smile or laugh. In response, Pohl yelled, "What are you laughing at, you dog?" Without any other provocation, he hit the flyer several times, aiming his punches to the airman's face. Several other civilians in the crowd then jumped toward the prisoners and started to beat them. A local doctor who was in the crowd and waiting to board the bus yelled for the crowd to stop. Within a few minutes, the guards managed to regain order. The doctor spoke to the guard in charge and suggested that they walk to Wiesbaden, which was around three miles away. The guard agreed and escorted the prisoners on foot.[8]

A trial was held in May 1946 at Ludwigsburg and tried Pohl for assaulting one of the flyers. He was a thirty-three-year-old gardener who had joined the Nazi Party in 1937. The court initially sentenced him to one year in prison (commencing January 16, 1946) and ordered him to pay 1,000 reichsmarks. However, the review board received several letters asking for clemency—for example, one letter was from a minister who verified that he was a "good church member and repeatedly contradicted any attempts of the party to cause him to leave the church." Taking these letters into consideration, the review board reduced his sentence to six months and remitted his fine. Pohl was released from prison one month after his trial since he had been held in confinement since January 16, 1946.

Kissenbrück (May 10, 1944)[9]

Around May 10, 1944, an unknown American flyer bailed out of his disabled aircraft and was taken into custody by a German farmer near the village of Kissenbrück—located a few miles south of Wolfenbüttel. He sprained his ankle upon landing, and as a result, it was quite difficult for him to walk, especially since he was forced to carry his heavy parachute. While en route to the police station in Kissenbrück, they met Ortsgruppenleiter Ludwig Kremling and two soldiers home on leave—Erich Mette was a sergeant in the Waffen SS and Otto Peters was a corporal in the navy. Both soldiers were in their early twenties. Kremling ordered the farmer to turn the captured flyer over to him, which the farmer was happy to do, as he needed to return to his farm. The three men then proceeded to escort the flyer to Kissenbrück to the home of the police chief. Upon seeing the airman in front of his house, the police chief informed Kremling that he would take the flyer to Wolfenbüttel after he ate his dinner. Meanwhile, the four men waited outside. After a few minutes, Kremling approached the house again—irritated by the police chief's lack of urgency. Uncertain that he would "properly" deal with the aviator, Kremling informed him to take his time eating dinner because the two soldiers would escort the captured flyer to Wolfenbüttel. Kremling then gave Mette a pistol and ordered him to shoot the flyer along the way. Allegedly, the Kreisleiter in Wolfenbüttel had informed his subordinates in the region that no enemy flyer should be captured alive.

Because of the airman's sprained ankle, the soldiers found a bicycle on which he could rest his parachute. The flyer used the bike as a crutch, as they walked out of town. Along the way, they passed through the small village of Neindorf—located between Kissenbrück and Wolfenbüttel (see fig. 5.2). Just a few hundred meters outside of the village, Mette shot and killed the airman. They moved his body a few feet away to the roadside ditch and covered it with the parachute to prevent anyone from seeing what they had done. Mette, using the bicycle, then proceeded to Wolfenbüttel to report the incident while Peters remained at the crime scene to guard the flyer's body.

When Mette arrived at the police station in Wolfenbüttel, the officer already knew about the downed airman as well as the order to kill him. Kremling had already called and informed him. As a reward for killing the airman, the soldiers received twenty cigarettes from the police chief. Upon returning to the scene of the crime, Mette took the flyer's belongings (i.e., his gloves, compass, maps, money, and any form of identification) to the mayor of Neindorf. This was likely a form of compensation for the aviator's body to be buried in his town.

Displaced Polish workers alerted the US military after the war about the killing of this flyer and an investigation immediately began; however, it took until January 1947 for a trial to be convened. It was difficult to collect evidence and identify, locate, and capture the accused perpetrators as many went into hiding and were unknowingly already detained (under false identities) as POWs throughout Europe. Mette, for example, was captured and held as a POW in France and Peters was apprehended in northern Germany. While the two soldiers were arrested, Kremling was never brought to justice for his actions. Both soldiers testified that before they were allowed to go on leave they had to sign a

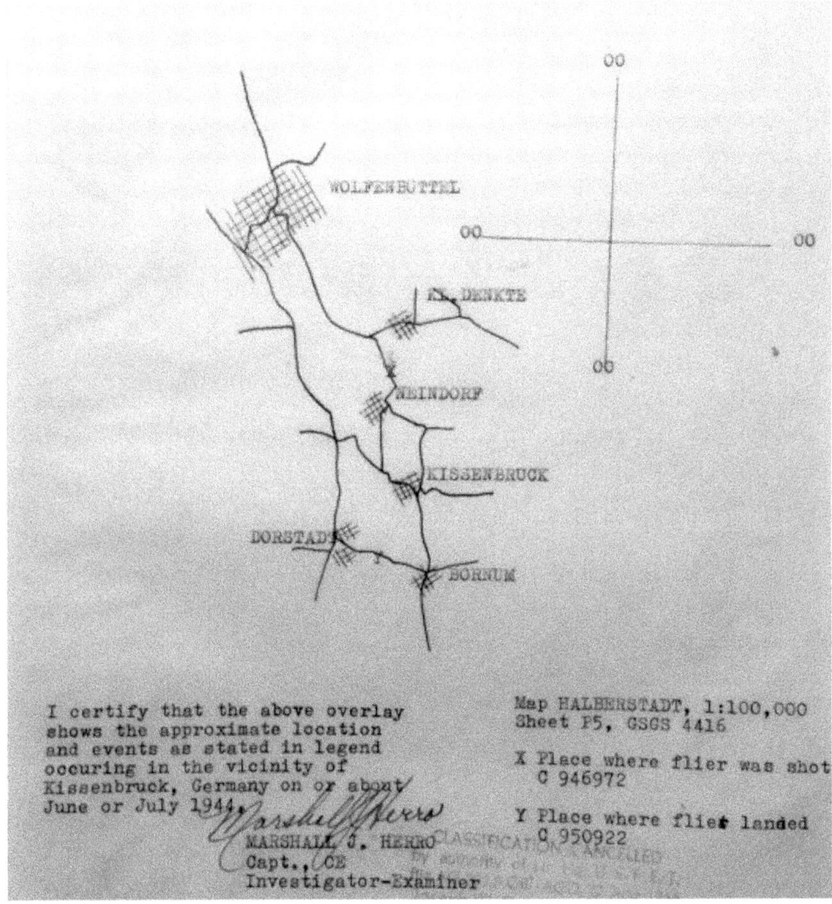

Figure 5.2. Exhibit 15 from trial 12-1812. Map of villages described in this case. The letter *Y* indicates where the flyer landed, while *X* indicates where the flyer was shot. *Exhibit 15, Case No. 12-1812, Record of U.S. Army Europe, War Crimes Case Files (Cases Tried), April 23, 1947; RG 549; Entry 290; Box 187, Declassification No. NND 775032, NARA.*

paper that confirmed they would report directly to the Ortsgruppenleiter once they arrived home and that they would obey his orders.

While Mette stated that the flyer had attempted to escape (in an attempt to justify shooting him), Peters refuted this claim. This fits with the numerous instances of flyers being "shot while attempting to escape," which was often a euphemism for murder and execution. Peters was somewhat remorseful for his actions following the incident. His father testified that when they discussed what happened, his son said, "We did unjust. I am sorry we did it but I can't change it now." Upset that his young son (who was only twenty-one years old) was put in such an iniquitous situation, the father confronted Kremling a few days after the incident. Kremling was quite agitated and refused to be criticized for his actions. In a most direct and clear manner, he allegedly threatened to send Peters's father to a concentration camp if he ever discussed the incident again.[10]

A witness who testified at the postwar trial—a Lutheran pastor—indicated that Kremling was "ambitious, false from his heart, and an ardent Nazi; and [that he] . . . ordered a plaque [be] placed above the grave of the flyer with the inscription 'Here rests a murderer pilot.'"[11] The two soldiers clearly acted on orders from the Ortsgruppenleiter; however, the court determined that superior orders offered insufficient justification to reduce their culpability or their sentences. Moreover, the court found that evidence was lacking to confirm that Kremling was in a position of superior authority over the soldiers. Despite this outcome, the increased role of high-ranking Nazi Party members in ordering and carrying out Lynchjustiz and other crimes, as well as their ability and desire to influence and control German society, is apparent from this case.

Mette was initially sentenced to death by hanging, but this was reduced to life imprisonment due to his young age. He was eventually paroled in October 1954. Peters was sentenced to life imprisonment, but after two years in prison, he was given a reduced sentence of twenty years based on "compassionate grounds," according to the review board. This sentence was further reduced to fifteen years (commencing on May 8, 1945); he was ultimately released by order of parole in December 1953.[12]

Vienenburg (May 19, 1944)[13]

Following a bombing attack on the area around Vienenburg on May 19, 1944, three unknown American airmen parachuted from their damaged aircraft. They landed safely and were quickly captured by a local hunter near the village of Bettingerode and escorted to the courthouse of Vienenburg—located four miles away.

Günther B.—the commanding officer of the airbase in Goslar (located seven miles away from Vienenburg)—was notified of the enemy airmen who had landed in his jurisdiction, and he immediately sought to arrest them and secure any crashed aircraft. Günther contacted authorities in Vienenburg and inquired about the flyers; however, local political officials refused to give him any information. He reported this to his superiors, as the Luftwaffe had jurisdiction over enemy airmen. After the Kreisleiter of Goslar, Wilhelm Pfeiffer, was informed of Günther's investigation about the whereabouts of the enemy flyers, he informed Günther that Günther was supposed to contact him, Pfeiffer, in such matters and that he severely disapproved of Günther questioning his actions. Again, Günther informed his superiors, this time about Pfeiffer's comments regarding the proper procedure in dealing with enemy flyers. A few days later, Günther was allegedly punished by a Luftwaffe general and sentenced to five days' confinement for "causing difficulties." In addition, he was relieved of his command at the airbase in Goslar.[14]

Meanwhile, the three flyers were interrogated by party officials in a guarded room of the courthouse. Pfeiffer summoned a local civilian to act as interpreter. Despite being beaten during the interrogation, the airmen refused to give any information other than their names, ranks, and serial numbers, which irritated the German officials. According to the interpreter, these officials included the Kreisleiter, Ortsgruppenleiter, members of the Gendarmerie and OrPo, and a high-ranking member of the Luftwaffe. Before the Luftwaffe officer left, the interpreter heard him tell the others to "see that these men are taken to the airbase in Goslar." However, as the two flyers were escorted out of the courthouse and into an awaiting car, he also overheard Pfeiffer tell the guards: "Make sure that they do not arrive in Goslar alive." Acting on Pfeiffer's orders, three men—members of the Gendarmerie and OrPo—tied the flyers' hands behind their backs and drove them to the forest on the edge of the town, where they were subsequently shot and killed. The perpetrators left the bodies where they fell and returned to Vienenburg.[15]

The next day, while hunting, a civilian discovered the bodies of the American flyers. Surely startled by what he saw, he immediately informed the police. A short time later, a policeman picked him up at his house, and they drove to the woods, where the man indicated the location of the bodies. Once they arrived, he suggested that the bodies should be taken to the morgue in Vienenburg; however, the policeman refused and said that they would have to be buried. The men then buried the flyers' bodies in shallow graves next to a footpath in the woods.

On the same day that these airmen were killed, two additional American aviators bailed out of their disabled aircraft—possibly crewmembers of the aforementioned flyers—and landed near the village of

Lochtum—located just two miles southwest of Vienenburg. Similar to the previous incident, these airmen were captured and taken to the police station in Lochtum, where they were beaten and interrogated by party and police officials. A short time later, Pfeiffer arrived and was incensed that the aviators were still alive. He immediately ordered three local policemen to deal with the enemy prisoners. They then drove the Americans to a field outside the village of Lochtum.

A shepherd who was tending to his sheep "saw the two American flyers with three men . . . on the side of a hill as shots were fired. . . . [Then] the flyers fell to the ground." He immediately went and asked a policeman what had happened. The police officer responded that the flyers had "attempted to escape." A post office employee (Otto P.) testified that he witnessed the bodies of the American flyers as they were brought to the local fire department. He stated that "during the loading of the bodies, I noticed that one flyer was moving." Otto allegedly suggested that they should call a doctor; however, but a fireman told him that it "was not necessary." Later in the day, the bodies were buried in an unmarked grave in the Lochtum cemetery.[16]

These were not the only incidents of Lynchjustiz to occur in this area or by these perpetrators. Several months later, for example, on September 28, 1944, two additional instances occurred in the villages surrounding Vienenburg. Similar to the previous cases, the Kreisleiter's power and influence were instrumental in the mistreatment of downed airmen.

In Heiningen, an American aviator was captured and taken to the mayor's office. At the time, Mayor August Reinecke was at the train station, but he quickly returned to his office after he was informed about the prisoner. Along the way, he met the Ortsgruppenleiter of Burgdorf, Ernest Königsdorf, who informed him of Pfeiffer's order to shoot enemy aviators. Reinecke acknowledged this order and retrieved his pistol before going to his office. He then took the flyer, accompanied by two policemen, and proceeded to walk along a road that led out of town. As soon as the mayor felt they were far enough out of the village—away from prying eyes—he shot and killed the airman.

Later in the day, in the village of Burgdorf, a flyer was captured as soon as he landed and placed in police custody. Königsdorf and his deputy, Hermann Landwehr, took custody of the prisoner and subsequently led him out of town toward the village of Schladen. After driving about a quarter of a mile down the road, Landwehr stopped the car and Königsdorf shot and killed the airman.

A war crime trial was held from August to October 1947 and tried the Kreisleiter of Goslar (Wilhelm Pfeiffer), his driver (Hartmann Lauterbacher), Ortsgruppenleiter Ernest Königsdorf, his deputy (Hermann Landwehr), the mayor of Heiningen (August Reinecke), two police officers (Robert Schottke and Otto Reinhardt), and three civilian men. The trial is of particular significance as the tribunal established that there was a "common plan and design of the Leadership Corps of the Nazi Party . . . to subject Allied prisoners of war to killings, beatings, tortures, abuses, and indignities."[17]

At the trial, an SS police chief (Benno M.) from Wehrkreis number thirteen (Nuremberg) testified that while "in the first years of the war, the police could investigate a Kreisleiter, in 1944–45 police could only make investigations about the Kreisleiter if the Gauleiter approved of it. The Kreisleiter was practically outside the jurisdiction of the police in cases where the Gauleiter did not give his approval."[18]

Pfeiffer, Königsdorf, Reinecke, and Reinhardt were sentenced to life in prison; however, they were all released on parole by April 1957. The policeman, Schottke, received a fifteen-year imprisonment but was eventually released in June 1953. The deputy Ortsgruppenleiter, Landwehr, was sentenced to five years in prison. The three civilians and the Kreisleiter's driver were acquitted of committing any crime.

Georgia Peach/Black Puff Polly (May 28, 1944)[19]

In the early afternoon on May 28, 1944, a bomber was shot down following a bombing attack on Dessau. While returning to base in England, the aircraft received heavy damage caused by flak and the radio operator (Technical Sergeant Walter W. Wagoner) was killed. Realizing that they were not going to make it back to friendly territory, the pilot (First Lieutenant Rudolph M. Stohl) ordered his crew to bailout over northwestern Germany (fig. 5.3).

Stohl landed near Osterholz—located sixteen miles north of Bremen. He was immediately captured by German civilians and beaten by several of them. One man (Otto Rueger)—a private in the army—arrived and joined in the melee. Allegedly, he even used a hatchet to beat Stohl, inflicting a wound on his head that covered his face with blood.

Another crewmember (copilot Second Lieutenant David W. Schellenger) landed near Verden—twenty miles east of Bremen—and, after being captured, was taken directly to the site of his crashed bomber. Upon reaching the crash site, he was placed in the back of a truck with

Figure 5.3. Crew of the *Georgia Peach/Black Puff Polly* (42-97067). First Lieutenant Rudolph M. Stohl (pilot), Second Lieutenant David W. Schellenger (copilot), Second Lieutenant John O. Millham (navigator), and Second Lieutenant James E. Thomas (bombardier); Master Sergeant Robert C. Kreite (top turret gunner), Technical Sergeant Walter W. Wagoner (radio), Sergeant William F. Bemus (right waist gunner), Sergeant Sheldon J. Moore (ball turret gunner), Staff Sergeant Irwin A. Welling (left waist gunner), and Sergeant Charles L. Stewart (tail gunner). *Flight Crews of the 457th Bomb Group, August 8, 2006, http://www.457thbombgroup.org/aircrews/pilotnames4.html#S, accessed June 5, 2018.*

the rest of the captured crew. While sitting in the truck, as a group of civilians, police officers, and soldiers were gathered around the wreckage, a police sergeant, Wilhelm Schroeder, ordered Schellenger to get out. Schroeder gave an order in German, but because Schellenger did not understand the language, he did not obey the order. Schroeder then punched Schellenger in the face and commanded his dog to bite Schellenger's leg. A short time later, Schellenger was loaded back into the truck, and the crew left the crash site. Eventually, the flyers were sent to Dulag Luft and then to various POW camps, where they managed to survive the war. In June 1947 Rueger, Schroeder, and a civilian, August Tidow, were tried for their actions in beating the American bomber crew. After just two days, the court found Rueger and Schroeder guilty of assaulting the flyers and sentenced them to three and two and a half years' imprisonment, respectively. Tidow was acquitted of any wrongdoing.

Hell's Belle (July 20, 1944)[20]

Hours before Claus von Stauffenberg's failed attempt to assassinate Hitler on July 20, 1944, the Fifteenth Air Force carried out a bombing raid against the Zeppelin Works factory in Friedrichshafen. The town is located along the picturesque Lake Constance, which forms a natural border between Germany, Austria, and Switzerland at the base of the Alps. A mere ten miles south of Friedrichshafen, across the lake, was neutral Switzerland, which offered a much better chance of positive treatment for downed Allied airmen.

During the air raid, several B-24 bombers, one of which was nicknamed *Hell's Belle*, were hit by flak. The hit damaged the *Hell's Belle* controls as the pilot (Second Lieutenant Howland J. Hamlin) and copilot (Second Lieutenant Richard V. S. Newhouse) were on a westward route heading over the middle of the lake (fig. 5.4). The pilots noticed that gasoline was leaking inside the fuselage, and in fear of an imminent fire, they signaled the crew to bailout. Nervous and filled with adrenaline, the nine men jumped out of the damaged aircraft as it flew over the lake.[21] Everyone successfully bailed out and the majority were in good health upon landing. However, it is believed that Staff Sergeant John A. Boardsen's parachute failed to open, and as a result, he did not survive the fall. As if the danger of bailing out was not grave enough, Swiss officials reported that Germans were shooting at the bomber crew as they descended in their parachutes. The aircraft continued flying and the wreckage was found near Hemishofen, Switzerland (roughly forty-five miles east of Friedrichshafen). Allegedly, as the aircraft crossed into Swiss territory, Swiss antiaircraft guns shot it out of the sky.

Three flyers (believed to be Staff Sergeant Aaron C. Slaughter, Staff Sergeant Ronald W. Cherrington, and Staff Sergeant Raymond C. Ertel) landed in the vicinity of Konstanz—located directly on the border with Switzerland and less than twenty miles west of Friedrichshafen—near a German army barracks (Cherisy Caserne), which housed the 195th Reserve Battalion (fig. 5.5). German soldiers quickly took the airmen into custody and escorted them through town. A short time later, the commander of the barracks, Albert Heim, arrived by car with three subordinate officers (one of whom was Fritz Saalmueller). Heim was also responsible for the defense of the region (Boden peninsula), especially against enemy airborne troops.

After Heim and his fellow officers exited the vehicle, they approached the airmen, who were being beaten unconscious by the

Figure 5.4. Photograph of Second Lieutenant Richard V. S. Newhouse. Photo was attached to a letter from Newhouse's mother to the US military tribunal in Dachau, November 16, 1947. *Deputy Theater Judge Advocate's Office, War Crimes Branch, Case No. 12-43; RG 153; Entry 143; Box 164, Declassification No. NND 735027, NARA.*

crowd. Heim remarked to Saalmueller: "Airborne troops. They must be killed." Reconfirming that he had correctly understood, Saalmueller asked: "I am to shoot him right now?" To which Heim replied: "Tell him that he is a gangster; that is sufficient." Heim then informed the crowd of roughly fifty individuals (mostly civilians) that all of the "American gangsters" must be shot immediately. Without waiting for the prisoner to be killed, Heim left in his car. Not hesitating, Saalmueller then shot and killed the flyers.[22]

Figure 5.5. Map of Lake Constance. The X indicates the location where *Hell's Belle* crashed. *Created by author.*

In the crowd was another Wehrmacht officer, Herbert Kunze, who was riding his bike to the barracks and stopped to see what was happening. After the flyers were shot, Kunze (a twenty-three-year-old former schoolteacher) proceeded to the barracks. When he arrived, he noticed two Luftwaffe soldiers escorting another captured flyer (most likely a crewmember of *Hell's Belle*). Remembering the commander's instructions, Kunze approached the detained flyer and ordered the guards to lead the prisoner toward a ditch near the barracks gate. He dismissed the guards and then pushed the airman forward, which the flyer likely assumed meant to walk. As the flyer's back was turned, Kunze drew his pistol and shot the prisoner several times. The prisoner fell forward toward the ditch and rolled onto his back. An unknown witness yelled: "Shoot again; he is not dead yet!" Kunze aimed his pistol again at the severely wounded flyer and shot him two more times in his chest. After the war, he testified that he allegedly shot the airman "so that he would not suffer." Yet the possibility of the airman suffering clearly did not deter him enough from initially attacking him. His deliberateness was evident to the war crime tribunal.[23]

Meanwhile another flyer (believed to be Second Lieutenant George T. Hunter Jr.—bombardier aboard *Hell's Belle*) had landed in the Untersee (Lower Lake). Swiss fishermen were in the area and repeatedly attempted to rescue this helpless flyer as he treaded water in his heavy flight suit and boots, fighting against his tangled parachute, which was pulling him closer to death. However, every rescue attempt was driven off by a German boat, which shot in the direction of the flyer and the Swiss fishermen when they approached. Soon after, the German boat plucked his lifeless body out of the water.

Two additional crewmembers (believed to be pilot Second Lieutenant Howland J. Hamlin and copilot Second Lieutenant Richard V. S. Newhouse) were captured and held in the jails of Öhningen and Wangen. SS officer Eduard Mack received a message from his superior (Kurt Gross), which indicated that he should send Adolf Mattes and Rudolf Spletzer to pick up the two enemy flyers and "shoot them when escaping." Using a wood-burning truck driven by Thomas Aschner, Mattes and Spletzer proceeded to Öhningen and then to Wangen to pick up the captured airmen. They drove through a small wooded area between Gundholzen and Iznang on their way back to Radolfzell. Once they were in a secluded area, Mattes ordered his men to get their pistols ready. The guards were told previously of the order that the flyers were not to be brought back alive.[24]

Mattes told Aschner to stop the truck and ordered the prisoners to exit the back of the truck. The airmen were then told to walk along the dirt road. With the flyers' backs to the guards, Mattes and Spletzer shot them in the back of the head. Their bodies were loaded into the back of the truck and taken to Radolfzell, where a doctor confirmed (in a written report) that the airmen were dead. The bodies were picked up later in the day and sent to Wollmatingen (near Konstanz). For carrying out the order to kill the enemy airmen, Mattes received a commendation in the daily bulletin of the Wehrmacht barracks.

Mack arranged for the flyers' remains to be buried in a mass grave; however, he allegedly ordered the burial to take place at night "because of the alert that resulted from the attempt on Hitler's life." He admitted as well, after the war, that he had a sign placed on the flyers' grave that read: "Here lies two American Gangsters." As the Allies advanced through Germany and took control of the region, the local civilians removed the sign in fear of retribution for the crimes committed against the flyers (fig. 5.6).[25]

Hell's Belle's nose gunner, Staff Sergeant Tonnes E. Tonnessen, also landed in the lake; however, he was far more fortunate than his comrades as he landed closer to the Swiss border and was picked up by Swiss fishermen. Top turrent gunner Technical Sergeant Donald W. Anderson

Figure 5.6. Graves of Richard Newhouse and Howland Hamlin in Radolfzell. The headstone was provided by the US military. *Graves of flyers in Radolfzell, Deputy Theater Judge Advocate's Office, War Crimes Branch, Case No. 12-43; RG 153; Entry 143; Box 164, Declassification No. NND 735027, NARA.*

landed along the lake in Swiss territory and was captured by Swiss frontier guards. These two flyers were held as internees in Adelboden and Münsingen and were the only crewmembers to survive the war.

After the war, two trials were held at Dachau to bring the perpetrators to justice for their actions in murdering six American flyers.

It was discovered that roughly a month before the crew of *Hell's Belle* were murdered, Albert Heim had addressed a group of noncommissioned officers at a meeting, where he emphasized that no enemy flyers were to be brought back alive to the barracks. At a later meeting with officers, he read out a strict order that enemy agents, saboteurs, and airborne troops were to be shot immediately upon capture. While airborne troops are considered paratroopers—and, therefore, not downed airmen—they were often incorrectly identified as air crewmembers who parachuted from stricken aircraft. Questioned by criminal investigators after the war, Heim stated that his predecessor had passed on this order when he took over the barracks in May 1943. Regarding the airmen murdered on July 20, 1944, he stated without remorse that it was his "duty to have them killed."[26]

The first trial took place in December 1946 and tried Heim, Saalmueller, and Kunze for their involvement in killing the first four airmen. Heim was sentenced to death by hanging and executed on February 2, 1949, for ordering his subordinates to kill captured flyers. Saalmueller, who had shot and killed the initial airman, was sentenced to life imprisonment. This sentence was later reduced to twenty-five years. Kunze—the twenty-three-year-old SS officer who removed the second aviator from Luftwaffe guards and shot him several times—was sentenced to death by hanging for the excessive manner in which he killed the prisoner. He was executed on October 22, 1948.[27]

The second trial was not held until September and October 1947 and tried Gross, Mattes, Mack, Spletzer, and Aschner for their involvement in killing the final two crewmembers of *Hell's Belle*. Gross and the two SS officers who shot the flyers, Mattes and Spletzer, all received life imprisonment; however, they were all eventually paroled in April 1954. Mack, who had relayed Gross's order that the flyers were to be killed, was sentenced to five years in prison. Finally, the driver of the truck, Aschner, was initially sentenced to three years for his involvement in the crime; however, a review board later acquitted him of all charges due to insufficient evidence.[28]

Weisenbach (August 9, 1944)[29]

Shortly before noon on August 9, 1944, three American aviators parachuted from their crippled bomber near the village of Weisenbach—located near the German-French border and around thirty miles northeast of Strasbourg (fig. 5.7). The first airman, twenty-five-year-old

Figure 5.7. B-17 (42-102962) crew shot down on August 9, 1944. *Left to right, back row*: Flight Officer Robert W. Day (bombardier), Second Lieutenant Harry F. Bowling (pilot), Second Lieutenant Harold C. Shackleton (copilot), and Second Lieutenant Furman J. Davis (navigator); *front row*: Sergeant Robert A. McDonough (tail gunner), Sergeant William E. Evans (ball turret gunner), Staff Sergeant Robert L. Harmon (radio), Staff Sergeant John B. Novota (top turret gunner), Sergeant Kenneth L. Palmer (waist gunner), and Sergeant Roy C. Ashes (was not on board for this mission). *Courtesy of William E. Evans's family. See also Steffan Killinger, "Der Fliegermord von Weisenbach und Obertsrot"* Badisches Tagblatt, *August 9, 2011.*

Staff Sergeant Robert L. Harmon, landed on a hill called "Weinerbuckel," located outside the village of Weisenbach. Harmon was quickly captured and received treatment for his minor wounds. He was then escorted to the courthouse in Weisenbach, where he was locked in an office by the mayor.

A short time later, two SA members (one of whom was Johann Schneider) and a member of the NSKK, Wilhelm Karcher, arrived from Gernsbach—just a few miles away—and severely beat Harmon with rubber hoses, metal wrenches, and other objects. The trio were ordered by Ortsgruppenleiter Adolf Eiermann to commit the offense. After several minutes of mercilessly beating him, Harmon was taken outside to the courtyard, where the beating continued. After he was unconscious, Harmon was shot and killed in the presence of Eiermann and

Blockleiter Matthaus Goetzmann. The body was removed a short time later to the local cemetery and buried.

The second flyer—nineteen-year-old Sergeant Robert A. McDonough—landed on a wooded hilltop known as the "Schöllkopf," located near the village of Weisenbach. McDonough was severely wounded from hitting numerous trees when he landed and quickly surrendered in hopes of receiving medical attention. Three men (a medic, a Blockleiter named Hermann Krieg, and a nineteen-year-old Hitler Youth leader named Rudolf Merkel) climbed up the steep terrain to carry McDonough back down.

By this time, word had spread among the local population about the downed enemy flyers. Eiermann quickly arrived to question McDonough with the local education leader and grammar school teacher (Franz Weiland) acting as interpreter. McDonough offered little information—due, likely, to his severe injuries. Eiermann then ordered that he was not to leave the woods alive. Without hesitation, Eiermann, the three men who captured McDonough and several other bystanders (including civilians) viciously attacked the wounded flyer. It resulted in McDonough being shot and killed. His body was then buried in the cemetery in Weisenbach.

The third member of the bomber crew (twenty-one-year-old Sergeant Kenneth L. Palmer) landed in the vicinity of the train station in Hilpertsau, located a mile north of Weisenbach. Palmer was slightly wounded and was quickly approached by a crowd who started to beat him. Not long after, a policeman (Weingärtner) arrived on the scene. He ordered the crowd to stop beating Palmer and took custody of him. Despite being wounded, Palmer was able to walk, and the two men proceeded north toward Gernsbach. They safely passed through the villages of Hilperstau and Obertsrot (less than a mile away); however, just prior to reaching Gernsbach, they were stopped by a Jagdkommando. The group included several party officials who had traveled by bicycle from Obertsrot to apprehend the prisoner. A melee immediately ensued as the men forcibly took Palmer from the custody of Weingärtner. They pushed Palmer off the road and into a nearby field and savagely beat him to death. The group departed as quickly as they had arrived, leaving Palmer's body in the field. Later in the day, his body was removed, and it was eventually taken to the Weisenbach cemetery.

At the postwar trial, sixteen men (who were mostly Alte Kämpfer) were charged with participating "in a common plan or design to . . . encourage, aid, abet, order and participate in, or took a consenting part in the subjection of members of the armed forces of the United States of America, who were surrendered and unarmed prisoners of war . . . to cruelties and mistreatment, including killings, beatings, tortures, abuses, and indignities." Indication of this "common plan" to kill downed flyers was evident with the discovery of mobile search units (*Rollkommando*) to effectively capture and kill downed enemy flyers. The Kreisleiter of Rastatt (Heinrich Dieffenbacher)—who, for reasons unknown, was never tried for his role in these (and likely many other) crimes—personally selected men who were all ardent supporters of the regime.[30]

Evidence indicated that during town meetings, Ortsgruppenleiter Eiermann emphasized Kreileiter Hans Rothacker's orders to kill downed enemy airmen. Rothacker testified that he received a directive from Martin Bormann (on May 30, 1944) that indicated that "party members should get the population into a mood for 'spontaneous action' against captured Allied flyers." Rothacker described that he understood the directive to mean that the "flyers were to be killed." After receiving this order, he informed the Ortsgruppenleiter within his district—both verbally and in writing. This was similarly done throughout all districts. However, Rothacker claimed that "it was his intention that the order be carried out in case of an emergency." Although instances of Lynchjustiz committed against Allied airmen surely occurred in his district, Rothacker was only sentenced to three years in prison and eventually extradited to France to stand trial for additional crimes. The US military court did not believe that Ortsgruppenleiter Eiermann was a participant in the "common design" alleged in the charges brought against him.[31]

Most perpetrators chose not to testify during the trial; however, Blockleiter Isidor Klumpp attempted to clarify his actions. He claimed that "it was propaganda that caused me to be involved in the killing [of McDonough] on the Schöllkopf." While Klumpp's testimony was made in an attempt to seek a lighter sentence, the power and impact of propaganda surely influenced his actions. Nevertheless, the tribunal did not believe it was a justifiable excuse to warrant clemency. For his role in killing the wounded prisoners, Ortsgruppenleiter Eiermann was sentenced to death by hanging, as were the two Blockleiter Klumpp and Goetzmann and SA sergeant Johann Schneider. Wilhelm Karcher, member of the NSAKK, was also sentenced to death. These five men were found guilty of participating in a common design to murder downed American airmen and were consequently executed in November 1948.[32]

A party official in charge of radio and film in Hilperstau, Julius Ratzke, was sentenced to twenty years in prison, as was the teacher, Franz Weiland. They were both released from prison by September 1950, having served just over two years of their sentences. Xavier Goetz, who was a civilian member of the group who beat McDonough, was sentenced to five years in prison and the Ortsgruppenleiter of Au-Murgtal, Maurus Haitzler, received a four-year sentence. The mayor and Ortsgruppenleiter of Gernsbach, Heinrich Stichling, was sentenced to life in prison for his role in facilitating the "common design" to kill Allied flyers, but he was eventually paroled in August 1954. Similarly, the nineteen-year-old Hitler Youth leader, Rudolf Merkel, was sentenced to life for killing McDonough; however, due to his young age, he was released in September 1950.

Hard to Get (August 28, 1944)[33]

During the afternoon of August 26, 1944, crewmembers of the B-17 *Hard to Get* were shot down after their bomber was hit by flak during a bombing mission over Gelsenkirchen. First Lieutenant Dean C. Allen (pilot), Second Lieutenant Charles H. Evans Jr. (navigator), Staff Sergeant James R. Carvey (tail gunner), and Staff Sergeant Richard C. Huebotter (waist gunner) landed safely in the vicinity of Rheinberg (roughly fifteen miles north of Duisburg). They were immediately taken into custody and transported to a nearby Luftwaffe airfield, where they were held in jail cells overnight. The next morning, they were transported via train to Dulag Luft. During the morning of August 28, Evans and Purkey were able to escape from the train near the village of Trebur when the train stopped at a small station and their guards were sleeping. However, they were quickly recaptured by German civilians and driven to the nearby town of Gross-Gerau by an escort that included at least one uniformed member of the Luftwaffe. Gross-Gerau is located four miles east of Trebur and eight miles south of Rüsselsheim, where the most infamous instance of Lynchjustiz occurred just three days prior to this incident.

The population was in a "state of great excitement," according to witnesses, because it had experienced a heavy air raid a few days before in which twenty-seven individuals—mostly women and children—were killed. To the misfortune of the airmen, the funeral for the individuals killed in the air raid was scheduled on this ill-fated day. As if the death and destruction caused by the air raid was not enough for individuals to seek revenge, the unfortunate timing of the airmen's presence with the memorial—alongside the Nazi regime condoning and often urging German citizens to seek revenge—would quickly give the aviators reason to worry for their safety.[34]

An enraged mob of civilians quickly gathered, which included several hundred people according to witnesses. The crowd savagely beat the flyers unconscious with their fists along with boards, metal pipes, bricks, and virtually anything at hand. One woman even used her shoe to beat an airman, directing the blows at his eyes. After the attack, she was reported to have said: "I never got my shoe off that quickly before." The spontaneity and the ferocity of the violence was alarming.[35]

Word of the enemy flyers' presence—and especially their mistreatment—quickly spread throughout the town. Margot Zeeck (fig. 5.8), who was a member of the mob and participated in beating the airmen, stated in her postwar testimony:

> my mother called me several times to come on the street. I said a few times, "Leave me alone," but then my mother said, "Look how they are beating the flyers." I went on the street and saw a big crowd. . . . I walked to the crowd and was in the vicinity of the flyers. The people were crowding one of them, and he seemed to protect himself from the blows, and in doing so, I was struck in the face. I did strike back because in my excitement I thought that he struck me intentionally. During this, I was pushed and lost my shoe, and I then used it to do the beating. It was a rubber shoe with a heel. All of a sudden, my mother asked me, if I was crazy and if I was not ashamed as a woman to do such a thing. At this moment, I realized my behavior.[36]

Standing at the window of her family's house, a ten-year-old girl watched as the crowd mercilessly beat the flyers. She did not understand what exactly was occurring but viewed her neighbor Margot Zeeck involved in the quarrel. The girl immediately cried out to her father, Heinrich Deubert (fig. 5.9): "Daddy, come out; Margot is having a quarrel and is being beaten." Deubert ran out of the house toward the crowd and, according to his postwar statement,

> under the impression of the words of my daughter . . . struck a man with my hand [who] . . . then fell down. When the man was lying on the ground, I saw that he wasn't a German. I was

Left, Figure 5.8. Photograph of Margot Zeeck taken by criminal investigators. *Photo of Margot Z., Case No. 12-793, Record of U.S. Army Europe, War Crimes Case Files (Cases Tried), August 3, 1945, August 15, 1945, July 28–29, 1947; War Crimes Trials Case Files, 1947–1958; RG 549; Entry 290; Box 121, Declassification No. NND 775032, NARA.*

Right, Figure 5.9. Photograph of Heinrich Deubert taken by criminal investigators. *Photo of Heinrich D., Case No. 12-793, Record of U.S. Army Europe, War Crimes Case Files (Cases Tried), August 3, 1945, August 15, 1945, July 28–29, 1947; War Crimes Trials Case Files, 1947–1958; RG 549; Entry 290; Box 121, Declassification No. NND 775032, NARA.*

informed that they were flyers. On account of the shouts I lost my head and struck the flyer, I can't say exactly, four or five times on the neck and in the face with my hand. The flyer jumped up, I struck him once, and he fell to the ground. He immediately got up again. . . . I sprang after the flyer and pushed him a few meters.[37]

Another woman involved in the violence, Anna-Margarete Solomon (fig. 5.10), stated in her trial testimony that "one of the flyers was beaten with a lath by the ones that were standing the closest. A woman lost a lath. I ran to it, picked it up, and I struck the flyer several times on his rear. . . . But a man rushed me and took the lath from my hand. I strongly presume that it was Heinrich. After this, I left the street. . . . I picked up a towel, which was lying on the street. Mrs. L. stated that one of the flyers had it hanging around him." Hours later, Anna was reported to have said that the towel was "a souvenir."[38]

Two SiPo officers and the Kreisleiter arrived after they were informed of the large spectacle and briefly discussed among themselves what should be done with the enemy airmen. One police officer stated the "flyers should be taken away" and be placed in protective custody of the police; however, the other policeman argued that the flyers should be given "to the population. Let them lynch them and beat them to death!" The Kreisleiter agreed with the latter opinion and contended that the airmen "should be given to the people."[39]

Shortly thereafter, the chief of the SiPo arrived, and he emphatically demanded, "Why haven't they been beaten to death?!" Police Chief Nikolaus Fachinger then ordered the two policemen to remove the airmen to the courtyard of the city hall. All the while, the irate civilians continued to beat the aviators. Deubert's wife, who was pregnant and was supposed to be bedridden at the time, went outside and witnessed the melee just as Fachinger was removing the flyers to the city hall. She had an argument with a female nurse, according to trial testimonies, because she said "the flyers should be bandaged, and the nurse called her an enemy of the state."[40]

Barring the crowd from the courtyard (including the two aforementioned police officers), Fachinger ordered the windows and doors facing the courtyard to be closed. Only two other men—a twenty-four-year-old civilian named Heinrich Flauaus and Georg Sturm, a Luftwaffe soldier who was tasked with escorting the downed flyers—were allowed in the courtyard. Both men were fully aware of the implications of the events that were about to unfold.

A woman attempted to enter the courtyard but was abruptly stopped by Fachinger. He told her: "This is nothing for you. We can only use strong men." He even locked a fireman in an adjoining building in his attempt to prevent any onlookers from seeing not only what was about to occur and the degree of brutality but also who was going to commit

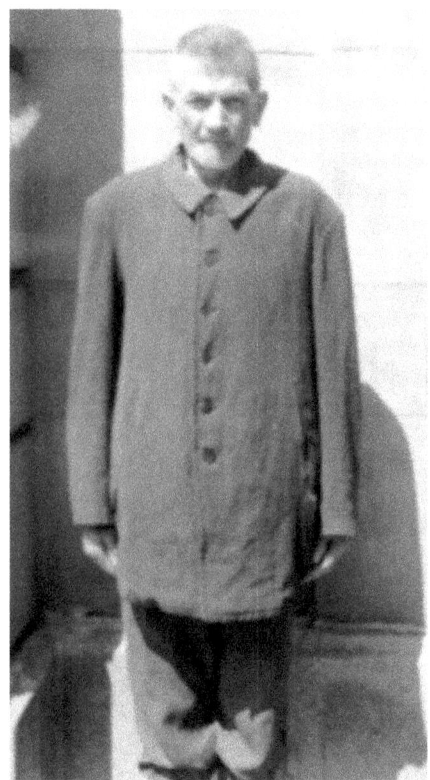

Left, Figure 5.10. Photograph of Anna-Margarete Solomon taken by criminal investigators. *Photo of Margot Z., Case No. 12-793, Record of U.S. Army Europe, War Crimes Case Files (Cases Tried), August 3, 1945, August 15, 1945, July 28–29, 1947; War Crimes Trials Case Files, 1947–1958; RG 549; Entry 290; Box 121, Declassification No. NND 775032, NARA.*

Right, Figure 5.11. Photograph of Peter Schindel taken by criminal investigators. *Photo of Peter S., Case No 12-793, Record of U.S. Army Europe, War Crimes Case Files (Cases Tried), August 3, 1945, August 15, 1945, July 28–29, 1947; War Crimes Trials Case Files, 1947–1958; RG 549; Entry 290; Box 121, Declassification No. NND 775032, NARA.*

the violence. Searching for an object that could be used to inflict horrific and decisive blows upon the airmen, Fachinger found iron bars and ordered the two men in the courtyard to beat the flyers to death. The men were eager to oblige, using the heavy iron bars to mercilessly murder the aviators. The airmen were then buried at the local cemetery in Gross-Gerau. Their remains were eventually reinterred at the Ardennes American Cemetery in Belgium.

After the war, former forced workers informed the American forces stationed in the area of the crimes committed against the unknown flyers. The War Crimes Commission was quickly informed and began investigating. Three separate trials were held and prosecuted seven German citizens. The first two trials were held in Munich in August 1945. The first two perpetrators brought to trial were Fachinger and Flauaus. During the trial, Fachinger attempted to argue that he took the airmen into the courtyard to "protect them from the mob; that he chased his own policemen away because he had no confidence in them and was afraid they might beat the prisoners." Flauaus admitted that he beat one of the airmen to death "with five or six blows to the neck." However, he offered no defense at the trial for his actions other than that he was following orders.[41]

The war crimes tribunal determined that it was "highly improbable" that the two men in the courtyard would have beaten the flyers to death unless Fachinger had "affirmatively ordered, arranged for, or tacitly authorized the killings." Moreover, the prosecution submitted that Fachinger "preferred that strangers perform the unlawful acts, and that as few person as possible witness the violence. . . . All the actions of the chief . . . portray a man who was planning and surreptitiously aiding in the commission of illegal acts, which, because of his official position, he could not himself or publicly approve." Both men were sentenced to death by hanging and were executed on April 1, 1946.[42]

The second trial, held a few weeks later, tried four civilians—Anna-Margarete Solomon, Margot Zeeck, Heinrich Deubert, and Peter Schindel (fig. 5.11)—for their involvement in the crowd that beat the downed flyers. According to his trial testimony, Deubert and his family (which included six children) were bombed out of their house in March 1944 and forced to move in with another family. This physical and psychological impact on Deubert was worsened by the death of his son following the air raid that occurred a few days before the downed airmen were killed on August 29, 1944. Deubert stated that he initially acted without thinking and that once he realized what was occurring sought to help the airmen by pushing them "away from the street." However, his alleged help occurred after he had beat the flyers for several minutes. He also attempted to place blame on another member of the crowd who "beat the prisoner with a lath [and] . . . wore a pair of SA trousers." Yet this alleged perpetrator was never identified and was, therefore, an easy attempt to divert accountability.[43]

Anna-Margarete attempted to justify her actions by stating that although she did beat the flyer several times with a board, she did not do this "because I wanted to hit him, but because I wanted to remove the lath." However, this was clearly not believed by the court. She and Schindel were each sentenced to a one-year imprisonment.[44] While Margot was initially sentenced to one and a half years in prison, this was quickly reduced to six months by the review board, which convened fifteen days after the initial trial. Deubert was initially sentenced to fifteen years in prison. However, after repeated appeals for a review of his case by his brother (who had been imprisoned as a political prisoner in Dachau from November 11, 1936, until January 20, 1939) and his wife, he was eventually paroled on December 6, 1952.

The final trial was held in July 1947 in Dachau and tried Georg Sturm—a thirty-three-year-old Nazi Party member (since 1934) and a member of the Luftwaffe who had escorted the flyers to Gross-Gerau and participated in beating the airmen to death in the courtyard of the city hall. A witness reported during the trial that while he accompanied Sturm back to Trebur after the airmen were killed, Sturm remarked: "My brother has got his revenge now." Also, a woman testified that as Fachinger started to close the gate to the courtyard, she heard a man (who was identified as Sturm) say: "I am coming along. Now I have a different pair of trousers. Now I can do the beating better. I am not allowed to do it in uniform."[45]

Sturm testified on his own behalf and stated that "in 1945 I was injured in an air raid and was unconscious four or five days from a brain concussion. . . . Due to the brain injury, I cannot remember anything that occurred since 1942 or 1943." He continued that he "did not ever remember having been at Gross-Gerau or Trebur and remembered nothing of having participated in the beating of flyers on August 29, 1944." The court had this information verified by a doctor and took this information into consideration in determining his sentence. For his direct involvement in beating two airmen to death, Sturm received a mere three-year prison sentence.[46]

Comparing the trials for the Lynchjustiz case in Gross-Gerau and the Rüsselsheim massacre is quite interesting; both incidents occurred within days and a few miles of each other as well as involved a similar form of violence carried out mostly by German civilians. Yet a key difference between the cases is the sentences imposed on the perpetrators. Although the trial for the incident in Rüsselsheim and the first two trials for the case in Gross-Gerau occurred within a few weeks of each other,

Figure 5.12. Memorial Plaque for Harvey J. Purkey and Charles H. Evans Jr. in Gross-Gerau. In August 2018, seventy-four years after the murders, a memorial was dedicated to Evans and Purkey in the local museum in Gross-Gerau. The plaque states: "We commemorate the American Air Force soldiers who died on August 29, 1944, here in the courtyard of the former town hall after an angry crowd had driven the US soldiers through the streets. We remember the occurrence with disgust. May the death of the American soldiers be a reminder of humanity, reconciliation, and peace." *Photo courtesy of Cornelia Benz, Presse- und Öffentlichkeitsarbeit, Kreisstadt Gross-Gerau.*

the sentences were considerably harsher for the perpetrators of the Rüsselsheim massacre. This was possibly due to the increased publicity that the incident in Rüsselsheim received. The third trial for the airmen killed in Gross-Gerau was held over two years after the initial trial and the desire to quickly move beyond the violent past is discernable in the records, as Sturm, who aided in beating the flyers to death with iron bars, only received a three-year prison sentence. While the court took into consideration the fact that the perpetrator suffered from alleged memory loss from concussions he received during an aerial attack, his coperpetrator, Flauaus, who was tried in 1945, received the death penalty and was executed in April 1946. Had Sturm been identified, found, and tried in 1945, it is not improbable that he would have received the death penalty as well (fig. 5.12).

Figure 5.13. Major James B. Cheney. *Bottisham Airfield Museum, Object Number UPL 18393.*

Scat-Cat (October 15, 1944)[47]

On the morning of Sunday, October 15, 1944, Major James Briggs Cheney and his wingman Second Lieutenant Claire P. Chennault were on a patrol mission near Münster (fig. 5.13). While they identified a few targets of opportunity (such as trucks and cars on the road) to strafe, it was a rather uneventful mission. However, as they made their way back to Little Walden air base in England, Cheney's plane began to emit smoke due to an oil leak, and not long after, the engine of his P-51 Mustang (nicknamed *Scat-Cat*) quit. Cheney was forced to bail out and landed near Dorsten. Upon landing, Cheney was captured and taken to the headquarters of the Forty-Sixth Regiment, which was located on the third floor of the Franciscan Monastery in Dorsten. While there, he was interrogated for about an hour by the ranking officers.

Meanwhile, German soldiers had gathered in the hallway and were enraged at the strafing of a passenger train and farmers working in the fields earlier that day, an attack that killed roughly twenty people. Calls for Cheney to be killed could be heard from the hallway and from an angry, hostile crowd of civilians that had gathered outside the monastery. Members of the crowd were armed with spades and shovels and demanded reprisal against the "murderer." While the commanding officer, Lieutenant Colonel Hubert von Svoboda, was against killing Cheney, who might have important information, he made it clear to his subordinates that he wanted the flyer to be beaten. Second Lieutenant Werner Hess, who was a Protestant minister before the war, ordered the soldiers in the hallway to line up and prepare to punish the flyer. They were armed with leather belts, clubs, and batons.

Cheney was then pushed into the hallway. Certain that they intended to inflict severe harm, Cheney attempted to run through the hall and down the stairs as fast as he could. He fell, however, as he made his way down the steps. Once he landed at the bottom, he was met by more punishment as two civilians and a policeman continued beating and kicking him. Shortly thereafter von Svoboda intervened and placed Cheney in a car waiting in the courtyard. The soldiers were forced to hold back the angry mob outside the gates, and Cheney was quickly driven away. He was taken to a hospital in Essen and eventually sent to a POW camp, where he survived the war.

During the two-day postwar trial in 1947, Hess and von Svoboda were charged with wrongfully encouraging the assault on Cheney. Hess attempted to defend his actions by claiming that his unit had captured roughly one hundred flyers during the war, and with the exception of the incident involving Cheney, all had been treated well. He even alleged that the flyers had all received proper food, cigarettes, medical attention, and beer. Von Svoboda also kept a guest book that many of the flyers had signed, "some adding humorous remarks." Nevertheless, the court found Hess guilty and sentenced him to six months in prison. For reasons unknown, von Svoboda was never tried for his role in allowing Cheney to be mistreated.[48]

Libby B (December 24, 1944)[49]

During a bombing mission to strike German airfields on Christmas Eve in 1944, escort aircraft (P-51 Mustangs) were tasked with fending off any possible attacks by German fighter aircraft. Over the city of Fulda, American aircrews came under attack by German fighters (FW-190s), and an intense air battle ensued. One pilot, believed to be

Figure 5.14. Captain William H. Mooney (right) in front of his P-51 Mustang (44–11198), *Libby B. "357th Fighter Group 'Yoxford Boys,'" http://www.cebudanderson.com/357thkia.htm.*

Captain William H. Mooney, was eventually forced to parachute from his disabled aircraft and landed near Freienseen—roughly thirty-five miles west of Fulda (fig. 5.14).

Not long after landing, the flyer was taken into custody by a member of the Landwacht, Otto Heene, and a crowd gathered after word spread throughout the village that an American pilot had been captured. Heene escorted Mooney to the neighboring village of Laubach, where he intended to turn him over to the Kreisleiter. Along the way, Ortsgruppenleiter Emil Hofmann decided to assist and accompanied Heene. However, Hofmann did not intend to bring the flyer to Laubach alive.

Not long thereafter, Hofmann pulled out his pistol and shot Mooney in the back. Dazed and in shock from what just happened, the flyer staggered and turned to face the men. Heene then grabbed him by the arm, likely to prevent him from collapsing, and Hofmann shot again. This time hitting Mooney in the upper chest. The flyer's leg buckled underneath of him, and he fell to the ground. Hofmann ordered Heene to remain with the body while he returned to Freienseen to secure some means to transport the body to Laubach. He returned a while later with a horse-drawn wagon. Later that day, the flyer's remains were buried in Laubach.

After the war, a war crimes trial convened from April 15 to April 21, 1947, and tried both Heene and Hofmann for killing the POW. Heene was eventually acquitted of any wrongdoing; however, Hofmann was found guilty. Although Hofmann attempted to justify his actions by stating the flyer was shot while trying to escape, the court did not believe him, especially given Heene's testimony, and sentenced him to death. He was ultimately executed on October 22, 1948.

Silver Slipper (March 21, 1945)[50]

During the afternoon of March 21, 1945 (seven weeks before the celebration of victory in Europe, or VE, Day), six American flyers arrived by bus in the town of Neckarsulm.[51] Four of these men likely belonged to the crew of a B-25 nicknamed *Silver Slipper*, which was shot down near Ora, Italy, on March 10. The flyers were being transported to Dulag Luft in Oberursel—over one hundred miles north of Neckarsulm and over four hundred miles from where they were shot down in Italy—by three Luftwaffe officers.

In Neckarsulm, the bus stopped at the corner of Neckar and Urban Streets around 5:00 p.m. (located about a block north of the main train station), and the flyers, along with their guards, exited the bus. The prisoners stood in a straight line at the edge of the nearby park on Neckar Street. Two guards left for unknown reasons, leaving one man to guard the six airmen. Even though the flyers clearly showed no sign of hostility, one man to guard six flyers is not enough.

The Nazi Party house of Neckarsulm was located on Salinen Street—across from the small park where the POWs were standing. After the flyers had been stretching their legs for a few minutes, Ortsgruppenleiter Heinz Endress and his deputy, Clemens Funder, noticed the them outside and quickly left (armed with pistols) to confront them. As he approached the airmen, Endress yelled to the guard: "These people should be shot! They destroyed my house on the first of March." As he neared within ten feet, Endress removed his pistol from his pocket and pointed it toward the prisoners. The guard immediately came to the defense of the flyers. He told Endress: "Don't touch these men." Endress stopped and put his pistol in the right pocket of his pants. He took a few steps back, considering his options. Then he suddenly drew his pistol again, said, "They must be shot!" and fired two shots toward the prisoners.[52]

The flyers' worst fears came true. They jumped back in shock and immediately raised their hands above their heads, afraid that a wrong move could be their last. A few flyers took cover behind some nearby trees in the park; however, one airman was hit by the two initial shots fired by Endress. He grimaced in pain, fell to the ground, and rolled partially into the street. Another airman allegedly attempted to run away—or made a sudden move—and Endress shot him from behind. The prisoner fell to the ground and remained motionless. Funder also wanted to partake and attempted to shoot at this same prisoner; however, his gun misfired, and he sought to fix the issue.

Meanwhile, a third flyer attempted to hide behind some trees in the nearby park. Yet there was little chance of evading in the small park, which was located in the middle of the town. Endress pursued this prisoner. Frantic to find any means of refuge, the airman ran and shielded himself behind a nearby civilian man who had watched the events unfold. Aiming his weapon at both men, Endress yelled to the civilian: "Move away so I can shoot!" In fear for his life, the civilian bent over. Realizing what was about to happen, the prisoner ran for his life. As Endress shot, the flyer collapsed near a tree. Having fixed his weapon,

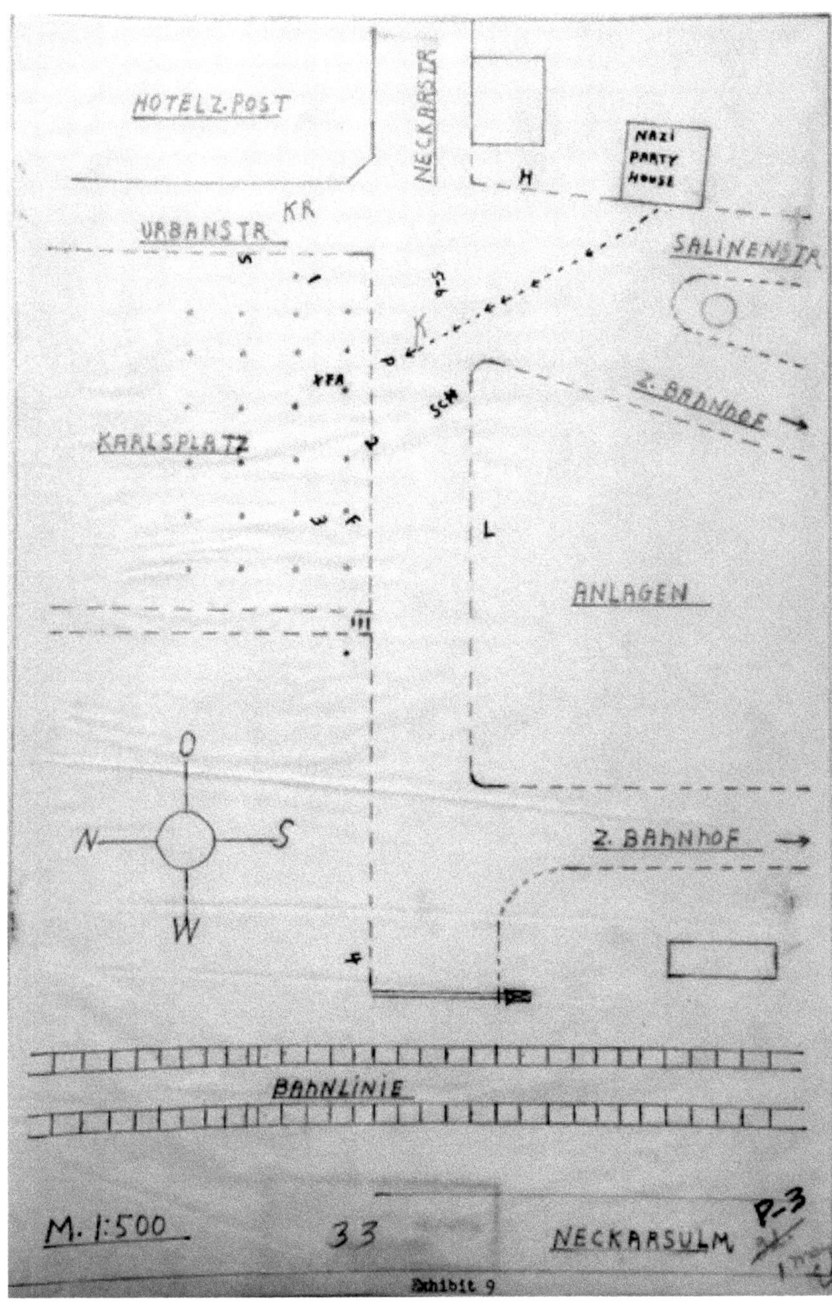

Figure 5.15. Exhibit 9 from trial 12-1182-2. Diagram of the crime scene in Neckarsulm. The numbers 1 through 4 indicate the location of the first four airmen's bodies when they were killed and the order in which they were killed. The dotted line indicates the path taken by the Ortsgruppenleiter and where they made initial contact with the prisoners and guard. *Exhibit 9, Map of the crime scene, Case No. 12-1182-2, Record of U.S. Army Europe, War Crimes Case Files (Cases Tried), November 6, 1945; RG 549; Entry 290; Box 151, Declassification No. NND 775032, NARA.*

Figure 5.16. Exhibit 10 from trial number 12-1182-2. Photograph of the crime scene. Each arrow indicates each murdered flyer and the number indicates the order in which they were killed. *Exhibit 10, Photo of the crime scene, Case No. 12-1182-2, Record of U.S. Army Europe, War Crimes Case Files (Cases Tried), November 6, 1945; RG 549; Entry 290; Box 151, Declassification No. NND 775032, NARA.*

Funder rejoined Endress as they approached the aviator who was still very much alive. Funder then drew his pistol and shot, administering the "coup de grace," at Endress's urging[53]

As this was unfolding, a fourth airman attempted to escape. He ran toward a nearby railroad crossing about two blocks west on Neckar Street. When Endress realized this, he ordered the guard: "Shoot! It's too far for me." Ignoring his order to guard the prisoners, the soldier raised his rifle and shot twice. The flyer's lifeless body collapsed near the railroad tracks (figs. 5.15 and 5.16). Endress and the guard walked toward the body of this flyer, which was the farthest away (several hundred feet). As they proceeded, they walked past the body of the airman who had first been shot. They noticed that he was still alive, and both men shot and killed the prisoner. The bodies of the flyers were buried in a mass grave near Neckarsulm.[54]

There were still two airmen alive (believed to be Sergeant Roscoe Harvey and Captain S. K. Anderson) who had not been shot (fig. 5.17).

Figure 5.17. Exhibit 6 in trial 12-1182-2. The two airmen who survived the initial attack on March 21, 1944, believed to be Captain S. K. Anderson and Staff Sergeant Roscoe W. Harvey. *Exhibit 6, Photo of two airmen who survived the initial attach, Case No. 12-1182-2, Record of U.S. Army Europe, War Crimes Case Files (Cases Tried), November 6, 1945; RG 549; Entry 290; Box 151, Declassification No. NND 775032, NARA.*

Seeing one of them, Endress attempted to shoot him, but the Wehrmacht guard intervened and prevented him from doing so. The two exchanged some words, and Endress and Funder returned to the Nazi Party house across the street. Once inside, they asked a female secretary (who had witnessed the incident from her office window, as had many other civilians): "Well, how did the village leaders do?" Although it was a rhetorical question, Endress's arrogance and desire for praise was evident. Another witness in the Nazi Party house was told by Endress: "Now I have finally avenged my wife." His wife had been killed and his house destroyed in an air raid on March 1, 1945. Apparently his actions did not satisfy him, because he then reloaded his weapon and said: "This is for the next ones." Later in the evening, Endress met a captain in the Wehrmacht who was stationed in Neckarsulm and a few other prominent men of the town in the guest room of the Hotel Post (across the street from the park where the airmen were killed). The Wehrmacht captain immediately reproached Endress and Funder for their actions against the POWs, to which Endress snapped back: "If you can't do it, we will. In Bavaria they slap them to death and then stabbed them to death." Before going home, Funder called Kreisleiter Richard Drauz, who was stationed five miles away in Heilbronn, and told him what he had done to the Terrorflieger reporting that "we shot some escaped Americans."[55]

The local commander of the Wehrmacht barracks, Lieutenant Colonel Karl Otto, ordered a few of his men to escort the surviving two flyers to the nearby army barracks, where they spent the night. In the early hours of following morning (around 5:00 a.m.), the prisoners were escorted to the train station under the pretenses of taking a train to Frankfurt and then eventually to Oberursel; however, shortly before they reached the train, Endress and Funder appeared again and opened fire on the prisoners. One flyer (believed to be Sergeant Roscoe Harvey) was shot in the stomach while the other (believed to be Captain S. K. Anderson) managed to escape despite the Wehrmacht commander sending approximately two hundred soldiers to search for him.

The wounded flyer, who needed surgery in order to survive, was taken to the nearby army barracks, where the commander refused to allow the prisoner to be treated. Medical personnel at the barracks repeatedly requested that the prisoner be transferred to a hospital, but the camp commander denied any form of medical care. The troop doctor even attempted to have the flyer removed by ambulance to a hospital, but the ambulance was ordered to return to the army barracks on orders from Drauz. Believing that the prisoner would survive if he received proper medical treatment, the doctor immediately went to see Drauz, in whose company he also met Endress. The doctor attempted to clarify that the "flyer's chance of survival was good, providing a prompt operation was performed." Drauz's initial recommendation was to give the prisoner poison. The doctor adamantly refused, and Endress offered to shoot the flyer in the cellar; however, Drauz refused this offer because he did not want it done in his house. He assured the doctor that the flyer would be removed, and the doctor returned to the barracks. At around 7:00 p.m., the commander allowed the wounded airman to be removed from the army barracks by truck but continued to bar any medical personnel from attending to the prisoner. Shortly after departing the barracks, the truck was stopped by an unknown military policeman, who then shot and killed the flyer in the back of the vehicle. The airman's body was subsequently buried in the cemetery of Heilbronn.

Two days later, Drauz was notified by a member of the Gestapo that a state policeman had captured Anderson in Brackenheim (located roughly fourteen miles southwest of Neckarsulm). The following day, Drauz, Endress, and three other men drove to Dürrenzimmern (located a mile from where the flyer was being held), where Drauz and Endress exited the vehicle and waited while the others proceeded to Brackenheim for the prisoner.

On the way back to Neckarsulm with the downed airman, they drove through Dürrenzimmern and stopped in the woods just outside of the village. Here, they met Drauz and Endress, who were waiting for them. The flyer was handcuffed and made no attempt to escape; he surely had a bad feeling about being brought to a secluded area by individuals who had murdered his fellow airmen. The flyer was then shot twice in the back of the head. Callous and remorseless, the men departed, leaving the body where it rested. Sometime later, by unknown individuals, the flyer's remains were buried in an unmarked grave in the woods (fig. 5.18).

While there was some question about who shot this prisoner, a witness stated that he saw Drauz with a pistol immediately after he heard the shot. In an attempt to save himself from a certain death sentence, Drauz testified during his postwar trial that his assistant, who had conveniently died by the time the trial began, had shot the flyer. A US war crimes tribunal convicted Drauz for murder and sentenced him to death on December 11, 1945. He was subsequently executed by hanging on December 4, 1946.

A trial for the four American airmen who were killed on March 21, 1945, in Neckarsulm was held in Dachau in November 1945. At the time, Ortsgruppenleiter Endress was the only perpetrator who was identified and in custody; Funder had committed suicide. Using testimony from over thirty witnesses, the court determined that the flyers

Figure 5.18. Exhibit 64 from trial 12-1182-2. An unknown German man points to the unmarked grave of an airman (believed to be Captain S. K. Anderson) killed in the woods outside Dürrenzimmern. *Exhibit 64, German man indicating location of flyers' remains, Case No. 12-1182-2, Record of U.S. Army Europe, War Crimes Case Files (Cases Tried), November 6, 1945; RG 549; Entry 290; Box 151, Declassification No. NND 775032, NARA.*

were not attempting to escape, as the deputy alleged, but rather sought safety from the accused's illegal attempts on their lives.[56] Moreover, the accused even admitted that his motive was to avenge the death of his wife. Even the accused's attorney conceded that his client's actions were "planned, deliberate, and vengeful." Despite Endress's plea for mercy, the court concluded: "This was no killing in self-defense or in the heat of anger. It was calculated murder and deserves no clemency." He was initially sentenced to death by decapitation; however, this was amended in January 1946 by a review board, which ordered that he be executed by hanging. Endress was eventually hanged on December 4, 1946. A final trial was held in May 1947 and charged Karl Otto, the commander of the Wehrmacht barracks in Neckarsulm. Despite the fact that he surely knew what would happen to the flyer when he left the barracks on the truck, Otto was sentenced to a mere five years in prison for his refusal to allow the wounded prisoner medical treatment. He was subsequently released in May 1950 at the age of fifty-two and received twenty deutsche marks to begin his life anew.[57]

Figure 5.19. Exhibit 38 in trial 12-1182-2. A member of the war crimes investigation team points to five pairs of boots that belonged to the flyers killed in this case. *Exhibit 38, Photo of war crimes investigator with boots that belonged to five flyers, Case No. 12-1182-2, Record of U.S. Army Europe, War Crimes Case Files (Cases Tried), November 6, 1945; RG 549; Entry 290; Box 151, Declassification No. NND 775032, NARA.*

While the bodies were too badly decomposed—and any personal identification had been removed by the perpetrators—to identify the young men, the pathologist relied on the type of clothing remnants and any manufacturer labels to identify that the bodies were at least American airmen. For example, flight jackets and air corps coveralls were discernable. Investigators were eventually able to recover the airmen's boots, which had been looted by the perpetrators (fig. 5.19).

Cape Cod Express (April 16, 1945)[58]

One of the last known cases of Lynchjustiz in Germany was committed on April 16, 1945, against Captain Chester E. Coggeshall Jr. near the small Bavarian village of Sillersdorf, located five miles northwest of Freilassing and seven miles from Salzburg. This case occurred just three weeks before the end of the war in Europe. At around 2:30 in the afternoon, Coggeshall (accompanied by two wingmen) attacked an airfield just west of Salzburg. During the low-level strafing mission, Coggeshall's P-51 Mustang—nicknamed *Cape Cod Express*—was hit by flak

Figure 5.20. Captain Chester E. Coggeshall Jr. (center) and his P-51 Mustang, *Cape Cod Express* (Russ Abbey and Frank Birtciel). *"55th Fighter Group Website," Russ Abbey and Frank Birtciel, http://www.station131.co.uk/55th/Pilots/343rd%20Pilots/Coggeshall%20Chester%20E.%20Jr.%20Capt.htm.*

and smoke immediately billowed from his aircraft (fig. 5.20). His two wingmen, Second Lieutenant Jack A. Bevington and First Lieutenant Walter Strauch, watched helplessly as Coggeshall's aircraft went into a slow turn and rapidly lost altitude. They reported that Coggeshall attempted a high-speed belly landing in an open field, but as his aircraft approached the ground, the right wing dug into the dirt, which forced the aircraft to cartwheel into a small building located at the edge of the field.

Slightly wounded, Coggeshall climbed out of the wreckage, hoping to evade capture; however, members of the local Gendarmerie and military personnel immediately captured him. He was then escorted to the courthouse of Freilassing. When he arrived, the mayor and Ortsgruppenleiter, August Kobus, denied Coggeshall first aid treatment. Kobus then informed the individuals present that he had orders from the Kreisleiter of Berchtesgaden, Bernhard Stredele, to "finish" any flyers captured in the area. Shortly thereafter, in the early evening, Coggeshall was placed in a car—guarded by two German soldiers (Karl Boehm and Rudiger von Massow)—and taken out of town by Kobus. As they reached the woods outside Freilassing, Kobus shot Coggeshall twice in the head.

Kobus was tried in November 1945 for "wrongfully and unlawfully killing an officer of the United States Army." He was initially sentenced to death by firing squad, but this sentence was later changed in February 1946 to death by hanging. He was subsequently executed on March 15, 1946. Two additional trials were held for the killing of Coggeshall. One was from February to March 1946 and tried Kreisleiter Stredele for war crimes. While he was initially sentenced to death, this sentence was reduced to life imprisonment by the review board in May 1947. Stredele was, however, paroled in April 1957 after serving twelve years.[59]

The final trial was held in June 1947 and tried the two German soldiers (Boehm and von Massow) who escorted Coggeshall to the woods, where he was killed. The court determined that there was "insufficient evidence to implicate [von Massow] . . . as an active participant in the killing." As for Boehm, despite knowing about the order to kill captured flyers, the evidence was also insufficient "to establish that he participated in the killing." For these reasons, the two men were acquitted.[60]

Notes

1. Case No. 12–2058; Deputy Theater Judge Advocate's Office, War Crimes Branch, April 23, 1947; Records of the Office of the Judge Advocate General (Army), RG 154; Entry 143; Box 407, National Archives at College Park, College Park, MD.

2. Missing Air Crew Report (MACR) # 282, Records of the Office of the Quartermaster General, 1774–1985, RG 92, Entry A1 2109B, NARA, https://catalog.archives.gov/id/90890504, accessed June 5, 2018.

3. Exhibit 7, Testimony by Lieutenant Cook, Case No. 12-2058, Deputy Theater Judge Advocate's Office, War Crimes Branch, April 23, 1947, RG 153; Entry 143, Box 407, NARA.

4. Exhibit 2, Testimony of Paul F., Case No. 12-2058, Deputy Theater Judge Advocate's Office, War Crimes Branch, April 23, 1947, RG 153, Entry 143, Box 407, NARA.

5. Exhibit 7, Testimony by Lieutenant Cook, Case No. 12-2058; Deputy Theater Judge Advocate's Office, War Crimes Branch, April 23, 1947, RG 153, Entry 143, Box 407, NARA.

6. Review and Recommendations for Case No. 12-2058, Deputy Theater Judge Advocate's Office, War Crimes Branch, April 23, 1947, RG 153, Entry 143, Box 407, NARA.

7. Case No. 12-1880, Deputy Theater Judge Advocate's Office, War Crimes Branch, April 20, 1946, RG 153, Entry 143, Box 397, NARA.

8. Ibid.

9. Case No. 12-1812, Record of U.S. Army Europe, War Crimes Case Files (Cases Tried), January 16, 1947, RG 549, Entry 290, Boxes 186–87, NARA.

10. Review and Recommendations for Case No. 12-1812, Record of U.S. Army Europe, War Crimes Case Files (Cases Tried), April 23, 1947, RG 549, Entry 290, Box 187, NARA.

11. Ibid.

12. Ibid.

13. Review and Recommendations for Case No. 12-1837; Record of U.S. Army Europe, War Crimes Case Files (Cases Tried), August 20–25, September 22–October 2, 1947, RG 549, Entry 290, Box 139, NARA.

14. Ibid.

15. Ibid.

16. Ibid., 5.

17. Ibid., 1.

18. Ibid., 7–8.

19. Case No. 12-57, Deputy Theater Judge Advocate's Office, War Crimes Branch, June 4, 1947, RG 153, Entry 143, Box 167, NARA.

20. Case No. 12-43 and 12-45, Record of U.S. Army Europe, War Crimes Case Files (Cases Tried), September 26–October 8, 1947, and December 16–18, 1946, RG 153, Entry 143, Box 164, NARA.

21. The crew consisted of Second Lieutenant Howland J. Hamlin (pilot), Second Lieutenant Richard V. S. Newhouse (copilot), Second Lieutenant George T. Hunter Jr. (bombardier), Staff Sergeant Aaron C. Slaughter (radio operator), Technical Sergeant Donald W. Anderson (engineer), Staff Sergeant Ronald W. Cherrington (left waist gunner), Staff Sergeant John A. Boardsen (right waist gunner), Staff Sergeant Raymond C. Ertel (ball turret gunner), and Staff Sergeant Tonnes E. Tonnesen (tail gunner).

22. Review and Recommendations for Case No. 12-45, Record of U.S. Army Europe, War Crimes Case Files (Cases Tried), September 26–October 8, 1947, and December 16–18, 1946, RG 153, Entry 143, Box 164, NARA.

23. Ibid.

24. Review and Recommendations for Case No. 12-43, Record of U.S. Army Europe, War Crimes Case Files (Cases Tried), September 26–October 8, 1947, and December 16–18, 1946, RG 153, Entry 143, Box 164, NARA.

25. Ibid.

26. Ibid.

27. Review and Recommendations for Case No. 12-45, Record of U.S. Army Europe, War Crimes Case Files (Cases Tried), September 26–October 8, 1947, and December 16–18, 1946, RG 153, Entry 143, Box 164, NARA.

28. Review and Recommendations for Case No. 12-43, Record of U.S. Army Europe, War Crimes Case Files (Cases Tried), September 26–October 8, 1947, and December 16–18, 1946, RG 153, Entry 143, Box 164, NARA.

29. Case No. 12-2036, Deputy Theater Judge Advocate's Office, War Crimes Branch, May 12–29, 1947, RG 153, Entry 143, Box 407, NARA.

30. Review and Recommendations for Case No. 12-2036, Deputy Theater Judge Advocate's Office, War Crimes Branch, May 12–29, 1947, RG 153, Entry 143, Box 407, NARA.

31. Exhibit 30, page 2, Case No. 12-2036, Deputy Theater Judge Advocate's Office, War Crimes Branch, May 12–29, 1947, RG 153, Entry 143, Box 407, NARA.

32. Testimony by Isidor K., Case No. 12-2036, Deputy Theater Judge Advocate's Office, War Crimes Branch, May 12–29, 1947, RG 153, Entry 143, Box 407, NARA.

33. Case Nos. 12-793, 12-793-1, 12-793-2, Record of U.S. Army Europe, War Crimes Case Files (Cases Tried), August 3, 1945, August 15, 1945, July 28–29, 1947, RG 549, Entry 290, Box 121, NARA. The crew consisted of First Lieutenant Dean C. Allen (pilot), First Lieutenant Charles U. Rapp Jr. (copilot), Second Lieutenant Charles H. Evans Jr. (navigator), First Lieutenant Michael L. Vlahos (nose gunner), Technical Sergeant Harvey J. Purkey Jr. (top turret), Technical Sergeant Robert B. Newsbigle (radio), Staff Sergeant Eugene W. Le Vegue (ball turret gunner), Staff Sergeant Richard C. Huebotter (waist gunner), and Staff Sergeant James R. Carey (tail gunner). First Lieutenant Vlahos, Technical Sergeant Newsbigle, and Staff Sergeant Le Veque died in the crash.

34. Ibid.

35. Ibid.

36. Margot Zeeck's testimony, July 20, 1945, Case No. 12-793, Record of U.S. Army Europe, War Crimes Case Files (Cases Tried), August 3, 1945, August 15, 1945, July 28–29, 1947, RG 549, Entry 290, Box 121, NARA.

37. Heinrich Deubert's testimony, June 20, 1945, Case No. 12-793, Record of U.S. Army Europe, War Crimes Case Files (Cases Tried), August 3, 1945, August 15, 1945, July 28–29, 1947, RG 549, Entry 290, Box 121, NARA.

38. Anna-Margarete Solomon's testimony, June 20, 1945, Record of U.S. Army Europe, War Crimes Case Files (Cases Tried), August 3, 1945, August 15, 1945, July 28–29, 1947, RG 549, Entry 290, Box 121, NARA.

39. Review and Recommendations for Case No. 12-793, 12-793-1, 12-793-2, Record of U.S. Army Europe, War Crimes Case Files (Cases Tried), August 3, 1945, August 15, 1945, July 28–29, 1947, RG 549, Entry 290, Box 121, NARA.

40. Ibid.

41. Ibid.

42. Ibid.

43. Review and Recommendations for Case No. 12-793-2, Record of U.S. Army Europe, War Crimes Case Files (Cases Tried), August 3, 1945, August 15, 1945, July 28–29, 1947, RG 549, Entry 290, Box 121, NARA.

44. Anna S.'s testimony, June 20, 1945, Record of U.S. Army Europe, War Crimes Case Files (Cases Tried), August 3, 1945, August 15, 1945, July 28–29, 1947, RG 549, Entry 290, Box 121, NARA.

45. Review and Recommendations for Case No. 12-793-2, Record of U.S. Army Europe, War Crimes Case Files (Cases Tried), August 3, 1945, August 15, 1945, July 28–29, 1947, RG 549, Entry 290, Box 121, NARA.

46. Ibid.

47. Case No. 12-1292, Deputy Theater Judge Advocate's Office, War Crimes Branch, November 10, 1947, Records of the Office of the Judge Advocate General (Army), RG 153, Entry 143, Box 397, NARA.

48. Ibid.

49. Case No. 12-1774, Record of U.S. Army Europe, War Crimes Case Files (Cases Tried), April 15–21, 1947, RG 549, Entry 290, Box 386, NARA.

50. Case No. 12-1182, Record of U.S. Army Europe, War Crimes Case Files (Cases Tried), November 6, 1945, RG 549, Entry 290, Box 151, NARA.

51. The criminal investigators believed that the flyers were Second Lieutenant Edward A. Martiniak, Staff Sergeant Roscoe Harvey, Staff Sergeant Donald O. Griffith, Staff Sergeant Richard H. Palmer, and Captain S. V. Anderson.

52. Review and Recommendations for Case No. 12-1182, Record of U.S. Army Europe, War Crimes Case Files (Cases Tried), November 6, 1945, RG 549, Entry 290, Box 151, NARA.

53. Ibid.

54. Ibid. Analysis of investigation files indicates that three of these four flyers were likely Second Lietuenant Edward A. Martiniak, Staff Sergeant Donald O. Griffith, and Staff Sergeant Richard H. Palmer.

55. Ibid.

56. There were over thirty witnesses who testified at the three trials with ages ranging from seventeen to sixty-eight. The average age of witnesses was forty-one and their occupations included sexton, doctor, Wehrmacht soldiers, policemen, mechanics, salesmen, housewives, farmers, party officials, mayor, contractor, and even a Catholic nun.

57. Review and Recommendations for Case No. 12-1182-2, Record of U.S. Army Europe, War Crimes Case Files (Cases Tried), November 6, 1945, RG 549, Entry 290, Box 151, NARA.

58. Case No. 12-1155, Deputy Theater Judge Advocate's Office, War Crimes Branch, February 6, 1946, Records of the Office of the Judge Advocate General (Army), RG 153, Entry 143, Box 414, NARA.

59. Review and Recommendations for Case No. 12-1155, Deputy Theater Judge Advocate's Office, War Crimes Branch, February 6, 1946, Records of the Office of the Judge Advocate General (Army), RG 153, Entry 143, Box 414, NARA.

60. Ibid.

Chapter 6

Examining the Motives of Lynchjustiz

Inter arma enim silent leges
"In times of war, the laws are silent"

Marcus Tullius Cicero[1]

Copious representations of evil exist throughout history, and there are numerous theories that attempt to explain them. Likely, the most well-known example of the twentieth century is the Holocaust. Various notions exist regarding the uniqueness of the Holocaust and the ways in which this atrocity was permitted to occur, especially in a modern society. These theories involve the role of not only Hitler but also the German people. While historians continue to examine events and individuals in an attempt to clarify theories and lasting questions, there remains no definite answer to how an entire society could allow such violence to be carried out. Some historians have proposed that Hitler did not have the initial intent (or a master plan) to eliminate European Jews and that there was no unique aspect of German antisemitism.[2] Moreover, these historians often believe that the Holocaust grew out of situational and psychological factors that were compounded through a "cumulative radicalization," as German historian Hans Mommsen described.[3] In contrast, other historians contend that not only did Hitler initially have the intent to eliminate Jews but also that German society exhibited "eliminationist antisemitism," as political scientist Daniel Goldhagen has argued.[4] Yet there are additional scholars who have attempted to synthesize these opposing theories, suggesting that the Holocaust resulted from officials and citizens "working towards the Führer," as historian Ian Kershaw reasons.[5] Thus, as legal historian James Q. Whitman suggests the Nazi regime "insisted on a kind of liberty for the individual . . . to act independently 'in the spirit of Hitler.'"[6]

The key to understanding Nazi terror and violence, whether concerning the Holocaust or Lynchjustiz committed against American airmen, centers on examining the individuals within German society. Since the 1990s, studies have increasingly focused on the role of "ordinary" citizens in Nazi Germany's war of atrocities.[7] Yet the violence committed against downed flyers, including those who committed the crimes and for what reasons, largely remains overlooked. The looming Cold War, arduous denazification process, and the complex historical memory of the air war overshadowed and hampered the prosecution of "lesser" war criminals and their significance in historical memory. More recently, historians have begun to shed light on these important trials, which permits a better understanding of low-level perpetrators' actions and an increased attempt to explore their motives and rationalizations.[8] These low-level criminals aid in understanding not only how atrocities like Lynchjustiz occurred but also how such violence may be prevented in the future.

Analysis of the postwar crime trials revealed that three specific motivations elicited Lynchjustiz: namely, the radicalization of war, obedience to figures of authority, and endorsement by the regime.[9] While each of these could result in the mistreatment of American flyers, the combination of several, or even all, motives was often at play. They potentiated each other and increased the probability of airmen being killed. Outside and personal influences uniquely elicited each perpetrating group into committing violence against flyers. While party officials, security forces, and police largely committed the controlled and often premeditated murder of airmen, civilians were most likely to act spontaneously and carry out nondeadly assaults, according to the flyer trials. This further supports research that indicates that German civilians played a significant role in the war.[10]

Perpetrators participated in violence against downed airmen as a way to advance what they believed were irreproachable causes—namely, to punish the alleged criminals for the devastation caused by the air war. The approach and rationale were similar to lynchings in the United States, especially the frontier justice (also known as vigilante justice) of the nineteenth century. The radicalization of the war in Nazi Germany led to near-frontier conditions, as characterized by the traditional notion of the frontier, but more so in its political and psychological states than a specific spatiality or geography, as was common in the context of the United States (i.e., the West). Similar to early lynchings in the United States, Lynchjustiz in Germany committed against American flyers occurred in response to perceived transgressions against property, homicide, or other heinous crimes and often occurred despite the presence of a legal apparatus. Similar examples of organizations using armed vigilante groups to eliminate adversaries include some nineteenth-century oil and steel barons in the American frontier and the social and political movement of the Ku Klux Klan [KKK] in the United States during the twentieth century. Lynching was used as a weapon of vengeance in an attempt to psychologically and physically combat the perceived "Other" was usually condoned by local officials. Similar to violence in the United States, lynchings in Germany occurred throughout the nation but most predominately in rural locations. Although Lynchjustiz did not deter airmen from taking part in air raids, knowledge of them increased flyers' anxiety about the possibility of being shot down and their potential contact with the German public.[11]

Studies analyzing the voting patterns and the success of the Nazi Party in the Weimar Republic have indicated that "the swing towards the NSDAP in the 1930s had a rural basis, and it was more pronounced in counties with higher proportions of agrarian middle classes. . . . This is due to the remarkable congruence between the programmatic offers of the Nazi Party and the politico-economic interests of this segment."[12] This could signify that these areas were more likely to be won over early on by Nazi Party rhetoric.[13] Given the extended support of the Nazi regime in these areas, its propensity to radicalize throughout the war is conceivable. However, this is by no means attempting to reduce the role of urban inhabitants carrying out violence. As cities often experienced the main force of the Allied air war, urban citizens frequently relocated to rural areas, bringing with them additional stories and rumors about the air war and animosity toward downed airmen.[14] In addition, flyers were more likely to land in the countryside, and therefore, Lynchjustiz was more likely to occur in rural areas with long histories of supporting the Nazi Party. But violence was not isolated to rural areas, and executions and lynchings, of not only downed airmen but also foreign workers and Soviet POWs, became more frequent in urban areas after the fall of 1944 in the wake of heavy air raids.[15]

Analysis of the flyer trials indicated that over 62 percent of Lynchjustiz cases occurred in rural towns with populations fewer than fifteen thousand. Thus, the historical significance of rural areas supporting the Nazi Party and an amplified amount of contact between downed airmen and German citizens in these areas led to an increased likelihood of rural citizens committing Lynchjustiz. Despite international laws established by The Hague (1899 and 1907) and the Geneva Conventions (1929), the radicalizing war, which was the main point of divergence between the phenomenon of lynching in the United States and Germany, obscured the border of legality and criminality, as the introductory quote by Cicero indicates.

As the air war intensified, feelings of security were quickly replaced with blind rage across the country. Lynchjustiz was most likely to occur throughout the final year of the war, even in areas that had hardly been bombed before 1944.[16] Historian Nicholas Stargardt confirmed that while "Germans did not have to be Nazis to fight for Hitler, . . . it was impossible to remain untouched by the ruthlessness of the war and the apocalyptic mentality it created."[17] As the war continued, it became more defensive for Germans, and as a result, the regime's orders became more draconian. The continuous bombings and unfilled promises by the regime—such as the much-anticipated Vergeltungswaffen—along with its inability to defend adequately against the air war, were "catalysts of radical transformation," which were reflected in the continuance of Lynchjustiz.[18] In addition, the devastating loss at Stalingrad in February 1942, the defeat in North Africa in May 1943, and the Allied invasion of Italy and France were turning points in the war against Germany—both strategically and psychologically—and facilitated the Allied advances across Europe. Yet, as Stargardt demonstrated, "the failures of the regime to defend the home front seemed to galvanize people into taking more initiative themselves. It was the regime's failures rather than its successes which imprinted the moral brutality of its core values on so many who did not see themselves as Nazis."[19]

Moreover, the failed assassination attempt on Hitler's life, on July 20, 1944, changed Hitler's attitude with regard to imposing total war, which Joseph Goebbels had promoted for years. Nazi leadership imbued an even more radical sense of purpose following the attempt on Hitler's life. Goebbels was appointed plenipotentiary for total war measures, which resulted in an increasing amount of responsibility for the defense of Germany to the various Gauleiter, who were, for example, involved in expressing the regime's desire to lynch downed airmen. In addition, local autonomy increased among police, party officials, and security forces; for example, RSHA in Berlin delegated decisions about executions to local Gestapo offices.[20] The final step in mobilizing German society for total war was the establishment of the Volkssturm in September 1944. This fully incorporated the remainder of civilians (mostly young boys, old men, and women) into the war effort. Thus, as Stargardt identified, "so many German men and women played active roles in the mass organizations of the party that no sharp line can be drawn between regime and society."[21]

During the war, there was no debate regarding the rationale among perpetrators because their actions were consistent with state-sponsored conduct. The Nazi regime created an environment that enabled and propelled people to commit immoral actions, bolstered considerably by the power and influence of indoctrination. Goebbels pushed the terroristic air war agenda through radio broadcasts, public speeches, and printed publications. People killed or at least abetted in the mistreatment of airmen as a way to seek revenge for personal losses (whether the destruction of property or loss of family) or due to orders given by figures of authority. Often both of these factors influenced perpetrators, which helped counter any hesitation they otherwise might have had.

While the Nazi regime's public promotion of Lynchjustiz, beginning largely in mid-1944, surely escalated the participation of the German population, the violence had already been occurring for at least a year. Even for individuals who were not necessarily ardent Nazis, the devastation caused by the air war united individuals in combat. Perpetrators often shifted the blame for their actions onto the airmen; this was a common perception even decades after the war and resembles what psychologist Jo-Ann Tsang described as "moral rationalization," a process wherein individuals reinterpret their immoral actions as moral.[22] Influenced by psychologist Ervin Staub's theory of the "continuum of destruction,"[23] Tsang stated, "When small acts of harm are committed, perpetrators dehumanize their victims to rationalize their harmful behavior. This dehumanization further obscures the relevance of morality, paving the way for more intense harm."[24]

One of the critical requirements for the success of Nazi Germany's totalitarian regime was obedience, whether through force or acquiescence. The Nazi regime represented one of the most lethal forms of nationalism and attempted to indoctrinate Germans with not only the need to fulfill their duty to the government and the national community but also satisfactorily carry out their desires. Two very well-known psychological studies were undertaken in 1963 and 1971 in an attempt to understand obedience and power, for example how perpetrators carried out the Holocaust, an event that should have left a substantial psychological and moral burden in the minds of perpetrators. The first was psychologist Stanley Milgram's well-known obedience studies, which sought to understand obedience in the context of the Holocaust.[25] Milgram described individuals being in an "agentic state," where they act for an authority they view as legitimate or they are willing to accept responsibility for what occurs; however, individuals acting as agents for the authority often pass the responsibility of the consequences to people who are higher in the authority.[26] The second well-known study was psychologist Philip Zimbardo's 1971 Stanford Prison Experiment, which examined the psychological perception of power.[27] Zimbardo's study revealed that individuals would conform to their expected social roles. Both Milgram and Zimbardo attempted to understand perpetrators' rationalizations in carrying out horrific acts, such as the Holocaust, yet the theories and knowledge learned from these studies is also helpful in rationalizing the actions of perpetrators of Lynchjustiz.

Three key aspects that were vital to the success of the Nazi regime achieving obedience among the German population included role orientation, depersonalization of the individual, and displacement of responsibility. Role orientation meant people acted based on what they perceived the Nazi regime and Hitler would want. People with this characteristic were far less likely to question the moral consequences of an order or their actions; instead, they focused on being a proper and obedient member of the national community. Although not all perpetrators were Nazi Party members, analysis of tried perpetrators revealed an increased implication of role orientation, as over 50 percent belonged to the party.

Depersonalization of the individual was a result of being obedient, as many Nazi Party members saw themselves as tools for a greater cause. According to Tsang, "they felt stripped of volition to choose between good and evil and [therefore] no longer saw themselves as responsible for their actions."[28] By legalizing Lynchjustiz, or at least not punishing Germans for mistreating downed airmen, public involvement became morally justifiable because of governmental support. In addition to the stimulation from war, "feelings of transcendence and anonymity from being a member of an organization such as the Nazi Party could have deindividualized people by obscuring cognitions of discrepancies and responsibility, making it harder for individuals to interpret the situation as morally relevant."[29] Because of this "increase in anonymity [,] an increase in immoral behavior occurred by reducing cues for social evaluations and self-evaluation."[30] This is likely why the written orders for Lynchjustiz only went as far as the Ortsgruppenleiter, while lower-level officials (within the political hierarchy) received orders verbally. This was important for the Nazi regime's desperate desire to combat the Allied air war, as well as the cohesion of society, and that Germans, especially civilians, acted (or were perceived to act) spontaneously against downed airmen with mob violence. The discussion of mistreating airmen in propaganda and especially war experiences sufficed for civilians to partake in Lynchjustiz. Individuals who carried out violence displaced responsibility by redirecting the blame for the violence to those who gave the orders. As renowned political theorist Hannah Arendt described in her analysis of Adolf Eichmann, Eichmann attempted to rationalize his behavior for himself and those judging him at the trial in a similar way. He claimed that he had merely followed orders and that "what he had done was a crime only in retrospect."[31]

Similar defenses were attempted by many Germans in the flyer trials; however, tribunals ruled against any defense based on superior orders. For example, on July 29, 1944, an American bomber was shot down near the village of Ottmannshausen, near the city of Weimar. According to the deposition of Ortsgruppenleiter Fritz Haehnert, German citizens had captured five flyers (most likely crewmembers of the B-17 *Liberty Belle*) immediately upon landing and escorted them to Ottmannshausen to be "lynched and publicly shot" on orders from Kreisleiter Albert Hendrich. Arriving in the village, Hendrich, Haehnert, and security forces (which included Karl Grosch) took the airmen to the house of a woman killed during a previous air raid where the five flyers were "mercilessly beaten and tortured by various persons."[32] While the perpetrators likely chose this house because it was empty and offered a way to deal with the flyers in private, the choice seemed symbolic, especially since the culprits publicly executed the airmen after their mistreatment in the abandoned house. Afterward, the perpetrators hastily buried the bodies in a common grave in the local cemetery at Ottmannshausen; however, the story of these five airmen did not end there. Three days later, local officials had the bodies exhumed and transported to a crematorium in

Weimar (six miles away), where they cremated the flyers' remains. Seeking to conceal the murders, the perpetrators had the remains reburied in the same graves, where they remained until the end of the war.

Two additional cases that offer corroborating examples occurred in October 1944. Three American flyers (believed to be Second Lieutenant Terrel L. Hollis, First Lieutenant Martin J. Mullane, and Technical Sergeant Hoover C. Baucom) parachuted from their bomber and landed near Engenhahn, thirty miles northwest of Frankfurt am Main. Local officials initially captured one airman near Niederseelbach (less than two miles from Engenhahn) and placed him in a room of the local kindergarten "for safekeeping," according to the testimony of the local mayor, Robert Schauer. He ordered two local officials (Ruecker and Willi Christ) to escort the other two flyers from Engenhahn to Niederseelbach. While escorting the two airmen, Ruecker and Christ discussed among themselves the proper treatment of enemy airmen. Ruecker was of the opinion that the flyers should be considered POWs, whereas Christ, influenced by the devastation in nearby Frankfurt caused by the air war, felt that they should be killed. Arriving in Niederseelbach, Schauer ordered Christ and Fritz Amstutz (a longtime member of the Nazi Party and SA) to take each airman individually out of town, under the pretense of taking them to a POW camp, and then execute them, alleging that they had attempted escape.

An unusual aspect of this case, however, is the fact that numerous civilians criticized the mistreatment of the airmen. In fact, while the first captured flyer sat in the room of the local kindergarten, a young girl brought the flyer a glass of tea. Upon discovering this "act of treason," Schauer immediately scolded the girl and said that the Kreisleiter would have her shot if he knew about her "disloyalty."[33] Although the Nazi Party exerted control over the German populace, the regime coerced obedience through situational and psychological circumstances.

That same day, three additional American flyers (First Lieutenant Edmund L. Dornburgh, First Lieutenant Wallace W. Bengson, and Staff Sergeant Franklin W. Adams Jr.) bailed out of their failing bomber near Wieseck, part of the city of Giessen, forty-five miles north of Frankfurt am Main. German citizens immediately captured the crewmembers and escorted them to the local police station at Wieseck. Police director Julius Lassak ordered the local police chief to turn the flyers over to Nazi Party members; however, the police chief refused multiple times because the airmen were POWs and should have been handed over to the Luftwaffe to be imprisoned in a POW camp. Nevertheless, four men, acting on orders from Lassak and Kreisleiter Brueck, forcibly removed the flyers and executed them. Despite acknowledging the directive to turn captured airmen over to the Luftwaffe, Lassak alleged in his trial deposition that failure to adhere to Gestapo and party orders meant certain death.[34] Analysis of the trials indicated that public officials were the most likely to justify their actions by claiming they were following orders.

Curiously, the condoning of Lynchjustiz by the Nazi regime was rarely used by perpetrators as a means to justify their involvement in the violence, at least in trial testimonies and interviews. However, propaganda was relatively identifiable with a significant portion of the German population, especially Goebbels's articles and speeches that portrayed the bombing of Germany as exterminatory. As Stargardt demonstrated, citizens openly referred to the Allied aerial attacks as "Jewish retaliation" for the regime's mistreatment of the Jews.[35] Whether openly discussing the mass execution in letters or privately in diaries, Stargardt revealed that knowledge of what would later be known as the Holocaust was relatively widespread among the German home front. However, the "comments were not a direct commentary on the murder of the Jews. Instead, they came only when people felt that they were being held to account for it by an external power that would retaliate on the victims' behalf."[36] Similar thoughts surely existed regarding Lynchjustiz, as the air war remained a constant and primary concern for the entire population.

Four key tactics that aided perpetrators in rationalizing Lynchjustiz were denunciation, dehumanization, moral exclusion, and advantageous comparisons. The regime "had a strong hand in recognizing the 'will of the *Volk*' and then stirring up and reigning in passions and providing [an authorized] framework for attacks," according to historian S. Johnathan Wiesen.[37] The legality of Lynchjustiz was never officially codified, yet the authorization and promotion of lynching downed airmen resulted in complicity at all levels of German society and throughout German territory. Although the Nazis were relinquishing a degree of power by permitting the German public to seek personal vengeance against downed flyers, they did so only because it served the goals of the regime.

Building on the dehumanization of airmen—for example in portraying American aviators as rapacious African Americans, corrupt mercenaries manipulated by plutocrats, or enemies influenced by a Jewish and Bolshevik struggle for world domination—fed into preexisting Nazi propaganda themes. The Nazi regime utilized tactics in its portrayal of American airmen in propaganda that were similar to the approaches used to promote antisemitism and aiding in constructing an environment that desired and promoted active participation. By attacking the alleged subculture of America, this approach took away the human qualities of the airmen or represented them as subhuman with animal-like traits. This was a common tactic used by governments throughout the world to desensitize their armies to the killing of the enemy or to gather support from the home front for the war effort. In addition, moral exclusion was key in isolating American airmen even further than the traditional enemy, due to German perceptions that airmen carried out an air war that specifically targeted German cities and civilians; something that was conveyed to be outside the realm of German understandings of morality. Thus, propaganda used an advantageous comparison, making Lynchjustiz justifiable because the Allies had allegedly initiated the violence with the air war, which was far more devastating and immoral than the retributive violence against the downed flyers.[38] As strong motivations came into conflict with moral principles, it was more costly for individuals to act morally.[39]

The Nazi government also attempted to justify Lynchjustiz by designating downed airmen as terrorists, as opposed to POWs, in order to legally circumvent the contradiction of unlawful treatment. This was also possibly an attempt to deal with the moral plight that perpetrators could encounter. Although there may have been strafing raids that targeted civilians, especially given the radicalization of the war, their prevalence is impossible to determine due to lack of evidence. Nevertheless, Nazi propaganda used this in its interpretation of the Allied air war, calling for the lynching of flyers who attacked civilians and hospitals. Similar to the discourse about lynching African Americans to avenge the alleged rape of white women at the beginning of the twentieth century in the United States, Nazi propaganda portrayed American flyers as criminals and African Americans who directly targeted German women and children. Perpetrators who defended their actions as merely following superior orders often acknowledged Goebbels's article from May 1944, as well as his weekly radio broadcasts, which openly promoted and urged Germans to seek revenge against Allied flyers. Influenced by the portrayal of American airmen in Nazi propaganda, dysphemisms such as Luftgangster, Terrorflieger, and Kindermörder became a common synonym for describing Allied flyers.

Euphemisms, according to Bandura, provided a "convenient device for masking reprehensible activities. Through convoluted verbiage, destructive conduct is made benign and those who engage in it are relieved of a sense of personal agency."[40] Heavily laden terms, such as Lynchjustiz, *Volksjustiz*, Luftgangster, or Kindermörder, were used to denounce the Allied air war, rile up the German public, and ultimately justify the so-called loyal actions committed against airmen. As Hannah Arendt described, "Language rules are not used to keep people ignorant of massacres but to prevent them from equating massacres with their old, 'normal' knowledge of murder."[41]

The radicalization of war, obedience to figures of authority, and endorsement by the regime, elicited not only the possibility of Lynchjustiz but also moral rationalization of such violence. As Bandura accurately clarified, "Given appropriate social conditions, decent, ordinary people can be led to do extraordinarily cruel things."[42] The correlation between war experience and Lynchjustiz was by far the most compelling of all the outside variables. Analysis of the trials indicated that war experiences particularly influenced civilians and military personnel as they attempted to justify their role in committing Lynchjustiz against downed airmen. Ultimately, the difficult living conditions and the escalation of the war were key to elicit involvement in Lynchjustiz, where average individuals could become criminals by redefining morally acceptable boundaries (both personal and societal) in an attempt to rationalize the shocking and horrific atrocities they perpetrated.[43]

Notes

1. From a speech by Marchus Tillius Cicero given in 52 BCE, *Pro Tito Annio Milone ad iudicem oratio*

2. Christopher Browning, *Ordinary Men: Reserve Police Battalion 101 and the Final Solution in Poland* (New York: Harper Perennial, 1992).

3. Hans Mommsen, "Der Nationalsozialismus: Kumulative Radikalisierung und Selbstzerstörung des Regimes," in *Meyers Enzyklopädisches Lexikon*, vol. 16 (Mannheim: Inter Alia, 1976), 785–90.

4. Daniel Goldhagen, *Hitler's Willing Executioners: Ordinary Germans and the Holocaust* (New York: Vintage Books, 1997).

5. Ian Kershaw, "'Working Towards the Führer' Reflections on the Nature of the Hitler Dictatorship," in *The Third Reich*, ed. Christian Leitz (London: Blackwell, 1999), 240; see also Ian Kershaw, *The Nazi Dictatorship: Problems & Perspectives of Interpretation* (Oxford: Oxford University Press, 2000); Ian Kershaw, *The "Hitler Myth": Image and Reality in the Third Reich* (Oxford: Oxford University Press, 2001); Ian

Kershaw, *Hitler, the Germans, and the Final Solution* (New Haven: Yale University Press, 2009); Ian Kershaw, *Hitler: A Biography* (New York: W. W. Norton, 2010).

6. Whitman, *Hitler's American Model*, 149.

7. Examples include Goldhagen, *Hitler's Willing Executioners*; Barnett, *Bystanders*; Johnson, *Nazi Terror*; Robert Gellately, *Backing Hitler: Consent and Coercion in Nazi Germany* (Oxford: Oxford University Press, 2002); Eric A. Johnson and Karl-Heinz Reuband, *What We Knew: Terror, Mass Murder, and Everyday Life in Nazi Germany* (New York: Basic Books, 2005).

8. Sigel, *Im Interesse der Gerechtigkeit*; Arieh J. Kochavi, *Prelude to Nuremberg: Allied War Crimes Policy and the Question of Punishment* (Chapel Hill: University of North Carolina Press, 1998); Ute, "Die Dachauer Prozesse Und Ihre Bedeutung Im Rahmen Der Alliierten Strafverfolgung Von NS-Verbrechen," 227–35; Neliba, *Lynchjustiz an amerikanischen Kriegsgefangenen in der Opelstadt Rüsselsheim (1944)*; Nigro, *Wolfsangel*; Greene, *Justice at Dachau*; Hilton, *Dachau Defendants*; Mallmann, "Nationalsozialistische Gewaltverbrechen Im Deutschen Reich," 211–12; Riedel, "U.S. War Crimes Tribunals at the Former Dachau Concentration Camp: Lessons for Today," 554–609; Ludwig Eiber and Robert Sigel, *Dachauer Prozesse: NS-Verbrechen vor amerikanischen Militärgerichten in Dachau 1945–48* (Göttingen: Wallstein, 2007); Yavnai, "Military Justice"; James J. Weingartner, *Americans, Germans and War Crimes Justice: Law, Memory, and "The Good War"* (Santa Barbara: Praeger, 2011); Hoffmann, *Fliegerlynchjustiz*.

9. These three influences were influenced by Morton Deutsch, "Psychological Roots of Moral Exclusion," *Journal of Social Issues* 46, no. 1 (1990): 21–25.

10. Hannah Arendt, *Eichmann in Jerusalem: A Report on the Banality of Evil* (New York: Penguin Books, 2006); Browning, *Ordinary Men*; Goldhagen, *Hitler's Willing Executioners*; Johnson, *Nazi Terror*.

11. For example, see Beck, *Fighter Pilot*; Simmons, *Kriegie*; Sommers, *European Story*; Tom Bird, *American POWs in World War II: Forgotten Men Tell Their Stories* (Westport, CT: Praeger, 1992); Bard, *Forgotten Victims*; Colin Burgress, *Destination: Buchenwald* (Kenthurst, Australia: Kangaroo Press, 1995); Thomas Childers, *Wings of Morning* (New York: Addison-Wesley Publishing, 1995); Philip Ardery, *Bomber Pilot: A Memoir of World War II* (Lexington: University Press of Kentucky, 1996); Charles W. Dryden, *A-Train: Memoirs of A Tuskegee Airman* (Tuscaloosa: University of Alabama Press, 1997); Gatewood and Belkham, *Kriegie 7956*; Bodson, *Downed Allied Airmen and Evasion of Capture*; Jefferson and Carlson, *Red Tail Captured, Red Tail Free*; Robert F. Dorr and Thomas D. Jones, *Hell Hawks!: The Untold Story of the American Fliers Who Savaged Hitler's Wehrmacht* (Minneapolis: Zenith Press, 2008).

12. Paul W. Thurner, Andre Klima, and Helmut Küchenhoff, "Agricultural Structure and the Rise of the Nazi Party Reconsidered," *Political Geography* 44 (2015): 62; for more information, see Jürgen W. Falter, "Die 'Märzgefallenen' von 1933: Neue Forschungsergebnisse zum sozialen Wandel innerhalb der NSDAP-Mitgliedschaft während der Machtergreifungsphase," *Historical Social Research/Historische Sozialforschung*, supplement, no. 25, Zur Soziographie des Nationalsozialismus: Studien zu den Wählern und Mitgliedern der NSDAP (2013): 280–302; Jürgen W. Falter, "The Young Membership of the NSDAP between 1925 and 1933: A Demographic and Social Profile," *Historical Social Research/Historische Sozialforschung*, supplement, no. 25, Zur Soziographie des Nationalsozialismus: Studien zu den Wählern und Mitgliedern der NSDAP (2013): 260–79; Jürgen W. Falter, "'Anfälligkeit' der Angestellten—'Immunität' der Arbeiter? Mythen über die

Wähler der NSDAP," *Historical Social Research/Historische Sozialforschung*, supplement, no. 25, Zur Soziographie des Nationalsozialismus: Studien zu den Wählern und Mitgliedern der NSDAP (2013): 90–110; Jürgen W. Falter, "Wählerbewegungen zur NSDAP 1924–1933: Methodische Probleme—Empirisch abgesicherte Erkenntnisse—Offene Fragen," *Historical Social Research/Historische Sozialforschung*, supplement, no. 25, Zur Soziographie des Nationalsozialismus: Studien zu den Wählern und Mitgliedern der NSDAP (2013): 49–89; John O'Loughlin, "The Electoral Geography of Weimar Germany: Explanatory Spatial Data Analysis (ESPDA) of Protestant Support for the Nazi Party," *Society for Political Methodology* 10, no. 3 (2002): 217–43; Colin Flint, "A Timespace for Electoral Geography: Economic Restructuring, Political Agency and the Rise of the Nazi Party," *Political Geography* 20, no. 3 (2001): 301–29; Colin Flint, "Electoral Geography and the Social Construction of Space: The Example of the Nazi Party in Baden, 1924–1932," *GeoJournal* 51, no. 3 (2000): 145–56; Brian Ault and William Brustein, "Joining the Nazi Party: Explaining the Political Geography of NSDAP Membership, 1925–1933," *American Behavioral Scientist* 41, no. 9 (1998): 1304–23; Colin Flint, "Forming Electorates, Forging Spaces: The Nazi Party Vote and the Social Construction of Space," *American Behavioral Scientist* 41, no. 9 (1998): 1282–1300; John O'Loughlin, Colin Flint, and Luc Anselin, "The Geography of the Nazi Vote: Context, Confession, and Class in the Reichstag Election of 1930," *Annals of the Association of American Geographers* 84, no. 3 (1994): 351–80; Thomas Childers, ed., *The Formation of the Nazi Constituency, 1919–1933* (New York: Routledge, 1986).

13. See Nicholas Stargardt, *The German War: A Nation under Arms, 1939–1945* (New York: Basic Books, 2015), 11.

14. According to historian Jill Stephenson, "perhaps ten million German women and children were evacuated [to rural areas in the south and east] by the end of the war" (Jill Stephenson, "The Home Front in 'Total War': Women in Germany and Britain in the Second World War," in *A World at Total War: Global Conflict and the Politics of Destruction, 1937–1945*, ed. Roger Chickering, Stig Förster, and Bernd Greiner [Cambridge: Cambridge University Press, 2004], 218; see also Stargardt, *German War*, 375).

15. Stargardt, *German War*, 360, 374–75; Nicholas Stargardt, "Legitimacy through War?" in *Beyond the Racial State: Rethinking Nazi Germany*, ed. Devin O. Pendas, Mark Roseman, and Richard F. Wetzell (Cambridge: Cambridge University Press, 2017), 411.

16. Stargardt, *German War*, 506.

17. Ibid., 7.

18. Ibid., 8.

19. Ibid., 463.

20. Ibid., 514.

21. Ibid., 517.

22. Jo-Ann Tsang, "Moral Rationalization and the Integration of Situational Factors and Psychological Processes in Immoral Behavior," *Review of General Psychology* 6, no. 1 (2002): 34–35.

23. Ervin Staub, *The Roots of Evil: The Origins of Genocide and Other Group Violence* (New York: Cambridge University Press, 1989), 17.

24. Tsang, "Moral Rationalization," 44–45.

25. Milgram, *Obedience to Authority*.

26. Ibid.
27. Haney, Banks, and Zimbardo, "Interpersonal Dynamics in a Simulated Prison," 69–97.
28. Tsang, "Moral Rationalization," 30.
29. Ibid., 30.
30. Ibid., 30; see also Philip G. Zimbardo, "The Psychology of Evil: A Situationist Perspective on Recruiting Good People to Engage in Anti-Social Acts," *Japanese Journal of Social Psychology* 11, no. 2 (1995): 125–33.
31. Arendt, *Eichmann in Jerusalem*, 24.
32. Review and Recommendations for Case No. 12-1395, Deputy Theater Judge Advocate's Office, War Crimes Branch, Dachau, April 14, 1947, RG 153, Entry 143, Box 357, NARA.
33. Review and Recommendations for Case No. 12-1742, Deputy Theater Judge Advocate's Office, War Crimes Branch, Ludwigsburg, May 13, 1946, RG 153, Entry 143, Box 385, NARA.
34. Review and Recommendations for Case No. 12-1871, Deputy Theater Judge Advocate's Office, War Crimes Branch, Dachau, October 3, 1947, RG 153, Entry 143, Box 396, NARA.
35. Stargardt, *German War*, 375.
36. Stargardt, "Legitimacy through War?," 407.
37. Wiesen, "American Lynching in the Nazi Imagination, 45.
38. Albert Bandura, "Selective Activation and Disengagement of Moral Control," *Journal of Social Values* 46, no. 1 (1990): 33–34.
39. As Bandura emphasized, "Cognitive restructuring of behavior through moral justifications and palliative characterizations is the most effective psychological mechanism for disengagement of moral self-sanctions. . . . Moral restructuring not only eliminates self-deterrents but engages self-approval in the service of destructive exploits. What was once morally condemnable becomes a source of self-valuation. After destructive means become invested with high moral purpose, functionaries work hard to become proficient at them and take pride in their destructive accomplishments" (Bandura, "Selective Activation and Disengagement of Moral Control," 33).
40. Ibid., 31.
41. Arendt, *Eichmann in Jerusalem*, 86.
42. Bandura, "Selective Activation and Disengagement of Moral Control," 40.
43. Ervin Staub, "Genocide and Mass Killings: Origins, Prevention, Healing and Reconciliation," *Political Psychology* 21, no. 2 (2000): 367–82; Albert Bandura, "Social Cognitive Theory of Moral Though and Action," in *Handbook of Moral Behavior and Development*, vol. 1, ed. W. M. Kurtines and J. L. Gewirtz (Hillsdale: Erlbaum, 1991), 45–104; Albert Bandura, "Moral Disengagement in the Perpetration of Inhumanities," *Personality and Social Psychology Review* 3, no. 3 (1999): 193–209.

Conclusion

During the final months of the war, German propaganda focused on future Allied justice and sought to summon a final resistance among the German public. This resulted, according to Norbert Frei, in "a kernel of suspicion to be planted that any justice meted out by the victors was bound to be triumphalist and vengeful."[1] However, the Allies earnestly desired to target individual offenders, the groups to which they belonged, and military and government elites (as opposed to placing blame on German society en masse). The goal was to seek justice for the numerous men, women, and children murdered by the regime, as well as continue the development of international law. The process of un-indoctrinating millions of individuals was one of determination and directness but lacked commitment by occupying nations and the newly formed West German government. The trials did little, however, to dissuade the suspicion of victors' justice as Germans viewed the trials as a burden of occupation.[2] By the end of the 1940s, the trials had fallen "into the same basic disrepute as had denazification, . . . as Germans began working with great determination for an end to the war-crimes trials," according to Frei.[3]

The German public did not believe that only Germans had committed crimes during the war and, therefore, believed they should not be the only ones on trial. They viewed the Allied air war in general as a crime against humanity—for example, the bombing of Dresden in February 1945, which had no military significance and killed tens of thousands of civilians, and of Hiroshima, which was the first use of an atomic weapon in combat. Members of both Catholic and Protestant churches in Germany were vocal in their attempt to end the war crime trials. Director of the Chancellery of the German Protestant Church Hans Asmussen wrote in February 1948 that:

> No rational person, let alone a Christian, can doubt that crimes committed in war ought to be expiated through courts and punishment. But we now have to confront the undeniable fact that public opinion, not only in Germany but also in other countries, says, "Today the generals are on the dock; with a shift in the power balance it would be the generals of the former victorious nations." No power in the world can presently pass equal judgment on *all* those who have committed crimes against humanity over recent years. The legal basis for the trials differs from one country to the next. But without exception, the proceedings are directed at the vanquished. While the intent of the war crimes trials was to render the world's conscience more acute, the result has been the opposite.[4]

With the establishment of the Federal Republic of Germany and the German Democratic Republic in 1949, as well as the emergence of the Cold War, the western Allies, especially the United States, were concerned more about the security of Western Europe. By 1950, the Allies were no longer willing to prosecute the thousands of Germans suspected of war crimes, and it was unlikely that Germany would assume the daunting task that the Allies had abandoned. The lack of "sufficient political will," according to historian David Cohen, from the western Allies and Germany hindered attempts to obtain justice.[5] The extent of Lynchjustiz cases committed within the borders of the German Democratic Republic remains even more uncertain as many cases were never investigated or brought to trial and the documents that existed were either destroyed or lost.[6] According to Günther Wieland (former prosecutor for the Attorney General Office of the German Democratic Republic), "The number of cases dismissed in the German Democratic Republic greatly exceeded those in the Federal Republic of Germany."[7]

Through the Amnesty Laws passed in 1949 and again in 1954, the Federal Republic of Germany pardoned tens of thousands of war criminals in an attempt to move on from the Nazi past by integrating Germans into the new democratic society.[8] In light of the evidence ascertained by the postwar crime trials, the "murder, torture, corporal punishment, and medical or scientific experiments" (Article 32) as well as reprisals

(Article 33) were finally outlawed by the Fourth Geneva Convention in 1949. It was not until 1977, however, that international law prohibited the indiscriminate bombing of civilian targets (Protocol I, Article 51) and attacks on pilots and aircrew (Article 42).[9] This was greatly influenced by the mistreatment of American POWs during the Vietnam War. Despite this, the mistreatment of downed airmen continues to be a potential aspect of present-day wars.

The main problem in understanding the dimensions of Lynchjustiz is due to the lack of remaining documents. This hindered the ability of Allied officials in postwar trials to determine the scale and explanation of the violence. Three main constraints hampered the flyer trials (and the Dachau trials in general): namely, legal limitations (only focusing on violations of the laws of war, which failed to set Lynchjustiz within the greater Nazi system), a lack of resources (relying heavily on imperfect witness testimonies and untrained investigators), and large prosecution load within a relatively short timeframe.

The postwar war crime trials, along with the denazification process, show the great difficulty of an effective judicial response coinciding with a political reintegration process. Ultimately, the trials allowed for an immediate judicial response to the Nazi crimes and helped delegitimize the Third Reich by reeducating and reorientating the German public. Although even Harold Zink, the former chief historian for the United States High Commissioner in Germany, stated, "The achievement [of the postwar crime trials] seems small indeed,"[10] Elisabeth Yavnai defended that they "provided the earliest glimpse into the identity of 'ordinary' war criminals . . . and the attitudes of the German population toward captured American prisoners of war. [Thus] their importance rested in their timing rather than the completeness of evidence or historical narrative."[11]

Only recently have historians started to consider how Lynchjustiz fits into the larger context of organized violence under the Nazi regime.[12] Interestingly, these studies parallel research on German society's experiences living under the bombs. One of the most well-known studies is by historian Jörg Friedrich, who argued that the Allied bombing of Germany was mass murder.[13] While Friedrich attempted unjustly to compare the Allied air war to the Holocaust, the debate that followed, as Hoffmann described, "expanded the limits of the air war discourse to include the effect of the air war on society, leadership, as well as how it had since been remembered."[14]

Figure 7.1. Memorial plaque to the seven airmen killed on the island of Borkum (Second Lieutenant Havey M. Walthall, Second Lieutenant William J. Myers, Second Lieutenant Howard S. Graham, Sergeant Kenneth Faber, Sergeant James W. Danno, Sergeant William F. Dold, and Sergeant William W. Lambertus). *Courtesy of SPBer (July 19, 2012) / Creative Commons / CC BY-SA 3.0 / https://de.wikipedia.org/wiki/Datei: Gedenktafel_B_-17_Borkum.JPG.*

While the issue of Lynchjustiz remained largely overlooked for more than fifty years after the war, beginning in the early 2000s German communities started to research the topic through explorations of local and regional histories during the war.[15] The war generation's descendants, who had little to no direct experience with the air war and who had different perspectives on the war in general (though they still lived with its effects), began to question the memories of the war. Gradually, the discourse pertaining to Lynchjustiz committed against downed airmen is becoming less taboo; however, it often remains an open secret. The willingness and openness to discuss this extralegal violence are still wanting.

As a result of this initial research about Lynchjustiz, German communities began to create memorials in the early 2000s for the Allied airmen victimized during the war. The earliest known memorial (fig. 7.1) was commemorated on August 4, 2003, on the island of Borkum and listed the names of the seven American airmen who "were killed under tragic circumstances" on August 4, 1944 (fifty-nine years later to the day). The local Rotary Club in Borkum sponsored the memorial.

Figure 7.2. Front side of the memorial to the eight American flyers beaten in Rüsselsheim. *Taken by the author on February 3, 2018.*

The following year, the city of Rüsselsheim commemorated a memorial (nearly sixty years to the day) to the eight American bomber crewmembers who were beaten (six of whom died) on August 26, 1944 (figs. 7.2 and 7.3). One side of the memorial offers images of each flyer, and the reverse is constructed of the original brick wall against which the flyers were executed.

In 2009, an ongoing art project initiated by German artist Gunter Demnig to commemorate victims of the Holocaust, and Nazi terror in general, included several cases of Lynchjustiz against downed Allied airmen in Germany. As the world's largest decentralized memorial, *Stolpersteine* (stumbling stones) are concrete cubes covered in brass and engraved, for example, with the victim's name, date of birth, date of death, and last known whereabouts or location of death (fig. 7.4). Demnig places the Stolpersteine, financed largely by private donations, at the individual's last known residence before becoming a victim of Nazi terror. The Stolpersteine for Allied flyers mark the location where they were mistreated. While there are over fifty-six thousand Stolpersteine throughout Europe, to this point there are only six known in

Figure 7.3. The memorial to the eight American flyers beaten in Rüsselsheim. *Left to right, top*: Sergeant Elmore L. Austin, Sergeant William A. Dumont, Second Lieutenant Norman J. Rogers Jr., and Second Lieutenant John N. Sekul; *bottom*: Field Officer Haigus Tufenkjian, Staff Sergeant Thomas D. Williams Jr., Sergeant William A. Adams, and Sergeant Sidney Eugene Brown. *Taken by the author on February 3, 2018.*

remembrances of British flyers murdered in Germany (and none for US airmen).

As communities continue to support local historical research, additional memorials are gradually being created to honor the victims, which assists in bringing these forgotten crimes into the public discourse. In Gross-Gerau, for example, a plaque in the town museum was commemorated in August 2018 to Second Lieutenant Charles H. Evans Jr. and Technical Sergeant Harvey J. Purkey Jr., who were murdered on August 29, 1944. In September 2018, a plaque was dedicated in Essen to three British airmen (Field Officer Michael Gisby, Field Officer Leon Milner, and Sergeant Harry Mawson) who were murdered on December 13, 1944, by a mob of civilians by being thrown from a bridge and then shot.[16] Most recently, the city of Wolfsburg is working on a memorial for Second Lieutenant Sydney A. Benson, who was murdered on June 29, 1944.

Figure 7.4. The Stolperstein dedicated to British flyer Cyril W. Sibley in Dirmstein, where he was murdered on February 21, 1945. *Courtesy of Albert H. Keil (March 20, 2011) / Creative Commons / CC BY-SA 3.0/ https://de.wikipedia.org/wiki/ Datei:2009-Dirmstein-Sibley.jpg#filelinks.*

Throughout the postwar era, holes where buildings no longer stood dotted the cityscapes of Germany and were a constant reminder of the air war.[17] Even after cities were rebuilt, Germans frequently discovered Allied bombs, often during construction projects and excavations. In fact, evacuations caused by Allied bombs still remain a regular occurrence (several per a month) throughout Germany; tens of thousands of individuals are forced from their homes, schools, and places of business for several hours while the bombs are defused. Occasionally, officials have no choice but to detonate the bomb, which can cause severe damage.

While the continual discovery of bombs is a recurring reminder of the Nazi past and the persistent influence of the air war on present-day Germany, the constant disruptions and inconveniences to normal life still have not facilitated a significant change to the limited discourse of Lynchjustiz. Despite this, Germany has made great strides in coming to terms with its National Socialist past. The continual discovery and identification of downed airmen's remains, along with German communities' support for local historical research and further analysis by historians, should greatly assist in raising awareness of Lynchjustiz—the extent to which it occurred and its historical significance. While it is important to remember the horrific violence that downed airmen faced, it is also key to recognize these instances within the context of the air war and the experiences of those living under the bombs. As the memorial inscription in Rüsselsheim urges, we, as humans, must "recall our common humanity."[18]

Identifying the boundaries of radicalization in war and acknowledging and learning from the past are the best methods to prevent similar escalations in the future. Analyzing the violence of Lynchjustiz can, therefore, provide an understanding of the nature of dictatorial terror as well as evil itself.[19] Moreover, understanding the process of Lynchjustiz permits further clarification about the complex relationship between war and society. As exhibited in the hundreds of known cases of violence committed against American airmen during World War II, moral rationalization could be altered relatively quickly in an attempt to justify the radicalizing violence. While Lynchjustiz committed against flyers was horrific and widespread, it represented a minority of downed airmen. This indicates that the effects of the radicalized war did not perversely destroy people's sense of morality, ethics, and the rule of law, as one might have thought, given the scale of atrocities committed by Germany during the war.

The air war, compelled by the radicalization of Nazi atrocities, removed any form of security on the German home front. As a consequence, the Nazi regime sought to harness the outrage of the German population, redirecting its anger explicitly against downed flyers. The regime took advantage of German citizens' vulnerability in the overwhelming and ever more lethal air war that erased nearly all boundaries between battlefront and home front. While a large portion of German society likely desired retribution against downed airmen for their role in the war, a minority of Germans—largely, Alte Kämpfer and other ardent supporters of the regime, along with individuals who were deeply affected by the devastating air war or influenced by propaganda and those in positions of authority—actually resorted to carrying out Lynchjustiz.

While many perpetrators argued that they were ordered to partake in the violence and that any opposition would have resulted in death, it is important to remember that these criminals, especially party officials and security forces, created these false and self-serving characterizations in an attempt to escape prosecution after the war. An interpretation that points to limited civilian involvement in Lynchjustiz is similarly misguided. As when, for example, historians published in studies from the 1990s, German citizens willingly took part in violence under the Nazi regime, which itself relied heavily on voluntary and emphatic civilian participation.[20] This fact should not obscure, however, the enormous culpability of lower-level officials, for example police, party officials, and security forces, in ordering and personally carrying out the violence against downed airmen.

Although Nazi Germany was a police state, it "allowed most of its citizens considerable room . . . for the venting of everyday frustrations," as Eric A. Johnson has stressed.[21] Lynchjustiz is a significant example of this. The regime allowed violence against downed airmen to ease the mounting pressure within the German population, as living under the bombs and among the ruins increased anxiety, fear, and anger.[22] Moreover, this form of violence facilitated the Nazi regime's pursuit of maintaining control over German society. Thus, Lynchjustiz not only offered a professed line of defense in the drastic downfall of the Third Reich but also provided an ancillary attempt for citizens to seek revenge, soothe public anger, and put fear in the minds of airmen flying over Germany.

Notes

1. Frei, *Adenauer's Germany and the Nazi Past*, 93.
2. For a German public opinion study, see Richard L. Merritt, *Democracy Imposed: U.S. Occupation Policy and the German Public 1945–1949* (New Haven: Yale University Press, 1995).
3. Frei, *Adenauer's Germany and the Nazi Past*, 94.
4. Evangelisches Zentralarchiv (EZA), 2/265, Asmussen to Bell, February 14, 1948 (italics in original), from Frei, *Adenauer's Germany and the Nazi Past*, 100.
5. David Cohen, "Transitional Justice in Divided Germany After 1945," in *Retribution and Reparation in the Transition to Democracy*, ed. Jon Elster (Cambridge: Cambridge University Press, 2006), 75–77.
6. According to a collection of German war crime trials edited by C. F. Rüter and D. W. de Mildt, there were at least six trials (including seven American airmen) held by the Federal Republic of Germany and eight trials (including eleven American airmen) held by the German Democratic Republic. For more information, see C. F. Rüter and D. W. de Mildt, eds., *DDR-Justiz und NS-Verbrechen: Sammlung Ostdeutsche Strafurteile wegen Nationalsozialistische Tötungsverbrechen, 1945–1999, Bd.*

1–14 (Rüter: Amsterdam University Press, 1968–2012); C. F. Rüter and D. W. de Mildt, eds., *Justiz und NS-Verbrechen: Sammlung Deutscher Strafurteile wegen Nationalsozialistische Tötungsverbrechen, 1945–1999, Bd. 1–49* (Rüter: Amsterdam University Press, 1968–2012).

7. Letter from Günther Wieland to Prof. Dr. Olaf Groehler (Zentralinstitut für Geschichte der Akademie der Wissenschaften der DDR), March 30, 1984, Bundesarchiv Berlin-Lichterfelde DP 3/2223. The original German text states: "Obwohl demgegenüber in der Bundesrepublik Deutschland allenfalls gegen an der Tötung alliierter Flieger beteiligte Personen Anklage erhoben wurde, liegen die in der Deutsche Demokratische Republik ausgeworfenen Strafen ganz wesentlich über denen in der Bundesrepublik Deutschland."

8. German historian Norbert Frei characterized this as *Vergangenheitspolitik* (policy of the past) (*Adenauer's Germany and the Nazi Past*, 33). See also Norbert Frei, *Vergangenheitspolitik* (Munich: Verlag C.H. Beck, 1997).

9. International Committee of the Red Cross, "Treaties, States Parties and Commentaries: Convention (IV) Relative to the Protection of Civilian Persons in Time of War. Geneva, 12 August 1949," https://ihl-databases.icrc.org/ihl/385ec082b509e76c41256739003e636d/6756482d86146898c125641e004aa3c5, accessed May 24, 2016; International Committee of the Red Cross, "Treaties, States Parties and Commentaries: Protocol Additional to the Geneva Conventions on 12 August 1949, and Relating to the Protection of Victims of International Armed Conflicts (Protocol I), 8 June 1977," https://ihl-databases.icrc.org/ihl/INTRO/470, accessed May 24, 2016.

10. Harold Zink, *The United States in Germany, 1944–55* (Princeton, NJ: D. Van Nostrand, 1957), 164; Cohen, "Transitional Justice," 75.

11. Yavnai, "Military Justice," 252–53.

12. Hoffmann, *Fliegerlynchjustiz*, 369.

13. Friedrich, *Fire*.

14. Hoffmann, *Fliegerlynchjustiz*, 371. Original German text: "Die Folge war eine Perspektivenerweiterung, die sich besonders in der Thematisierung der Wirkungen des Bombekrieges auf die Gesellschaft aber auch auf 'Herrschaft' sowie Erinnerung manifestierte."

15. Neliba, *Lynchjustiz an amerikanischen Kriegsgefangenen in der Opelstadt Rüsselsheim (1944)*; Nigro, *Wolfsangel*.

16. For more information, see Sean Feast and Marc Hall, *Missing—Presumed Murdered: One Raid, Two Trials, Three Lost Airmen* (Hitchin, UK: Fighting High, 2018).

17. These are known as *Bombenlücke*.

18. Anglican priest Paul Oestreicher's speech at the commemoration of the memorial (August 26, 2004) to the eight American flyers lynched in Rüsselsheim.

19. Johnson, *Nazi Terror*, 464.

20. For example, see Browning, *Ordinary Men*; Goldhagen, *Hitler's Willing Executioners*.

21. Johnson, *Nazi Terror*, 485.

22. Hoffmann, *Fliegerlynchjustiz*, 189.

Appendix A
Lynchjustiz Documents

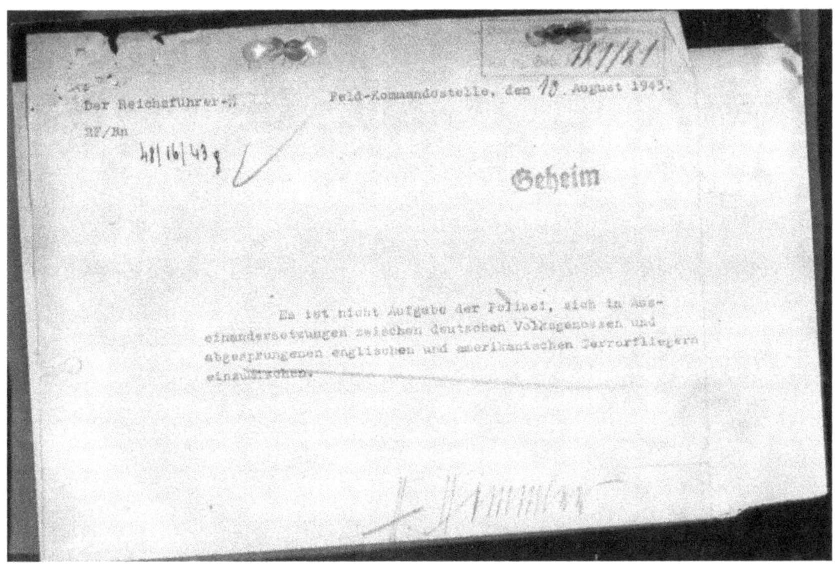

Der Reichsführer-SS
RF/Bn

Feld-Kommandostelle, den 10. August 1943.

Geheim

Es ist nicht Aufgabe der Polizei, sich in Auseinandersetzungen zwischen deutschen Volksgenossen und abgesprungenen englischen und amerikanischen Terrorfliegern einzumischen.

Figure A.1 Secret circular from Heinrich Himmler to SS officials and commanders of the OrPo and SiPo, August 10, 1943. *Order from Heinrich Himmler, August 10, 1943, Case Number 12-2000, Vol 36: Treatment of Enemy Terror Fliers and Sabotage Troops, RG 549, Entry A1 2238, Microfilm T1021, Roll 10, Frame No. 771, NARA, https://catalog.archives.gov/id/40957462.*

German Transcription

Es ist nicht Aufgabe der Polizei, sich in Auseinandersetzungen zwischen deutschen Volksgenossen und abgesprungenen englischen und amerikanischen Terrorfliegern einzumischen.

English Translation

"It is not the job of the police to interfere between the German folk [*Volksgenossen*] and downed English and American terror flyers."

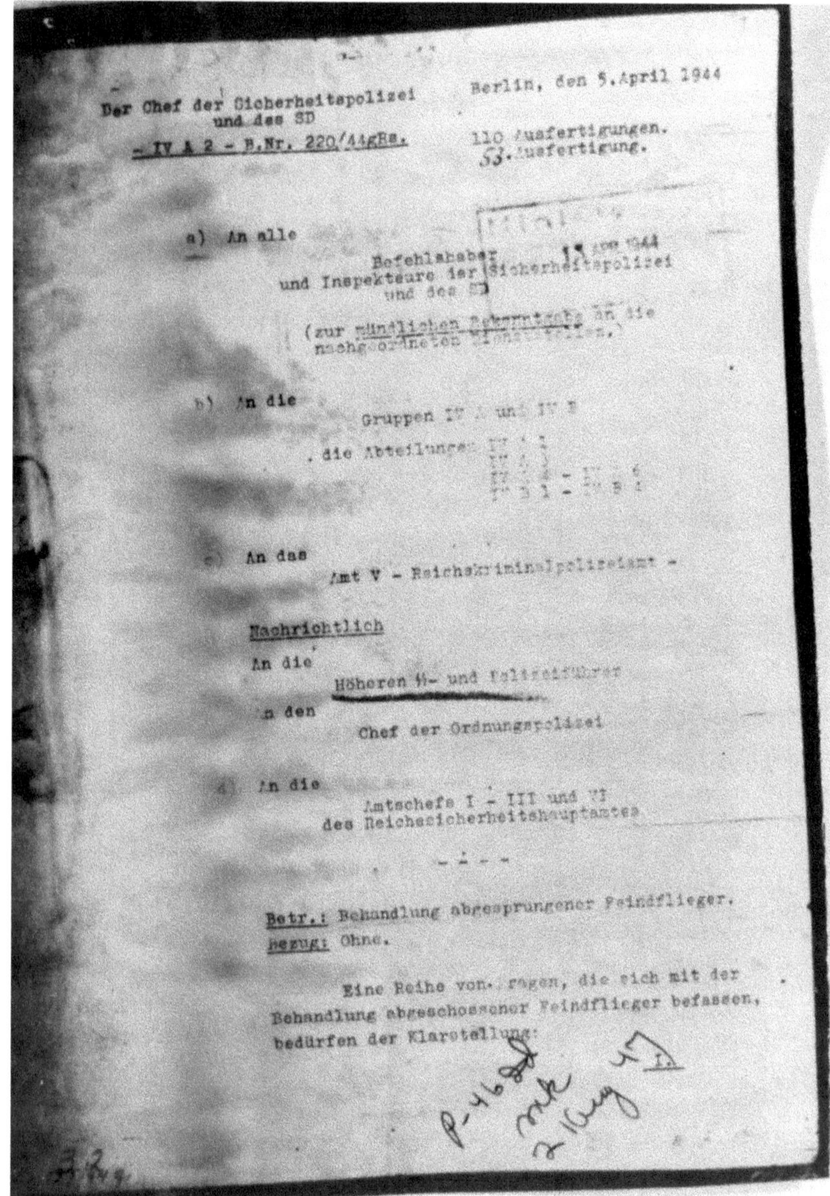

Der Chef der Sicherheitspolizei
und des SD
- IV A 2 - B.Nr. 220/44gRs.

Berlin, den 5.April 1944

110 Ausfertigungen.
53. Ausfertigung.

a) An alle
Befehlshaber
und Inspekteure der Sicherheitspolizei
und des SD
(zur mündlichen Bekanntgabe an die
nachgeordneten Dienststellen.)

b) An die
Gruppen IV A und IV B
die Abteilungen [illegible]

c) An das
Amt V - Reichskriminalpolizeiamt -

Nachrichtlich

An die
Höheren SS- und Polizeiführer

An den
Chef der Ordnungspolizei

d) An die
Amtschefs I - III und VI
des Reichssicherheitshauptamtes

- 1 -

Betr.: Behandlung abgesprungener Feindflieger.
Bezug: Ohne.

Eine Reihe von Fragen, die sich mit der Behandlung abgeschossener Feindflieger befassen, bedürfen der Klarstellung:

Figure A.2–A.5 "Treatment of Downed Enemy Flyers." Directive from the chief of the SiPo and the SD in Berlin to all commanders of the SiPo and the SD, RSHA, SS, and Polizeiführer; chief of the OrPo; and the chiefs of the RSHA, April 5, 1944. *Case Number 12-1077, Vol 8: Treatment of Captured Enemy Pilots and Lynch Law, RG 549, Entry A1 2238, Microfilm T1021, Roll 10, Frame No. 000465–000468, NARA, https://catalog.archives.gov/id/40957462.*

I.

Aufgegriffene feindliche Flieger sind grundsätzlich zu f e s s e l n. Diese Maßnahme ist erforderlich und geschieht in voller Billigung des Chefs des Oberkommandos der Wehrmacht

a) zur Verhinderung der häufigen Fluchtfälle und
b) im Hinblick auf die äusserst angespannte Personallage bei den Erfassungsorganen.

II.

Feindliche Flugzeugbesatzungen, die

a) bei Festnahme Widerstand leisten oder
b) unter der Uniform Zivilkleidung tragen,

unmittelbar bei Festnahme zu erschiessen.

III.

Feindflieger – insbesondere der anglo-amerikanischen Luftwaffe – führen meist Fluchtsäcke gefüllt [illegible], verschiedensten Arten von Landkarten, [illegible]mitteln[illegible], Ausbruchswerkzeugen usw. bei [illegible].

Fluchtsäcke sind vor Polizeiorganen unbedingt [illegible]zustellen, da sie wichtigste Fahndungs-Hilfs[illegible] darstellen. Weiterleitung an Luftwaffe erforderlich.

IV.

Der Reichsführer-SS Befehl vom 10.8.1943 findet [illegible]teil keine Beachtung, da er bis zu den unter[illegible] Polizei-Dienststellen wahrscheinlich nicht [illegible] befohlen – mündlich übermittelt worden ist. [illegible]rd daher wiederholt:

"Es ist nicht Aufgabe der Polizei, sich in Auseinandersetzungen zwischen deutschen Volksgenossen und abgesprungenen englischen und amerikanischen Terrorfliegern einzumischen."

V.

83

V.

Bei der Leiche eines abgeschossenen englischen Fliegers wurde eine Armbinde mit Aufschrift "Deutsche Wehrmacht" und gültigem Stempel gefunden. Diese Armbinde wird nur von Kombattanten getragen und gibt dem Träger in den verschiedenen Operationsgebieten überall Zugang zu militärischen und strategisch wichtigen Punkten. Abgesetzte feindliche Agenten werden vermutlich Gebrauch von diesem neuen Tarnungsmittel machen.

VI.

Einzelfälle der letzten Monate haben gezeigt, dass die deutsche Bevölkerung zwar Feindflieger festnimmt, aber dann diesen gegenüber bis zur Ablieferung bei Polizei oder Wehrmacht nicht den entsprechenden Abstand wahrt. Zu harte staatspolizeiliche Maßnahmen gegen diese Volksgenossen würden abhalten, sich bei Festnahme von Feindfliegern vorbehaltlos einzusetzen, zumal diese Fälle nicht verwechselt werden dürfen mit dem Verbrechen einer Unterstützung flüchtiger Feindflieger.

Reichsführer-SS hat folgende Maßnahmen gegen Volksgenossen, die sich aus böser Absicht oder falsch verstandenem Mitleid gegenüber gefangengenommenen feindlichen Fliegern würdelos verhalten, befohlen:

1.) In besonders krassen Fällen Einweisung in ein Konzentrationslager. Bekanntgabe in den Zeitungen des Bezirks.
2.) In leichteren Fällen Schutzhaft nicht unter 14 Tagen bei der zuständigen Staatspolizeistelle. Einsatz zu Aufräumungsarbeiten in den Schadensgebieten.

Falls

34

Falls im Bereich einer Staatspolizeistelle zum Einsatz geeignete Schadensgebiete nicht vorhanden sind, ist die kurzfristige Schutzhaft bei der nächstgelegenen Staatspolizeistelle zu vollstrecken. Da es sich dabei immer um leichtere Fälle handelt, bestehen, um unnötige Belastungen der Dienststellen zu vermeiden, keine Bedenken dagegen, wenn der Betreffende auf Grund einer staatspolizeilichen Auflage auf eigene Kosten ohne Begleitung zu der ihm benannten Staatspolizeistelle fährt und sich dort zur Verbüssung der Schutzhaft meldet.

Die Entscheidung, ob es sich um einen krassen oder um einen leichten Fall handelt, ist nach Ermittlungen und Anhörung der Partei, unter Gesamtwürdigung der Persönlichkeit des Täters von dem Leiter der zuständigen Staatspolizeistelle zu treffen. Kurzbericht (nicht FS.) mit Personalien des Täters und Angabe, ob leichter oder krasser Fall, an Reichssicherheitshauptamt.

Reichsführer-SS hat sich in dieser Angelegenheit an Reichsleiter B o r m a n n gewandt und darauf hingewiesen, dass es Aufgabe der Hoheitsträger der Partei ist, aufklärend auf die Bevölkerung zu wirken, den unbedingt notwendigen Abstand gegenüber Feindfliegern zu wahren.

\- - - -

Den Befehlshabern und Inspekteuren der Sicherheitspolizei und des SD stelle ich anheim, den Absatz V und VI des vorstehenden Erlasses auch schriftlich an die nachgeordneten Dienststellen weiterzugeben.

gez. Dr. K a l t e n b r u n n e r.

Beglaubigt:
Rose
Kanzleiangestellte.

German Transcription

I

Aufgegriffene feindliche Flieger sind grundsätzlich zu fesseln. Diese Maßnahme ist erforderlich und geschieht in voller Billigung des Chefs der Oberkommando der Wehrmacht.

A. *Zur Verhinderung der häufigen Fluchtfälle und*

B. *im Hinblick auf die* äußerst *angespannte Personallage bei den Erfassungsorgangen.*

II

Feindliche Flugzeugbesatzungen, die

A. *bei Festnahme Widerstand leisten oder*

B. *unter der Uniform Zivilkleidung tragen, unmittelbar bei Festnahme zu erschießen.*

III

Feindflieger—insbesondere der anglo-amerikanischer Luftwaffe—führen meist Fluchtsäcke gefüllt mit [illegible], *verschiedensten Arten von Landkarten, Lebensmittelmarken, Ausbruchewerkzeugen usw. bei sich. Fluchtsäcke sind von Polizeiorganen unbedingt sicherzustellen, da sie wichtigste Fahndungs-Hilfsmittel darstellen. Weiterleitung an Luftwaffe erforderlich.*

IV

Der Reichsführer-SS Befehl vom 10.8.1943 findet zum Teil keine Beachtung, da er bis zu den untergeordneten Polizei-Dienststellen wahrscheinlich nicht—wie befohlen—mündlich übermittelt worden ist.

Er wird daher wiederholt:

"Es ist nicht Aufgabe der Polizei, sich in Auseinandersetzungen zwischen deutschen Volksgenossen und abgesprungenen englischen und amerikanischen Terrorflieger einzumischen."...

V

Bei der Leiche eines abgeschossenen englischen Fliegers wurde eine Armbinde mit Aufschrift "Deutsche Wehrmacht" und gültigem Stempel gefunden. Diese Armbinde wird nur von Kombattanten getragen und gibt dem Träger in den verschiedenen Operationsgebieten überall Zugang zu militärischen und strategisch wichtigen Punkten. Abgeordnete feindliche Agenten werden vermutlich Gebrauch von diesem neuen Tarnungsmittel machen.

VI

Einzelfälle der letzten Monate haben gezeigt, dass die deutsche Bevölkerung zwar Feindflieger festnimmt, aber dann diesen gegenüber bis zur Ablieferung bei Polizei oder Wehrmacht nicht den entsprechenden Abstand wahrt. Zu harte staatspolizeiliche Maßnahmen gegen diese Volksgenossen würden sie abhalten, sich bei Festnahme von Feindfliegern vorbehaltlos einzusetzen, zumal diese Fälle nicht verwechselt werden dürfen mit dem Verbrechen einer Unterstützung flüchtiger Feindflieger.

Reichsführer-SS hat folgende Maßnahmen gegen Volksgenossen, die sich aus böser Absicht oder falsch verstandenem Mitleid gegenüber gefangengenommenen feindlichen Fliegern würdelos verhalten, befohlen:

1. *In besonders krassen Fällen Einweisung in ein Konzentrationslager. Bekanntgabe in den Zeitungen des Bezirks.*

2. *In leichteren Fällen Schutzhaft nicht unter 14 Tage bei der zuständigen Staatspolizeistelle. Einsatz zu Aufräumungsarbeiten in den Schadensgebieten.* <\>

Falls im Bereich einer Staatspolizeistelle zum Einsatz geeignete Schadensgebiete nicht vorhanden sind, ist die kurzfristige Schutzhaft bei der nächstgelegenen Staatspolizeistelle zu vollstrecken. Da es sich dabei immer um leichtere Fälle handelt, bestehen, um unnötige Belastungen der Dienststellen zu vermeiden, keine Bedenken dagegen, wenn der Betroffene auf Grund einer staatspolizeilichen Auflage auf eigene Kosten ohne Begleitung zu der ihm genannten Staatspolizeistelle fährt und sich dort zur Verbüßung der Schutzhaft meldet.

Die Entscheidung, ob es sich um einen krassen oder einen leichten Fall handelt, ist nach Ermittlungen und Anhörung der Partei, unter Gesamtwürdigung der Persönlichkeit des Täters von dem Leiter der zuständigen Staatspolizeistelle zu treffen. Kurzbericht (nicht FS.) mit Personalien des Täters und Angabe, ob leichter oder krasser Fall, an Reichssicherheitshauptamt.

Reichsführer-SS hat sich in dieser Angelegenheit an Reichsleiter Bormann gewandt und darauf hingewiesen, dass es Aufgabe der Hoheitsträger der Partei ist, aufklärend auf die Bevölkerung zu wirken, den unbedingt notwendigen Abstand gegenüber Feindfliegern zu wahren.

English Translation

I

In principle, captured enemy airmen are to be restrained. This measure is required and fully approved by the Chief of the High Command of the Wehrmacht.

A. To prevent frequent escapes and

B. In view of the extremely tense staff situation at the registration office.

II

Hostile air crews who

A. Offer resistance during their arrest or

B. Wear civilian clothes under their uniform, are to be shot immediately upon arrest.

III

Enemy flyers—especially the English and American Air Forces—usually carry escape bags filled with various types of maps, food stamps, escape tools, etc. Escape bags must always be secured by police, as they are the most important tools to escape. Forwarding to the Luftwaffe is necessary.

IV

The Reichsführer-SS order from August 10, 1943 is partially ignored, as it probably was not sent to the subordinate police departments—as ordered—verbally.

It is therefore repeated:

"It is not the job of the police to interfere between *Volksgenossen* and downed English and American terror flyers." . . .

V

An armband with the inscription "Deutsche Wehrmacht" and a valid stamp was found on the corpse of a downed English flyer. This armband is worn only by combatants and gives the wearer full access to military and strategically important points in various areas. Enemy agents will likely make use of this new means of disguise.

VI

In recent months, individual cases have shown that the German population detains enemy flyers but then does not maintain the appropriate distance from them for delivery to the police or Wehrmacht. Measures by the police that are too harsh toward these citizens would discourage their unconditional involvement in the capture of enemy flyers. These cases must not be confused with the crime of supporting fleeing enemy airmen.

Reichsführer-SS has ordered the following measures against citizens who behave dubiously, maliciously or who show pity toward captured enemy airmen:

1. In particularly blatant cases, admission to a concentration camp. Announcement in the newspapers of the district.

2. In minor cases, protective custody not less than 14 days at the responsible state police station. Use for cleanup work in the damaged areas.

If there are no suitable areas of damage to clean up in the jurisdiction of the state police, the short-term protective custody is to be enforced at the nearest state police station. Since these are always lighter cases, in order to avoid unnecessary burdens on the units, there are no objections if, on the basis of a state police order, the person concerned drives at his own expense (unaccompanied) to the state police station and serves his sentence.

After an investigation and hearing by the party, which takes into consideration the personality of the perpetrator, the decision as to whether it is an extreme or a mild case, is decided by the head of the state police department. Send a short report with personal details of the offender and decision, whether mild or harsh case, to the Reich Main Security Office (RSHA).

Concerning this matter, Reichsführer-SS turned to Reichsleiter Bormann and pointed out that it is the party's responsibility to educate the population accordingly and to maintain a necessary distance from enemy airmen."

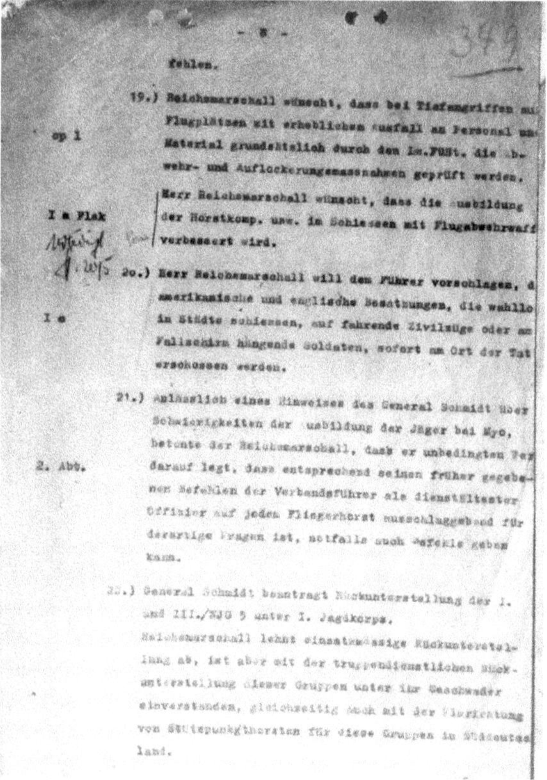

- 8 -

fehlen.

19.) Reichsmarschall wünscht, dass bei Tiefangriffen au Flugplätzen mit erheblichem Ausfall an Personal und Material grundsätzlich durch den Lw.Füst. die Abwehr- und Auflockerungsmassnahmen geprüft werden.

op 1

I a Flak

Herr Reichsmarschall wünscht, dass die Ausbildung der Horstkomp. usw. im Schiessen mit Flugabwehrwaff verbessert wird.

I e

20.) Herr Reichsmarschall will dem Führer vorschlagen, d amerikanische und englische Besatzungen, die wahllo in Städte schiessen, auf fahrende Zivilzüge oder am Fallschirm hängende Soldaten, sofort am Ort der Tat erschossen werden.

2. Abt.

21.) Anlässlich eines Hinweises des General Schmidt über Schwierigkeiten der Ausbildung der Jäger bei Nyo, betonte der Reichsmarschall, dass er unbedingten Wer darauf legt, dass entsprechend seinen früher gegebenen Befehlen der Verbandsführer als dienstältester Offizier auf jedem Fliegerhorst ausschlaggebend für derartige Fragen ist, notfalls auch Befehle geben kann.

22.) General Schmidt beantragt Rückunterstellung der I. und III./NJG 5 unter I. Jagdkorps.
Reichsmarschall lehnt einsatzmässige Rückunterstellung ab, ist aber mit der truppendienstlichen Rückunterstellung dieser Gruppen unter ihr Geschwader einverstanden, gleichzeitig auch mit der Einrichtung von Stützpunktthorsten für diese Gruppen in Süddeutschland.

Figure A.6 "Jägerbesprechung beim Reichsmarschall Göring." Notes from Meeting with Hermann Göring, General Galland, Generalmajor Schmidt, and Generalmajor Kreipe, May 19, 1944. *Notes from Meeting with Göring and Luftwaffe Officials, May 19, 1944, RG 549, Entry A1 2238, Microfilm T1021, Roll 10, Frame No. 487–495, NARA, https://catalog.archives.gov/id/40957462.*

German Transcription

Herr Reichsmarschall (Göring) *will dem Führer vorschlagen, dass amerikanische und englische Besatzungen, die wahllos in Städte Schießen, auf fahrende Zivilszuge oder am Fallschirm hängende Soldaten, sofort am Ort der Tat erschossen werden.*

English Translation

Reichsmarschall (Göring) wants to suggest to the Führer that American and British crews who indiscriminately target towns, passenger trains, or soldiers in parachutes are to be shot immediately upon capture.

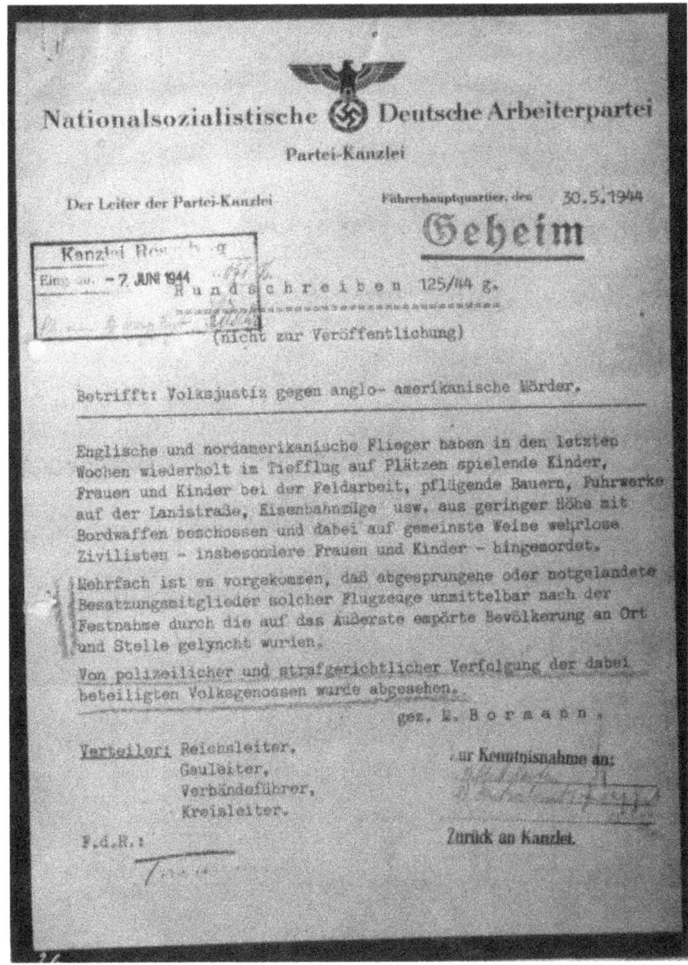

Nationalsozialistische Deutsche Arbeiterpartei

Partei-Kanzlei

Der Leiter der Partei-Kanzlei

Führerhauptquartier, den 30.5.1944

Geheim

Kanzlei Ros[illegible]
Eing. – 7. JUNI 1944

Rundschreiben 125/44 g.

(nicht zur Veröffentlichung)

Betrifft: Volksjustiz gegen anglo- amerikanische Mörder.

Englische und nordamerikanische Flieger haben in den letzten Wochen wiederholt im Tiefflug auf Plätzen spielende Kinder, Frauen und Kinder bei der Feldarbeit, pflügende Bauern, Fuhrwerke auf der Landstraße, Eisenbahnzüge usw. aus geringer Höhe mit Bordwaffen beschossen und dabei auf gemeinste Weise wehrlose Zivilisten – insbesondere Frauen und Kinder – hingemordet.

Mehrfach ist es vorgekommen, daß abgesprungene oder notgelandete Besatzungsmitglieder solcher Flugzeuge unmittelbar nach der Festnahme durch die auf das Äußerste empörte Bevölkerung an Ort und Stelle gelyncht wurden.

Von polizeilicher und strafgerichtlicher Verfolgung der dabei beteiligten Volksgenossen wurde abgesehen.

gez. M. Bormann.

Verteiler: Reichsleiter,
Gauleiter,
Verbändeführer,
Kreisleiter.

[Z]ur Kenntnisnahme an:

Zurück an Kanzlei.

F.d.R.:

Figure A.7. "Volksjustiz against Anglo-American Murderers," secret circular (not for publication) from Martin Bormann to Reichsleiter, Gauleiter, Verbändeführer, and Kreisleiter, May 30, 1944. *Order from Martin Bormann to Reichsleiter, Gauleiter, Verbändeführer, and Kreisleiter, May 30, 1944, Case Number 12-2000, Vol 36: Treatment of Enemy Terror Flyers and Sabotage Troops, RG 549, Entry A1 2238, Microfilm T1021, Roll 10, Frame No. 000764, NARA, https://catalog.archives.gov/id/40957462.*

German Transcription

Englische und nordamerikanische Flieger haben in den letzten Wochen wiederholt in Tiefflug auf Plätzen spielende Kinder, Frauen und Kinder bei der Feldarbeit, pflügende Bauern, Fuhrwerke auf der Landstraße, Eisenbahnzüge usw. aus geringer Höhe mit Bordwaffen beschossen und dabei auf gemeinste Weise wehrlose Zivilisten—insbesondere Frauen und Kinder—hingemordet.

Mehrfach ist es vorgekommen, dass abgesprungene oder notgelandete Besatzungsmitglieder solcher Flugzeuge unmittelbar nach der Festnahme durch die auf das Äußerte empörte Bevölkerung an Ort und Stelle gelyncht wurden.

Von polizeilicher und strafgerichtlicher Verfolgung der dabei beteiligten Volksgenossen wurde abgesehen.

English Translation

In recent weeks, English and North American airmen have repeatedly shot at children playing, women and children working in the fields, peasants working on farms, wagons on the road, etc., during low-level strafing attacks. This is the most awful way to murder defenseless civilians—especially women and children.

It has often occurred that downed crewmembers of such aircraft were immediately arrested and lynched on the spot by the outraged population.

Police and criminal prosecution of the people involved were omitted.

Facing, Figure A.8. Letter to Gauleiter and Kreisleiter regarding Circular 125/44g from Bormann, May 30, 1944. *Letter to Gauleiter and Kreisleiter regarding Circular 125/44g from Bormann, May 30, 1944, Case Number 12-2000, Vol 36: Treatment of Captured Enemy Pilots and Lynch Law, RG 549, Entry A1 2238, Microfilm T1021, Roll 10, Frame No. 000765, NARA, https://catalog.archives.gov/id/40957462.*

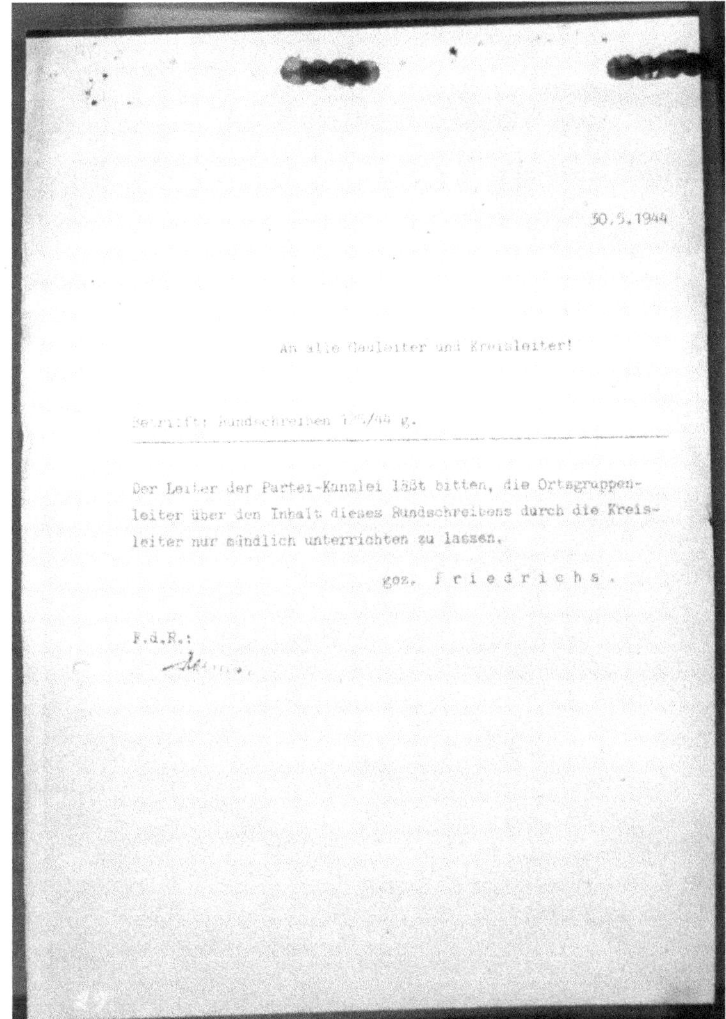

30.5.1944

An alle Gauleiter und Kreisleiter!

Betrifft: Rundschreiben [illegible]/44 g.

Der Leiter der Partei-Kanzlei läßt bitten, die Ortsgruppenleiter über den Inhalt dieses Rundschreibens durch die Kreisleiter nur mündlich unterrichten zu lassen.

gez. F r i e d r i c h s .

F.d.R.:

German Transcription

Der Leiter der Partei-Kanzlei lässt bitten, die Ortsgruppenleiter über den Inhalt dieses Rundschreibens durch die Kreisleiter nur mündlich unterrichten zu lassen.

English Translation

The head of the party chancellery requests that the Ortsgruppenleiter only be informed of the content of this circular verbally by the Kreisleiter.

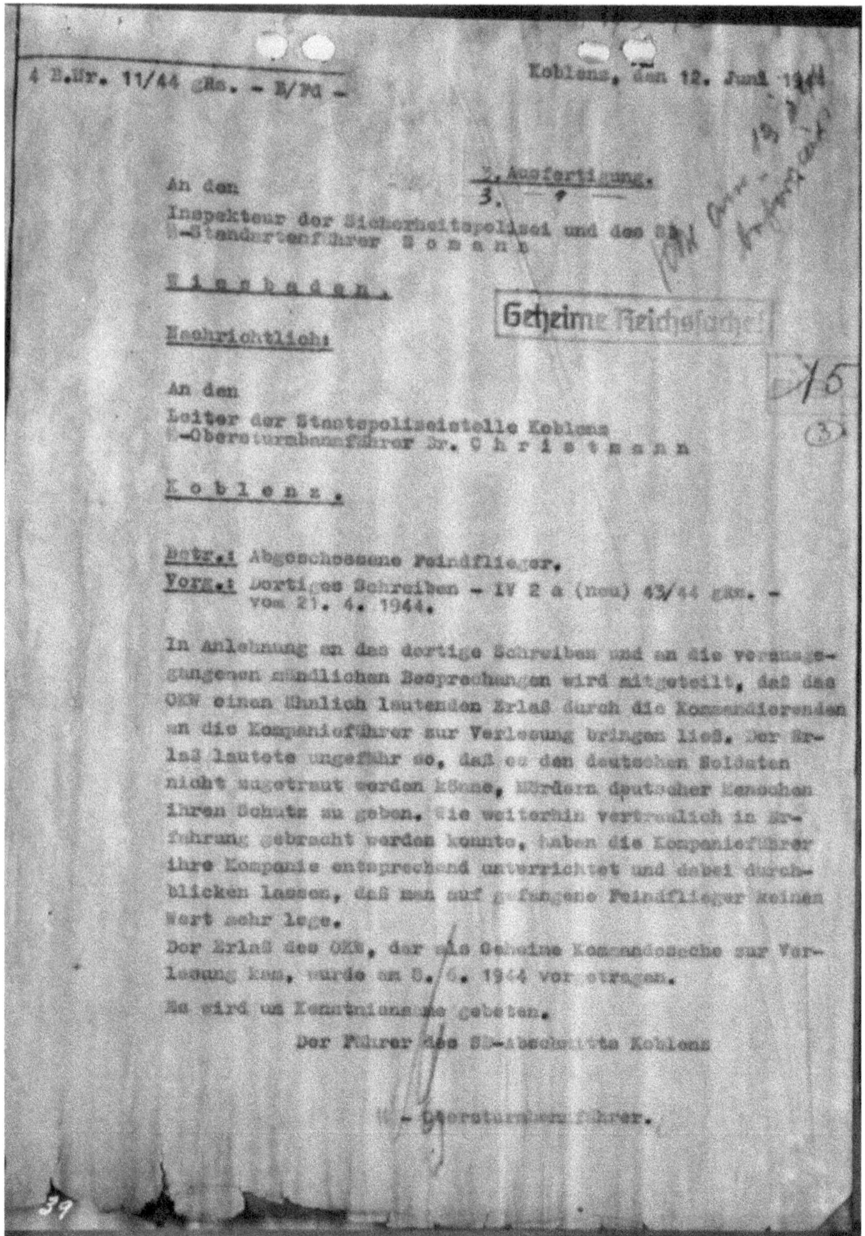

4 B.Nr. 11/44 gRs. - B/Pd -

Koblenz, den 12. Juni 1944

2. Ausfertigung.
3.

An den
Inspekteur der Sicherheitspolizei und des SD
SS-Standartenführer S o m a n n

W i e s b a d e n.

Geheime Reichssache!

Nachrichtlich:

An den
Leiter der Staatspolizeistelle Koblenz
SS-Obersturmbannführer Dr. C h r i s t m a n n

K o b l e n z.

Betr.: Abgeschossene Feindflieger.
Vorg.: Dortiges Schreiben - IV 2 a (neu) 43/44 gRs. - vom 21. 4. 1944.

In Anlehnung an das dortige Schreiben und an die vorausgegangenen mündlichen Besprechungen wird mitgeteilt, daß das OKW einen ähnlich lautenden Erlaß durch die Kommandierenden an die Kompanieführer zur Verlesung bringen ließ. Der Erlaß lautete ungefähr so, daß es den deutschen Soldaten nicht zugetraut werden könne, Mördern deutscher Menschen ihren Schutz zu geben. Wie weiterhin vertraulich in Erfahrung gebracht werden konnte, haben die Kompanieführer ihre Kompanie entsprechend unterrichtet und dabei durchblicken lassen, daß man auf gefangene Feindflieger keinen Wert mehr lege.
Der Erlaß des OKW, der als Geheime Kommandosache zur Verlesung kam, wurde am 6. 6. 1944 vorgetragen.

Es wird um Kenntnisnahme gebeten.

Der Führer des SD-Abschnitts Koblenz

SS-Obersturmbannführer.

Figure A.9. "Downed Enemy Flyers, " secret letter from the head of the SD in Koblenz to the head of the Staatspolizei in Koblenz, June 12, 1944. *Letter from the head of the SD in Koblenz to the head of the Staatspolizei in Koblenz, June 12, 1944, Case Number 12-2000, Vol 36: Treatment of Captured Enemy Pilots and Lynch Law, RG 549, Entry A1 2238, Microfilm T1021, Roll 10, Frame No. 000769, NARA, https://catalog.archives.gov/id/40957462.*

German Transcription

In Anlehnung an das dortige Schreiben und an die vorausgegangenen mündlichen Besprechungen wird mitgeteilt, dass das OKW einen ähnlich lautenden Erlass durch die Kommandierenden an die Kompanieführer zur Verlesung bringen ließ. Der Erlass lautete ungefähr so, dass es den deutschen Soldaten nicht zugetraut werden könne, Mördern deutscher Menschen ihren Schutz zu geben. Wie weiterhin vertraulich in Erfahrung gebracht werden konnte, haben die Kompanieführer ihre Kompanie entsprechend unterrichtet und dabei durchblicken lassen, dass man auf gefangene Feindflieger keinen Wert mehr lege.

Der Erlass des OKW, der als Geheime Kommandosache zu Verlesung kam, wurde am 8.6.1944 vorgetragen.

English Translation

Based on the previous letter [previous document] and on the previous verbal discussion, it is reported that the OKW ordered a similar decree to be read to the company commanders. The decree approximately stated that German soldiers could not be trusted to give protection to murderers of German people. The company commanders instructed their company accordingly, pointing out that no value was placed on captured enemy airmen.

The decree from the OKW, which was received as a secret commando matter, was delivered on June 8, 1944.

Oberkommando der Wehrmacht Entwurf F.H.Qu., den 15.6.1944.
Nr.771793/44 g.K.Chefs.II.Ang.
WFSt / Qu. (Verw. 1)

Geheime Kommandosache
2 Ausfertigungen
2. Ausfertigung.

Betr.: Behandlung der feindl. Terrorflieger.

Chefsache!
Nur durch Offizier!

An den
Oberbefehlshaber der Luftwaffe,
z.Hd. Oberst d.G. v. Brauchitsch.

I. Auf Grund der geführten Vorbesprechungen und nach Benehmen mit dem Reichsaussenminister und dem Chef der Sicherheitspolizei und des S.D. sollen folgende Tatbestände als Terrorhandlungen angesehen werden, die bei der Veröffentlichung eines Falles von Lynchjustiz zu beachten sind bzw. die Übergabe von kriegsgefangenen feindlichen Fliegern aus dem Fliegeraufnahmelager Oberursel an den S.D. zur Sonderbehandlung rechtfertigen:

1.) Bordwaffenangriffe auf die Zivilbevölkerung, und zwar sowohl auf Einzelpersonen wie auf Ansammlungen;

2.) Beschuss von am Fallschirm hängenden abgeschossenen eigenen (deutschen) Flugzeugbesatzungen;

3.) Bordwaffenangriffe auf Personenzüge des öffentlichen Verkehrs;

4.) Bordwaffenangriffe auf Lazarette, Krankenhäuser und Lazarettzüge, die mit dem Roten Kreuz deutlich gekennzeichnet sind.

Es wird gebeten, die Zustimmung des Herrn Reichsmarschalls zu dieser Formulierung der Tatbestände herbeiführen sowie gegebenenfalls den Kommandanten des Fliegeraufnahmelagers Oberursel zu entsprechendem Verfahren mündlich anzuweisen.

3/ 95 - 2 -

Figure A.10. "Treatment of the Enemy Terror Flyers," secret letter from the High Command of the Wehrmacht (OKW) to the commander in chief of the Luftwaffe, June 15, 1944. *Letter from the High Command of the Wehrmacht (OKW) to the commander in chief of the Luftwaffe, June 15, 1944, Case Number 12-2000, Vol 36: Treatment of Captured Enemy Pilots and Lynch Law, RG 549, Entry A1 2238, Microfilm T1021, Roll 10, Frame No. 000758, NARA, https://catalog.archives.gov/id/40957462.*

German Transcription

. . . folgende Tatbestände sollen als Terrorhandlungen angesehen werden, die bei der Veröffentlichung eines Falles von Lynchjustiz zu beachten sind bzw. die Übergabe von kriegsgefangenen feindlichen Fliegern aus dem Fliegeraufnahmelager Oberursel an den S.D. zur Sonderbehandlung rechtfertigen:

Bordwaffenangriffe auf die Zivilbevölkerung, und zwar sowohl auf Einzelpersonen wie auf Ansammlungen;

Beschuss von am Fallschirm hängenden abgeschossenen eigenen (deutschen) Flugzeugbesatzungen;

Bordwaffenangriffe auf Personenzüge des öffentlichen Verkehrs;

Bordwaffenangriffe auf Lazarette, Krankenhäuser und Lazarettzüge, die mit dem Roten Kreuz deutlich gekennzeichnet sind.

English Translation

. . . the following facts are to be regarded as acts of terrorism, which have to be taken into account in the publication of Lynchjustiz and the handing over of enemy airmen POWs from the flyer holding center at Oberursel to the SD to justify Sonderbehandlung:"

Attacks on the civilian population, both on individuals and on groups;

Attacks on German air crews who are parachuting to the ground;

Attacks on passenger trains and public transportation;

Attacks on military field hospitals, public hospitals and hospital trains, which are clearly marked with a Red Cross."

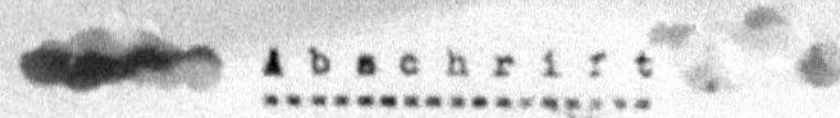

A b s c h r i f t

Der Befehlshaber
der Sicherheitspolizei und des SD
Rhein / Westmark
III - 1829/44

Wiesbaden, den 6. Okt. 1944.

An die Geheime Staatspolizei, Staatspolizeistellen
in Frankfurt a.M.,
Koblenz,
Darmstadt,
Saarbrücken und
Metz,

an die Kriminalpolizeileitstelle in Frankfurt a.M.,
Kriminalpolizeistelle in Darmstadt,
Koblenz,
Trier,
Saarbrücken
Metz,

an die SD - Abschnitte in Frankfurt a.M.
Koblenz und
Saarbrücken.

Betrifft: Verhalten der Wehrmacht gegenüber abgesprungenen Terrorfliegern.

Vorgang: Ohne.

Wie aus verschiedenen Berichten hervorgeht, verhindert die Wehrmacht häufiger ein entsprechendes Vorgehen der Bevölkerung gegen abgesprungene Terrorflieger durch Fest- und Inschutznahme derselben. In Zukunft sind alle derartigen Fälle umgehend nach hier unter möglichst eingehender Schilderung des einzelnen Falles und unter Angabe der Personalien des betr. Streifenführers bezw. unter näherer Bezeichnung der betr. Einheit zu berichten.

In Vertretung:
gez. Unterschrift
SS-Obersturmbannführer

133

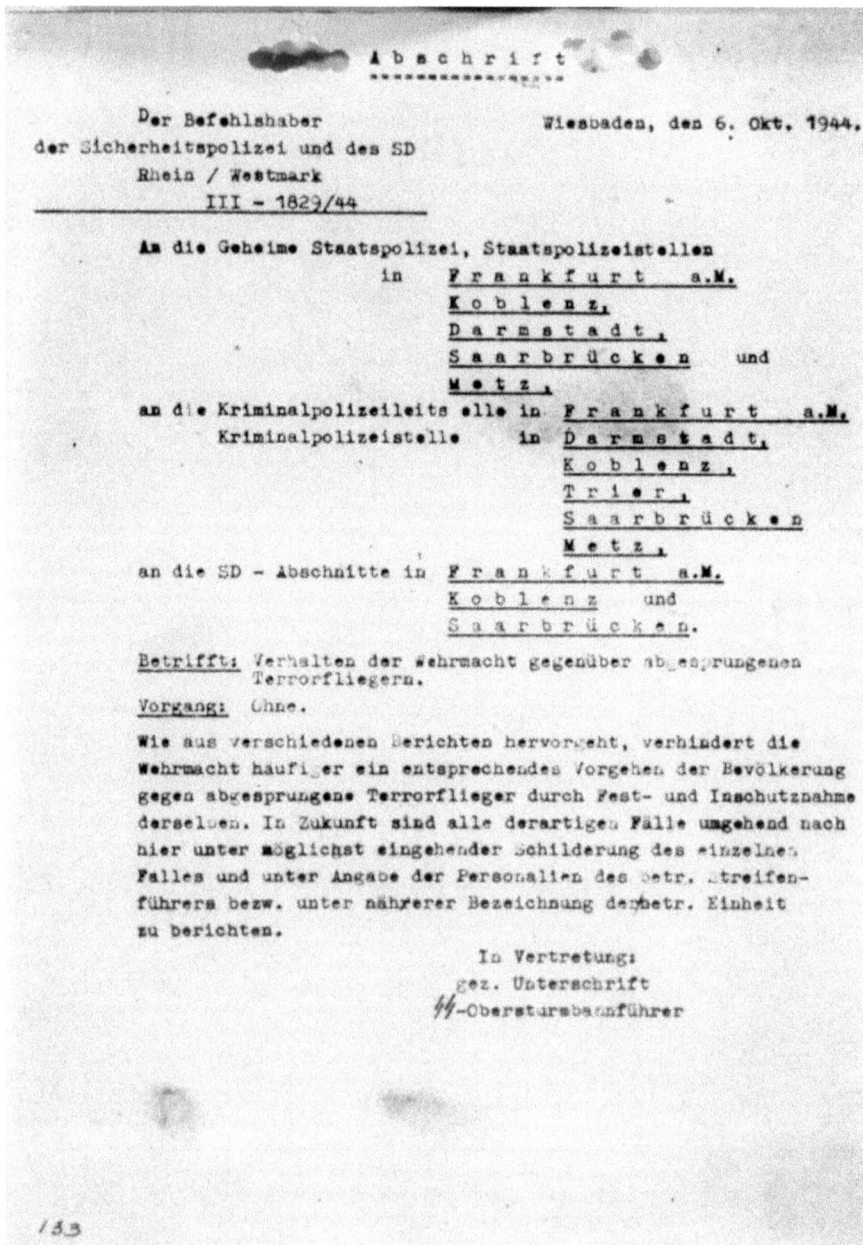

Figure A.11 "Behavior of the Wehrmacht with downed Terror Flyers" *Order from the Commander of the SiPo and the SD Rhein/Westmark to the Gestapo, Staatspolizei, KriPo, and SD, October 6, 1944, Case Number 12-2000, Vol 36: Treatment of Captured Enemy Pilots and Lynch Law, RG 549, Entry A1 2238, Microfilm T1021, Roll 10, Frame No. 000790, NARA, https://catalog.archives.gov/id/40957462.*

German Transcription

Wie aus verschiedenen Berichten hervorgeht, verhindert die Wehrmacht häufiger ein entsprechendes Vorgehen der Bevölkerung gegen abgesprungene Terrorflieger durch Fest- und Inschutznahme derselben. In Zukunft sind alle derartigen Fälle umgehend nach hier unter möglichst eingehender Schilderung des einzelnen Falles und unter Angabe der Personalien des betr. Streifenführers bzw. unter näherer Bezeichnung der betr. Einheit zu berichten.

English Translation

As various reports have shown, the Wehrmacht often prevents a corresponding action by the population against downed Terrorflieger by protecting them. In the future, all such cases are to be reported here immediately with a detailed description of the individual case and personal details of the respective patrol leader and unit.

Dr. Goebbels: „Ein Wort zum feindlichen Luftterror"

Berlin, 26. Mai. (dnb) Der „Völkische Beobachter" veröffentlicht unter der Überschrift: „Ein Wort zum feindlichen Luftterror" einen Aufsatz von Reichsminister Dr. Goebbels, in dem es heißt:

Es wird heute von keiner Seite mehr bestritten, daß der feindliche Luftterror fast ausschließlich das Ziel verfolgt, die Moral der deutschen Zivilbevölkerung zu brechen. Der Feind führt Krieg gegen Wehrlose, in der Hauptsache Frauen und Kinder, um damit die Männer unseres Landes zur Nachgiebigkeit zu zwingen. Diese seine Absicht wird einerseits durch die Tatsachen selbst, andererseits durch die in Hülle und Fülle vorliegenden publizistischen Äußerungen der Feindseite bewiesen.

Was die Tatsachen anlangt, so braucht man nur im Reichsgebiet oder in den besetzten Gebieten eine oft bombardierte Stadt zu besichtigen, um durch eigenen Augenschein zweifelsfrei festzustellen, daß unser Kriegspotential durch den feindlichen Luftterror vielleicht zu einem Prozent getroffen wird, die übrigen 99 Prozent aber eindeutig auf den zivilen Sektor entfallen. Kürzlich haben sich die maßgebenden Vertreter des französischen und belgischen Episkopats, die gewiß nicht in dem Verdacht stehen, nach deutschen Befehlen zu handeln, an die internationale Öffentlichkeit gewandt und in flammenden Protesten Einspruch gegen diese barbarische Art der feindlichen Luftkriegsführung eingelegt, die Greise, Frauen und Kinder tötet sowie Kirchen, ehrwürdige Kulturdenkmäler und dichtbesiedelte Wohnviertel der Zivilbevölkerung niederlegt, ohne daß dabei ein militärischer Zweck ersichtlich wäre.

Die britisch-amerikanischen Terrorflieger sind in den letzten Wochen dazu übergegangen, neben der wahllosen Bombardierung der Wohnviertel unserer Städte die deutsche Zivilbevölkerung offen, direkt und ohne jede auch nur äußerliche Respektierung der internationalen Kriegsgesetze anzugreifen, sie mit Bordwaffen zu beschießen und kaltblütig hinzumorden. Ausreden können hier nicht mehr vorgebracht werden, daß die Feindflugzeuge in geringer Höhe über Dörfer, Äcker und Landstraßen einherstreichen und ihre Maschinengewehrläufe in harmlos ihres Weges gehende Menschengruppen hineinhalten. Das hat nichts mehr mit Krieg zu tun, das ist nackter Mord. Es gibt keine völkerrechtliche Regelung, auf die sich die Feindseite dabei berufen könnte. Die britisch-amerikanischen Piloten stellen sich mit einer solchen verbrecherischen Kampfesweise außerhalb international anerkannter Kriegsgesetze. Am vergangenen Sonntag beispielsweise wurden, um nur eines aus tausend Beispielen herauszugreifen, in sächsischen Landkreisen spielende Kindergruppen durch Bordwaffenbeschuß angegriffen, wodurch unter ihnen erhebliche Verluste entstanden.

Niemand wird sich darüber wundern, daß sich der betroffenen Bevölkerung, die, wie in der ganzen Welt bekannt ist, für jede soldatische Art der Kriegsführung jedes Verständnis hat, angesichts dieser zynischen Verbrechen eine rasende Wut bemächtigt. Es ist nur mit Hilfe der bewaffneten Macht möglich, bei solchen Angriffen abgeschossene Feindpiloten in ihrem Leben zu sichern, da sie sonst von der heimgesuchten Bevölkerung totgeschlagen würden. Wer hat hier Recht, die Mörder, die nach ihren feigen Untaten noch eine humane Behandlung seitens ihrer Opfer erwarten, oder die Opfer, die sich nach dem Grundsatz zur Wehr setzen wollen: Auge um Auge, Zahn um Zahn! Diese Fragen dürften nicht schwer zu beantworten sein. Jedenfalls wäre es zuviel von uns verlangt, wenn man von uns forderte, daß wir deutsche Soldaten zum Schutz für Kindermörder einsetzen, gegen die die von rasender Wut ergriffenen Eltern, die gerade ihr kostbarstes Gut durch den brutalen Zynismus des Feindes verloren haben, zur Selbstwehr schreiten. Wenn die Engländer und Amerikaner, wie sie das ja selbst sagen, uns wie lästige Eingeborenenstämme ansehen und behandeln wollen, so ist es unsere Sache, ob wir uns das gefallen lassen. Das deutsche Volk ist in der ganzen Welt bekannt dafür, daß es dem Krieg gibt, was der Krieg von ihm verlangt. Aber was zuviel ist, ist zuviel; und hier sind die Grenzen des Erträglichen weit überschritten.

Unsere Feinde machen aus ihren dahingehenden A b s i c h t e n a u c h g a r k e i n H e h l. Man braucht nicht lange in der britischen oder USA-Presse herumzusuchen, um dafür beweiskräftige Unterlagen zu finden. „Legt die großen Städte in Trümmer, und ihr werdet den Willen zum Krieg zerschmettern!" So schrieb schon 1930 der e n g l i s c h e Luftsachverständige I. M. Spaight in seinem Buche „Air Power and the Cities". An dieser Tendenz der britischen Luftkriegsführung hat sich seitdem nichts geändert. „Es ist nicht möglich, eine Trennungslinie zwischen der Zivilbevölkerung und der kämpfenden zu ziehen." Mit dieser feigen Aussage sucht die „Daily Mail" diese rohe und gemeine Art der feindlichen Kriegsführung öffentlich zu rechtfertigen. Sehr viel deutlicher wird ein maßgebender britischer Seeoffizier, der in der englischen Militärzeitschrift „The Army quarterly" erklärt: „Gibt es denn überhaupt den Begriff des Nichtkämpfers? Ein kleines Kind ist weder im Frieden noch im Kriege ein nützliches Glied der Volksgemeinschaft. Niemand hat in Wirklichkeit das Recht, für sich Unverletzlichkeit zu beanspruchen, wenn er auch den Versuch dazu im Namen der Menschlichkeit machen kann. Deutschland muß wüster werden als die Sahara."

Die A m e r i k a n e r sind nicht weniger robust. Einer ihrer ersten Wortführer, Raymond Clapper, schreibt mit sichtlichem Behagen: „Terror und Brutalität sind die besten Seiten des Luftkrieges." Man wird hier vielleicht einwenden, so dächten nicht alle maßgebenden Engländer und Amerikaner. Fehlgeschossen! Sogar die anglikanische Hochkirche erklärt in ihrem amtlichen Organ „Church of England" am 28. Mai 1943: „Es ist eine perverse Ansicht der Christenheit zu wähnen, daß Zivilisten nicht getötet werden dürften." Ja sogar der Erzbischof von York, Dr. Cyrill Garbett, segnet die barbarischen Methoden des britisch-amerikanischen Luftterrors in seinem Hirtenbrief vom Juni 1943 mit den Worten: „Es ist nur ein geringes Übel, die deutschen Zivilisten zu bombardieren."

Wir treffen diese Feststellungen in aller Sachlichkeit. Unser Volk denkt in diesen Fragen viel radikaler wie seine Regierung. Es ist immer unser Wunsch gewesen, daß der Krieg sich in ritterlichen Formen abspielt. Der Feind scheint das nicht zu wollen. Die ganze Welt ist Zeuge dafür. Sie würde bei Anhalten dieses empörenden Zustandes auch Zeuge dafür werden, daß wir Mittel und Wege zu finden wissen, um uns gegen diese Verbrechen zur Wehr zu setzen. Wir sind das unserem Volke schuldig, das anständig und tapfer sein Leben verteidigt und keinesfalls verdient, dafür zum Freiwild feindlicher Menschenjagd erklärt zu werden.

Figure A.12. "Dr. Goebbels: A Word Regarding the Enemy Air Terror," (here from) *Völkischer Beobachter* (Munich) May 28, 1944. This article was subsequently published in newspapers throughout German occupied territory, including in, for example, *Kölnische Zeitung*, *Leipziger Neueste Nachrichten*, *Gumbinner Allgemeine Zeitung* (East Prussia), *Teltower Kreisblatt*, and *Neue Vetschauer Zeitung*.

German Transcription (of Selected Area)

Niemand wird sich darüber wundern, dass sich der betroffenen Bevölkerung, die, wie in der ganzen Welt bekannt ist, für jede soldatische Art der Kriegsführung jedes Verständnis hat, angesichts dieser zynischen Verbrechen eine rasende Wut bemächtigt. Es ist nur mit Hilfe der bewaffneten Macht möglich, bei solchen Angriffen abgeschossene Feindpiloten in ihrem Leben zu sichern, da sie sonst von der heimgesuchten Bevölkerung totgeschlagen würden. Wer hat hier recht, die Mörder, die nach ihren feigen Untaten noch eine humane Behandlung seitens ihrer Opfer erwarten, oder die Opfer, die sich nach dem Grundsatz zur Wehr setzen wollen: Auge um Auge, Zahn um Zahn? Diese Fragen dürften nicht schwer zu beantworten sein. Jedenfalls wäre es zu viel von uns verlangt, wenn man von uns forderte, dass wir deutsche Soldaten zum Schutz für Kindermörder einsetzen, gegen die die von rasender Wut ergriffenen Eltern, die gerade ihr kostbarsten Gut durch den brutalen Zynismus des Feindes verloren haben, zur Selbstwehr schreiten."

Es ist immer unser Wunsch gewesen, dass der Krieg sich in ritterlichen Formen abspielt. Der Feind scheint das nicht zu wollen. Die ganze Welt ist Zeuge dafür. Sie würde bei Anhalten dieses empörenden Zustandes auch Zeuge dafür werden, dass wir Mittel und Wege zu finden wissen, um uns gegen diese Verbrechen zur Wehr zu setzen.

English Translation

Nobody will be surprised that the affected population, which, as is known throughout the world, has every understanding for every type of military warfare, is in a rage over these cynical crimes. It is only possible to protect the lives of downed enemy pilots with the use of armed forces, as they would otherwise be killed by the afflicted population. Who is right here? The murderers who, after their cowardly misdeeds, still expect humane treatment on the part of the victims or the victims who want to defend themselves according to the principle of an eye for an eye and a tooth for a tooth. This question is not difficult to answer. In any case, it would be intolerable to use German soldiers to protect child murderers from the rage-stricken parents who resort to self-defense after having just lost their most precious possessions through the brutal cynicism of the enemy.

It has always been our wish that the war be fought in chivalrous forms. The enemy does not seem to want that. The whole world is witness to it. Upon halting this revolting situation, the world would also witness that we know how to find ways and means to defend ourselves against these crimes."

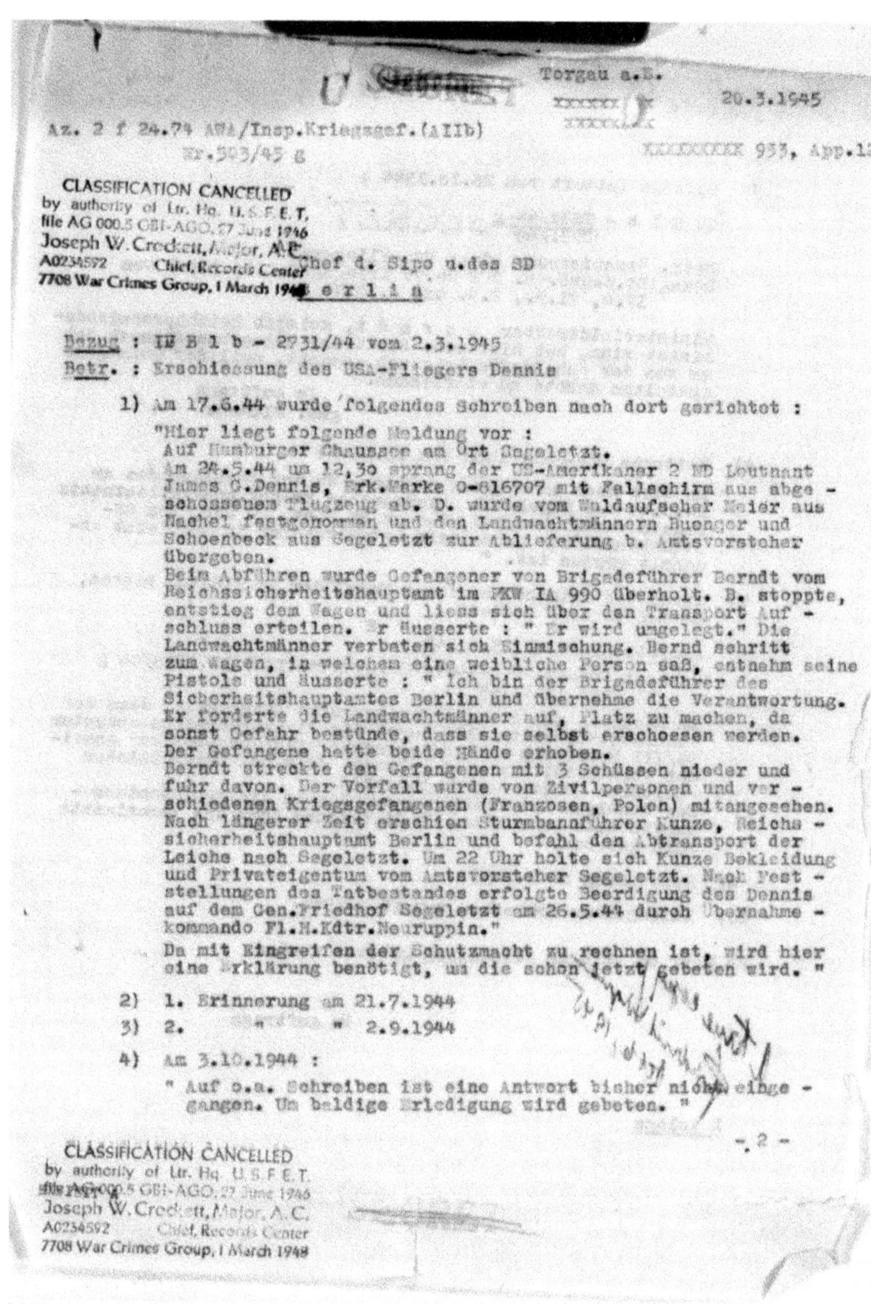

Torgau a.E.

20.3.1945

Az. 2 f 24.74 AWA/Insp.Kriegsgef.(AIIb)
Nr.593/45 g

XXXXXXXXX 933, App.128

CLASSIFICATION CANCELLED
by authority of Ltr. Hq. U.S.F.E.T.
file AG 000.5 GBI-AGO, 27 June 1946
Joseph W. Crockett, Major, A.C.
A0234592 Chief, Records Center
7708 War Crimes Group, 1 March 1948

Chef d. Sipo u.des SD
B e r l i n

Bezug : IV B 1 b - 2731/44 vom 2.3.1945
Betr. : Erschiessung des USA-Fliegers Dennis

1) Am 17.6.44 wurde folgendes Schreiben nach dort gerichtet :

"Hier liegt folgende Meldung vor :
Auf Hamburger Chaussee am Ort Segeletzt.
Am 24.5.44 um 12,30 sprang der US-Amerikaner 2 ND Leutnant James G.Dennis, Erk.Marke 0-816707 mit Fallschirm aus abge - schossenem Flugzeug ab. D. wurde vom Waldaufseher Meier aus Nachel festgenommen und den Landwachtmännern Buenger und Schoenbeck aus Segeletzt zur Ablieferung b. Amtsvorsteher übergeben.
Beim Abführen wurde Gefangener von Brigadeführer Berndt vom Reichssicherheitshauptamt im PKW IA 990 überholt. B. stoppte, entstieg dem Wagen und liess sich über den Transport Auf - schluss erteilen. Er äusserte : " Er wird umgelegt." Die Landwachtmänner verbaten sich Einmischung. Bernd schritt zum Wagen, in welchem eine weibliche Person saß, entnahm seine Pistole und äusserte : " Ich bin der Brigadeführer des Sicherheitshauptamtes Berlin und übernehme die Verantwortung. Er forderte die Landwachtmänner auf, Platz zu machen, da sonst Gefahr bestünde, dass sie selbst erschossen werden.
Der Gefangene hatte beide Hände erhoben.
Berndt streckte den Gefangenen mit 3 Schüssen nieder und fuhr davon. Der Vorfall wurde von Zivilpersonen und ver - schiedenen Kriegsgefangenen (Franzosen, Polen) mitangesehen.
Nach längerer Zeit erschien Sturmbannführer Kunze, Reichs - sicherheitshauptamt Berlin und befahl den Abtransport der Leiche nach Segeletzt. Um 22 Uhr holte sich Kunze Bekleidung und Privateigentum vom Amtsvorsteher Segeletzt. Nach Fest - stellungen des Tatbestandes erfolgte Beerdigung des Dennis auf dem Gen.Friedhof Segeletzt am 26.5.44 durch Übernahme - kommando Fl.H.Kdtr.Neuruppin."

Da mit Eingreifen der Schutzmacht zu rechnen ist, wird hier eine Erklärung benötigt, um die schon jetzt gebeten wird. "

2) 1. Erinnerung am 21.7.1944
3) 2. " " 2.9.1944
4) Am 3.10.1944 :

" Auf o.a. Schreiben ist eine Antwort bisher nicht einge - gangen. Um baldige Erledigung wird gebeten. "

- 2 -

CLASSIFICATION CANCELLED
by authority of Ltr. Hq. U.S.F.E.T.
file AG 000.5 GBI-AGO, 27 June 1946
Joseph W. Crockett, Major, A.C.
A0234592 Chief, Records Center
7708 War Crimes Group, 1 March 1948

Figure A.13–A.14. "Shooting of US-Flyer Dennis," March 20, 1945. *"Shooting of US-Flyer Dennis," Report from OKW to SiPo and SD in Berlin, March 20, 1945, RG 549, Entry A1 2238Microfilm T1021, Roll 13, Frame No. 421–423, NARA, https://catalog.archives.gov/id/40957462.*

5) Dortige Antwort vom 26.10.1944 :

"IV B 1 b - 7637/44 g
2731/44

Betr. Erschiessung eines USA-Fliegers.
Bezug: Dt.Schrb.Az. 2 f 24.77 Kriegsgef.Allg (IIa) vom
17.6, 21.7., 2.9. und 3.10.44

Ministerialdirektor B e r n d t, zuletzt Reichspropagandaministerium, hat hier eine Erklärung abgegeben. Danach hat er von der Schußwaffe Gebrauch gemacht, weil der Gefangene Anstalten machte zu entfliehen.

Im Auftrage
gez. Clemens "

6) Weiteres OKW-Schreiben vom 13.11.44 :

" Es wird noch um Meldung gebeten, wo der Nachlass des am 24.5.44 bei Segeletzt erschossenen kr.gef.amerik.Leutnants Dennis verblieben ist, das am 24.5.44, 22 Uhr, von SS-Sturmbannführer Kunze beim Amtsvorsteher in Segeletzt abgeholt worden ist. "

7) Anruf von Kriminalkommissar Mohr, der um Klärung bittet, um was es sich handelt .

8) Schreiben OKW v. 25.11.44 :

"Bezug : OKW Az. 2 f 24.74 Kriegsgef.(IIb) Nr.2645/44 g
vom 13.11.44

Im Nachgang zum Bezugsschreiben wird mitgeteilt, dass der Wehrmachtauskunftstelle durch die Fliegerhorstkommandantur 25/III Neuruppin als Todesursache "Flugzeugabsturz" gemeldet worden ist. Es wird gebeten, dies bei irgendwelchen weiteren Rückfragen zu beachten.
Der Nachlass ist bestimmungsgemäss an die Wehrmachtauskunftstelle zu senden. Um Mitteilung über das Veranlasste wird gebeten. "

9) Erinnerung am 5.1.45

10) Anliegendes Schreiben vom 16.2.1945.

Es darf um baldige Erledigung gebeten werden.

Im Auftrage

A true copy
Friedrich Wegner
Oct 6, 1945

1 Anlage

CLASSIFICATION CANCELLED
by authority of the Hq. U.S.F.E.T.
...
Joseph W. Crimp...
7708 War Crimes Group, March 1948

German Transcription

Am 24.5.1944 um 12:30 sprang der US-Amerikaner 2nd Leutnant James G. Dennis mit Fallschirm aus abgeschossenem Flugzeug ab. Dennis wurde vom Waldaufseher Meier aus Nachel festgenommen und den Landwachtmännern Buenger und Schoenbeck aus Segeletzt zur Ablieferung bei Amtsvorsteher übergeben.

Beim Abführen wurde Gefangener von Brigadeführer Berndt vom RSHA im PKW überholt. Berndt stoppte, entstieg dem Wagen und ließ ich über den Transport Aufschluss erteilen. Er äußerte: "Er wird umgelegt." Die Landwachtmänner verbaten sich Einmischung. Berndt schritt zum Wagen, . . . entnahm seine Pistole und äußerte: "Ich bin der Brigadeführer des Sicherheitshauptamtes Berlin und übernehme die Verantwortung." Er forderte die Landwachtmänner auf, Platz zu machen, da sonst Gefahr bestünde, dass sie selbst erschossen werden. Der Gefangene hatte beide Hände erhoben.

Berndt streckte den Gefangenen mit 3 Schüssen nieder und fuhr davon. Der Vorfall wurde von Zivilpersonen und verschiedenen Kriegsgefangenen (Franzosen, Polen) mitangesehen. Nach längerer Zeit erschien Sturmbannführer Kunze (RSHA, Berlin) und befahl den Abtransport der Leiche nach Segeletzt. Um 22 Uhr holte sich Kunze Bekleidung und Privateigentum vom Amtsvorsteher Segeletzt. Nach Feststellungen des Tatbestandes erfolgte Beerdigung des Dennis auf dem Friedhof Segeletzt am 26.5.1944 durch Übernahmekommando Fliegerhorstkommandantur Neuruppin.

Da mit Eingreifen der Schutzmacht zu rechnen ist, wird hier eine Erklärung benötigt . . .

(Page 2)

5) Dortige Antwort vom 26.10.1944:

"Ministerialdirektor Berndt, zuletzt Reichspropagandaministerium, hat hier eine Erklärung abgegeben. Danach hat er von der Schusswaffe Gebrauch gemacht, weil der Gefangene Anstalten machte zu entfliehen."

8) Schreiben OKW vom 25.11.1944:

"Im Nachgang zum Bezugsschreiben wird mitgeteilt, dass der Wehrmachtsauskunftstelle durch die Fliegerhorstkommandantur Neuruppin als Todesursache 'Flugzeugabsturz' gemeldet worden ist. Es wird gebeten, dies bei irgendwelchen weiteren Rückfragen zu beachten."

English Translation

On May 24, 1944, at 12:30 p.m. the American flyer, 2nd Lt. James G. Dennis, parachuted from his damaged aircraft. Dennis was arrested by the forest ranger Meier (from Nachel) and handed over to two Landwacht officials (Buenger and Schoenbeck from Segeletzt), who were to delivery him to a public official (Amtsvorsteher) in Segeletzt.

En route, Brigadeführer Berndt (RSHA) passed the two guards and Dennis in his car and stopped them. Berndt got out of the car and the guards informed him of their orders to transport the captured flyer. Berndt said: "He's going to be killed," and he ordered the guards to not interfere. Berndt approached the car, took out his pistol and said: "I am the Brigadeführer of the RSHA and take over responsibility." He ordered the guards to make room and hand over the flyer, otherwise they themselves would be shot. The prisoner had both hands raised above his head.

Berndt then shot the prisoner three times and drove away. The incident was witnessed by civilians and various prisoners of war (French and Polish). After a while, Sturmbannführer Kunze (RSHA, Berlin) arrived at the scene and ordered the removal of the corpse to Segeletzt. At 10 p.m., Kunze gathered the clothing and property of the flyer from a public official (Amtsvorsteher) in Segeletzt. A few days later, on May 26, 1944, the remains were buried in the cemetery in Segeletzt -following orders from Luftwaffe officials from the airbase in Neuruppin.

Since intervention by the protective powers is to be expected, an explanation is needed here . . ."

(Page 2)

5) Reply, October 26, 1944:

"Ministerialdirektor Berndt, formerly Brigadeführer of the RSHA, issued an explanation. He used his firearm because the prisoner was attempting to escape."

8) Letter from the OKW, November 25, 1944:

"It is reported that the Wehrmacht Information Agency (Wehrmachtsauskunftstelle) was informed by the Fliegerhorstkommandantur Neuruppin that the cause of death was due to the 'plane crash.' It is requested to keep this in mind if there are any further inquiries . . ."

Appendix B
Newspaper Examples

Headlines and Articles Concerning Downed Airmen

Berliner Ausgabe

„Freiheit und Brot“

Berliner Ausgabe

VÖLKISCHER BEOBACHTER

Kampfblatt der nationalsozialistischen Bewegung Großdeutschlands

Feindliche Durchbruchsversuche auf der Krim gescheitert

Briten und Nordamerikaner

die geborenen Mörder!

Ein englischer Major lehrt von amtswegen: „Deutsche umbringen belastet nicht mehr als Fliegen zerquetschen — man schläft wie ein Baby danach“

Stolz und Verachtung

Figure B.1. "British and Americans, the Born Murderers!" *Völkischer Beobachter* (Berlin), February 5, 1944.

Berliner Ausgabe

Berliner Ausgabe

VÖLKISCHER BEOBACHTER

Kampfblatt der nationalsozialistischen Bewegung Großdeutschlands

Beförderungen in der Wehrmacht

Das Eichenlaub für den Kampf um Kowel

Von den Deutschen gerettet – von den Briten zerstört

Ein Meisterstück der Luftbarbaren

Britische Bomben auf die Kathedrale von Rouen

Der Luftsieg der Waffenbrüder

Figure B.2. "Save by the Germans—Destroyed by the British. A Masterpiece of the Barbarians of the Sky," *Völkischer Beobachter* (Berlin), February 21, 1944.

Neue Bestialität der Luftgangster

Zwei Jungen in Köln von einem durch Feindflieger abgeworfenen Drehbleistift mit Sprengladung schwer verletzt

Köln, 25. April

Am Freitag, 21. April, wenige Stunden nach dem britischen Terrorangriff auf die Hansestadt Köln, fand in einem Kölner Vorort ein sechsjähriger Junge beim Spiel auf einer Anlagenwiese einen Drehbleistift. Er hob ihn auf und drehte daran. Mit einer für den kleinen Gegenstand unverhältnismäßig starken Detonation explodierte der Bleistift — ein in dieser Gestalt von britisch-amerikanischen Mordbrennern abgeworfenen Sprengkörper — in der Hand des Jungen, der ihn aufgehoben hatte. Dem Jungen wurden dabei mehrere Finger abgerissen und die Hand bis zum Handballen hinunter zerfleischt. Ein gleichaltriger Spielgefährte, der dabei stand, erlitt erhebliche Gesichtsverletzungen.

Der Arbeiter H. Z., der diesen Vorfall als Augenzeuge schildert, sagte dazu: „Ich hatte es nie so recht glauben können, wenn die Zeitungen davon schrieben, daß die Briten und Amerikaner so verwerfliche Methoden anwenden. Das ist ja keine Kriegführung mehr, so etwas können doch nur Verbrecher tun. Es war furchtbar, die verletzten Kinder zu sehen."

Weitere der mit Sprengstoff gefüllten Drehbleistifte, die wenige Meter von dem explodierten Spengkörper entfernt lagen, konnten sichergestellt und unschädlich gemacht werden.

Diese neue infame Bestialität der anglo-amerikanischen Luftgangster zeigt wiederum, daß es kein Verbrechen gibt, zu dem diese Mordbanditen nicht fähig wären. Diese heimtückischen Gangstermethoden sind für deutsches Empfinden einfach unfaßbar. Nicht genug damit, daß die Luftbanditen ihre Sprengstoffe und Phosphorbrände gegen die Wohnstätten der Zivilbevölkerung schleudern, mit raffinierter Heimtücke machen sie sich auch den Spieltrieb der Kinder zunutze und wenden damit Methoden an, die jeder Menschlichkeit Hohn sprechen. An alle Eltern ergeht deshalb die dringende Aufforderung, ihre Kinder nach einem Luftangriff zu äußerster Vorsicht zu ermahnen. Füllfederhalter, Drehbleistifte und andere von Feindfliegern abgeworfene Gegenstände bergen vor allem für die Kinder tödliche Gefahren. Es ist deshalb dringend nötig, die Kinder vor dem Aufheben solcher Gegenstände immer wieder zu warnen. **Die tierische Verbrecherfratze unserer Feinde enthüllt sich täglich aufs neue. Gegen diese Verbrecher kann es in der Zukunft kein Mitleid und keine Rücksicht mehr geben. Das deutsche Schwert wird sie unschädlich machen, wenn die Stunde dafür gekommen ist.**

Figure B.3. "New Bestiality of the Gangsters of the Sky," *Westdeutscher Beobachter* (Aachen), April 25, 1944.

German Transcription (of Selected Area)v

Der Arbeiter H.Z., der diesen Vorfall als Augenzeuge schildert, sagte dazu: "Ich hatte es nie so recht glauben können, wenn die Zeitungen davon schrieben, daß die Briten und Amerikaner so verwerfliche Methoden anwenden. Das ist ja keine Kriegführung mehr, so etwas können doch nur Verbrecher tun. Es war furchtbar, die verletzten Kinder zu sehen. . . .

Diese neue infame Bestialität der anglo-amerikanischen Luftgangster zeigt wiederum, daß es kein Verbrechen gibt, zu dem diese Mordbanditen nicht fähig wären. Diese heimtück-isches Gangstermethoden sind für deutsches Empfinden einfach unfaßbar. . . .

Die tierische Verbrecherfratze unserer Feinde enthüllt sich täglich aufs neue. Gegen diese Verbrecher kann es in der Zukunft kein Mitleid und keine Rücksicht mehr geben. Das deutsche Schwert wird sie unschädlich machen, wenn die Stunde dafür gekommen ist."

English Translation

Work H.Z., who was a witness to this incident, said: 'I never quite believed it when the newspapers wrote that the British and Americans were using such reprehensible methods. That is no longer warfare; it is only something criminals can do. It is terrible to see the injured children. . . .

This new infamous bestiality of the Anglo-American gangsters of the sky shows again that there is no crime to which these homicidal bandits would not be capable. These malicious gangster methods are simply unfeasible for German sentiment. . . .

The bestially criminal grimace of our enemies reveals itself daily. There can be no pity or consideration for these criminals in the future. The German sword will make them harmless when the hour comes."

Neue verbrecherische Methode des Luftterrors

Tiefangriffe der Luftgangster gegen die Zivilbevölkerung

Berlin, 24. April

Seit einigen Tagen ist in der Anwendung des englisch-amerikanischen Luftterrors eine neue verbrecherische Methode festzustellen. In einigen Gauen des Reichsgebiets haben die Luftgangster den Terror gegen die Zivilbevölkerung durch Tiefangriffe erweitert. Jagdflugzeuge beschossen mit Maschinengewehren aus geringer Höhe Frauen und Kinder in den Straßen der Städte und Bauern auf dem Felde.

Dabei muß festgestellt werden, daß es sich nicht um Einzelaktionen mordgieriger Luftbanditen handelt, die ihrem Trieb zum „Killen" in jeder Form nachgehen wollen. Es handelt sich vielmehr um bewußte und systematische Anwendung einer neuen Taktik im Terror gegen die Zivilbevölkerung. Das deutsche Volk wird auf diese neue Art des Luftverbrechens mit der Haltung und Abwehrkraft antworten, die es seit jeher auch im verschärften Bombenkrieg der Welt eindrucksvoll dokumentiert hat.

Unter dem Eindruck der hohen Verluste bei den Einflügen der Bombengeschwader geht der Feind zu Methoden über, die in ihrer Sinnlosigkeit seiner Verzweiflung Ausdruck geben über die ausgebliebene Wirkung der Bombenangriffe auf das deutsche Volk. Es gibt kein Argument und keinen Vorwand militärischer Art für die Rechtfertigung dieser Methode. Wehrlose Frauen und Kinder in den Straßen niederzuknallen, das ist nicht mehr eine Angelegenheit der Kriegführung, sondern gehört in das Gebiet der Kriminalistik. Die Anwendung solcher Methoden kennzeichnet die Bolschewisierung des Krieges, der die Anglo-Amerikaner sich in ihrer geistigen und militärischen Haltung haben ausliefern müssen.

Denn ohne Zweifel liegt auch diesem Vorgehen die Erkenntnis zugrunde, daß das deutsche Volk weder mit den Waffen noch durch den Bombenterror auf die Knie zu zwingen ist. Ausweglos und ratlos werden nunmehr aus dem Musterkoffer kolonialer Patente diejenigen hervorgeholt, mit denen man ehedem in Afrika oder Indien billige Triumphe errungen hat. Die Vorstellung aber, auf diese Art und Weise das deutsche Volk besiegen zu können, ist närrisch. Sie zeigt, daß es dem Gegner zwar möglich ist, seine Kriegsmittel zu brutalisieren, daß er aber in der geistigen und verstandesmäßigen Form der Kriegführung jenem Schrumpfungsprozeß unterliegt, der in Teheran begonnen hat und dem raschen Altern seiner Staatsmänner entspricht.

Neditsch zu den Terrorangriffen

Belgrad, 24. April

Ministerpräsident Generaloberst Neditsch besuchte am Montag die von den anglo-amerikanischen Terrorangriffen betroffenen Stadtteile Belgrads. Einem Mitarbeiter der „Novo Vreme" erklärte der Ministerpräsident: „Das serbische Volk wird auch diese schweren Opfer überleben, weil es an sich selbst glaubt. Die anglo-amerikanischen Kapitalisten haben einem Gelichter aus aller Herren Ländern Flugzeuge gegeben, um die wehrlose Bevölkerung hinzumorden zu dem Zweck, sie zur Kapitulation zu zwingen. Aber unser Glaube an uns selbst wird uns vor dem Tod retten, den uns die anglo-amerikanischen Plutokraten wünschen."

„Die Antwort auf die Frage, warum die Anglo-Amerikaner Belgrad bombardieren, ist in unserer Kampfeinstellung gegen den Bolschewismus zu suchen", schreibt „Nowo Vreme" an anderer Stelle. „Die Nordamerikaner, England, Stalin und Tito sind alle gleichmäßig daran schuldig. Sie wollen uns vernichten, weil wir sie durchschaut und trotz ihrer zahlreichen Masken ihr wahres Gesicht erkannt haben."

Figure B.4. "New Criminal Methods of the Air Terror. Low-Level Attacks of the Gangsters of the Sky against the Civilian Population," *Völkischer Beobachter* (Berlin), April 26, 1944.

German Transcription (of Selected Area)

Seit einigen Tagen ist in der Anwendung des englisch-amerikanischen Luftterrors eine neue verbrecherische Methode festzustellen. In einigen Gauen des Reichsgebiets haben die Luftgangster den Terror gegen die Zivilbevölkerung durch Tiefangriffe erweitert. Jagdflugzeuge beschossen mit Maschinengewehren aus geringer Höhe Frauen und Kinder in den Straßen der Städte und Bauern auf dem Felde.

Dabei muß festgestellt warden, daß es sich nicht um Einzelaktionen mordgieriger Luftbanditen handelt, die ihrem Trieb um 'Killen' in jeder Form nachgehen wollen. Es handelt sich vielmehr um bewußte und systematische Anwendung einer neuen Taktik im Terror gegen die Zivilbevölkerung. . . .

Es gibt kein Argument und keinen Vorwand militärischer Art für die Rechtfertigung dieser Methode. Wehrlose Frauen und Kinder in den Straßen niederzuknallen, das ist nicht mehr eine Angelegenheit der Kriegführung sondern gehört in das Gebiet der Kriminalistik. Die Anwendung solcher Methoden kennzeichnet die Bolschewisierung des Krieges, der die Anglo-Amerikaner sich in ihrer geistigen und militärischen Haltung haben ausliefern müssen. . . .

Die Nordamerikaner, England, Stalin und Tito wollen uns vernichten, weil wir sie durchschaut und trotz ihrer zahlreichen Masken Ihr wahren Gesicht erkannt haben.

English Translation

For several days a new criminal method has been noticed in the English-American air terror. In some districts of the Reich the gangsters of the air have extended the terror against the civilian population with strafing attacks. Fighters fired machine guns from a low altitude at women and children in the streets of towns and farmers in the fields.

It must be noted that these are not individual actions of murderous bandits of the sky who want to pursue their drive for killing in any form. Rather, it is a deliberate and systematic application of a new tactic in the terror against the civilian population. . . .

There is no argument or pretext of a military nature to justify this method. Gunning down defenseless women and children in the streets is no longer a matter of warfare but belongs to the field of criminology. The use of such methods characterizes the Bolshevization of the intellectual and military attitudes of war that Anglo-Americans must deliver. . . .

The North Americans, England, Stalin and Tito want to destroy us because we have seen through them and, despite their numerous masks, have recognized their truce face.

USA.-Gangster deckt das alliierte Kriegsziel auf:

Morden, zerstückeln, versklaven . . .

Wir werden den Vansittarts gebührend antworten

VB Berlin, 5. Mai

Im Mai-Heft der amerikanischen Zeitschrift „See" lobt ein Major Malcolm Wheeler Nicolson seinen wütenden Haß gegen das deutsche Volk spaltenlang aus und faßt seine Forderungen nach völliger Auslöschung Deutschlands wie folgt zusammen:

„Die Freiheit der friedliebenden Völker fordert es, daß die militärische Junkerkaste ausgelöscht wird, daß Preußen von seinen dort gebürtigen Einwohnern gesäubert und das Land an Bevölkerungen mit friedlicheren Tendenzen verteilt wird. Auch andere strategische deutsche Gebiete sollen durch Nichtdeutsche bevölkert werden, und Korridore mit friedlichen Rassen besiedelt, sollten errichtet werden, um die kriegsliebenden Teutonen von einander zu trennen. Die deutsche Mentalität sollte durch die Verheiratung deutscher Frauen mit Mitgliedern der Besatzungskräfte geheilt werden. Deutsche Kinder sollten getrennt von ihren Nazi-Eltern erzogen werden."

Hier findet man alles wieder, was Vansittart unter ungeteiltem Beifall der Briten verlangt. Dem verfolgungswahnsinnigen Yankee gelingt es sogar, sein englisches Vorbild noch zu übertrumpfen, indem er die USA-Neger auf deutsche Frauen loslassen und ihnen ihre Kinder rauben will, ganz im Geist der jüdischen Mädchenhändler und Kidnapper, die in den USA ihr Wesen treiben. Man muß sich darüber klar sein, daß hier keineswegs ein verrückter Außenseiter spricht, sondern daß diese sadistischen Phantasien in den USA weiteste Kreise beschäftigen, die von den Juden unablässig in diesem Sinn bearbeitet worden sind. Dieses Subjekt, das sich selbst natürlich von der Front fernhält und andere bluten läßt, „begründet" seinen Kannibalismus damit, daß die Deutschen sich nicht widerstandslos ergeben, sondern kämpfen, um zu leben. So etwas läuft also drüben als „Major" verkleidet herum! Offenbar bildet sich dieser Gangster ein, daß sein Wutschrei uns einschüchtern könnte. Wir sind ihm nur dankbar dafür, daß er die Karten des Roosevelt-Gesindels so offen auf den Tisch legt.

Die Antwort wird der deutsche Soldat geben und mit ihm das ganze deutsche Volk, dem dieses verächtliche Pack ans Leben greift. Sie wird so ausfallen, daß die Welt von der Gefahr befreit wird, dauernd unter dem erpresserischen Druck solcher Kanaillen zu stehen, die im jüdischen Auftrag einen Krieg nach dem anderen anzetteln und sich an der unsauberen Vorstellung berauschen, ein großes Volk wie die Indianer behandeln zu können, die sie bis auf einige Museumsstücke ausgerottet haben.

Wenn es noch eines Beweises bedurft hätte, daß die Geldsackdemokratie die ideale Brutstätte für völlige moralische Verlumpung ist, so ist es dem Mister Nicolson aus USA. gelungen, diesen Beweis zu erbringen und aller Welt klarzumachen, wovor sie der deutsche Sieg bewahren wird.

Figure B.5. "USA-Gangsters Reveal the Allied War Aims: Murder, Dismember, Enslave . . . ," *Völkischer Beobachter* (Berlin), May 6, 1944.

German Transcription (of Selected Area)

Dem verfolgungswahnsinnigen Yankee gelingt es sogar sein englisches Vorbild noch zu übertrumpfen indem er die USA Neger auf deutsche Frauen loslassen und ihnen ihre Kinder rauben will, ganz im Geist der jüdischen Madchenhandler und Kindnapper, die in den USA ihr Wesen treiben.

English Translation

The persecution maniac Yankee has even succeeded in outdoing his English role model by releasing the USA Negro on German women and robbing them of their children in the spirit of the Jewish girl-traders and kidnappers, who pursue their activity in the USA.

Die Verbrecher des James Doolittle

VB **Berlin**, 22 Mai

Wie um dem Vorwurf ihrer unsoldatischen Grausamkeit im Luftkrieg eine unbestreitbare Spezifikation zu geben, erweiterten die anglo-amerikanischen Barbaren ihr europäisches Flugprogramm in der jüngsten Zeit um die Tiefangriffe mit Bordwaffen auf die Bevölkerung. der Wehrmachtbericht erwähnt sie jetzt zum erstenmal in der ausgewogenen Zweckmäßigkeit seiner Formulierung kaum ohne Grund. Als ob es den vieltausendfachen Mördern am friedlichen Leben nicht genügte, mit der Schuld des wahllosen Bombenwurfs aus großen Höhen und bei unsichtigem Wetter durch geschlossene Wolkendecken ohne Zielmöglichkeit belastet zu sein, griffen die Engländer und Amerikaner vor allem bei ihren tiefräumigen Vorstößen mit Jagdverbänden zu den Maschinengewehren und Kanonen, die sie gegen das harmloseste, das wehrloseste, das fürwahr von jeder militärischen Bedeutung am weitesten entfernte Ziel richteten, gegen den einzelnen Spaziergänger, gegen Bauern bei der Feldarbeit, gegen Kinder auf dem Schulweg, gegen Frauen, die in ihren Markttaschen kaum Objekte von militärischer Wichtigkeit bei sich trugen, gegen den Menschen und seine Menschlichkeit schlechthin.

Die zynische Deutlichkeit des feindlichen Terrors überschlägt sich je weniger wichtig diese jüngsten Ziele der Luftoffensive dem gesunden soldatischen Empfinden in kriegerischer Hinsicht erscheinen mußten, desto weniger schützte man sie — denn wer dächte unverdorbenen Sinnes daran, daß die friedliche Harmlosigkeit gerade wegen dieses Charakters zum bevorzugten Opfer der feindlichen Verbrecher werden könnte? Soweit wir uns mit dem Gedanken abfanden, daß der Krieg für viele Männer den Tod bedeuten muß, so fern standen wir dem Mord, den er unter den Hoheitszeichen der Engländer und Amerikaner an Frauen und Kindern verübt. Wir werden aus dieser grausamen Lehre lernen müssen.

Die Sühne für die Vernichtung des abendländischen Kulturguts, für die Brandstiftung in den europäischen Wohnstädten, für die erschlagenen und verbrannten Opfer eines rasenden Irrsinns wird sich einmal aus den Ruinenfeldern ihr Recht beweisen. Der Meuchelmord auf offener Straße aber muß rechtzeitig mit seinen Daten festgehalten werden, um zu den Anklageakten zu kommen. Wir erheben die Forderung nach der verdienten Strafe, die vielleicht die Geschichte an den feigen Tätern bald vollziehen mag, nicht nur in Bausch und Bogen, sondern wissen Beispiele für das abzuurteilende Verbrechen, leider, in Hülle und in Fülle. Von den vielen aus den jüngsten Tagen nur diese:

Aus Hützel im Kreise Soltau wird ein Tiefangriff auf den Kleinbahnhof gemeldet;

bei Langenhagen im Kreise Harburg-Land fielen die Luftgangster über die Bauern auf den Feldern her;

ein Gehöft in Wiebertsdorf im mecklenburgischen Kreise Ludwigslust wurde mit Bordwaffen beschossen, der Bauer wurde getötet;

Kratzeburg im pommerschen Kreise Stargard zählte unter den Opfern eines Tiefangriffes besonders Frauen;

ein Rittergut im Kreise Malchin, das mit Bordwaffen beschossen wurde, hatte zwei Verletzte zu beklagen;

in der Stadt Hagenau schossen die Terrorflieger in die Wohnhäuser;

sonntägliche Spaziergänger in der Nähe der Reichshauptstadt wurden unter das Feuer der Bordwaffen genommen, und in einem Ausflüglerzug der Strecke Bernau—Eberswalde wurden drei Fahrgäste getötet, einer schwer und einer leicht verletzt.

Diese Liste läßt sich lang fortsetzen. Es sei versichert, daß uns kein Anklagepunkt unter den Tisch fallen wird, und daß wir auf den Tag bewahren, was uns der feige Meuchelmord jetzt niederträchtig antut. Ob die Ausflügler, die am Sonntag in der überfallenen Heidekrautbahn die Einschläge feindlicher MG.-Garben prasseln hörten, ob die Bauern in Neu-Löwenberg oder die Einwohner von Wensickendorf, denen Mühle, Scheunen, Ställe, ja die Kirche ihres Ortes in Brand gesetzt wurden, ob die Schnitter von Lehnitz bei Berlin oder die Überlebenden des zwischen Neu-Ruppin und Wildberg überfallenen Reichsbahnomnibus, die fünf aus ihrer Mitte fallen sahen und sechs schwer verletzt bargen — alle werden eines Tages als Zeugen auftreten, wenn die Gerechtigkeit der Geschichte ihr Urteil fällen wird. Noch ist die Welt nicht so weit im jüdischen Blutrausch versunken, daß jeder heimtückische Mörder seiner Straflosigkeit schon sicher sein darf!

Doch so schuldig sich jeder einzelne Schütze machte, der seine Waffe auf die unverteidigte Harmlosigkeit richtete, so schwer beschuldigen diese Schandtaten das System der feindlichen Kriegführung, ihre Gesinnung, und vor allem ihre Verantwortlichen. Über den kaltblütigen Mord aus den tief über den Straßen preschenden Jagdflugzeugen regiert nicht ein einmal verzeihlicher Irrtum, nicht die schon sträfliche Leichtfertigkeit, sondern die brutale Absicht, ein eiskalter und mit der nüchternen Klarheit des haßgetriebenen Wahnsinns gefaßter, vorbereiteter und durchgeführter Plan. Der Feind bekennt sich dazu schamlos in der voreiligen Überheblichkeit des vermeintlichen Siegers.

Als amerikanische Flieger, die von Flugzeugträgern gestartet waren, wie in anderen japanischen Städten auch in Tokio Passanten in den Straßen ermordet hatten, beförderte Roosevelt den Organisator und Anführer der feigen Mordtat, James Doolittle, zum General. Er wurde vom pazifischen auf den europäischen Kriegsschauplatz versetzt. Er hat dort angesichts aller vielfältigen Möglichkeiten zum soldatischen Waffengang die unsoldatischen Methoden des Tokioter Mordraids nicht verabscheuen gelernt, sondern sie zu uns importiert. Er vergißt, daß die Stufenleiter so verdienter Rangerhöhungen am Galgen enden mag.

Denn weder die Vernunft noch das menschliche Gewissen rechtfertigen dem Träger einer Uniform ein Verhalten, das ihn den Verbrechern gleichstellt — um nicht mit unseren Worten unsere Empörung auszudrücken, sondern mit dem Sinn etwa eines Hirtenbriefes, den am Sonntag von den Kanzeln aller belgischen Kirchen der Kardinal van Roey, Primas von Belgien und Erzbischof von Mecheln, gegen die Brutalität des anglo-amerikanischen Luftterrors verlesen ließ. Gerade an der Sanftmut seiner Ueberzeugung gemessen, lieh der kirchliche Würdenträger seiner Empörung eine ungewöhnliche Schärfe. Er wies nachdrücklich darauf hin, wie die Wirklichkeit alle Erklärungen aus London und Washington Lügen straft, daß die Zerstörungen an Besitz und Leben durch den Luftkrieg eine unvermeidbare Folge militärischer Operationen darstellten. Nicht zur Vernichtung von Verkehrsmitteln und Fabriken, sondern von wenigen Fällen abgesehen, blindlings und unterschiedslos auf ganze Quadratkilometer dichtbebauter Wohngebiete würfe der Feind die Lasten seiner Spreng- und Brandbomben, und offensichtlich ohne alle mindesten Vorsichtsmaßnahmen, die unerläßlich seien, um das Leben unschuldiger Menschen zu schonen. Die Welt, sagt der Kardinal van Roey in seinem Hirtenbrief, wird solches Handeln mit Abscheu erwidern.

Mit Abscheu. Mit Ekel. Mit Verachtung. Mit dem Gefühl der unvermeidlichen Pflicht, sich dieser Attentäter auf Recht und Gewissen ihrer Kultur und Zivilisation zu entledigen. Mit jener notgezwungenen Anstrengung also, die schließlich das Joch der unmenschlichen Barbarei von ihren Schultern schüttelt. Denn Recht und Unrecht, Leben oder Mord dürfen nebeneinander keinen Platz haben. Wenn schon einer, und notfalls mit dem Aufgebot der härtesten Mittel, weichen muß, so das Unrecht des feigen Mordes unserem Recht auf unser freies Leben.

Figure B.6. "The Crimes of James Doolittle," *Völkischer Beobachter* (Berlin) May 23, 1944.

German Transcription (of Selected Area)

Die Sühne für die Vernichtung des abendländischen Kulturguts, für die Brandstiftung in den europäischen Wohnstädten, für die erschlagenen und verbrannten Opfer eines rasenden Irrsinns wird sich einmal aus den Ruinenfeldern ihr Recht beweisen. Der Meuchelmord auf offener Straße aber muß rechtzeitig mit seinem Daten festgehalten werden, um zu den Anklageakten zu kommen. Wir erheben die Forderung nach der verdienten Strafe, die vielleicht die Geschichte an den feigen Tätern bald vollziehen mag, nicht nur in Bausch und Bogen, sondern wissen Beispiele für das abzuurteilende Verbrechen, leider, in Hülle und in Fülle. . . .

Als amerikanische Flieger, die von Flugzeugträgern gestartet waren, wie in anderen japanischen Städten auch in Tokio Passanten in den Straßen ermordet hatten, beförderte Roosevelt den Organisator und Anführer der feigen Mordtat, James Doolittle, zum General. Er wurde vom pazifischen auf den europäischen Kriegsschauplatz versetzt. Er hat dort angesichts aller vielfältigen Möglichkeiten zum soldatischen Waffengang die unsoldatischen Methoden des Tokioter Mordraids nicht verabscheuen gelernt, sondern sie zu uns importiert.

English Translation

The atonement for the destruction of the occidental cultural heritage, for the arson in European cities, and for the slain and burned victims of a frenzied insanity will prove its right by the ruins. The insidious murder in open streets, however, must be recorded in order to come to form an indictment. We demand the deserved punishment, which may soon make the story of the cowardly perpetrators known, not only completely but, unfortunately, include the abundance of examples of the condemned crimes. . . .

When American flyers, who had launched from aircraft carriers, killed civilians in the streets of Tokyo and other Japanese cities, Roosevelt promoted the organizer and leader of the cowardly murderous act, James Doolittle, to the rank of General. He was transferred from the Pacific to the European Theater of war. In view of all the various possibilities for military action, he did not abhor the unsoldierly methods of the Tokyo raid, but rather imported them to us.

So morden die Luftgangster Frauen und Kinder

Koblenz, 29. Mai

Bei den Angriffen amerikanischer Mordgangster auf Zivilpersonen, besonders auf Frauen und Kinder, im Gebiete des Rheins wurde bei Remagen ein Personendampfer der Köln-Düsseldorfer Schiffahrtsgesellschaft von drei zweimotorigen Jägern im Tiefflug mit Bordwaffen angegriffen. Der Passagierdampfer „Ostmark" war ohne weiteres aus der Höhe in der die Mordgangster über ihn hinwegflogen, als Ausflugdampfer zu erkennen. Bei dem Mordangriff wurden sechs Personen getötet, darunter drei Frauen und zwei Kinder. 19 Personen, darunter elf Frauen und ein Kind, wurden schwer verletzt. Außerdem wurden noch zahlreiche Personen leicht verletzt.

Im Strandbad Sinzig im Kreise Ahrweiler beschossen amerikanische Mordgangster badende Personen mit Bordwaffen. — Bei den weiteren Angriffen auf Zivilpersonen wurde in Hestrup bei Bentheim ein Kind durch Bordwaffenbeschuß schwer verletzt.

Auch bei Paris wurden, einer amtlichen französischen Meldung zufolge, Zivilpersonen in den Vororten im Departement Seine-et-Oise angegriffen. In einem Falle wurden 90 Reisende getötet und weit mehr als 100 verletzt. Heftige Angriffe richteten sich weiter gegen die ländliche Umgebung von Abbeville, wo ein Friedhof von Bomben buchstäblich umgewühlt wurde. Unter den angegriffenen Zielen befanden sich auch in Lyon und St. Etienne in erster Linie dichtbesiedelte Arbeiterviertel, Krankenhäuser, Schulen und Kirchen. In St. Etienne wurden in einer Kirche, in der gerade ein Trauung stattfand, etwa 100 Personen getötet. Ein Volltreffer in eine Schule begrub unter den Trümmern 30 Kinder mit ihren Lehrern. In Lyon wurden zwei Krankenhäuser getroffen und ein Gebäude der Universität zerstört. In Lyon wurden zum Zeichen der Trauer alle Vergnügungsstätten für einige Tage geschlossen.

Staatssekretär Henriot verurteilte mit schärfsten Worten die unmenschlichen Bombenangriffe der ehemaligen französischen Alliierten, die sich dabei nicht einmal scheuten, diese Barbarei als das Vorspiel der Befreiung zu bezeichnen. Mit Empörung vernahmen seine Zuhörer die Verlustzahlen von Lyon, St. Etienne, Chambery und Grenoble und die Schilderungen über die noch schwelenden Brände und Menschenverluste in Marseille, Avignon und Nimes am Sonnabend.

Ritterkreuz für Befehlshaber der ungarischen Ostfronttruppen

Berlin, 29. Mai.

Der Führer verlieh das Ritterkreuz des Eisernen Kreuzes an den Befehlshaber der ungarischen Ostfronttruppen, Generaloberst Vitez Geza Lakatos, in Anerkennung seiner Verdienste im Angriff sowie in der erfolgreichen Abwehr der feindlichen Angriffe im Raum von Kolomea.

Figure B.7. "This Is How Gangsters of the Sky Murder Women and Children," *Völkischer Beobachter* (Berlin), May 30, 1944.

German Transcription (of Selected Area)

Bei den Angriffes amerikanischer Mordgangster auf Zivilpersonen, besonders auf Frauen und Kinder, im Gebiete des Rheins wurde bei Remagen ein Personendampfer der Köln-Düsseldorfer Schiffahrtsgesellschaft von drei zweimotoriges Jägern im Tiefflug mit Bordwaffen angegriffen. Der Passagierdampfer "Ostmark" war ohne weiteren aus der Höhe in der die Mordgangster über ihn hinwegflogen, als Ausflugdampfer zu erkennen. Bei dem Mordangriff wurden sechs Personen getötet, darunter drei Frauen und zwei Kinder. 19 Personen, darunter elf Frauen und ein Kind, wurden schwer verletzt. Außerdem wurden noch zahlreiche Personen leicht verletzt.

Im Strandbad Sinzig im Kreise Ahrweiler beschossen amerikanische Mordgangster badende Personen mit Bordwaffen.—Bei den weiteren Angriffen auf Zivilpersonen wurde in Hestrup bei Bentheim ein Kind durch Bordwaffen beschuß schwer verletzt.

English Translation

In the attack of American gangsters on civilians, especially women and children, in the Rhine area a passenger steamer of the Köln-Düsseldorfer shipping company was attacked near Remagen by three two-engine fighters at low altitude. The passenger steamer "Ostmark" was clearly distinguishable as an excursion steamer from the height in which the gangsters flew. The murderous attack killed six people, including three women and two children. 19 people, including 11 women and one child, were seriously injured. In addition, many people were slightly injured.

In the beach resort Sinzig, in the district of Ahrweiler, American gangsters fired on people bathing. In another strafing attack on civilians in Hestrup (near Bentheim), a child was seriously injured.

Feindlicher Luftterror schon seit 1914

Vor 30 Jahren erfolgten die ersten Angriffe auf die deutsche Zivilbevölkerung / Von Otto Riebicke

Im allgemeinen herrscht die Auffassung, daß die Einbeziehung der Zivilbevölkerung in den Luftkrieg, wie er von der Gegenseite begonnen wurde, eine Erscheinung ist, die erst der Verlauf dieses Krieges sah. Hier liegt ein großer Irrtum vor. Der Einsatz des Terrors aus der Luft ist keine Erfindung des Luftmarschalls Harris oder anderer anglo-amerikanischer Luftwaffengenerale, sondern ein Kriegsmittel, das bereits im ersten Weltkrieg, und zwar schon seit den Jahren 1914 und 1915 ganz bewußt und skrupellos von der feindlichen Führung zum Einsatz gebracht wurde. Was wir also in der Gegenwart erlebt haben und noch immer erleben, hat seine Anfänge, die schon recht beachtlich sind, in der ersten großen Auseinandersetzung mit unseren westlichen Gegnern.

Der erste Fliegerangriff auf deutsches Reichsgebiet fand in der Nacht zum 23. August 1914 statt. Ein französisches Militärflugzeug näherte sich der offenen Stadt Müllheim i. B. und warf zwei Bomben ab, die jedoch nur einen geringen Sachschaden verursachten. Einen Monat später warf ein französischer Flieger bei Düsseldorf drei Bomben ab, die einen Menschen töteten. Am 8. Oktober erschien wieder ein französischer Flieger über Düsseldorf, seine Bomben töteten vier und verwundeten neun Menschen. Am 21. November versuchten zwei französische Flieger einen Angriff auf Friedrichshafen; während das eine Flugzeug durch die Bodenabwehr abgeschossen wurde, löste das andere eine Bombe mitten über der Stadt aus, durch die ein Zivilist getötet, zwei Frauen und ein Kind verletzt wurden.

Im Dezember 1914 wurde Freiburg i. Br. mehrere Male von Einzelfliegern angegriffen, durch den dritten Angriff, der am 13. Dezember aus einer Flughöhe von 1000 m erfolgte, wurden zwei Zivilisten getötet und 16 verletzt. Von nun an setzte eine gewisse Planmäßigkeit der feindlichen Luftangriffe ein; rücksichtslos wurden — nach einer Pause bis zum Frühjahr 1915 — Orte auch ohne militärische Ziele angegriffen. An neun Tagen des Monats April wurden 13 Ortschaften in Württemberg und Baden mit insgesamt 82 Fliegerbomben belegt; 24 Tote und 29 Verletzte waren das Opfer. In dieser Zeit fanden auch die ersten Nachtangriffe statt. Die Feindmächte steigerten die rücksichtslosen, völkerrechtswidrigen Luftangriffe nun offen gegen die Zivilbevölkerung. In Freiburg wurden Bomben in eine Kinderschar geworfen, die bei Schulschluß auf die Straße stürmte, in Kandern eine Bombe mitten in einen Schulhof, auf dem eine große Anzahl von Kindern spielte. Waren es bis dahin meist nur Einzelflugzeuge, die terroristische Angriffe gegen die Zivilbevölkerung flogen, so wandelte sich das Bild im Sommer 1915.

Am 15. Juni 1915 fand der erste Terror-Großangriff statt, der nur zu diesem Zweck geplant war. In der Morgenfrühe dieses Tages starteten dreiundzwanzig Flugzeuge — eine für die damalige Zeit sehr große Zahl — gegen Karlsruhe mit dem ausdrücklichen, im französischen amtlichen Bericht zugegebenen Befehl, die Hauptstadt des Großherzogtums Baden, besonders das Schloß, zu bombardieren. Terrorflieger trafen zwischen 5.50 und 6.20 Uhr über der Stadt ein.

Obwohl auf der Feindseite bekannt war, daß das Schloß außer der ehrwürdigen Großherzogin Luise seit mehreren Wochen auch die Königin von Schweden beherbergte, wurde die Residenz angegriffen. Etwa hundert Häuser wurden durch den Abwurf von 107 Bomben beschädigt, darunter das Großherzogliche Schloß und das Palais des Prinzen Max von Baden. Unter den 30 Toten und 59 Verletzten, die diesem Angriff zum Opfer fielen, befanden sich nur drei Soldaten, die dort in Lazarettpflege waren.

Fast genau ein Jahr darauf, am 22. Juni 1916, fand dann auf die gleiche Stadt der ruchlose Angriff statt, der als „Kindermord von Karlsruhe" den Abscheu der ganzen gesitteten Welt erregte. An diesem Tage — es war Fronleichnamstag — griff ein französischer Verband die offene Stadt, ohne irgendein militärisches Ziel im Auge zu haben, an. Aus großer Höhe wurden die Bomben über mehrere Stadtviertel abgeladen. Sie richteten insbesondere vor dem Zirkus Hagenbeck, kurz vor Beginn einer Kindervorstellung, in wenigen Minuten ein grausiges Blutbad an; von den dort getroffenen 154 Kindern blieben 82 tot am Platze; insgesamt wurden 254 Zivilisten verletzt, davon 120 tödlich.

Die Gewissenlosigkeit der feindlichen Luftkriegführung, an sich schon einwandfrei festgestellt, geht auch aus einer Agentennachricht an den Chef des Generalstabes des Feldheeres vom 2. August 1916 hervor, in der als Auffassung der französischen Heeresleitung mitgeteilt wird, „man verfolge mit den Fliegerangriffen den Zweck, durch ständige Beunruhigung die deutsche Bevölkerung noch schneller reif für den Frieden zu machen; man könne im Hinblick auf dieses Ziel keine Rücksicht auf unschuldige Opfer nehmen; es seien weitere Fliegerangriffe auf deutsche Städte und Ortschaften vorgesehen . . ."

Ohne Zweifel ist es dem Heimatluftschutz — in erster Linie durch Aufklärung der Bevölkerung über die Gefahren, seine Vorkehrungen und seine Sicherungsmaßnahmen — zu verdanken, daß die Verluste der Zivilbevölkerung in den letzten Jahren des ersten Weltkrieges zurückgingen; er hat uns viele Menschenleben und große Werte erhalten. Die unmittelbaren Schäden durch die Luftangriffe der Alliierten auf das Reichsgebiet betrugen 746 Tote und 1843 Verletzte, der Sachschaden wird auf 25 Millionen Mark beziffert.

Ein „Panther" erledigt drei „T 34"

Berlin, 24. August

Ein zur Erkundung angesetzter Panther war nordöstlich von Warschau in unübersichtlichem Gelände unerwartet auf drei bolschewistische Kampfwagen vom Typ T 34 gestoßen. Zugleich entdeckte der Panzerkommandant, Unteroffizier Grohner, zwei weitere T 34, die in einer Waldschneise Feuerstellung bezogen hatten.

Unteroffizier Grohner nahm den ungleichen Kampf sofort auf. Noch bevor die überraschten Bolschewisten ihre Panzertürme drehten, hatte die Panther-Besatzung ihnen ihre Sprenggranaten entgegengejagt, und wenig später gingen die drei Kolosse in Flammen auf. Als die Panther-Besatzung ihr Rohr auf die beiden Sowjets in der Waldschneise richten wollten, hatten diese sich bereits ins Dickicht zurückgezogen.

Figure B.8. "Enemy Air Terror since 1914," *Westdeutscher Beobachter* (Aachen), August 1944.

German Transcription (of Selected Area)

Im allgemeinen herrscht die Auffassung, daß die Einziehung der Zivilbevölkerung in dem Luftkrieg, wie er von der Gegenseite begonnen wurde, eine Erscheinung ist, die erst der Verlauf dieses Krieges sah. Hier liegt ein großer Irrtum vor. Der Einsatz des Terrors aus der Luft ist keine Erfindung des Luftmarschalls Harris oder anderer anglo-amerikanischer Luftwaffengenerale, sondern ein Kriegsmittel, das bereits im ersten Weltkrieg, und zwar schon zeit den Jahren 1914 und 1915 ganz bewußt und skrupellos von der feindlichen Führung zum Einsatz gebracht wurde. . . .

Am 22. Juni 1916, fand dann auf die gleiche Stadt (Karlsruhe) der ruchlose Angriff statt, der als "Kindermord von Karlsruhe" den Abscheu der ganzen gesitteten Welt erregte. An diesem Tage—es war Fronleichnamstag—griff ein französischer Verband die offene Stadt, ohne irgendein militärisches Ziel im Auge zu haben, an. Aus großer Höhe wurden die Bomben über mehrere Stadtviertel abgeladen. Sie richteten insbesondere vor dem Zirkus Hagenbeck, kurz vor Beginn einer Kindervorstellung, in wenigen Minuten ein grausiges Blutbad an. . . .

English Translation

In general, it is believed that the inclusion of the civilian population in the air war, as was started by our opponents, is a phenomenon that only was witnessed in this war. The use of terror from the air is not the invention of the Air Marshall Harris or other English-American Air Force generals, but rather an instrument of war that was already used in the First World War (already in 1914 and 1915) quite deliberately and unscrupulously by the enemy leadership. . . .

On June 22, 1916, the ruthless attack took place on the same city (Karlsruhe). Known as the "child murder of Karlsruhe," this attack aroused the disgust of the entire civilized world. On that day—it was during the observance of Corpus Christi—a French unit attacked the open city without any military purpose in mind. From a great height, the bombs were dropped over several neighborhoods, especially in front of the Hagenbeck circus, shortly before the beginning of a children's performance, where they inflicted a gruesome bloodbath in just a few minutes.

Appendix C
Index of Flyer Trials

Table C.1. Index of Flyer Trials[1]

Trial Number/ Location	Airmen	Aircraft/Unit	Date of Incident	Location	Treatment
12-25 Dachau	Sgt. Frank P. Pacylowsky (tail gunner)	44th B.G. 506th B.S. B-24(42-110034) *Southern Comfort II* MACR 7805	July 21, 1944	Bauerbach (Grabfeld)	Assaulted
	2nd Lt. Orville E. Flora, Jr. (bombardier)	44th B.G. 506th B.S. B-24(42-110034) *Southern Comfort II* MACR 7805			Assaulted
12-27 Dachau	2nd Lt. Richard G. Chapman (pilot)	351st B.G. 510th B.S. B-17 (42-107077) *Shoo Shoo Baby* MACR 7556	July 19, 1944	Obergünzburg	Assaulted
12-43 Dachau	Most likely: 2nd Lt. Howland J. Hamlin (pilot)	459th B.G. 756th B.S. B-24 (42-52358) *Hell's Belle* MACR 6851	July 20, 1944	Öhningen/ Radolfzell	Killed
	2nd Lt. Richard V. S. Newhouse (copilot)	459th B.G. 756th B.S. B-24 (42-52358) *Hell's Belle* MACR 6851			Killed
12-45 Dachau	Most likely: 2nd Lt. George Hunter (bombardier)	459th B.G. 756th B.S. B-24 (42-52358) *Hell's Belle* MACR 6851	July 20, 1944	Wolltmatingen (Constance)	Killed
	S/Sgt. Ronald W. Cherrington (ball turret)	459th B.G. 756th B.S. B-24 (42-52358) *Hell's Belle* MACR 6851			Killed
	S/Sgt. Raymond C. Ertel (tail gunner)	459th B.G. 756th B.S. B-24 (42-52358) *Hell's Belle* MACR 6851			Killed
	S/Sgt. Aaron C. Slaughter (radio)	459th B.G. 756th B.S. B-24 (42-52358) *Hell's Belle* MACR 6851			Killed

1. Names of the accused are spelled as they were recorded in court records. The outcome reflects the known changes made to the sentences by the US military review boards or the Federal Republic of Germany. Airmen's names and aircraft/unit information are based on court records, MACR reports, and Luftwaffe reports (e.g., the so-called KU and J Reports as well as documents from Dulag Luft).

Accused	Offender's Status	Age	Party Status	Profession	Sentencing	Outcome:
Karl Wilhelm Baumgärtner	Regional Police Chief	57	Unknown	Police	Acquitted	
Georg Ostenrieder	Civilian	37	Unknown	Unknown	2 years	
Kurt Gross	SS Major	35	Yes	Attorney	Life	Reduced to 25 years; Paroled April 1954
Adolf Mattes	SS 1st Lt.	35	Yes	Plumber	Life	Reduced to 25 years; Paroled April 1954
Eduard Mack	SS 2nd Lt.	41	Yes	Business-man	5 years	
Rudolf Spletzer	SS Mast.Sgt.	34	No	Carpenter	Life	Reduced to 25 years; Paroled April 1954
Thomas Aschner	SS Corp.	36	Yes	Farmer	3 years	Acquitted (Lack of Evidence)
Albert Heim	Army Major	54	Unknown	Unknown	Death	Executed February 2, 1949
Fritz Saalmueller	Army 1st Lt.	42	Unknown	Mayor	Life	Reduced to 25 years
Herbert Kunze	Army 1st Lt.	23	Unknown	School Teacher	Death	Executed October 22, 1948

Trial Number/ Location	Airmen	Aircraft/Unit	Date of Incident	Location	Treatment
12-57 Dachau	1st Lt. Rudolph Melvin Stohl (pilot)	457th B.G. 749th B.S. B-17 (42-97067) *Georgia Peach/Black Puff Polly* MACR 5297	May 28, 1944	Bremen (Verden, Osterholt)	Assaulted
	2nd Lt. David W. Schellenger (copilot)	457th B.G. 749th B.S. B-17 (42-97067) *Georgia Peach/Black Puff Polly* MACR 5297			Assaulted
	2nd Lt. James Earl Thomas (bombardier)	457th B.G. 749th B.S. B-17 (42-97067) *Georgia Peach/Black Puff Polly* MACR 5297			Assaulted
	2nd Lt. James O. Millham (navigator)	457th B.G. 749th B.S. B-17 (42-97067) *Georgia Peach/Black Puff Polly* MACR 5297			Assaulted
	S/Sgt. Robert Charles Kreite (top turret)	457th B.G. 749th B.S. B-17 (42-97067) *Georgia Peach/Black Puff Polly* MACR 5297			Assaulted
	S/Sgt. Irwin Arthur Welling (waist gunner)	457th B.G. 749th B.S. B-17 (42-97067) *Georgia Peach/Black Puff Polly* MACR 5297			Assaulted
12-80 Dachau	1st Lt. James E. Dale (pilot)	446th B.G. 707th B.S. B-24 (42-94994) *Dissipated Duck* MACR 6933	July 11, 1944	Ludenhausen	Killed
12-336 Dachau	S/Sgt. Herbert Gebers (waist gunner)	482 B.G. 813th B.S. B-17 (42-3357) MACR 2781	June 10, 1944	Frankfurt a.M. (Gestapo HQ)	Assaulted
12-413-1 Dachau	2nd Lt. Jack Rives (pilot)	404th F.G. 507th F.S. P-47 (42-26285) MACR13620	March 1, 1945	Quirnbach	Killed
12-468 Heidelberg	2nd Lt. Thomas Knapp Kohlhaas (copilot)	384th B.G. 544th B.S. B-17 (43-37713) *Grewsome Crewsome* MACR11129	December 1, 1944	Beltershain/ Gruenberg	Killed
	S/Sgt. John Joseph Bellovary (ball turret)	384th B.G. 544th B.S. B-17 (43-37713) *Grewsome Crewsome* MACR11129			Killed
	T/Sgt. Milton Benjamin Erich (top turret)	384th B.G. 544th B.S. B-17 (43-37713) *Grewsome Crewsome* MACR11129			Killed
	1st Lt. Hugh Legar Evans (pilot)	384th B.G. 544th B.S. B-17 (43-37713) *Grewsome Crewsome* MACR11129			Killed
12-472 Dachau	Sgt. Ferdinand E. Flach (nose/turret gunner)	445th B.G. 701st B.S. B-24 (41-28922) *Texas Rose* MACR 9386	September 27, 1944	Hattenrod	Killed
	Sgt. Lee R. Huffman (waist gunner)	445th B.G. 701st B.S. B-24 (41-28922) *Texas Rose* MACR 9386			Killed
12-481 Heidelberg	S/Sgt. Charles E. Hollenbeck Jr. (waist gunner)	392nd B.G. 578th B.S. B-24 (41-29002) MACR 10206	September 21, 1944	Wollendorf (Neuwied)	Killed

Accused	Offender's Status	Age	Party Status	Profession	Sentencing	Outcome:
Otto Rueger	Army Private	43	Yes	Baker	3 years	
Wilhelm Schroeder	Police Sgt.	56	Yes	Police	2½ years	
August Tidow	Civilian	41	Unknown	Mechanic	Acquitted	
Josef Stern	Civilian	25	Unknown	Unknown	Acquitted	
Ludwig Dösch	Gestapo	35	Unknown	Unknown	4 years	
Hans Heitkamp	Gestapo	35	Unknown	Banker	Life	Reduced to 25 years
Karl Dressler	Gestapo	38	Unknown	Distillation Expert	Death	Reduced to Life; Paroled August 1954
Karl Block	Blockleiter	43	Yes (1937)	Farmer	Death	Executed January 12, 1946
Karl Neunobel	Civilian		Unknown	Unknown	10 years	
Herman Noack	HJ Camp Leader	34	No	Athletic Instructor	Death	Executed March 21, 1947
Karl Georg Böss	Fire Brigade	42	Yes (1927)	Butcher	8 years	Paroled January 1951
Dominikus Thomas	Volkssturm	51	Unknown	Shoemaker	Death	Executed January 12, 1946

Trial Number/ Location	Airmen	Aircraft/Unit	Date of Incident	Location	Treatment
12-485 Ludwigsburg	1st Lt. Robert Dykeman (copilot)	100th B.G. 350th B.S. B-17 (42-31537) *Randie Lou* MACR 7809	July 30, 1944	Altenburg	Killed
12-489 Ludwigsburg	S/Sgt. William W. Lambertus (tail gunner)	486th B.G. 832nd B.S. B-17 (43-37909) MACR 7711	August 4, 1944	Borkum Island	Killed
	2nd Lt. William J. Myers (copilot)	486th B.G. 832nd B.S. B-17 (43-37909) MACR 7711			Killed
	Sgt. James W. Danno (ball turret)	486th B.G. 832nd B.S. B-17 (43-37909) MACR 7711			Killed
	Sgt. William F. Dold (waist gunner)	486th B.G. 832nd B.S. B-17 (43-37909) MACR 7711			Killed
	2nd Lt. Harvey M. Walthall (pilot)	486th B.G. 832nd B.S. B-17 (43-37909) MACR 7711			Killed
	Sgt. Kenneth Faber (radio)	486th B.G. 832nd B.S. B-17 (43-37909) MACR 7711			Killed
	2nd Lt. Howard S. Graham (bombardier)	486th B.G. 832nd B.S. B-17 (43-37909) MACR 7711			Killed
12-489-1 Dachau					
12-524 Ludwigsburg	1 Unknown		November 1, 1944	Between Wallhausen & Sangerhausen	Assaulted
12-531 Dachau	Sgt. William H. Kane (top turret)	457th B.G. 748th B.S. B-17 (42-31615) *Snafusk Shamrock* MACR 6003	June 20, 1944	Neu-Wulmstorf (Hamburg)	Killed
12-551 Dachau	2nd Lt. John W. Cowgill (navigator)	445th B.G. 702nd B.S. B-24 (42-50383) *King Kong* MACR 9390	September 27, 1944	Nentershausen work camp	Killed
	2nd Lt. Hector V. Scala (bombardier)	445th B.G. 702nd B.S. B-24 (42-50383) *King Kong* MACR 9390			Killed

Accused	Offender's Status	Age	Party Status	Profession	Sentencing	Outcome:
Ernst Mueller	Political Official	51	Yes (1933)	Police	Death	Executed June 10, 1947
Kurt Goebell	Navy	50	No	Chemist	Death	Paroled February 1956
Walter Krolikovski	Flak Member	41	Unknown	Navy	Life	Paroled March 1952
Erich Wentzel	Flak Member	45	No	Merchant	Death	Executed December 3, 1948
Karl Weber	Flak Member	42	No	Navy	25 years	Paroled December 1951
Jakob Valentine Seiler	Flak Member	39	Yes (1932)	Salesman	Death	Executed October 15, 1948
Johann Josef Schmitz	Flak Member	52	Unknown	Foreman	Death	Executed October 15, 1948
Johann Pointer	Flak Member	24	Unknown	Butcher	5 years	
Günther Albrecht	Flak Member	23	Unknown	Shipyard Worker	6 years	Paroled July 1950
Karl Geyer	Flak Member	34	Unknown	Farmer	4 years	
Heinz Witzke	Flak Member	35	Unknown	Postman	11 years	Reduced to 6 years
Jan J. Akkermann	Ortsgruppenleiter & Mayor	54	Yes (1930)	Merchant	Death	Executed October 15, 1948
Heinrich Rommel	Police Chief -Borkum	54	Yes (1937)	Police	2 years	Acquitted
Gustav Mammenga	Private Security	52	Unknown	Telephone Operator	20 years	Paroled August 1952
Heinrich Heinemann	Navy	29	Yes	Butcher	18 years	Reduced to 10 years
August Haesiker	RAD Captain	39	Yes (1932)	Merchant	10 years	Paroled December 1952
Klaus Meyer-Gerhards	Air Raid Police		Unknown	Unknown	Acquitted	
Otto Rudolph	Civilian	49	No	Railroad Worker	7 years	Reduced to 2 years
Ernst Böhrs	Civilian	38	Yes	Farmer	7 years	
Peter Brümmer	Civilian	47	Yes	Factory Foreman	20 years	Paroled June 1957
Hermann Dammann	Volkssturm	52	Yes (1933)	Teacher	Death	Reduced to 33 years
Josef Ehlen	Nenters-hausen Camp Commander	33	Unknown	Labor Camp Leader	Death	Reduced to Life
August Viehl	Civilian	47	Unknown	Miner	Death	Executed January 14, 1949

Trial Number/ Location	Airmen	Aircraft/Unit	Date of Incident	Location	Treatment
	Likely: T/Sgt. John J. Donahue (Radio)	445th B.G. 703rd B.S. B-24 (41-29579) *Clay Pigeon* MACR 9387			Killed
12-581 Dachau	Captain Everett S. Lindley (pilot)	1st F.G. 94th F.S. P-38 (44-24132) MACR 13799	April 15, 1945	Mühldorf	Assaulted
12-643 Heidelberg	1st Lt. Paul J. Roberts Jr. (pilot)	356th F.G. 361st F.S. P-47 (42-76177) MACR 9264	October 27, 1944	Buchenau	Assaulted
12-658 Dachau	S/Sgt. William K. Forsythe (waist gunner)	303rd B.G. 459th B.S. B-17 (42-31213) *Pistol Packin' Mama* MACR 5341	May 30, 1944	Lelm (Königslutter am Elm)	Killed
	S/Sgt. Ralph E. Ledogar (radio)	303rd B.G. 459th B.S. B-17 (42-31213) *Pistol Packin' Mama* MACR 5341			Killed
	2nd Lt. William A. Sysel (copilot)	303rd B.G. 459th B.S. B-17 (42-31213) *Pistol Packin' Mama* MACR 5341			Killed
	Sgt. John K. Barry (tail gunner)	303rd B.G. 459th B.S. B-17 (42-31213) *Pistol Packin' Mama* MACR 5341			Killed
12-714 Ludwigsburg	1 Unknown		September 19, 1944	Erbach (on Mariannenau Island in Rhein River)	Assaulted
12-765 Dachau	2nd Lt. George F. Brown, Jr. (pilot)	44th B.G. 506th B.S. B-24 (44-40158) *Tinker Belle* MACR 14110	March 29, 1945	Bergisch-Gladbach	Killed
12-779 Dachau	2nd Lt. Charles E. Woolf (navigator)	305 B.G. 365 B.S. B-17 (42-97350) *Strictly From Hunger* MACR 7276	July 21, 1944	Schollach & Urach	Killed
	S/Sgt. Frank L. Misiak (tail gunner)	305 B.G. 365 B.S. B-17 (42-97350) *Strictly From Hunger* MACR 7276			Killed
	S/Sgt. Meredith M. Mills Jr. (ball turret)	305 B.G. 365 B.S. B-17 (42-97350) *Strictly From Hunger* MACR 7276			Killed
	1st Lt. Leonard A. Kornblau (pilot)	305 B.G. 365 B.S. B-17 (42-97350) *Strictly From Hunger* MACR 7276			Killed
	2nd Lt. Bernard E. Radomski (copilot)	305 B.G. 365 B.S. B-17 (42-97350) *Strictly From Hunger* MACR 7276			Killed

Accused	Offender's Status	Age	Party Status	Profession	Sentencing	Outcome:
Franz Mueller	Civilian	48	Unknown	Miner	6 years	
Martin Baesse	Rural Police	50	Unknown	Police	6 years	
Paul Winkler	District Mining Inspector	51	Yes	District miner inspector	Death	Executed August 5, 1947
Karl Eggert	Gestapo	50	No	Truck driver	Death	Executed November 14, 1947
Matthias Zierhut	Mayor	53	Yes	Mayor	Life	Reduced to 25 years; Paroled June 1955
Johann Gilch	Civilian	59	Yes	Machinist	10 years	Paroled October 1952
Wilhelm Dieterman	Gendarmerie	55	Yes (1932)	Quarry Laborer	Death	Executed January 12, 1946
Andreas Ebling	Civilian			Unknown	Acquitted	
Waldemar Feldmeier	Kreisleiter	37	Yes	Merchant	Death	Executed November 5, 1948
Otto Behme	Ortsgruppen-leiter	45	Yes	Farmer	Acquitted	
Wilhelm Bausch	Civilian		Unknown	Unknown	5 years	
Otto Brehm	Ortsgruppen-leiter		Yes	Unknown	5 years	
Christian Menrath	Ortsgruppen-leiter & Volkssturm	56	Yes	Metal Worker	Death	Executed December 5, 1947
Otto Knopp	Volkssturm	46	Yes	Clerk	Death	Executed December 5, 1947
Gottlieb Werner	Local Party Official	60	Yes	Tax Inspector	Death	Executed December 5, 1947
Max Matthes	SA	53	Yes	Tax Secretary	Life	Paroled February 1954
Heinrich Birnbreier	Local Party Official	33	Yes	Kreis-personal-amtsleiter	Death	Executed December 5, 1947
Josef Eisele	SA	46	Yes	Factory Supervisor	Life	Paroled October 1954
Arthur Faller	Gendarmerie	53	No	Baker	20 years	Paroled February 1954
Friedrich Heim	Blockleiter	42	Yes	Engineer	Acquitted	
Fritz Kuner			Unknown	Unknown	Not found	

Trial Number/ Location	Airmen	Aircraft/Unit	Date of Incident	Location	Treatment
	T/Sgt. James T. Fields (radio)	445th B.G. 702nd B.S. B-24 (42-50383) *King Kong* MACR 9390			Killed
	Likely: T/Sgt. John J. Donahue (Radio)	445th B.G. 703rd B.S. B-24 (41-29579) *Clay Pigeon* MACR 9387			Killed
12-581 Dachau	Captain Everett S. Lindley (pilot)	1st F.G. 94th F.S. P-38 (44-24132) MACR 13799	April 15, 1945	Mühldorf	Assaulted
12-643 Heidelberg	1st Lt. Paul J. Roberts Jr. (pilot)	356th F.G. 361st F.S. P-47 (42-76177) MACR 9264	October 27, 1944	Buchenau	Assaulted
12-658 Dachau	S/Sgt. William K. Forsythe (waist gunner)	303rd B.G. 459th B.S. B-17 (42-31213) *Pistol Packin' Mama* MACR 5341	May 30, 1944	Lelm (Königslutter am Elm)	Killed
	S/Sgt. Ralph E. Ledogar (radio)	303rd B.G. 459th B.S. B-17 (42-31213) *Pistol Packin' Mama* MACR 5341			Killed
	2nd Lt. William A. Sysel (copilot)	303rd B.G. 459th B.S. B-17 (42-31213) *Pistol Packin' Mama* MACR 5341			Killed
	Sgt. John K. Barry (tail gunner)	303rd B.G. 459th B.S. B-17 (42-31213) *Pistol Packin' Mama* MACR 5341			Killed
12-714 Ludwigsburg	1 Unknown		September 19, 1944	Erbach (on Mariannenau Island in Rhein River)	Assaulted
12-765 Dachau	2nd Lt. George F. Brown, Jr. (pilot)	44th B.G. 506th B.S. B-24 (44-40158) *Tinker Belle* MACR 14110	March 29, 1945	Bergisch-Gladbach	Killed
12-779 Dachau	2nd Lt. Charles E. Woolf (navigator)	305 B.G. 365 B.S. B-17 (42-97350) *Strictly From Hunger* MACR 7276	July 21, 1944	Schollach & Urach	Killed
	S/Sgt. Frank L. Misiak (tail gunner)	305 B.G. 365 B.S. B-17 (42-97350) *Strictly From Hunger* MACR 7276			Killed
	S/Sgt. Meredith M. Mills Jr. (ball turret)	305 B.G. 365 B.S. B-17 (42-97350) *Strictly From Hunger* MACR 7276			Killed
	1st Lt. Leonard A. Kornblau (pilot)	305 B.G. 365 B.S. B-17 (42-97350) *Strictly From Hunger* MACR 7276			Killed
	2nd Lt. Bernard E. Radomski (copilot)	305 B.G. 365 B.S. B-17 (42-97350) *Strictly From Hunger* MACR 7276			Killed

Accused	Offender's Status	Age	Party Status	Profession	Sentencing	Outcome:
Reinhard Beck	Civilian	48	No	Banker	4 years	Acquitted (Lack of Evidence)
Franz Mueller	Civilian	48	Unknown	Miner	6 years	
Martin Baesse	Rural Police	50	Unknown	Police	6 years	
Paul Winkler	District Mining Inspector	51	Yes	District miner inspector	Death	Executed August 5, 1947
Karl Eggert	Gestapo	50	No	Truck driver	Death	Executed November 14, 1947
Matthias Zierhut	Mayor	53	Yes	Mayor	Life	Reduced to 25 years; Paroled June 1955
Johann Gilch	Civilian	59	Yes	Machinist	10 years	Paroled October 1952
Wilhelm Dieterman	Gendarmerie	55	Yes (1932)	Quarry Laborer	Death	Executed January 12, 1946
Andreas Ebling	Civilian			Unknown	Acquitted	
Waldemar Feldmeier	Kreisleiter	37	Yes	Merchant	Death	Executed November 5, 1948
Otto Behme	Ortsgruppen-leiter	45	Yes	Farmer	Acquitted	
Wilhelm Bausch	Civilian		Unknown	Unknown	5 years	
Otto Brehm	Ortsgruppen-leiter		Yes	Unknown	5 years	
Christian Menrath	Ortsgruppen-leiter & Volkssturm	56	Yes	Metal Worker	Death	Executed December 5, 1947
Otto Knopp	Volkssturm	46	Yes	Clerk	Death	Executed December 5, 1947
Gottlieb Werner	Local Party Official	60	Yes	Tax Inspector	Death	Executed December 5, 1947
Max Matthes	SA	53	Yes	Tax Secretary	Life	Paroled February 1954
Heinrich Birnbreier	Local Party Official	33	Yes	Kreis-personal-amtsleiter	Death	Executed December 5, 1947
Josef Eisele	SA	46	Yes	Factory Supervisor	Life	Paroled October 1954
Arthur Faller	Gendarmerie	53	No	Baker	20 years	Paroled February 1954

Trial Number/ Location	Airmen	Aircraft/Unit	Date of Incident	Location	Treatment
12-788 Dachau	2nd Lt. George Calvin Padgett (bombardier)	379 B.G. 525 B.S. B-17 (42-29937) MACR 1051	March/April 1945	Wiesbaden jail	Assaulted
	2nd Lt. Harmon Smith Jr. (navigator)	93rd B.G. 328th B.S. B-24 (42-40930) MACR 2366			Assaulted
12-793 Munich	2nd Lt. Charles H. Evans Jr. (navigator)	306th B.G. 368th B.S. B-17 (42-97946) *Hard To Get* MACR 8464	August 29, 1944	Gross-Gerau	Killed
	T/Sgt. Harvey J. Purkey Jr. (top turret)	306th B.G. 368TH B.S. B-17 (42-97946) *Hard To Get* MACR 8464			Killed
12-793-1 Munich					
12-793-2 Dachau					
12-819 Ludwigsburg	2nd Lt. Paul C. Davenport (pilot)	406th F.G. 513th F.S. P-47 (44-20730) MACR 12284	February 2, 1945	Wiesbaden (West of Rhein River)	Assaulted
12-926/ 12-926-1 Ludwigsburg	T/Sgt. Charles Bernard Goldstein (radio)	388th B.G. 563rd B.S. B-17 (44-8437) MACR 12414	February 17, 1945	Hanau	Killed
	S/Sgt. Warren George Hammond (engineer)	388th B.G. 561st B.S. B-17 (43-38623) *Easy Does It* MACR 12432			Killed
	1 Unknown				Killed
12-931 Dachau	2nd Lt. Arthur M. Scott (bombardier)	454th B.G. 738th B.S. B-24 (42-5228) *Hairless Joe* MACR 6971	July 20, 1944	Ailingen/ Friedrichshafen	Killed
12-932 Ludwigsburg	1 Unknown		September 28, 1944	Hornburg	Assaulted
12-1022 Dachau	1 Unknown		May 30, 1944	Rühen	Assaulted
12-1034 Dachau	1st Lt. Edward J. Lower (bombardier)	385th B.G. 548th B.S. B-17 (42-31638) *Big Gas Bird* MACR 8907	September 12, 1944	Ruppertshütten	Killed

Accused	Offender's Status	Age	Party Status	Profession	Sentencing	Outcome:
Friedrich Heim	Blockleiter	42	Yes	Engineer	Acquitted	
Fritz Kuner			Unknown	Unknown	Not found	
Karl Thoma	Police Sgt.	54	No	House painter	1 year	
Heinrich Flauaus	Civilian	24	Unknown	Unknown	Death	Executed April 1, 1946
Nikolaus Fachinger	Police (SiPo)	40	Unknown	Police	Death	Executed April 1, 1946
Anna-Margarete Solomon	Civilian		Unknown	Unknown	2 years	Reduced to 1 year
Margot Zeeck	Civilian		Unknown	Unknown	1 1/2 years	Reduced to 1 year
Peter Schindel	Civilian		Unknown	Unknown	1 year	Reduced to 6 months
Heinrich Deubert	Civilian	44	Unknown	Laborer	15 years	Paroled December 1952
Georg Sturm	Luftwaffe - M.Sgt.	33	Yes (1934)	Unknown	3 years	
Friedrich Katz	Police	56	Unknown	Police	10 years	Reduced to 5 years
Emil Geisser	Civilian	25	Unknown	Unknown	5 years	Reduced to 2½ years
Karl Nerge	Police	52	Unknown	Unknown	5 years	Reduced to 2½ years
Karl Neuber	Gestapo	38	Yes	Driver	7 years	Paroled August 1950
Julius Schulze	Police (KriPo)	41	Unknown	Police	Life	Reduced to 25 years; Paroled December 1953
Adolf Weger	Gestapo	31	Yes	Administration Official	Death	Reduced to life; Paroled October 1954
Hans Seibold	Kreisleiter	43	Yes (1927)	Engineer	Life	Reduced to 30 years; Paroled May 1955
Albert Schraff	Ortsgruppen-leiter	49	Yes (1933)	Farmer & Mayor	Life	Reduced to 20 years; Paroled October 1954
Albert Friedrich Mueller	SS	42	Yes (1929)	Mason	Death	Reduced to life; Paroled February 1954
Wilhelm Foerster	Zellenleiter	43	Yes (1932)	Unknown	2 years	
Otto Winter	Rural Police	62	Unknown	Farmer	Acquitted	
Christian Blum	Police (KriPo)	39	Yes (1937)	Police	1 year	

Trial Number/ Location	Airmen	Aircraft/Unit	Date of Incident	Location	Treatment
12-1034 Dachau	1st Lt. Edward J. Lower (bombardier)	385th B.G. 548th B.S. B-17 (42-31638) *Big Gas Bird* MACR 8907	September 12, 1944	Ruppertshütten	Killed
	1st Lt. Ramon H. Newman (pilot)	385th B.G. 548th B.S. B-17 (42-31638) *Big Gas Bird* MACR 8907			Killed
	2nd Lt. Harvey Dater (copilot)	385th B.G. 548th B.S. B-17 (42-31638) *Big Gas Bird* MACR 8907			Killed
	T/Sgt. Robert E. Kuhn (radio)	385th B.G. 548th B.S. B-17 (42-31638) *Big Gas Bird* MACR 8907			Killed
	Sgt. John J. Smith Jr. (radio)	94th B.G. 410th B.S. B-17 (42-31906) MACR 7739			Killed
12-1068 Dachau	1st Lt. Theodore D. Nielson (pilot)	364th F.G. 384th F.S. P-51 (44-13766) MACR 7620	August 9, 1944	Saulgau	Killed
12-1077 Dachau	1 Unknown		September 28, 1944	Burgdorf	Killed
12-1035 Dachau	1 Unknown		September 28, 1944	Heiningen	Killed
12-1837 Dachau	3 Unknown		May 19, 1944	Vienenburg	Killed
	2 Unknown		May 19, 1944	Lochtum	Killed
12-1086 Ludwigsburg	1st Lt. William M. Couch (navigator)	303rd B.G. 359th B.S. B-17 (42-102484) *Heller's Angel* MACR 11201	November 21, 1944	Hausen (Ginnheim)	Killed
12-1093 Dachau	9 Unknown	Likely members of the following crew: 92nd B.G. 327th B.S. B-17 (42-38025) *Flak Happy* MACR 7565	June 16, 1944	Mittenwald	Assaulted

Accused	Offender's Status	Age	Party Status	Profession	Sentencing	Outcome:
Christian Blum	Police (KriPo)	39	Yes (1937)	Police	1 year	
Kurt Hans	Kriminalrat	35	Yes	Police	Acquitted	
Gottlob Hohloch	Police (KriPo)	48	No	Police	Acquitted	
Josef Huber	SA	39	Yes	Locksmith	Life	Paroled November 1954
Walter Kaiser	SA	31	Unknown	Unknown	Acquitted	
Friedrich Wilhelm Altena	SS Major	45	Yes	Unknown	Life	Paroled April 1957
Wilhelm Pfeiffer	Kreisleiter	38	Yes (1927)	Merchant	Life	Paroled April 1957
Ernst Hermann August Königsdorf	Ortsgruppen-leiter	55	Yes	Teacher	Life	Paroled February 1955
August Reinecke	Mayor	56	Yes (1935)	Railroad Foreman	Life	Paroled November 1954
Hermann Ferdinand Albert Landwehr	Ortsgruppen-amtsleiter	51	Yes (1937)	Farmer	5 years	
Otto Reinhardt	Police Auxiliary	58	Yes (1933)	Police	Life	Paroled June 1956
Robert Schottke	Police Auxiliary	58	Yes (1937)	Interior Decorator	15 years	Paroled June 1953
Ernst Homann	Civilian	47	No	Gardner	Acquitted	
Hartmann Lauterbacher	SS	38	Yes	Merchant	Acquitted	
Arthur Lessmann	Civilian	50	No	Gardner	Acquitted	
Michael Schock	Civilian	37	No	Mechanic	Acquitted	
Wilhelm Heene	Ortsgruppen-leiter & Mayor	53	Yes	Electrical Engineer	Death	Executed April 18, 1947
Wilhelm Matthaei	RAD	44	Yes (1933)	Locksmith	Death	Executed April 18, 1947
Josef Klotz	Army (Home on furlough)		Unknown	Unknown	2 years	
Erhardt Erdt	Civilian		Unknown	Butcher	2 years	
Charlotte Battalo	Civilian		Unknown	Unknown	1 year	
Maria Hegele	Civilian		Unknown	Unknown	1 year	Reduced to 7 months

Trial Number/ Location	Airmen	Aircraft/Unit	Date of Incident	Location	Treatment
	1st Lt. Ramon H. Newman (pilot)	385th B.G. 548th B.S. B-17 (42-31638) *Big Gas Bird* MACR 8907			Killed
	2nd Lt. Harvey Dater (copilot)	385th B.G. 548th B.S. B-17 (42-31638) *Big Gas Bird* MACR 8907			Killed
	T/Sgt. Robert E. Kuhn (radio)	385th B.G. 548th B.S. B-17 (42-31638) *Big Gas Bird* MACR 8907			Killed
	Sgt. John J. Smith Jr. (radio)	94th B.G. 410th B.S. B-17 (42-31906) MACR 7739			Killed
12-1068 Dachau	1st Lt. Theodore D. Nielson (pilot)	364th F.G. 384th F.S. P-51 (44-13766) MACR 7620	August 9, 1944	Saulgau	Killed
12-1077 Dachau	1 Unknown		September 28, 1944	Burgdorf	Killed
12-1035 Dachau	1 Unknown		September 28, 1944	Heiningen	Killed
12-1837 Dachau	3 Unknown		May 19, 1944	Vienenburg	Killed
	2 Unknown		May 19, 1944	Lochtum	Killed
12-1086 Ludwigsburg	1st Lt. William M. Couch (navigator)	303rd B.G. 359th B.S. B-17 (42-102484) *Heller's Angel* MACR 11201	November 21, 1944	Hausen (Ginnheim)	Killed
12-1093 Dachau	9 Unknown	Likely members of the following crew: 92nd B.G. 327th B.S. B-17 (42-38025) *Flak Happy* MACR 7565	June 16, 1944	Mittenwald	Assaulted
12-1104 Ludwigsburg	Sgt. Sheppard Kerman (radio)	303rd B.G. 360th B.S. B-17 (43-37930) MACR 9406	September 28, 1944	Wolfenbüttel	Killed

Accused	Offender's Status	Age	Party Status	Profession	Sentencing	Outcome:
Kurt Hans	Kriminalrat	35	Yes	Police	Acquitted	
Gottlob Hohloch	Police (KriPo)	48	No	Police	Acquitted	
Josef Huber	SA	39	Yes	Locksmith	Life	Paroled November 1954
Walter Kaiser	SA	31	Unknown	Unknown	Acquitted	
Friedrich Wilhelm Altena	SS Major	45	Yes	Unknown	Life	Paroled April 1957
Wilhelm Pfeiffer	Kreisleiter	38	Yes (1927)	Merchant	Life	Paroled April 1957
Ernst Hermann August Königsdorf	Ortsgruppen-leiter	55	Yes	Teacher	Life	Paroled February 1955
August Reinecke	Mayor	56	Yes (1935)	Railroad Foreman	Life	Paroled November 1954
Hermann Ferdinand Albert Landwehr	Ortsgruppen-amtsleiter	51	Yes (1937)	Farmer	5 years	
Otto Reinhardt	Police Auxiliary	58	Yes (1933)	Police	Life	Paroled June 1956
Robert Schottke	Police Auxiliary	58	Yes (1937)	Interior Decorator	15 years	Paroled June 1953
Ernst Homann	Civilian	47	No	Gardner	Acquitted	
Hartmann Lauterbacher	SS	38	Yes	Merchant	Acquitted	
Arthur Lessmann	Civilian	50	No	Gardner	Acquitted	
Michael Schock	Civilian	37	No	Mechanic	Acquitted	
Wilhelm Heene	Ortsgruppen-leiter & Mayor	53	Yes	Electrical Engineer	Death	Executed April 18, 1947
Wilhelm Matthaei	RAD	44	Yes (1933)	Locksmith	Death	Executed April 18, 1947
Josef Klotz	Army (Home on furlough)		Unknown	Unknown	2 years	
Erhardt Erdt	Civilian		Unknown	Butcher	2 years	
Charlotte Battalo	Civilian		Unknown	Unknown	1 year	
Maria Hegele	Civilian		Unknown	Unknown	1 year	Reduced to 7 months
Georg Gruendel	Civilian		Unknown	Unknown	2 years	
Mathias Schandl	Civilian		Unknown	Farmer	1 year	
Gerd Beck	Army	23	Unknown	Baker	Death	Reduced to Life; Paroled September 1954

Trial Number/ Location	Airmen	Aircraft/Unit	Date of Incident	Location	Treatment
12-1104-1 Dachau					
12-1106 Dachau	1st Lt. James T. Hahn (pilot)	303rd B.G. 360th B.S. B-17 (42-97805) MACR 9412	September 28, 1944	Halchter	Killed
12-1109 Dachau	1 Unknown		January/ February 1945	Altwied	Killed
12-1115 Ludwigsburg	S/Sgt. Odis L. Apple Jr. (radio)	392nd B.G. 579th B.S. B-24 (42-50279) MACR 8848	September 13, 1944	Bingen	Killed
12-1119 Dachau	S/Sgt. Edward Supe (gunner)	486th B.G. 834th B.S. B-17 (43-36757) MACR 13887	April 8, 1945	Hof	Assaulted
12-1140 Dachau	1st Lt. Carl J. Hert (copilot)	445th B.G. 703rd B.S. B-24 (42-50729) MACR 11216	November 26, 1944	Springe	Killed
12-1145 Heidelberg	Sgt. Anthony B. Martin (tail gunner)	303rd B.G. 359th B.S. B-17 (42-102484) *Heller's Angel* MACR 11201	November 21, 1944	Ginnheim	Killed
12-1146 Ludwigsburg	1 Unknown		October 1, 1944	Cologne-Bickendorf	Killed
12-1149 Dachau	S/Sgt. Arthur W. Manosh (waist gunner)	97th B.G. 342nd B.S. B-17 (44-6188) MACR 6745	July 20, 1944	Moosinning	Killed
12-1149-1 Dachau					
12-1155 Ludwigsburg	Captain Chester E. Coggeshall Jr. (pilot)	55th F.G. 343rd F.S. P-51 (44-15608) *Cape Cod Express* MACR 13866	April 16, 1945	Freilassing	Killed

Accused	Offender's Status	Age	Party Status	Profession	Sentencing	Outcome:
Otto Weinreich	Ortsgruppen-leiter	46	Yes (1933)	Mechanic	Life	Paroled July 1954
Wilhelm Kanschat	Wehrmacht Reserve	57	Yes (1933)	Merchant	Death	Reduced to Life; Paroled November 1954
Wilhelm Bock	Rural Police Sgt.	50	Unknown	Police	Death	Executed April 3, 1947
Johann Gross	Gestapo	35	Yes (1933)	Police	Life	Paroled June 1953
Ludwig Firmenich	Civilian	54	Yes (1933)	Janitor in bank	Life	Paroled April 1954
Heinrich Overdick	Civilian	53	Yes (1933)	Janitor in commerce	Life	Paroled April 1954
Wilhelm Kraft	Ortsgruppen-leiter	48	Yes (1929)	Railway Inspector	10 years	Released February 1952
Philipp Jaeger	Civilian	52	Unknown	Farm Leader	6 years	Released Mach 1950
Adolf Knell	Civilian	57	Yes (1937)	Labor office worker	6 years	Released April 1950
Hugo Schuck	Civilian	22	No	Bank Employee	1 year	
Friedrich Hanselmann	Civilian	35	Unknown	Bricklayer	2 years	
Heinrich Rixen	Military	36	No	Textile Tanner	Death	Paroled April 1957
Clemens Wiegand	Ortsgruppen-leiter	46	Yes (1935)	Teacher	Death	Executed January 10, 1946
Anton Albishausen	Volkssturm	47	Unknown	Tailor	Life	Paroled August 1955
Josef Boullet	Ortsgruppen-leiter	43	Yes	Locksmith	Death	Reduced to Life; Paroled November 1955
Fritz Ohsiek	Civilian	53	No	Carpenter	Acquitted	
Anton Schosser	Kreisleiter	43	Yes (1933)	Unknown	Death	Executed
Josef Goldbrunner	Army	27	Yes	Unknown	Acquitted	
Alfons Jacob Wilm	Civilian		Yes	Accountant	Acquitted	
Emil Breitenstein	Kreisleiter	47	Yes	Unknown	Acquitted	
August Kobus	Ortsgruppen-leiter & Mayor	45	Yes (1931)	Unknown	Death	Executed March 15, 1946

Trial Number/ Location	Airmen	Aircraft/Unit	Date of Incident	Location	Treatment
12-1155-1 Ludwigsburg					
12-1155-2 Dachau					
12-1160 Dachau	1 Unknown		September 12, 1944	Warsleben	Assaulted
12-1168 Dachau	2nd Lt. Homer W. Goff (bombardier)	303rd B.G. 427th B.S. B-17 (44-8335) MACR 9405	September 25, 1944	Cramme	Killed
12-1182 Dachau	Most likely the following crew: 2nd Lt. Edward A. Martiniak (copilot)	310th B.G. 428th B.S. B-25 (43-27529) MACR 12920	Between March 10-21, 1945	Neckarsulm	Killed
	S/Sgt. Richard H. Palmer (radio & gunner)	310th B.G. 428th B.S. B-25 (43-27529) MACR 12920			Killed
	S/Sgt. Donald O. Griffith (top turret)	310th B.G. 428th B.S. B-25 (43-27529) MACR 12920			Killed
	1 Unknown				
12-1182-1 Dachau	Captain S.K. Anderson		Between March 10–24, 1945	Brackenheim/ Dürrenzimmern	Killed
12-1182-2 Dachau	S/Sgt. Roscoe W. Harvey (tail gunner)	310th B.G. 428th B.S. B-25 (43-27529) MACR 12920	Between March 10–22, 1945	Neckarsulm	Killed
12-1203 Dachau	Sgt. Rubin F. Harkey (gunner)	460th B.G. 760th B.S. B-24 (42-50888) MACR 8739	September 22, 1944	Palling	Killed
12-1217 Dachau	2nd Lt. Robert Leslie Van Horn (pilot)	55th F.G. 338th F.S. P-51 (44-14598) MACR 13397	March 18, 1945	Winterkasten	Killed
12-1247 Dachau	2nd Lt. Robert E. Delavan (navigator)	467th B.G. 789th B.S. B-24 (41-29363) MACR 7377	August 5, 1944	Hohenhausen	Killed
	2nd Lt. Louis E. Younkin (bombardier)	467th B.G. 789th B.S. B-24 (41-29363) MACR 7377			Killed
	3 Unidentified crewmembers				Killed
12-1292 Dachau	Major James Briggs Cheney (pilot)	361st F.G. 376th F.S. P-51 (44-14219) *Scat-Cat* MACR 9502	October 15, 1944	Dorsten	Assaulted

Accused	Offender's Status	Age	Party Status	Profession	Sentencing	Outcome:
Bernhard Stredele	Kreisleiter	34	Yes (1930)	Unknown	Death	Reduced to life; Paroled April 1957
Karl Boehm	Army	27	Unknown	Optician	Acquitted	
Rüdiger von Massow	Civilian	25	Unknown	Student	Acquitted	
Karl Polus	Civilian	34	Unknown	Unknown	1½ years	
Wilhelm Luethje	Police	55	Yes (1929)	Police	Life	Paroled December 1954
Heinz Endress	Leader of NSU Works	44	Yes	Unknown	Death	Executed December 4, 1946
Richard Drauz	Kreisleiter	51	Yes (1930)	Unknown	Death	Executed December 4, 1946
Karl Otto	Army Lt. Col.	49	Yes (1930)	Unknown	5 years	Released May 1950
Siegfried Scholz	Army Captain	36	No	Unknown	Acquitted	
Erich Hinkel	Gestapo	38	Yes (1932)	Apprentice in Father's Business	20 years	Paroled April 10, 1954
Adolf Schmidt			Unknown	Unknown	Stay of Proceeding	
Gustav Stork	Rural Police	47	Unknown	Police	Death	Executed June 20, 1947
Gustav Deppe	Rural Police	53	Unknown	Grocery Store worker	Death	Executed June 20, 1947
Franz Durschke	Rural Police	45	Unknown	Chimney Sweeper	Death	Executed June 20, 1947
Heinrich Jurgens			Unknown	Unknown	Stay of Proceeding	
Werner Hess	Army 2nd Lt.	32	No	Protestant minister	6 months	
Hubert von Svoboda	Army		Unknown	Unknown	Stay of Proceeding	

Trial Number/ Location	Airmen	Aircraft/Unit	Date of Incident	Location	Treatment
12-1299 Ludwigsburg	3 Unknown		October 1, 1944	Schwickers-hausen/ Nordheim	Killed
12-1307 Dachau	Most likely: S/Sgt. Jack Steiner Patrick (tail gunner)	381st B.G. 532nd B.S. B-17 (44-6020) *Underground Farmer* MACR 7882	August 6, 1944	Lübeck-Siems	Killed
12-1368/69 Dachau	Most likely the following crew: T/Sgt. Frank Borchick (radio)	467th B.G. 790th B.S. B-24 (42-52497) *Osage Express* MACR 6235	June 21, 1944/ September 1944	Veelböken/ Pingelshagen/ Klink/Mollin/ Schwerin	Killed
	S/Sgt. Stanley E. Brzezowski (gunner)	467th B.G. 790th B.S. B-24 (42-52497) *Osage Express* MACR 6235			Killed
	S/Sgt. Thomas A. Gensert (ball turret)	467th B.G. 790th B.S. B-24 (42-52497) *Osage Express* MACR 6235			Killed
	1st Lt. Edwin M. Helton (pilot)	467th B.G. 790th B.S. B-24 (42-52497) *Osage Express* MACR 6235			Killed
	2nd Lt. Richard J. Ludka Jr. (bombardier)	467th B.G. 790th B.S. B-24 (42-52497) *Osage Express* MACR 6235			Killed
	2nd Lt. Maurice E. Nelson (copilot)	467th B.G. 790th B.S. B-24 (42-52497) *Osage Express* MACR 6235			Killed

Accused	Offender's Status	Age	Party Status	Profession	Sentencing	Outcome:
Friedrich Salzmann	Gendarmerie Captain	61	Unknown	Police	Death	Reduced to life; Paroled June 1955
Wilhelm Anding	Police Reserve	54	Unknown	Merchant	Life	Released January 1954
Albert Singer	Gendarmerie	60	Unknown	Police	Death	Reduced to life; Died in Prison October 25, 1949
Walter Schneider	Gendarmerie	53	No	Painter	Life	Paroled June 1954
Richard Hammer	Civilian	38	Yes (1929)	Machinist	Life	Paroled March 1954
Hans Ohrt	Civilian	42	No	Shipbuilder	1 year	
Gotthard Parzyk	Blockleiter	45	Yes (1931)	Machinist	Death	Reduced to life; Paroled March 1954
Willi Voight	Air raid Warden	38	Unknown	Machinist	10 years	Released March 1952
Paul Doose	SS 1st Lt.	41	Yes	Factory Policeman	3 years	Acquitted (Lack of evidence)
Ernst Hachmeier	SS	43	Yes (1937)	River Work Supervisor	Life	Paroled March 1954
Otto Giese	Civilian	43	Yes (1937)	Machinist	Life	Paroled January 1954
Friedrich Lehmensick	Civilian	46	Yes (1936)	Machinist	3 years	
Karl Neeb	Civilian	45	Yes (1932)	Machinist	2 years	Acquitted (Lack of evidence)
Hertha Stapelfeldt	Civilian	39	Unknown	Housewife	21 months	
Christian Schutt	Civilian	40	Unknown	Unknown	Acquitted	
Hans Wahls	Civilian	46	Unknown	Unknown	Acquitted	
August Doose			Unknown	Unknown	Stay of Proceeding	
Karl Jentz			Unknown	Unknown	Stay of Proceeding	
Paul Sack			Unknown	Unknown	Stay of Proceeding	
Friedrich Hildebrandt	Gauleiter	48	Yes	Farmer	Death	Executed November 5, 1947
Wilhelm Bollow	Kreisleiter	49	Yes	Secretary	Death	Executed November 5, 1947
Karl Gronwaldt	Kreisamts-leiter	54	Yes	Merchant	Death	Executed November 5, 1947
Kurt Muller	Deputy Ortsgruppen-leiter	45	Yes	Farmer	Death	Executed November 5, 1947
Fritz Schroder	Blockleiter	47	Yes	Farmer	20 years	Released February 1952
Ewald Haselow	Ortsgruppen-leiter	50	Yes	Forester	Death	Executed November 5, 1947

Trial Number/ Location	Airmen	Aircraft/Unit	Date of Incident	Location	Treatment
	1st Lt. Edwin M. Helton (pilot)	467th B.G. 790th B.S. B-24 (42-52497) *Osage Express* MACR 6235			Killed
	2nd Lt. Richard J. Ludka Jr. (bombardier)	467th B.G. 790th B.S. B-24 (42-52497) *Osage Express* MACR 6235			Killed
	2nd Lt. Maurice E. Nelson (copilot)	467th B.G. 790th B.S. B-24 (42-52497) *Osage Express* MACR 6235			Killed
	S/Sgt. Charles L. Knowles Jr. (gunner)	467th B.G. 790th B.S. B-24 (42-52497) *Osage Express* MACR 6235			Killed
	S/Sgt. Carmine Margiasso (gunner)	467th B.G. 790th B.S. B-24 (42-52497) *Osage Express* MACR 6235			Killed
	T/Sgt. Warren C. Rankin (engineer)	467th B.G. 790th B.S. B-24 (42-52497) *Osage Express* MACR 6235			Killed
	Most likely the following crew: 2nd Lt. Arthur B. Majestic (copilot)	448th B.G. 713th B.S. B-24 (42-95186) MACR 6264			Killed
	2nd Lt. Victor D. Dolecek (bombardier)	448th B.G. 713th B.S. B-24 (42-95186) MACR 6264			Killed
	Sgt. George J. Grubisa (waist gunner)	448th B.G. 713th B.S. B-24 (42-95186) MACR 6264			Killed
	S/Sgt. Hershel O. Hamlin (radio)	448th B.G. 713th B.S. B-24 (42-95186) MACR 6264			Killed
	S/Sgt. Bertil S. Johnson (top turret)	448th B.G. 713th B.S. B-24 (42-95186) MACR 6264			Killed
	Sgt. Sammie D. Vinson (waist gunner)	448th B.G. 713th B.S. B-24 (42-95186) MACR 6264			Killed
12-1395 Dachau	Most likely the following crew: S/Sgt. Frank A. Caldwell (waist gunner)	100th B.G. 349th B.S. B-17 (42-107211) *Liberty Belle* MACR 7816	July 29, 1944	Ottmannshausen	Killed
	S/Sgt. Marccena F. Dottoviano (bombardier)	100th B.G. 349th B.S. B-17 (42-107211) *Liberty Belle* MACR 7816			Killed
	F/O Victor I. Kinkade (navigator)	100th B.G. 349th B.S. B-17 (42-107211) *Liberty Belle* MACR 7816			Killed
	S/Sgt. Jack C. Kromer (ball turret)	100th B.G. 349th B.S. B-17 (42-107211) *Liberty Belle* MACR 7816			Killed
	T/Sgt. Anthony G. Trebnik (radio)	100th B.G. 349th B.S. B-17 (42-107211) *Liberty Belle* MACR 7816			Killed
12-1397 Freising	T/Sgt. Donald L. Hein (radio)	445th B.G. 700th B.S. B-24 (44-10493) MACR 11087	December 12, 1944	Hanau	Killed

Accused	Offender's Status	Age	Party Status	Profession	Sentencing	Outcome:
Kurt Muller	Deputy Ortsgruppen-leiter	45	Yes	Farmer	Death	Executed November 5, 1947
Fritz Schroder	Blockleiter	47	Yes	Farmer	20 years	Released February 1952
Ewald Haselow	Ortsgruppen-leiter	50	Yes	Forester	Death	Executed November 5, 1947
Franz Penzien	Kreisstellen-leiter	51	Yes	Construction Official	Death	Executed November 5, 1947
Karl Grosch	SS	49	Yes (1933)	Locksmith	Life	Reduced to 25 years; Paroled February 1954
Fritz Erich Haehnert	Ortsgruppenleiter & Mayor	43	Yes (1933)	Mayor	Death	Executed July 15, 1947
Albert Hendrich	Kreisleiter	57	Yes (1933)	Unknown	20 years	Released January 1954
Albert Bury	Police	45	Unknown	Police	Death	Executed November 19, 1947

Trial Number/ Location	Airmen	Aircraft/Unit	Date of Incident	Location	Treatment
	S/Sgt. Charles L. Knowles Jr. (gunner)	467th B.G. 790th B.S. B-24 (42-52497) *Osage Express* MACR 6235			Killed
	S/Sgt. Carmine Margiasso (gunner)	467th B.G. 790th B.S. B-24 (42-52497) *Osage Express* MACR 6235			Killed
	T/Sgt. Warren C. Rankin (engineer)	467th B.G. 790th B.S. B-24 (42-52497) *Osage Express* MACR 6235			Killed
	Most likely the following crew: 2nd Lt. Arthur B. Majestic (copilot)	448th B.G. 713th B.S. B-24 (42-95186) MACR 6264			Killed
	2nd Lt. Victor D. Dolecek (bombardier)	448th B.G. 713th B.S. B-24 (42-95186) MACR 6264			Killed
	Sgt. George J. Grubisa (waist gunner)	448th B.G. 713th B.S. B-24 (42-95186) MACR 6264			Killed
	S/Sgt. Hershel O. Hamlin (radio)	448th B.G. 713th B.S. B-24 (42-95186) MACR 6264			Killed
	S/Sgt. Bertil S. Johnson (top turret)	448th B.G. 713th B.S. B-24 (42-95186) MACR 6264			Killed
	Sgt. Sammie D. Vinson (waist gunner)	448th B.G. 713th B.S. B-24 (42-95186) MACR 6264			Killed
12-1395 Dachau	Most likely the following crew: S/Sgt. Frank A. Caldwell (waist gunner)	100th B.G. 349th B.S. B-17 (42-107211) *Liberty Belle* MACR 7816	July 29, 1944	Ottmannshausen	Killed
	S/Sgt. Marccena F. Dottoviano (bombardier)	100th B.G. 349th B.S. B-17 (42-107211) *Liberty Belle* MACR 7816			Killed
	F/O Victor I. Kinkade (navigator)	100th B.G. 349th B.S. B-17 (42-107211) *Liberty Belle* MACR 7816			Killed
	S/Sgt. Jack C. Kromer (ball turret)	100th B.G. 349th B.S. B-17 (42-107211) *Liberty Belle* MACR 7816			Killed
	T/Sgt. Anthony G. Trebnik (radio)	100th B.G. 349th B.S. B-17 (42-107211) *Liberty Belle* MACR 7816			Killed
12-1397 Freising	T/Sgt. Donald L. Hein (radio)	445th B.G. 700th B.S. B-24 (44-10493) MACR 11087	December 12, 1944	Hanau	Killed
12-1418 Dachau	1st Lt. Donald E. Brent (pilot)	445th B.G. 702nd B.S. B-24 (42-50324) MACR 9388	September 27, 1944	Renda	Killed

Accused	Offender's Status	Age	Party Status	Profession	Sentencing	Outcome:
Franz Penzien	Kreisstellen-leiter	51	Yes	Construction Official	Death	Executed November 5, 1947
Karl Grosch	SS	49	Yes (1933)	Locksmith	Life	Reduced to 25 years; Paroled February 1954
Fritz Erich Haehnert	Ortsgruppenleiter & Mayor	43	Yes (1933)	Mayor	Death	Executed July 15, 1947
Albert Hendrich	Kreisleiter	57	Yes (1933)	Unknown	20 years	Released January 1954
Albert Bury	Police	45	Unknown	Police	Death	Executed November 19, 1947
Wilhelm Hafner	Police	50	Unknown	Police	Death	Executed November 19, 1947
Karl Henkel	Police		Unknown	Police	Acquitted	
Georg Kalte	Police		Unknown	Police	Acquitted	
Johann Loser	Police		Unknown	Landrat	Acquitted	
Wilhelm Plitt	Police		Unknown	Police	Acquitted	
Georg Schultheiss	Army Sgt.	54	Unknown	Unknown	Acquitted	

Trial Number/ Location	Airmen	Aircraft/Unit	Date of Incident	Location	Treatment
12-1422 Dachau	Captain Fletcher Eugene Adams (pilot)	357th F.G. 362nd F.S. P-51 (43-12468) *The Southern Belle* MACR 5200	May 30, 1944	Tiddische	Killed
12-1449 Dachau	5 Unknown		Fall of 1944	Munich	Killed
12-1457 Ludwigsburg	2nd Lt. Darwin R. Nichols (copilot)	351st B.G. 511th B.S. B-17 (42-97318) *Dina Mite* MACR 8898	March 27, 1945	Giessen	Killed
12-1497 Darmstadt	2nd Lt. John N. Sekul (copilot)	491st B.G. 854th B.S. B-24 (42-110107) *Wham! Bam! Thank You Ma'm!* MACR 8296	August 26, 1944	Rüsselsheim	Killed
12-2381	Sgt. William A. Dumont (ball turret)	491st B.G. 854th B.S. B-24 (42-110107) *Wham! Bam! Thank You Ma'm!* MACR 8296			Killed
	S/Sgt. Thomas D. Williams Jr. (radio)	491st B.G. 854th B.S. B-24 (42-110107) *Wham! Bam! Thank You Ma'm!* MACR 8296			Killed
	Sgt. Elmore L. Austin (waist gunner)	491st B.G. 854th B.S. B-24 (42-110107) *Wham! Bam! Thank You Ma'm!* MACR 8296			Killed
	F/O Haigus Tufenkjian (navigator)	491st B.G. 854th B.S. B-24 (42-110107) *Wham! Bam! Thank You Ma'm!* MACR 8296			Killed
	2nd Lt. Norman J. Rogers Jr. (pilot)	491st B.G. 854th B.S. B-24 (42-110107) *Wham! Bam! Thank You Ma'm!* MACR 8296			Killed
	Sgt. Sidney E. Brown (tail gunner)	491st B.G. 854th B.S. B-24 (42-110107) *Wham! Bam! Thank You Ma'm!* MACR 8296			
					Assaulted & Escaped
	Sgt. William M. Adams (nose gunner)	491st B.G. 854th B.S. B-24 (42-110107) *Wham! Bam! Thank You Ma'm!* MACR 8296			Assaulted & Escaped

Accused	Offender's Status	Age	Party Status	Profession	Sentencing	Outcome:
Gustav Heidmann	Volkssturm	47	Yes (1933)	Army	Death	Reduced to life; Paroled January 1954
Erich Schnelle	Civilian	46	Unknown	Farmer	20 years	Released March 1950
Kurt Wilhelm Martin	SS	30	Unknown	Unknown	Acquitted	
Rudolf Dirnagel	SS	35	Unknown	Unknown	Acquitted	
Hans Pietsch	SS		Unknown	Unknown	Stay of Proceeding	
Karl Loesch	Gestapo	47	Yes	Police	11 years	Released September 1952
Josef Hartgen	Local Propaganda Chief	41	Unknown	Opel Plant Worker	Death	Executed November 10, 1945
Franz Umstatter	Army	36	Unknown	Gardner	Death	Released March 1948
Heinrich Barthel	Civilian	43	No	Factory Worker	15 years	Paroled December 1953
Katharina Reinhardt	Civilian	39	No	Store Owner	Death	Reduced to 30 years; Paroled December 1953
Margarete Witzler	Civilian	50	No	Store Owner	Death	Reduced to 30 years; Paroled December 1953
Georg Daum	Civilian	50	No	Opel plant Worker	25 years	Paroled January 1954
Karl Fugmann	Civilian	42	Unknown	Locksmith	Acquitted	
Philipp Gutlich	Civilian		No	Farmer	Death	Executed November 10, 1945
Johann Opper	Civilian	60	No	Telephone Operator	Death	Executed November 10, 1945
Johannes Seipel	Civilian	67	Unknown	Farmer	Death	Executed November 10, 1945
August Wolf	Civilian	43	No	Opel Plant Manager	15 Years	Paroled December 1953
Friedrich Wust	Civilian	47	Yes	Opel Plant Worker	Death	Executed November 10, 1945

Trial Number/ Location	Airmen	Aircraft/Unit	Date of Incident	Location	Treatment
12-1502 Dachau	Cpl. William Harville Armstrong (radio)	313th T.C.G. 49th T.C.S. C-47 (43-16049) MACR 9913	September 17, 1944	Kranenburg	Killed
	T/Sgt. George Thomas Harrison (crew chief)	313th T.C.G. 49th T.C.S. C-47 (43-16049) MACR 9913			Killed
12-1534 Dachau	2nd Lt. Richard G. Lipinski (copilot)	491st B.G. 854th B.S. B-24 (44-40271) *House of Rumor* MACR 10766	November 26, 1944	Lauenau	Assaulted
	2nd Lt. Fred Willis Jr. (navigator)	491st B.G. 854th B.S. B-24 (44-40271) *House of Rumor* MACR 10766			Assaulted
12-1538 Ludwigsburg	Most likely: 2nd Lt. Raymond C. Hopp (copilot)	398th B.G. 600th B.S. B-17 (42-107218) *Agony Wagon II* MACR 7221	July 1944	Aken (Elbe)	Killed
12-1542 Dachau	Sgt. Robert W. Boynton (nose gunner)	485th B.G. 831st B.S. B-24 (42-52709) MACR 6388	June 13, 1944	Attenkirchen	Killed
	2nd Lt. Dennis H. Griggs (co-pilot)	485th B.G. 831st B.S. B-24 (42-52709) MACR 6388			Killed
12-1545 Dachau	Pvt. Jack A. Maxwell (waist gunner)	446th B.G. 706th B.S. B-24 (41-29177) *Ginger* MACR 8471	July 31, 1944/ August 25, 1944	Neunkirchen, Saarbruecken, Burbach	Killed
	Sgt. Willard R. Fetterhoff (tail gunner)	6th B.G. 706th B.S. B-24 (41-29177) *Ginger* MACR 8471			Killed
	Sgt. Ted Zemonek (waist gunner)	6th B.G. 706th B.S. B-24 (41-29177) *Ginger* MACR 8471			Killed
	T/Sgt. Charles E. Wyatt Jr. (top turret)	6th B.G. 706th B.S. B-24 (41-29177) *Ginger* MACR 8471			Killed

Accused	Offender's Status	Age	Party Status	Profession	Sentencing	Outcome:
Ludwig Kluettgen	SA Lt. Col.	38	Yes	Soldier	Death	Executed October 29, 1948
Carl Bruns	Mayor	59	Yes	Carpenter	2 years	
Karl Dierking	Civilian	55	Unknown	Merchant	2 years	
Fritz Hunke	Civilian	50	Unknown	Businessman	2 years	
Friedrich Meyer	Civilian	55	Unknown	Unknown	2 years	
Heinrich Schmedes	Civilian	48	Unknown	Electrician	2 years	
Wilhelm Mundo	Police Auxiliary	40	No	Merchant	Acquitted	
Erich Weiss	Police Auxiliary	42	No	Merchant	Acquitted	
Franz Friedl	Police	59	Yes	Rural Police Chief	7 years	Died in prison, May 1948
Therese Gebhardt	Frauenschaft Leader	45	No	Unknown	Life	Reduced to 10 years
Heinrich Heidenreich	County Administrator	65	Unknown	Unknown	Acquitted	
Johann Heilmeier	Kreisleiter chauffer & SA	30	Yes	Unknown	Life	Reduced to 10 years; Paroled January 1952
Maximilian Hermann	SS	48	Yes	Labor office	Death	Executed in December 1947
Korbinian Kaindl	Army	50	Yes	Farmer	Acquitted	
Hans Lechner	Mayor	48	Yes	Mayor	7 years	Reduced to 4 years
Hans Staudinger	Kreisleiter Assistant	44	Yes	Luftwaffe (1939–1942)	Death	Executed in December 1947
Josef von Gruen	Blockleiter & Rural Police Chief	55	Yes	Unknown	2 years	
Else Kreis	Civilian		Unknown	Unknown	Stay of Proceeding	
Fritz Dintinger	Lt. Col. SS	49	Yes (1936)	Police President	Life	Paroled September 1954
Fritz Dietrich	Sgt. SS	49	Yes (1936)	Mechanic & Electrician	Death	Executed October 29, 1948
Albert Eli	Corp. SS	38	Yes (1937)	Metal Worker	Life	Paroled October 1954
Karl Hunsicker	2nd Lt. SS	39	Yes (1935)	Merchant	Death	Executed October 29, 1948

Trial Number/ Location	Airmen	Aircraft/Unit	Date of Incident	Location	Treatment
	2nd Lt. John B. Good (copilot)	446th B.G. 706th B.S. B-24 (42-52467) *Hula Wahine II* MACR 7826			Killed
	1st Lt. Emil Berry Jr. (pilot)	446th B.G. 706th B.S. B-24 (42-52467) *Hula Wahine II* MACR 7826			Killed
	S/Sgt. Lewis E. Pulsipher (waist gunner)	446th B.G. 706th B.S. B-24 (42-52467) *Hula Wahine II* MACR 7826			Killed
12-1576 Dachau	Most likely the following crew members: F/O Lewis P. Martner (Bombardier)	447th B.G. 709th B.S. B-17 (42-31128) *Mohawk* MACR 7547	July 20/21, 1944	Teutleben (Gotha)	Killed
	T/Sgt. Frank T. Witek (top turret)	447th B.G. 709th B.S. B-17 (42-31128) *Mohawk* MACR 7547			Killed
12-1592 Ludwigsburg	1 Unknown		October 7, 1944	Billroda	Assaulted
12-1594 Ludwigsburg	1 Unknown		January 20, 1944	Alvessee	Assaulted
12-1595 Dachau	1st Lt. William C. Littlewood (pilot)	XII TAC 111th R.S. F-6 (42-103460) *Weenie Merchant II* MACR 11619	December 25, 1944	Bechtheim	Assaulted
12-1622 Ludwigsburg	1 Unknown		March 1945	Hastenbeck	Assaulted
12-1650 Dachau	1 Unknown		October 1944	Hoffnungsthal	Assaulted
12-1666 Dachau	1st Lt. William J. Simmons (pilot)	354th F.G. 355th F.S. P-51 (43-12486) MACR 4187	April 25, 1944	Michelfeld	Killed
12-1685 Dachau	2nd Lt. Peter Mandros Jr. (navigator)	351st B.G. 511th B.S. B-17 (42-102952) MACR 7817	July 28, 1944	Fauerbach	Killed
12-1733 Dachau	Captain Richard C. Smith (pilot)	357th F.G. 364th F.S. P-51 (43-6974) *Mr. Period* MACR 6260	June 29, 1944	Seesen	Killed
12-1740 Ludwigsburg	1 Unknown		August 13/14, 1944	Reiffenhausen	Assaulted

Accused	Offender's Status	Age	Party Status	Profession	Sentencing	Outcome:
Willy Stemmler	Col. SS	48	Yes (1928)	Merchant	Death	Executed October 29, 1948
Dr. Otto Zeitzer	Sgt. SS	39	Yes	Doctor	4 years	Acquitted (Lack of evidence)
Johann Klein	Police	56	Unknown	Clerk	Acquitted	
Richard Wandel	Police	64	Yes	Police	Acquitted	
Julius Bodenstein	Police SS	47	Yes (1937)	Unknown	Life	Paroled June 1955
Edmund Kürschner	Volkssturm	58	Yes (1942)	Unknown	20 years	Paroled June 1954
Richard Eck	Civilian	60	Unknown	Carpenter	1 1/2 years	Acquitted (Lack of evidence)
Wilhelm Roth	Civilian	62	Yes	Farmer	1 1/2 years	
Rudolf Haferburg	Volkssturm	57	Unknown	Farmer	1 year	
Albert Luechau	Political Official	48	No	Police	5 years	
Ludwig Schickert	Ortsgruppen-leiter & Mayor	45	Yes	Farmer	2 years	
Werner Kornalewicz	Civilian	30	No	Technician	1 year	
Hermann Loehmer	Political Official	51	Unknown	Police	1½ years	
Karl Mack	Civilian	46	Unknown	Farmer	Acquitted	
Willi Rieke	Volkssturm	56	Yes	Sports Instructor	Death	Executed October 15, 1948
Karl Schenk	Volkssturm	51	Unknown	Unknown	Acquitted	
Eduard Karl Ludwig Curdts	Police	56	Unknown	Police	Death	Executed July 15, 1947
Karl Stieg	Civilian	41	Unknown	Farmer	Acquitted	
Wilhelm Paland	Civilian	43	Unknown	Railroad Worker	2 years	Reduced to 1 year
Fritz Teuteberg	Ortsgruppen-leiter	50	Yes (1935)	Farmer	4 years	Reduced to 1 year

Trial Number/ Location	Airmen	Aircraft/Unit	Date of Incident	Location	Treatment
12-1742 Ludwigsburg	Most likely the following airmen: 1st Lt. Martin J. Mullane (pilot)	446th B.G. 704th B.S. B-24 (42-50681) *Slightly Dangerous* MACR 9633	October 19, 1944	Niederseelbach & Engenhahn	Killed
	T/Sgt. Hoover C. Baucom (radio)	446th B.G. 704th B.S. B-24 (42-50681) *Slightly Dangerous* MACR 9633			Killed
	2nd Lt. Terrel L. Hollis (navigator)	389th B.G. 567th B.S. B-14 (42-50842) *Betsy II* MACR 9482			Killed
12-1745 Ludwigsburg	2nd Lt. Samuel J. Levine (navigator)	392nd B.G. 579th B.S. B-24 (42-52160) *Ski Nose* MACR 7369	July 7, 1944	Kleinzerbst	Killed
	S/Sgt. Walter F. Dinsmore (engineer)	392nd B.G. 579th B.S. B-24 (42-52160) *Ski Nose* MACR 7369			Killed
	T/Sgt. John M. Chojecki (radio)	392nd B.G. 579th B.S. B-24 (42-52160) *Ski Nose* MACR 7369			Killed
12-1752	2nd Lt. Donald J. Lehmkuhl (bombardier)	487th B.G. 837th B.S. B-17 (43-8596) MACR 12550	February 20, 1945	Rothenbeck	Assaulted
	S/Sgt. Gilbert E. Hyatt (tail gunner)	487th B.G. 837th B.S. B-17 (43-8596) MACR 12550			Assaulted
	T/Sgt. Kay S. Taft (engineer)	487th B.G. 837th B.S. B-17 (43-8596) MACR 12550			Assaulted
12-1761	2nd Lt. Richard E. Johnston (pilot)	474th F.G. 428th F.S. P-38 (44-23161) MACR 12339	February 14, 1945	Brühl	Assaulted
12-1774 Dachau	Most likely: Captain William H. Mooney Jr. (pilot)	357th F.G. 362nd F.S. P-51 (44-11198) *Libby B* MACR 11329	December 24, 1944	Between Freienseen & Laubach	Killed
12-1790 Dachau	4 Unknown		January 1945	Issel	Killed
12-1807 Dachau	1 Unknown		Summer 1944	Geradstetten & Hebsack	Assaulted
12-1812 Dachau	1 Unknown		May 10, 1944	Neindorf (Wolfenbüttel)	Killed

Accused	Offender's Status	Age	Party Status	Profession	Sentencing	Outcome:
Fritz Amstutz	SA	40	Yes (1932)	Electrician	5 years	Released February 1950
Robert Schauer	Ortsgruppen-leiter & Mayor	42	Yes	Locksmith	13 years	Released December 1954
Willi Christ	Army	31	Unknown	Army	1 year	
Friedrich Pohla	Police	51	Yes (1939)	Police	Death	Reduced to life; Paroled June 1955
Ernst Otto Vogler	SD	43	Yes (1933)	Police	Death	Reduced to life; Paroled May 1955
Dr. Wilhelm Bork	Civilian	57	Unknown	Doctor	Acquitted	
Dr. Paul Eckert	Civilian	39	Unknown	Doctor	Acquitted	
Bernhardt Engelbrecht	Police Chief	41	Yes	Police	Acquitted	
Hugo Blessmann	Police (KriPo)	40	Unknown	KriPo Secretary	2 years	
Franz Johann Schmitz	Rural Police	57	Unknown	Unknown	Acquitted	
Wilhelm Karlsohn	Civilian	44	Unknown	Mechanic	1½ years	
Gottfried Segschneider	Civilian	48	Unknown	Bookkeeper	1 year	
Johann Adam Marx	Civilian	41	Unknown	Coal Miner	6 months	
Emil Hofmann	Ortsgruppen-leiter	53	Yes	Farmer	Death	Executed October 22, 1948
Otto Heene	Landwacht	55	No	Businessman	Acquitted	
Kurt Hartman	Civilian	51	Yes	Engineer	Acquitted	
Bernhard Schlarp	Army	32	Unknown	Army	Acquitted	
Karl Gottlieb Conzmann	Ortsgruppen-leiter & Mayor	57	Yes (1932)	Unknown	1½ years	
Erich Mette	SS.	23	Unknown	Hair Dresser	Death	Reduced to life; Paroled October 1954
Otto Peters	Navy Corporal	28	Unknown	Butcher	Life	Reduced to 20 years; Paroled December 1953

Trial Number/ Location	Airmen	Aircraft/Unit	Date of Incident	Location	Treatment
12-1813 Dachau	Sgt. Harold E. Churchill (top turret & engineer)	401st B.G. 613th B.S. B-17 (43-38607) *Lady Jane II* MACR 13137	March 18, 1945	Göddenstedt (Uelzen)	Killed
12-1814 Ludwigsburg	1 Unknown		July 16, 1944	Between Gutfreudenthal & Gertenbach	Killed
12-1821 Ludwigsburg	2 Unknown		September 9, 1944	Grossenlinden	Killed
12-1833 Dachau	2nd Lt. Wendell L. Hoenshel (bombardier)	1st Pathfinder B-26 (42-95933) MACR 12838	March 2, 1945	Langgöns	Killed
	S/Sgt. Robert H. Folsom (tail gunner)	1st Pathfinder B-26 (42-95933) MACR 12838			Killed
	T/Sgt. Henry M. Isenberg (radio)	1st Pathfinder B-26 (42-95933) MACR 12838			Killed
12-1848 Dachau	1 Unknown		September 11, 1944	Kleinlinden & Giessen	Killed
12-1851 Ludwigsburg	T/Sgt. Almo W. Dennerle (radio)	303rd B.G. 306th B.S. B-17 (44-8330) MACR 9404	September 28, 1944	Gross Dentke	Killed
12-1852 Dachau	Sgt. Patsy Rocco (radio)	303rd B.G. 358th B.S. B-17 (42-31183) *Bad Penny* MACR 8170	August 17, 1944	Between Idesheim & Bitburg	Killed
12-1866 Dachau	2nd Lt. Sidney A. Benson (copilot)	493rd B.G. 862nd B.S. B-24 (42-94812) *Little Warrior* MACR 6721	June 29, 1944	Wolfsburg	Killed
12-1871 Ludwigsburg	1st Lt. Edmund L. Dornburgh (pilot)	92nd B.G. 327th B.S. B-17 (43-38396) *Insomnia* MACR 9344	October 3, 1944	Giessen-Wieseck	Killed
12-1871-1 Dachau	1st Lt. Wallace W. Bengson (navigator)	92nd B.G. 327th B.S. B-17 (43-38396) *Insomnia* MACR 9344			Killed
	S/Sgt. Franklin W. Adams Jr. (waist gunner)	92nd B.G. 325th B.S. B-17 (43-38445) MACR 9346			Killed

Accused	Offender's Status	Age	Party Status	Profession	Sentencing	Outcome:
Siegfried Utermark	RAD Cmdr.	36	Yes	Sports Instructor	Life	Reduced to 30 years; Paroled March 1954
Justus Gerstenberg	Gendarmerie	49	Yes (1933)	Painter	Death	Executed September 12, 1946
Johann Melchior	SD Chief	40	Yes	Carpenter	Life	Paroled June 1955
Walter Hirschelmann	Kreisstellen-leiter	48	Yes	Merchant	Life	Paroled May 1955
Albert August Weil	Mayor	37	Yes (1932)	Farmer	25 years	Acquitted (Lack of Evidence)
Carl Muller	Mayor till 1944	62	Yes (1933)	Merchant	10 years	Acquitted (Lack of Evidence)
Ludwig Muller	Army Sgt. (Tank Corps)	29	Unknown	Office Clerk	15 years	
Otto Pfluger	Civilian	49	Yes	Night Watchman	20 years	
Otto Lechens	SA Alert Group	41	Yes	Mechanic/ Locksmith	10 years	Acquitted (Lack of Evidence)
Wilhelm Lang	Police (Auxiliary)	55	Unknown	Painter	Life	Died in Prison, March 6, 1947
Eugen Katzenmeier	Political Official	40	Yes	DAF	Life	Paroled April 1955
Otto Sukopp	Landrat-Wolfenbuttel	47	Yes (1941)	Farmer	12 years	Released June 1953
Kurt Kiehne	Army Private	24	No	Farmer	5 years	Released May 1950
Friedrich Scheilz	Police	54	No	Police	Life	Released after 2 years (Evidence indicated Flyer might have attempted to escape)
Helmut Lippmann	Major HJ	35	Yes (1941)	Factory Engineer	Death	Reduced to 25 years; Paroled April 1954
Kurt Kuhnert	SA	40	Yes (1933)	Mechanic	Life	Acquitted (Lack of Evidence)
Robert Buhler	Unknown			Unknown	Stay of Proceeding	
Ludwig Schardt	Volkssturm	55	Yes	Public Bath Attendant	Life	Paroled October 1954
Julius Lassak	SS Police Director	60	Yes (1925)	Police Director	Life	Unknown

Trial Number/ Location	Airmen	Aircraft/Unit	Date of Incident	Location	Treatment
12-1880 Ludwigsburg	1 Unknown		March 10, 1944	Schierstein/ Wiesbaden	Assaulted
12-1881 Dachau	T/Sgt. Harrel W. Fuller (waist gunner)	453rd B.G. 733rd B.S. B-24 (42-110138) *Stinky* MACR 8424	August 16, 1944	Stapelburg	Killed
	F/O Frank Mishaga (copilot)	453rd B.G. 733rd B.S. B-24 (42-110138) *Stinky* MACR 8424			
12-1885 Dachau	Sgt. Felix W. Kolasinski (waist gunner)	445th B.G. 701st B.S. B-24 (42-91506) MACR 12778	February 27, 1945	Ebnet (Freiburg)	Killed
12-1890 Ludwigsburg	1 Unknown		November 2, 1944	Witchensdorf	Assaulted
12-1894 Ludwigsburg	1st Lt. Ross S. Houston (navigator)	491st B.G. 853rd B.S. B-24 (44-40205) *The Moose* MACR 10765	November 26, 1944	Roloven	Assaulted
12-1898 Ludwigsburg	1 Unknown		September 1944	Hattenheim	Assaulted
12-1905 Dachau	1 Unknown		June 9, 1944	Mötzing	Assaulted
12-1911 Dachau	2nd Lt. Charles A. Norby (pilot)	390th B.G. 568th B.S. B-17 (42-97863) *Shack Rat* MACR 7821	July 29, 1944	Buttstadt (Weimar)	Killed
12-1915 Dachau	Likely: 2nd Lt. Newell W. Brainard (copilot)	445th B.G. 700th B.S. B-24 (43-110022) MACR 9399	September 27, 1944	Nentershausen	Killed
12-1930 Dachau	1 Unknown		July 31, 1944	Heddesheim	Assaulted
12-1930-1 Dachau					
12-1934 Dachau	Sgt. Robert J. Speir (waist gunner)	44th B.G. 66th B.S. B-24 (42-95124) *Sand Bomb Special* MACR 10835	December 4, 1944	Freiburg	Killed

Accused	Offender's Status	Age	Party Status	Profession	Sentencing	Outcome:
Hans Pohl	Civilian	33	Yes (1937)	Gardener	1 year	Reduced to 6 months
Walter Heinrich Ernst Rieseberg	SS	49	Yes (1930)	Unknown	Life	Acquitted (Lack of Evidence)
Kurt Friedrich Wilhelm Dilba	Civilian	48	Unknown	Bank Clerk	Acquitted	
Franz Weiss	Luftwaffe	47	Unknown	Construction Worker	Death	Paroled February 1954
Karl Weisshuhn	Civilian		Unknown	Unknown	3 years	
Alfred Koller	Civilian	45	Yes (1940)	Lab Tech	5 years	Reduced to 2 years
Wilhelm Krahn	Civilian		Unknown	Unknown	Acquitted	
Konrad Kremer	Civilian		Unknown	Unknown	5 years	
Johann Hemauer	Luftwaffe (Home on leave)	56	Unknown	Luftwaffe	1 year	
Rudolf Auburger	Civilian	33	Unknown	Carpenter	1 year	
Hermann Gustav Adolf Brückner	Police Auxiliary	55	Yes	Farmer	Life	Medical Parole January 1954
Arno Otto Börnschein	Civilian	52	Unknown	Glass Worker	Acquitted	
Paul Rubsamen	Civilian	45	Unknown	Miner	Death	Executed July 15, 1947
Paul Winkler	Civilian	51	Unknown	Mine Inspector	Death	Executed August 5, 1947
Martin Baesse	Civilian	50	No	Auto Painter	25 years	Released July 1952
Karl Schrader	Civilian	46	Unknown	Machinist	12 years	
Jakob Ehlen	Civilian	63	Unknown	Miner	3 years	
Reinhard Beck	Civilian	47	Unknown	Baker	2 years	
Joseph Crumbach	Civilian	59	Unknown	Unknown	Acquitted	
Peter Etsch	Police (SiPo)	59	Yes (1933)	Unknown	2 years	
Heinrich Schmitt	civilian	52	Yes (1933)	Unknown	2 years	
Karl Geggus	civilian	54	Unknown	Unknown	2 years	
Erwin Rudmann	Military	35	Unknown	Unknown	10 years	Released July 1953
Karl Rudmann			Unknown	Unknown	Stay of Proceeding	
Michael			Unknown	Unknown	Stay of Proceeding	

Trial Number/ Location	Airmen	Aircraft/Unit	Date of Incident	Location	Treatment
12-1949 Dachau	Most likely the following crew: S/Sgt. Raymond Gasperetti (waist gunner)	44th B.G. 68th B.S. B-24 (44-40098) *Lone Ranger* MACR 8273	August 24, 1944	Between Münstedt and Braunschweig	Killed
	2nd Lt. Arthur H. Dittmer (pilot)	44th B.G. 68th B.S. B-24 (44-40098) *Lone Ranger* MACR 8273			Killed
12-1950 Ludwigsburg	2 Unknown		July 21, 1944	Flehingen	Assaulted
12-1958 Dachau	1 Unknown		September 12, 1944	Stetten	Assaulted
12-1960 Dachau	Most likely the following crew: 2nd Lt. Anthony J. Santomiery (copilot)	389th B.G. 566th B.S. B-24 (42-50374) MACR 7364	July 7, 1944	Bad Harzburg	Killed
12-1960-1 Dachau	T/Sgt. Lawrence A. Hambel (top turret)	389th B.G. 566th B.S. B-24 (42-50374) MACR 7364			Killed
12-1961 Dachau	1 Unknown Lieutenant		July 18, 1944	Riestedt (Sangerhausen)	Assaulted
12-1966 Dachau	8 Unknown		August 26, 1944	Trebur/ Gross-Gerau/ Rüsselsheim	Assaulted
12-1967 Dachau	S/Sgt. Leroy Desmond Cruse (tail gunner)	351st B.G. 510th B.S. B-17 (42-31721) *Black Magic* MACR 5334	May 28, 1944	Elm	Killed
12-1968 Dachau	Sgt. Cecil F. Allen (engineer & gunner)	323rd B.G. 453rd B.S. B-26 (42-96261) MACR 13088	February 10, 1945	Kemel (Bad Schwalbach)	Killed
12-1973 Dachau	2nd Lt. Leslie Horace Hauss (copilot)	401st B.G. 613th B.S. B-17 (43-37511) *Jill's Jalopy* MACR 8204	August 24, 1944	Gross Lindern	Killed
12-1989 Dachau	T/Sgt. Richard C. Travers (radio)	460th B.G. 763rd B.S. B-24 (42-99763) MACR 6917	July 19, 1944	Solln (Munich)	Assaulted
	S/Sgt. James M. Greene (gunner)	460th B.G. 763rd B.S. B-24 (42-99763) MACR 6917		Pulloch (Munich)	Killed

Accused	Offender's Status	Age	Party Status	Profession	Sentencing	Outcome:
Heinz Franz Herbert Minx	SS	38	Unknown	Merchant	Acquitted	
Gustav Sauter	Agricultural Advisor & Blockleiter	47	Yes (1934)	Farmer	3 years	
Jakob Schwarz	Ortsgruppen-leiter	55	Yes (1932)	Farmer	21 months	
Ludwig Wolter	Gestapo	53	Yes	KriPo Secretary	Life	Medical Parole, December 1952
Leo Kowitzke	Gestapo Chief	53	Yes	Police Instructor	Death	Reduced to life; Released August 1950
Richard Franke	Civilian	57	Unknown	Farmer	2½ years	
Hermann Friedrich	Civilian	41	Unknown	Unknown	Acquitted	
Friedrich Schmidt	Civilian	58	Unknown	Unknown	1 year	
Karl Kraft	Civilian	53	Yes	Unknown	1½ years	
Anna Stein	Civilian	34	Unknown	Unknown	1 year	
Georg Dickhaut	Civilian	19	Yes	Unknown	1½ years	
Heinrich Luley	Civilian	66	Unknown	Unknown	1 year	
Karl Reinheimer	Civilian	45	Unknown	Fireman	1½ years	
Jacob Brueckmann	Civilian	39	Unknown	Unknown	20 months	
Peter Lietschuh	Civilian	44	Unknown	Fireman	3 years	
Georg Jaeger	Civilian	44	Yes (1937)	Unknown	3 years	
Richard Wegmann	Army	25	Unknown	Unknown	Death	Reduced to 30 years; Paroled August 1954
Heinrich Otte	Police	52	Yes (1937)	Police	Death	Executed September 1947
Willy Lang	Volkssturm	46	No	Farmer	1 year	
Hans Otto Seidel	Police	46	Unknown	Police	Acquitted	
Siegfried Utermark	RAD	36	Yes	RAD	Acquitted	
Josef Kolb	Civilian	63	Unknown	Unknown	2 months	
Albert Loerch	Army Tech. Sgt.	52	Unknown	Unknown	1 year	

Trial Number/ Location	Airmen	Aircraft/Unit	Date of Incident	Location	Treatment
12-1993 Dachau	S/Sgt. Stephen J. Andrews (gunner)	490th B.G. 849th B.S. B-17 (43-38128) *Bombo* MACR 8856	September 13, 1944	Fürth	Killed
12-2000 Dachau	2nd Lt. William Alfred Duke (pilot)	458th B.G. 754th B.S. B-24 (44-10491) *Iron Duke* MACR 12675	February 22, 1945	Bieber	Killed
	2nd Lt. Archibald B. Monroe Jr. (copilot)	458th B.G. 754th B.S. B-24 (44-10491) *Iron Duke* MACR 12675	February 22, 1945	Offenbach	Killed
	Captain Ray F. Herrmann (pilot)	339th F.G. 504th F.S. P-51 (44-11745) *Happy III* MACR 12682	February 15, 1945	Bensheim	Killed
	Sgt. Jimmie R. Heathman (waist gunner)	490th B.G. 849th B.S. B-17 (43-38046) MACR 13080	March 18, 1945	Wallrabenstein	Killed
	T/Sgt. Robert W. Garrison (engineer)	100th B.G. 349th B.S. B-17 (44-8514) *Lassie Come Home* MACR 11345	December 30, 1944	Delkenheim	Killed
	T/Sgt. Willard F. Perry (top turret & engineer)	446th B.G. 704th B.S. B-24 (42-50681) *Slightly Dangerous* MACR 9633	October 19, 1944	Wiesbaden	Killed
	Lt. William H. Forman		March 24, 1945	Bensheim	Killed
	Pvt. Robert T. McDonald		March 24, 1945	Bensheim	Killed
	1 Unknown		October 3, 1944	Giessen	Killed

Accused	Offender's Status	Age	Party Status	Profession	Sentencing	Outcome:
Adolf Feuerlein	Civilian	72	Unknown	Unknown	Acquitted	
Fritz Kolb	Civilian		Unknown	Unknown	Acquitted	
Otto Peschke	Army Sgt.	25	Unknown	Barber	Life	Paroled February 1954
Josef Schmitz	Army Lt.	28	Unknown	Technician	Acquitted	
Jürgen Stroop	SS Major	51	Yes (1932)	Unknown	Death	Extradited to Poland, Executed March 6, 1952
Hans Trummler	SS Col.	46	Yes (1928)	SS	Death	Executed October 22, 1948
Otto Somann	Police- SS Col.	47	Yes (1927)	SS	4 years	Released May 1949
Wilhelm Adolf Höhler	Gestapo	37	Yes (1931)	Police	Death	Reduced to Life; Paroled September 28, 1954
Arthur Führ	Gestapo	37	Yes	Mechanic	Death	Executed October 22, 1948
Hans Eichel	Police Director	56	Yes (1931)	Unknown	Death	Executed December 3, 1948
Joseph Johann Kiwitt	Police (OrPo)	52	Yes (1932)	Police	Death	Executed October 15, 1948
Wilhelm Albrecht	Police (OrPo)	57	Yes (1940)	Police	15 years	Paroled December 1953
Hermann Moeller	Police	45	Yes (1937)	Clerk	Death	Reduced to Life; Paroled October 1954
Paul Nahrgang	Fire Protection Police	46	No	Locksmith	5 years	Released February 1950
Philipp Hammann	Air Raid Police	51	No	Carpenter	15 years	Died in prison July 30, 1947
Bernard Fay	Air Raid Police	52	No	Merchant	5 years	
Georg Best	SS Police Chief	39	Yes (1932)	SS Police in France	15 years	Paroled March 1954
Erwin Goss	SS Director, Wehrwolf School	41	Yes (1939)	Economist	Death	Executed October 15, 1948
Heinrich Matthias Michely	SS Instructor, Wehrwolf school	33	Yes	Teacher	Death	Reduced to Life; Paroled August 3, 1954
Julius Lassak	Police (SiPo Director)	59	Yes (1925)	Railroad Inspector	3 years	Died in prison, March 26, 1950
Fritz Girke	Gestapo	35	Yes (1937)	Lawyer	Death	Executed October 15, 1948
Heinz Hellenbroich	Police (KriPo)	31	Yes (1933)	Lawyer	Death	Executed October 1948
Karl Franz Stattmann	Gestapo	35	Yes (1938)	Dental Assistant	Death	Executed October 22, 1948
Michael Raaf	Gestapo	41	Yes (1940)	Police	Death	Executed October 22, 1948
Wilhelm Friedrich Göhrendt	Police (SiPo)	53	No	Police	Acquitted	

Trial Number/ Location	Airmen	Aircraft/Unit	Date of Incident	Location	Treatment
12-2000, 1 Dachau					
12-2009 Ludwigsburg	1 Unknown		June 21, 1944	Kospa (Eilenburg)	Killed
12-2011 Dachau	Maj. John R. Reynolds (pilot)	339th F.G. 505th F.S. P-51 (44-14069) MACR 8695	September 10, 1944	Ingolstadt	Killed
12-2018 Dachau	2nd Lt. Donald Emerson Howie (pilot)	353rd F.G. 350th F.S. P-51 (44-15594) *Miss Kay* MACR 13971	April 16, 1945	Thanham	Killed
12-2025 Ludwigsburg	2 Unknown		January 1945	Raunheim	Assaulted
12-2034 Dachau	1 Unknown		August 1944	Wehrden	Assaulted
12-2036 Dachau	S/Sgt. Robert L. Harmon (radio)	305th B.G. 365th B.S. B-17 (42-102962) MACR 8066	August 9, 1944	Weisenbach	Killed
	Sgt. Robert A. McDonough (tail gunner)	305th B.G. 365th B.S. B-17 (42-102962) MACR 8066			Killed
	Sgt. Kenneth L. Palmer (waist gunner)	305th B.G. 365th B.S. B-17 (42-102962) MACR 8066			Killed

Accused	Offender's Status	Age	Party Status	Profession	Sentencing	Outcome:
Anton Josef Wrede	SS	39	Unknown	SS	6 years	
Erich Dietzschold	Army	28	No	Unknown	Acquitted	
Johann Georg Sponsel	Kreisleiter	52	Yes (1931)	Unknown	Death	Executed March 4, 1947
Walter Joseph Ziehnert	Kreisleiter	47	Yes (1936)	Unknown	Death	Executed March 4, 1947
Hans Toelle	Army	39	Unknown	Merchant	6 years	
Herbert Langner	Army	26	Unknown	Unknown	Acquitted	
Georg Hitzer	Civilian	41	Yes (1937)	Opel Factory Worker	4 years	Reduced to 2 years
Anton Doerr	Civilian	39	Yes	Electrician	17 months	
Aloys Neis	Civilian	34	Unknown	Mechanic	16 months	
Karl Mai	Civilian	52	Unknown	Miner	14 months	
August Sturm	Civilian	50	Unknown	Mine Foreman	Acquitted	
Hans Rothacker	Kreisleiter	43	Yes	Trade Employee	3 years	Extradited to France
Adolf Phillip Eiermann	Ortsgruppen-leiter & Volkssturm	54	Yes (1933)	Painter	Death	Executed November 19, 1948
Xavier Goetz	Army	49	Yes (1943)	Cardboard Cutter	5 years	Acquitted (Lack of Evidence)
Matthäus Goetzmann	Blockleiter	54	Yes (1934)	Post Secretary	Death	Reduced to Life; Paroled November 1954
Maurus Haitzler	Ortsgruppen-leiter	59	Yes (1933)	Polisher	4 years	Acquitted (Lack of Evidence)
Wilhelm Karcher	NSKK	49	Yes (1936)	Mechanic	Death	Executed November 19, 1948
Isidor Klumpp	Blockleiter	53	Yes (1940)	Mill Foreman	Death	Executed November 19, 1948
Hermann Wendelin Krieg	Blockleiter	36	Yes (1940)	Barrel Maker	10 years	Released (Insane Asylum) September 1951
Rudolf Merkel	HJ	19	Yes	Assistant Driver	Life	Reduced to 15 years; Released September 1951
Julius Ratzke	local Head of Film/ Radio	59	Yes (1933)	Electrician	20 years	Reduced to 2 years; Released February 1949
Johann Gotthilf Schneider	SA Sgt.	52	Yes (1937)	Mason	Death	Executed November 19, 1948

Trial Number/ Location	Airmen	Aircraft/Unit	Date of Incident	Location	Treatment
12-2052 Dachau	Most Likely: S/Sgt. Francis J. McAdam (waist gunner)	446th B.G. 706th B.S. B-24 (42-51115) MACR 11347	November 30, 1944	Wellesweiler	Assaulted
12-2058 Dachau	1st Lt. Eugene D. Cook (copilot)	91st B.G. 401st B.S. B-17 (42-5437) "Frank's Nightmare" MACR 282	August 17, 1943	Schleiden (Hergarten)	Assaulted
12-2064 Dachau	Most likely: 1st Lt. Francis P. Chinchilla (bombardier)	392nd B.G. 578th B.S. B-24 (41-29002) MACR 10206	September 21, 1944	Hüllenberg	Killed
12-2067 Ludwigsburg	1 Unknown		February 1945	Düsseldorf	Assaulted
12-2068 Dachau	1 Unknown		October 19, 1944	Eppstein/Taunus	Assaulted
12-2074 Ludwigsburg	S/Sgt. Calvin C. Ferrari (waist gunner)	305th B.G. 366th B.S. B-17 (42-31611) MACR 4870	May 11, 1944	Dillingen	Killed
12-2114 Dachau	1 Unknown		August 9, 1944	Waldrach	Assaulted
12-2119 Dachau	1 Unknown		July 19, 1944	Olching	Killed
12-2129 Dachau	1 Unknown		February 1945	Berlin	Killed
12-2150 Dachau	1 Unknown		August 1944	Schwalbach	Assaulted

Accused	Offender's Status	Age	Party Status	Profession	Sentencing	Outcome:
Heinrich Stichling	Ortsgruppen-leiter & Mayor	45	Yes (1933)	Hotel Manager	Life	Paroled August 1954
Franz Weiland	Local education leader	57	Yes (1933)	Grammar School Teacher	20 years	Reduced to 8 years; Released September 1950
Franz Deck			Unknown	Unknown	Stay of Proceeding	
Fritz Kern			Unknown	Unknown	Stay of Proceeding	
Kurt Overlack	Luftwaffe (later Volkssturm)	41	Unknown	Merchant	Acquitted	
Josef Pelizaeus	Volkssturm	49	Yes	Salesman	10 years	Acquitted (Lack of Evidence)
August Klaebe	Police	44	No	Police	8 years	Reduced to 3 years; Released May 1949
Ludwig Hollacher	Army	29	Unknown	Farmer	Death	Executed February 2, 1949
Friedrich Metz	Army	43	No	Deacon & Missionary	Death	Executed February 2, 1949
Alfred Bracht	Civilian	48	Yes (1931)	Gardener	2 years	Reduced to 14 months
Fritz Kroll	Civilian	44	Yes (1941)	Farmer	1½ years	Reduced to 1 year
Theodor Schillings	Civilian	39	No	Farmer	2 years	Reduced to 14 months
Hubert Mohlen	Civilian	62	Yes	Unknown	Acquitted	
Georg Adalbert Baum	Civilian	57	Yes (1937)	Innkeeper	1 year	
Ludwig Loeber	Civilian	47	Yes (1933)	Farmer	2½ years	
Otto Albrecht	Civilian		Unknown	Unknown	Stay of proceeding	
Nicholas Hartmann	Volkssturm	40	Unknown	Machinist	25 years	Paroled April 1954
Peter Scherf	Mayor	56	No	Mayor	5 years	Released December 1949
Karl Sonner	Gendarmerie	57	Yes (1933)	Painter	Acquitted	
Paul Kahnert	Army	42	Unknown	Locksmith	Life	Medical Parole, January 1956
Ferdinand Blum	Gendarmerie	54	Unknown	Unknown	4 years	
Hugo Langenfeld	Civilian	29	Unknown	Office Clerk	1 year	Acquitted (Lack of evidence)
Johann Trenz	Civilian	33	Unknown	Telephone Operator	1½ years	
Heinrich Rupp	Civilian	40	Unknown	Miner	2 years	

Trial Number/ Location	Airmen	Aircraft/Unit	Date of Incident	Location	Treatment
12-2157 Dachau	1 Unknown		September 6, 1943	Hülben	Killed
12-2175 Munich	S/Sgt. Jon Eggleston (waist gunner)	301st B.G. 352nd B.S. B-17 (44-8107) *Josephine* MACR 10894	December 28, 1944	Haimbuch	Killed
12-2185 Dachau	1 Unknown		October 1944	Niedernhausen	Assaulted
12-2202 Dachau	Sgt. John A. Star (radio & gunner)	95th B.G. 336th B.S. B-17 (42-87844) MACR 12948	March 9, 1945	Darmstadt	Assaulted
12-2218 Dachau	Maj. Robert M. Blackbourn (pilot)	405th F.G. 509th F.S. P-47 (44-33291) MACR 13577	March 25, 1945	Brackel	Killed
12-2261 Ludwigsburg	1 Unknown		August 15, 1944	Oberkail	Killed
12-2270 Dachau	3 Unknown		July 31, 1944	Dudweiler	Assaulted
12-2283 Dachau	T/Sgt. Forrest A. Peterson (radio)	390th B.G. 570th B.S. B-17 (42-107041) *Ain't Misbehavin'* MACR 11137	November 30, 1944	Küchen	Killed
12-2313 Dachau	1st Lt. Lloyd C. Carter (pilot)	453rd B.G. 793rd B.S. B-24 (42-95047) MACR 10177	October 19, 1944	Griesheim (Frankfurt a.M.)	Assaulted
12-2337 Dachau	Sgt. Robert Andrew Hildebrand (tail gunner)	388th B.G. 561st B.S. B-17 (42-97091) *Dear Mom* MACR 4956	May 22, 1944	Ascheburg	Killed
12-2400 Dachau	S/Sgt. Joseph C. Ward (bombardier)	381st B.G. 535th B.S. B-17 (42-97330) *Chug-A-Lug IV* MACR 10154	November 6, 1944	Bergdorf (Hamburg)	Assaulted

Accused	Offender's Status	Age	Party Status	Profession	Sentencing	Outcome:
Heinrich Reinhard	Civilian	51	Unknown	Miner	1½ years	
Edith Kohler	Civilian		Unknown	Unknown	Stay of proceeding	
Friedrich (Fritz) Schmauder	Army	27	No	Butcher	Life	Released June 1952
Ernst Waldmann	Army	43	Unknown	Shoemaker/ Farmer	Death	Executed November 19, 1945
Carl Feix	Civilian	50	Unknown	Mill Manager	1 year	
Franz Reininger	Civilian	49	Unknown	Factory Worker	1 year	
Alfred Romer	Civilian	38	Unknown	Unknown	1 year	
Paul Schult	Police	51	Unknown	Police	Acquitted	
Georg Mayer	Flak 1st Sgt. (9th Battery, 333d)	39	Yes	Soldier	Life	Died in Prison, March 9, 1956
Wilhelm Wanders	Civilian	41	Unknown	Miner	10 years	Released December 1951
Otto Paul Hellwing	Civilian	47	Unknown	Miner	3 years	Released January 1949
Heinrich Bäcker	Civilian	50	Unknown	Baker	10 years	Released July 1952
Matthias Zahnen	Army	48	Yes (1933)	Locksmith	15 years	Acquitted (Lack of evidence)
Jakob Zimmer	Police	51	Unknown	Police	1½ years	
Franz Goldinger	Civilian	65	Unknown	Unknown	1½ years	
Peter Klaes	Civilian	45	Unknown	Miner	2 years	
Albert Woll	Civilian	52	Unknown	Unknown	22 months	
Peter Schneider	Police	61	Unknown	Police	Acquitted	
Reinhard Moeller	Civilian	41	Unknown	Railroad Worker	Death	Executed May 2, 1947
Gustav Engelhardt	Volkssturm	52	Yes (1933)	Teacher	Death	Executed May 2, 1947
Karl Stoll	RAD	40	Yes	Brewer	10 years	Released January 1951
Alwin Reinke	Civilian	47	Unknown	Court Employee	Death	Executed August 15, 1947
Erwin Karl Heinrich Schlickau	Volkssturm	38	Yes (1941)	Coal Dealer	7 years	Released December 1949

Trial Number/ Location	Airmen	Aircraft/Unit	Date of Incident	Location	Treatment
12-2404 Dachau	Captain Jack McNider Beckman (pilot)	355th B.G. 350th B.S. P-51 (44-14230) *Trigger III* MACR 12835	March 1, 1945	Wassertrüdingen	Killed
12-2409 Dachau	Most likely: Sgt. Edward C. Holdren (tail gunner)	490th B.G. 849th B.S. B-17 (43-38046) MACR 13080	March 17, 1945	Engenhahn	Killed
12-2420 Dachau	2nd Lt. Stanford Gene Wolfson (copilot)	95th B.G. 335th B.S. B-17 (43-38814) *Cadet Nurse The 2nd* MACR 10308	November 6, 1944	Kaiserslautern	Killed
12-2422 Ahrweiler	Most likely: 2nd Lt. Lester E. Reuss (navigator)	303rd B.G. 358th B.S. B-17 (43-31183) *Bad Penny* MACR 8170	August 16, 1944	Preist	Killed
12-2422-1 Ahrweiler					
12-2581 Dachau	S/Sgt. Morris Peter Thompson (waist gunner)	388th B.G. 561st B.S. B-17 (44-6574) *Solid Sender* MACR 13871	April 9, 1945	Munich	Killed
12-2593 Dachau	2nd Lt. Ralph S. Brackens (pilot)	351st B.G. 511th B.S. B-17 (42-97492) *Slow Ball* MACR 7704	August 3, 1944	Huttersdorf (Saarbrücken)	Assaulted
12-2595 Dachau	T/Sgt. Robert R. DeKay (radio)	100th B.G. 418th B.S. B-17 (42-5860) *Escape Kit* MACR 675	August 17, 1943	Epplingen	Assaulted

Accused	Offender's Status	Age	Party Status	Profession	Sentencing	Outcome:
Georg Eckstein	Volkssturm	45	Yes (1937)	Mechanic	Death	Executed December 3, 1948
Ernst Ittameier	Civilian	54	Yes (1925)	Businessman	Death	Executed November 5, 1948
Fritz Stiegler	Civilian	45	Yes (1929)	Merchant	Life	Paroled December 1954
Johann Georg (Hans) Sturm	Army Sgt.	36	Yes (1928)	Butcher	Death	Executed November 5, 1948
Friedrich Tiefenbach	SS	41	Yes	Businessman	Acquitted	
Heinrich Franke	SS	48	Yes	Farmer	Death	Executed October 29, 1948
Albert Ningelgen	Police (KriPo)	38	No	Police	Life	Paroled Mach 1955
Peter Kohn	Civilian	33	Unknown	Railroad Worker	Death	Executed June 29, 1945
Matthias Gierens	Civilian	37	Yes	Railroad Worker	Death	Executed June 29, 1945
Peter Back	Landwacht	37	Yes (1937)	Unknown	Death	Executed June 29, 1945
Matthias Krein	Blockleiter	45	Unknown	Blacksmith	Death	Released March 1950
Franz Montscher	RAD	35	Yes	Unknown	Death	Reduced to Life; Paroled May 1955
Hans Schemm	RAD	36	Yes	Unknown	Life	Paroled December 1954
Johann Engelniederhammer	Civilian	42	Unknown	Railroad Official	Death	Executed January 14, 1949
Ludwig Obermayr	Civilian	42	No	Farmer	10 years	Acquitted (Lack of Evidence)
Bartholomaeus Misslinger	RAD	34	Unknown	Clerk	Life	Released September 1953
Karl Ruehling	RAD	36	Yes (1933)	Forest Laborer	7 years	Acquitted (Lack of Evidence)
Johann Eiser	Civilian	51	Unknown	Railroad Official	Acquitted	
Max Maier	Civilian	37	Unknown	Unknown	Acquitted	
Anton Pfeiffer	Civilian	38	Unknown	Unknown	Acquitted	
Peter Merten	Ortsgruppen-leiter	59	Yes	Accountant	2 years	
Matthias Lamerti	Civilian	51	Unknown	Carpenter	3 years	
Emil Dittgen	Civilian	40	Yes	Businessman	Acquitted	
Ernst Hofmann	Civilian	57	Unknown	Farmer	Acquitted	
Johann Hettinger	Civilian	52	Unknown	Farmer	Acquitted	

Trial Number/ Location	Airmen	Aircraft/Unit	Date of Incident	Location	Treatment
12-2616 Dachau	2 Unknown		July 16, 1944	Mörlach	Denied Medical Aid
12-2662 Dachau	2 Unknown		May 1944	Blofeld (Reichelsheim)	Assaulted
12-2694 Dachau	1 Unknown		March 1945	Mainz	Killed
12-2804 Dachau	1 Unknown		July 12, 1944	Garmisch	Assaulted
12-2823 Dachau	S/Sgt. Leon Synfelt (nose turret)	446th B.G. 707th B.S. B-24 (42-51356) *Lassie Come Home* MACR 10161	November 4, 1944	Bad Salzdetfurth	Killed
12-2823-1 Dachau					
12-2887 Dachau	Captain William Bohen (copilot)	381st B.G. 532nd B.S. B-17 (42-29976) *Sad Sack* MACR 128	July 25, 1943	Wulfsfelde	Assaulted
12-2971 Dachau	1 Unknown		Summer 1944	Walle	Assaulted
12-3121 Dachau	S/Sgt. Zigfryd Valentino Czarnecki (waist gunner)	379th B.G. 526th B.S. B-17 (42-102628) *G.I. Jane* MACR 5989	June 18, 1944	Appen	Killed
12-3193-B Dachau	S/Sgt. Hubert W. Burleigh Jr. (radio)	100th B.G. 349th B.S. B-17 (44-6306) MACR 9373	September 29, 1944	Bad Neustadt (Saale)	Killed

Accused	Offender's Status	Age	Party Status	Profession	Sentencing	Outcome:
Michael Kaiser	Gendarmerie	66	Yes (1935)	Unknown	1 year	Acquitted (Lack of Evidence)
Karl Hess	Civilian	66	Yes (1933)	Unknown	1½ years	
Rudolf Küfer	Civilian	56	Unknown	Unknown	2 years	
Karl Heinz Scherer	Army Panzer 1st Lt.	25	Yes	Bank Apprentice	25 years	
Michael Kuhn	Army	47	Unknown	Unknown	1 year	
Max Bruno Gartmann	Political Official	55	Yes	Rural Police	Death	Executed November 5, 1948
Willi Dehnbostel	Political Official	47	Unknown	Rural Police	10 years	Released November 1951
Josef Hutler	Volkssturm	49	Unknown	Gardner	Acquitted	
Friedrich Meyer	Political Official	43	Unknown	Rural Police	10 years	Released December 1952
Heinrich Hahne	Political Official	47	Unknown	Rural Police	10 years	Released November 1951
Heinrich Adler	Civilian	46	No	Window Cleaner	Acquitted	
Waldemar Freitag	Civilian	53	Yes	Farmer	2 years	
Heinrich Jaeger	Civilian	57	Unknown	Unknown	28 months	
Robert Kuennemann	Civilian	46	Unknown	Unknown	3½ years	
Hermann Gustav Schmidt	Civilian	43	Unknown	Unknown	2½ years	
Wilhelm Langeloh (Alias: Felix Bauer)	Kreis-organisation-sleiter	55	Yes	Clerk	Death	Executed October 10, 1947
Franz Josef Büchler	Gendarmerie	57	Yes	SS (Police)	10 years	Reduced to 5 years
Norbert Endres	Kreisleiter	48	Yes (1930)	School Teacher	Death	Reduced to Life; Died in prison, November 11, 1950
Heinrich Baumann	Gestapo	36	Yes (1932)	SS (Police)	Death	Executed November 26, 1948
Dr. Otto Hellmuth	Political Official	51	Yes (1927)	Gauleiter (Dentist)	Death	Reduced to Life; Paroled May 1955
Andreas Ingebrand	Political Official	44	Yes	Kreisleiter	Death	Executed November 26, 1948
Dr. Richard Schulze	Gestapo	48	Yes	Police	Death	Paroled December 1956
Albert Hammer	KriPo	38	Yes (1937)	Police	Death	
Kurt Hans	KriPo	36	Yes (1932)	Police	Death	
Karl Hellmuth	Civilian	45	Yes	Dentist	3 years	
Oswald Gundelach	SD	43	Yes (1937)	Police	Death	Reduced to Life
Georg Baumann	Gestapo	48	Unknown	Police	Acquitted	

Trial Number/ Location	Airmen	Aircraft/Unit	Date of Incident	Location	Treatment
12-3205 Dachau	6 Unknown		June and July 1944	Helmstedt (Marienthal Airport)	Killed

Accused	Offender's Status	Age	Party Status	Profession	Sentencing	Outcome:
Kurt Dreger	Army	38	Yes	Electrical Engineer	Life	Paroled November 1956
Waldemar Feldmeier	Volkssturm	37	Yes	Merchant	Life	Paroled December 1953
Erich Mueller	NSKK	44	Unknown	Mechanic	20 years	Paroled December 1953
August Schubert	NSKK	52	Unknown	Police	20 years	Paroled December 1953
Oswald Conrad	NSKK	47	Unknown	Police	20 years	Paroled December 1953
Harry Hauenschild	NSKK	45	Unknown	Clerk	20 years	Paroled December 1953
Karl Schroeder	NSKK	54	Unknown	Laborer	Life	Paroled December 1953
Hans Willi Finke	Unknown		Unknown	Unknown	Stay of proceeding	
Herbert Monsenheuer	Unknown		Unknown	Unknown	Stay of proceeding	

Appendix D
Unresolved Cases

Table D.1. Unresolved Cases[1]

Trial Number	Airmen	Aircraft/Unit	Date of Incident	Location
12-377	S/Sgt. Alvin William Brady (ball turret)	379th B.G. 524th B.S. B-17 (42-32093) *Big Barn Smell* MACR 7392	August 9, 1944	Schmitthof (near Walheim/Aachen)
	Unknown			
	T/Sgt. John C. Phillips (top turret)	379th B.G. 524th B.S. B-17 (42-32093) *Big Barn Smell* MACR 7392		
12-2109				
12-405	2nd Lt. William T. Neidhardt (copilot)	457th B.G. 751st B.S. B-17 (43-37562) MACR 6724	June 29, 1944	Borna
12-839	2nd Lt. Harry Weissman (navigator)	385th B.G. 551st B.S. B-17 (43-57888) MACR 10155	November 2, 1944	Merseburg

1. These represent examples of unresolved cases (or cases where the sentences and outcome are unknown) that involve American airmen who were killed or assaulted in Nazi Germany. Often, airmen reported being assaulted or crewmembers and former forced workers witnessed these atrocities and offered the only known reports of the mistreatment. When the cases appeared to be based on enough evidence (more than just hearsay), investigations attempted to apprehend the perpetrators and put them on trial; however, numerous cases remain unsolved due to the lack of witnesses as well as the identification and whereabouts of perpetrators. The incidents that do not have case numbers are based on the recently discovered remains of airmen or victims' and witness's statements, which reported (both personally and secondhand) assaults and murders. These cases were not included in the quantitative analysis of this study, as they are incomplete.

Treatment	Accused (Status)	Outcome
Assaulted (Stoned by civilians and beaten by police until he was handed over to Luftwaffe soldiers)	Johann Bergmann (KriPo)	
Assaulted (Stoned by civilians and beaten by police until he was handed over to Luftwaffe soldiers)	Magdalena Beus (civilian)	Unknown
	Gottfried Fieseler (civilian)	Unknown
	Paul Kappes (civilian)	Unknown
	Gustav Flasche (KriPo)	Unknown
	Hans Muhs (KriPo)	Unknown
	Josef Pesch (civilian)	Unknown
	Fritz Schwenke (KriPo director)	Unknown
	Max Stober (KriPo)	Unknown
	Johann Wink (KriPo)	Unknown
	Friedrich Steinnebecher (KriPo)	Unknown
	Johann Unger (civilian)	Unknown
	Rudolf Fried (civilian)	Unknown
Assaulted	Unknown civilians	No person identified/found
Killed (Crewmembers witnessed Weissman being taken out of a house by SS troops and a short time later heard shots.)	SS	Alleged perpetrators were dead or not found

Trial Number	Airmen	Aircraft/Unit	Date of Incident	Location
12-903	2nd Lt. Owen Howard Jorgensen (navigator)	401st B.G. 613th B.S. B-17 (42-31037) *Pistol Packin' Mama* MACR 7545	July 20, 1944	Wohlsborn
	S/Sgt. Donald H. Schmidli (tail gunner)	401st B.G. 613th B.S. B-17 (42-31037) *Pistol Packin' Mama* MACR 7545	July 20, 1944	Wohlsborn
	S/Sgt. Jerome Robertson (ball turret)	401st B.G. 613th B.S. B-17 (42-31037) *Pistol Packin' Mama* MACR 7545	July 20, 1944	Wohlsborn
	T/Sgt. Stanley Lesser (engineer)	401st B.G. 613th B.S. B-17 (42-31037) *Pistol Packin' Mama* MACR 7545	July 20, 1944	Wohlsborn
	S/Sgt. Howard Magnuson (waist gunner)	401st B.G. 613th B.S. B-17 (42-31037) *Pistol Packin' Mama* MACR 7545	July 20, 1944	Wohlsborn
12-1524	F/O Arthur N. Skarsten (bombardier) Cpl. George Bulgarelli (ball turret)	447th B.G. 711th B.S. B-17 (42-102441) *TNT Katie* MACR 9764 447th B.G. 711th B.S. B-17 (42-102441) *TNT Katie* MACR 9764	October 7, 1944	Merseburg
12-1552	2nd Lt. Walter Humphreys (bombardier)	384th B.G. 587th B.S. B-17 (42-29686) *Pie Eyed Piper* MACR 290	August 12, 1943	Gelsenkirchen
12-1560	T/Sgt. Patrick Negri Colosimo (radio)	44th B.G. 68th B.S. B-24 (42-51101) *Korky* MACR 12007	January 28, 1945	Dortmund
12-1604	1st Lt. David W. Thompson (pilot)	93rd B.G. 330th B.S. B-24 (41-24147) *The Duchess* MACR 2924	February 25–29, 1944	From Landau to Frankfurt a/M
12-1629	6 unknown		September 1944	Frankfurt a/M
12-1663	8 unknown		October/ November 1944	Neu Brandenburg
12-1702	1 unknown		September 12, 1944	Aderstedt
12-1707	T/Sgt. William J. Sloane (radio)	445th B.G. 703rd B.S. B-24 (42-51541) MACR 9394	September 27, 1944	Hersfeld (Fulda)

Treatment	Accused (Status)	Outcome
Killed (Crewmembers witnessed him land safely. He was beaten beyond recognition by civilians with rocks, clubs, and other implements. German officials reported he allegedly attempted to escape and was shot.)	Unknown	No person identified/found
Killed (Crewmembers witnessed him land safely. He was beaten beyond recognition by civilians with rocks, clubs, and other implements. German officials reported he allegedly attempted to escape and was shot.)	Unknown	No person identified/found
Assaulted (Forced to walk through a small village naked while civilians threw rocks, sticks, and other objects at him, spit on him, and beat him. Saved once soldiers took custody of him)	Unknown civilians	No person identified/found
Assaulted (Forced to walk through a small village naked while civilians threw rocks, sticks, and other objects at him, spit on him, and beat him. Saved once soldiers took custody of him)	Unknown civilians	No person identified/found
Assaulted (Forced to walk through a small village naked while civilians threw rocks, sticks, and other objects at him, spit on him, and beat him. Saved once soldiers took custody of him)	Unknown Civilians	No person identified/found
Killed (Shot by civilians)	Unknown	No person identified/found
Killed (Shot by civilians)		
Killed (Crew reported he was shot as he parachuted to the ground)	Unknown	No person identified/found
Assaulted (Landed with a broken leg and severe burns to his face. Beaten by a mob of civilians. Saved by German soldiers who intervened; however, while being escorted, a soldier kept pushing him, forcing him to fall to the ground, at which time the civilians seized the opportunity to continue beating him.)	Unknown	No person identified/found
Assaulted (He, along with several other captured airmen, was assaulted while they were being transported from Landau to Frankfurt a/M)	Unknown civilians	No person identified/found
Assaulted (He, along with three American, two British, and one Australian airmen, was assaulted by civilians as he was transported to Oberursel. Guards had to force the civilians away at gunpoint)	Unknown civilians	No person identified/found
Killed (Allegedly captured and taken to a hospital in Neu Brandenburg. On the night of their arrival, Gestapo agents took the flyers to a nearby woods and shot them.)	Unknown Gestapo	No person identified/found
Killed (Captured by Walter and Otto and forced the flyer to walk to a secluded area, where Otto shot him several times.)	Walter S. (Volkssturm)	Not found
	Otto K. (Police)	Not found
Assaulted	Unknown civilians	No person identified/found

Trial Number	Airmen	Aircraft/Unit	Date of Incident	Location
	3 unknown			
12-1729	Captain Caleb L. Reeder Jr. (pilot)	56th F.G. 62nd F.S. P-47 (42-74623) MACR 2841	March 8, 1944	Föckinghausen (Melle)
12-1782	2nd Lt. Gene O. Hubbartt (pilot)	392nd B.G. 576th B.S. B-24 (42-50387) MACR 12379	February 15, 1945	Mühlhausen (Nordhausen)
	F/O Calvin J. Carter Jr. (navigator)	392nd B.G. 576th B.S. B-24 (42-50387) MACR 12379		
	Cpl. Paul S. Glassman (tail gunner)	392nd B.G. 576th B.S. B-24 (42-50387) MACR 12379		
12-1794	T/Sgt. Eugene A. Pax (engineer)	493rd B.G. 863rd B.S. B-17 (43-38295) MACR 8867	September 12, 1944	Otterburg (Magdeburg)
	F/O John R. Hewitt (bombardier)	493rd B.G. 863rd B.S. B-17 (43-38261) MACR 8866		
	2nd Lt. Kenneth D. Evans (navigator)	493rd B.G. 863rd B.S. B-17 (43-38261) MACR 8866		
	T/Sgt. Harold W. Puetz (engineer)	493rd B.G. 863rd B.S. B-17 (43-38261) MACR 8866		
12-1811	Most likely: S/Sgt. Leroy D. Kucharski (waist gunner)	603rd B.G. 398th B.S. B-17 (42-102562) "Knock Out" MACR 10157	November 27, 1944	Polleben
	2 unidentified crewmembers			
	Wilhelm Z. (Gendarmerie)	Repeated attempts to extradite (from Russian Zone) were unsuccessful for unknown reasons		
12-1969	1 unknown		June 21, 1944	Berlin
12-1975	1 unknown		March 1945	Westerode

Treatment	Accused (Status)	Outcome
Killed (The three flyers were stripped of their clothes and put on horses with a noose tied around their necks; the ropes were put over a tree limb and tied to the base of the tree. Then the men slapped the horses, causing the flyers to fall off and be hanged)	Unknown soldiers	No person identified/found
Assaulted (Beaten by a mob of civilians for an extended period of time. Then his hands were tied behind his back, and he was forced to run several miles through a few villages and finally into a wooded area, where the rope was removed and a noose placed around his neck. He was questioned about why he was involved in the war against Germany. His answers were apparently satisfactory, as the rope was removed from his neck and he was taken to the local jail. The next day, he was handed over to the Luftwaffe.)	Unknown civilians	No person identified/found
Assaulted (Beaten by a soldier and two Gestapo officers)	Unknown	No person identified/found
Assaulted (Beaten unconscious and stuck with a pitchfork)	Unknown	No person identified/found
Assaulted (Beaten and stuck with a pitchfork. Then shot by a Hitler Youth boy)	Unknown	No person identified/found
Assaulted (Captured by soldiers and taken to a nearby woods, where he was shot and left for dead. Pax regained consciousness the next morning and walked, with the aid of sticks as crutches, for three days and nights before he was picked up by a German farmer who took him to a village where he was turned over to the Luftwaffe and received first aid. The other three flyers died.)	Unknown	No person identified/found
Killed		
Killed		
Killed		
Killed	Siegfried H. (Wehrmacht)	Repeated attempts to extradite (from Russian Zone) were unsuccessful for unknown reasons
Killed		
	Ortsgruppenleiter (name unknown)	Allegedly executed on the spot by an American firing squad after Wilhelm Z. confessed that the Ortsgruppenleiter murdered the two airmen.
Assaulted	Unknown civilians	No person identified/found
Killed	Unknown	No person identified/found

Trial Number	Airmen	Aircraft/Unit	Date of Incident	Location
12-1982	2 Unknown crewmembers	458th B.G. 754th B.S. B-24 (44-10491) "Iron Duke" MACR 12675	February 22, 1945	Mühlheim
	Sgt. Charles Frazer Jr. (waist gunner)	458th B.G. 754th B.S. B-24 (44-10491) *Iron Duke* MACR 12675	February 22, 1945	Bieber
12-1999	Sgt. John A. Cederlind (Ball Turret)	390th B.G. 571st B.S. B-17 (44-8319) MACR 11055	December 4, 1944	Langenlonsheim
12-2221	Sgt. Roland J. Bender (ball turret)	303rd B.G. 358th B.S. B-17 (42-97972) MACR 11200	November 26, 1944	Minden
12-2294	1st Lt. William Webb McElhare (pilot)	56th F.G. 62nd F.S. P-47 (42-26636) MACR 9163	September 18, 1944	Efferen
12-2354	1st Lt. John C. Saunders (pilot)	445th B.G. 703rd B.S. B-24 (42-50692) MACR 12883	March 3, 1945	St. Andreasberg
12-2569	2nd Lt. Victor Charles Cook (copilot)	96th B.G. 339th B.S. B-17 (42-3528) MACR 834	October 14, 1943	Mittenwald
12-2579	S/Sgt. Arthur Lane Blanchard (waist gunner)	95th B.G. 334th B.S. B-17 (42-39989) *Patches* MACR 4904	March 16, 1944	Freiburg
12-2881	S/Sgt. Richard C. Josephson (waist gunner)	483rd B.G. 817th B.S. B-17 (44-6741) MACR 13254	March 22, 1945	Ruhland

Treatment	Accused (Status)	Outcome
Assaulted (One flyer was captured by Karl Grob [police] and an unknown German soldier. As they were escorting the flyer to the police station, Bernhard encouraged the crowd to beat the flyer. Civilians Peter Winter, Adam Roth, and Heinrich Blank knocked the airman to the ground and repeatedly kicked him. The German soldier then pulled out his pistol and chased the crowd away.)	Jacob Bernard (Ortsgruppenleiter)	Unknown
(A second flyer was captured and brought to the Flak Battery, where members of the flak unit placed him under guard in a freight car at the railroad station. Here he was beaten by the flak members with a board.)	Peter Jordan (Kreisleiter of Frankfurt a/M)	Unknown
	Franz Winter (flak member)	Unknown
	Heinrich Blank (civilian)	Unknown
	Adam Roth (civilian)	Unknown
	Peter Winter (civilian)	Unknown
Killed (Shot while allegedly attempting to escape)	Policeman	Perpetrator never found
Killed (Initially captured by two Wehrmacht soldiers home on leave. August R. & Alfred R. came upon the men and the former order Alfred R. to shoot the flyer, which he did.)	Hugo August Rothfuchs (alias: Waldemar Knauf) (Oberführer of the Hitler Youth)	Released from custody in September 1947 without trial because of the death of a witness and lack of corroborating evidence (not because the investigation had cleared him of possible implication in the crime).
	Jakob Alfred Rueppel (civilian)	Deceased
Assaulted (Beaten unconscious by civilians and confined in the local jail. He was then sent to Oberursel)	Unknown civilians	No person identified/found
Assaulted (McElhare surrendered to soldiers and a policeman. After he was disarmed, he was led through the streets of the town and beaten brutally by a mob, losing four teeth in the melee. Even children were given stones to throw at the flyer.)	Johann A. (Blockleiter)	Unknown
	Agnes B. (housewife)	Unknown
	Johanna B. (housemaid)	Unknown
	Heinrich B. (police)	Unknown
	Josef J. (police)	Unknown
Killed	Unknown civilians	No person identified/found
Killed After they crash-landed in a small lake, the crew attempted to board lift rafts. As they started to paddle toward shore, they were fired on by members of the Hitler Youth. Cook was hit in the back and died the next day)	Unknown	No person identified/found
Assaulted (Beaten by civilians and Hitler Youth members)	Unknown	No person identified/found
Killed (Crewmembers were shot at as they descended in their parachutes)	Unknown	No person identified/found

Trial Number	Airmen	Aircraft/Unit	Date of Incident	Location
12-2956	S/Sgt. Hugh E. Winfree (tail gunner)	91st B.G. 401st B.S. B-17 (42-97519) *Spirit of Billy Mitchell* MACR 4048	April 19, 1944	Eschwege
	Sgt. Robert Nelson Kasch	91st B.G. 401st B.S. B-17 (42-97519) *Spirit of Billy Mitchell* MACR 4048		
	S/Sgt. Robert J. Schupp (tail gunner)	91st B.G. 401st B.S. B-17 (42-97519) *Spirit of Billy Mitchell* MACR 4048		
12-3090	1 unknown		February 1945	Mainz
	2nd Lt. John W. Herb (pilot)	359th F.G. 368th F.S. P-51 (44072260) "Mary Lou" MACR 13905	April 13, 1945	Rosien (Amt Neuhaus)
	1st Lt. Arlen Richard Baldridge (pilot)	359th F.G. 368th F.S P-51 (43-6962) MACR 5113 (J 1168)	May 21, 1944	Bad Doberan
	1st Lt. Kirby Monette Brown (pilot)	357th F.G. 364th F.S. P-51 (44-13698) *Shady Lady* MACR 8654	September 13, 1944	Burgwalde
	Sgt. Melvin Conrad Carlson (tail gunner)	303rd B.G. 427th B.S. B-17 (42-102544) *Sack Time* MACR 14168	April 17, 1945	Halsbrücke
	S/Sgt. Edward Gilbert Eschinger (bombardier)	303rd B.G. 427th B.S. B-17 (42-102544) *Sack Time* MACR 14168	April 17, 1945	Halsbrücke
	2nd Lt. Frank R. Hedeen (copilot)	490th B.G. 849th B.S. B-17 (43-38128) *Bombo* MACR 8856	September 13, 1944	Attenkirchen
	S/Sgt. Joseph G. Kralick (waist gunner)	381st B.G. 532nd B.S. B-17 (42-30013) *Lethal Lady* MACR 130	July 25, 1943	Neustadt (Hamburg)
	2nd Lt. Dale George Wendte (copilot)	381st B.G. 532nd B.S. B-17 (42-30013) *Lethal Lady* MACR 130	July 25, 1943	Neustadt (Hamburg)
	2nd Lt. George E. Lyford (navigator)	486th B.G. 835th B.S. B-17 (43-39163) *Happy Warrior* MACR 13889	April 7, 1945	Parchim
	S/Sgt. Frank W. Pikula (waist gunner)	486th B.G. 835th B.S. B-17 (43-39163) *Happy Warrior* MACR 13889	April 7, 1945	Parchim
	Likely Sgt. Leo F. Waldron (top turret)	303rd B.G. 359th B.S. B-17 (42-97187) *Miss Umbriago* MACR 9410	September 28, 1944	Wolfenbüttel
	Likely: 1st Lt. Teddy A. Smith (bombardier)	303rd B.G. 359th B.S. B-17 (42-97187) *Miss Umbriago* MACR 9410	September 28, 1944	Wolfenbüttel
	2nd Lt. Arthur Alexander Conn Jr. (navigator)	303rd B.G. 359th B.S. B-17 (42-97187) *Miss Umbriago* MACR 9410	September 28, 1944	Wolfenbüttel
	2nd Lt. William L. Howell (pilot)	445th B.G. 701st B.S. B-24 (42-78483) MACR 7385 (U 3187)	August 14, 1944	Saarbrücken
	Sgt. John Kanyak (tail gunner)	445th B.G. 701st B.S. B-24 (42-78483) MACR 7385 (U 3187)	August 14, 1944	Saarbrücken
	Sgt. Vance H. Murphy (waist gunner)	445th B.G. 701st B.S. B-24 (42-78483) MACR 7385 (U 3187)	August 14, 1944	Saarbrücken

Treatment	Accused (Status)	Outcome
Assaulted (Flyers were captured by civilians and taken to the mayor's home. A short time later, two Gendarmerie men arrived and beat the airmen.)	Gendarmerie and public official	No person identified/found
Assaulted (Flyers were captured by civilians and taken to the mayor's home. A short time later, two Gendarmerie men arrived and beat the airmen.)	Unknown civilians	No person identified/found
Killed (Shot by civilians between the eyes)	Unknown civilians	No person identified/found
Killed (Airman was lying wounded in the Robert Koch Street and was robbed by the civilian crowd that surrounded him. Kayser shot and killed the flyer, allegedly to avenge his parents who had been killed two weeks earlier in the aerial bombing of Mainz.)	Hermann Kayser (civilian—released from the Luftwaffe in 1943 due to head injury. After the war he enlisted in the French Foreign Legion)	Unknown
Killed (Allegedly shot as he climbed out of his wrecked aircraft, which he crash-landed.)	Unknown	Airman's remains weren't found until 2016. No person was identified/found. A local woman (Anna Waschke) tended Herb's grave in the woods until she died in the 1960s.
Killed (Shot while allegedly attempting to escape)	Police	Perpetrator and witnesses were believed to be in the Russian Zone of Occupation
Killed (The perpetrator allegedly shot Brown to seek revenge for the loss of his brother. The perpetrator then reported that Brown had been "shot while attempting to escape.")	Party Official	Unknown
Killed (Crewmembers believed they were killed by civilians)	Unknown	No person identified/found
Killed (Crewmembers believed they were killed by civilians)	Unknown	No person identified/found
Killed (Hedeen was beaten by civilians and then shot along with his crewmember S/Sgt. Stephen J. Andrews) (see 12-1993)	SS	No person identified/found
Killed	Unknown civilians	No person identified/found
Killed	Unknown civilians	No person identified/found
Killed	Unknown	No person identified/found
Killed	Unknown	No person identified/found
Killed	Unknown	No person identified/found
Killed	Unknown	No person identified/found
Killed	Unknown	No person identified/found
Killed (Shot while allegedly attempting to escape) Allegedly held at St. Avold Prison	Unknown	No person identified/found
Killed (Shot while allegedly attempting to escape) Allegedly held at St. Avold Prison	Unknown	No person identified/found
Killed (Shot while allegedly attempting to escape) Allegedly held at St. Avold Prison	Unknown	No person identified/found

Trial Number	Airmen	Aircraft/Unit	Date of Incident	Location
	2nd Lt. James G. Dennis (copilot)	(42-31941)	May 24, 1944	Wusterhausen/ Segeletz
	1st Lt. Joe H. Shelly (pilot)	392nd B.G. 578th B.S. B-24 (41-29002) MACR 10206	September 21, 1944	Vershoven (10 km east of Eurskirchen)
	2nd Lt. Robert C. Barton (copilot)	389th B.G. 566th B.S. B-24 (42-50617) MACR 7365	July 8, 1944	Near Dingelstedt
	Unknown	No person identified/found		
	2nd Lt. Wayne R. Davis (bombardier)	44th B.G. 68th B.S. B-24 (44-40098) *Lone Ranger* MACR 8273	August 24, 1944	Between Münstedt and Braunschweig

Treatment	Accused (Status)	Outcome
Killed (Captured by forest ranger and handed over to Landwacht members from Segeletzt. They were stopped in the car by Brigadeführer Berndt vom RSHA and announced, "He will be killed." He ordered the Landwacht men to not get involved. He then shot Dennis three times. Dennis was reported to the local Luftwaffe officials as having died in the plane crash.)	Political official and police	No person found
Killed (along with two other crewmembers) (see: 12-481 and 12-2064)	Unknown	No person identified/found
(Shot while allegedly attempting to escape)		
Assaulted (Captured by a soldier who allowed a civilian mob to beaten him.)	Unknown civilians	No person identified/found

Appendix E
Lists of Known Airmen Held at Prisons

Table Unit/Service Abbreviations

B.G.	Bomb Group	USAAF	United States Army Air Force
B.S.	Bomb Squadron	RAAF	Royal Australian Air Force
F.G.	Fighter Group	RCAF	Royal Canadian Air Force
F.S.	Fighter Squadron	RNZAF	Royal New Zealand Air Force
		RAF	Royal Air Force

Table E.1. List of Known US Airmen Held at Saint Gilles Prison in Brussels

Name	Report #	Date Shot Down
1st Lt. John J. Bradley	E&E 1590	Nov. 5, 1943
1st Lt. William G. Ryckman	E&E 1591	May 28, 1944
T/Sgt. James R. Dykes	E&E 1592	Jan. 29, 1944
Sgt. Hugh C. Bomar	E&E 1593	June 14, 1944
S/Sgt. Ray Smith	E&E 1594	June 23, 1944
2nd Lt. Alfred M. L. Sanders	E&E 1595	May 28, 1944
2nd Lt. Thomas P. Smith	E&E 1781	April 1, 1944
1st Lt. Jack Terzian	E&E 1789	May 22, 1944
2nd Lt. John William Brown	E&E 1841	Feb. 4, 1944
S/Sgt. William Row Muse	E&E 1846	April 29, 1944
2nd Lt. J. H. Singleton	E&E 1847	April 29, 1944
2nd Lt. James G. Levey	E&E 1848	April 29, 1944
Sgt. Harry J. Blair Jr.	E&E 1849	April 29, 1944
S/Sgt. Cecil D. Spence	E&E 1856	July 20, 1944
T/Sgt. Kenneth C. Holcomb	E&E 1858	July 20, 1944
S/Sgt. Donald H. Swanson	E&E 1861	July 12, 1944
S/Sgt. Charles C. Hillis	E&E 1862	July 12, 1944
S/Sgt. Ralph J. Lynch	E&E 1868	July 1, 1944
S/Sgt. James M. Wagner	E&E 1870	July 11, 1944
1st Lt. Henry W. Wolcott III	E&E 1877	May 28, 1944
1st Lt. William D. Grosvenor	E&E 1881	Nov. 30, 1943

Service	Aircraft	Unit	MACR
USAAF	B-17 (42-39831)	92nd B.G. 327th B.S.	1383
USAAF	B-24 (42-40550)	801st B.G. 406th B.S.	5239
USAAF	B-24 (42-7484)	392nd B.G. 579th B.S.	2548
USAAF	B-24 (44-40460)	493rd B.G. 862st B.S.	5909
USAAF	B-17 (42-97324)	95th B.G. 334th B.S.	5915
USAAF	B-24 (42-52764)	486th B.G. 832nd B.S.	5390
USAAF	P-47 (42-74737)	359th F.G. 370th F.S.	3733
USAAF	P-47 (42-25730)	353rd F.G. 351st F.S.	5101
USAAF	B-17 (42-39799)	100th B.G. 349th B.S.	2564
USAAF	B-17 (42-31116)	401st B.G. 614th B.S.	4344
USAAF	B-17 (42-31116)	401st B.G. 614th B.S.	4344
USAAF	B-17 (42-31116)	401st B.G. 614th B.S.	4344
USAAF	B-17 (42-31116)	401st B.G. 614th B.S.	4344
USAAF	B-24 (42-95117)	458th B.S. 752nd B.S.	7255
USAAF	B-24 (42-95117)	458th B.S. 752nd B.S.	7255
USAAF	B-24 (42-100365)	458th B.G. 755th B.S.	6930
USAAF	B-24 (42-100365)	458th B.G. 755th B.S.	6930
USAAF	B-24 (42-52758)	486th B.G. 835th B.S.	6771
USAAF	B-24 (42-94773)	445th B.G. 701st B.S.	6941
USAAF	B-24 (42-40550)	801ST B.G. 406th B.S.	5239
USAAF	P-47 (42-75216)	56th F.G. 61st F.S.	1542

Table E.2. List of Known US Airmen Held at Fresnes Prison in Paris, France and Sent to Buchenwald Concentration Camp (August 20, 1944–October 19, 1944)

Name	Buchenwald #	Date Shot Down
S/Sgt. William Joseph Alexander	78287	June 25, 1944
S/Sgt. Roy Allen	78357	June 14, 1944
2nd Lt. Stratton M. Appleman	78314	June 6, 1944
F/O Warren F. Bauder	78196	May 11, 1944
1st Lt. Levitt Clinton Beck Jr.	78286	June 29, 1944
Richard Berford	78283	
S/Sgt. Chasten L. Bowen	78336	July 8, 1944
Sgt. James Walter Bozarth	78340	Aug. 1, 1944
2nd Lt. Robert Harold Brown	78295	April 24, 1944
2nd Lt. Frederick Walter Carr	78318	June 25, 1944
F/O John A. Chalot	78278	March 11, 1944
2nd Lt. Park Chapman	78284	July 6, 1944
S/Sgt. Douglas Murrel Chesshir	78285	June 25, 1944
S/Sgt. Basil A. Coats	78308	June 5, 1944
2nd Lt. J. D. Coffman	78319	June 25, 1944
T/Sgt. Frank Kirby Cowan	78271	June 22, 1944
1st Lt. Marshall E. Crouch Jr.	78277	Jan. 29, 1944
1st Lt. Donat F. Dauteuil	78324	May 27, 1944
2nd Lt. Ralph H. Dearey	78316	June 19, 1944
2nd Lt. Joseph Charles Denaro	78269	July 5, 1944
2nd Lt. James H. Duncan	78300	June 8, 1944
Sgt. William L. Edge	78267	May 10, 1944
S/Sgt. Earl Ellsworth Fix	78313	June 25, 1944
F/O James William Fore	78349	July 8, 1944
2nd Lt. Elmer Clayton Freeman	78359	May 8, 1944
Sgt. Edward Joseph Friel	78309	July 2, 1944
2nd Lt. William Langley Granbery III	78312	July 4, 1944
John T. Hanson	78280	
Capt. James Dale Hastin	78354	June 8, 1944
S/Sgt. Lawrence A. Heimerman	78334	May 11, 1944
2nd Lt. Russell Dwayne Hilding	78326	July 13, 1944
2nd Lt. Robert B. Hoffman	78350	June 23, 1944
T/Sgt. Roy J. Horrigan	78321	June 22, 1944
2nd Lt. Glenn Lorenzen Horwege	78281	Aug. 9, 1944
1st Lt. Harry F. Hunter	78337	May 30, 1944
S/Sgt. Robert T. Johnson	78272	June 10, 1944
Capt. Myles A. King	78279	June 22, 1944
Capt. Merle E. Larson	78363	June 21, 1944
S/Sgt. Bruce S. Little	78301	June 16, 1944
S/Sgt. Everett F. Ludwig	78339	June 4, 1944
S/Sgt. John H. Maclanahan	78348	June 14, 1944

Aircraft	Unit	MACR #
B-24 (42-95249)	489th B.G. 845th B.S.	6987
CG-4A (Glider) (42-79200)	437th TC 85th TCS	13319
B-24 (42-94999)	44th B.G. 506th B.S.	4849
P-47 (42-8473)	406th F.G. 514th F.S.	6224
B-17 (42-97173)	91st B.G. 323rd B.S.	8323
B-17 (42-39873)	401st B.G. 615th B.S.	7824
B-17 (42-31346)	384th B.G. 544th B.S.	9355
B-24 (42-95249)	8th B.G. 489th B.S.	6987
P-51 (43-6554)	355th F.G. 358th F.S.	3105
B-26 (41-31897)	322ndB.G. 450th B.S.	15175
B-24 (42-95249)	8th B.G. 489th B.S.	6987
B-17 (42-97473)	390th B.G. 571st B.S.	5481
B-24 (42-95249)	8th B.G. 489th B.S.	6987
B-17 (42-102552)	96th B.G. 339th B.S.	5917
B-24 (42-7484)	392ndB.G. 579th B.S.	2548
B-26 (41-31716)	391st B.G. 574th B.S.	5135
P-51 (42-106615)	339th F.G. 503rd F.S.	5944
B-24 (42-95170)	801st B.G. 850th B.S.	6774
B-26 (42-96058)	394th B.G. 585th B.S.	4513
B-24 (42-95249)	8th B.G. 489th B.S.	6987
B-17 (42-97173)	91st B.G. 323rd B.S.	8323
B-26 (42-96143)	397th B.G. 596th B.S.	4429
B-24 (42-95310)	491st B.G. 852nd B.S.	5391
B-24 (42-95170)	801st B.G. 850th B.S.	6774
P-51 (43-6982)	361st F.G. 374th F.S.	5600
B-24 (41-29468)	487th B.G. 838th B.S.	4750
B-17 (43-37788)	447th B.G. 709th B.S.	6938
P-38 (42-67578)	55th F.G. 38th F.S.	6246
B-24 (42-52759)	493rd B.G. 862nd B.S.	5937
P-47 (42-76443)	362nd F.G. 377th F.S.	8441
P-47 (42-75688)	353rd F.G. 351st F.S.	5204
B-24 (44-40107)	448th B.G. 718th B.S.	5630
P-51 (42-103282)	355th F.G. 357th F.S.	5963
P-38 (42-67765)	474th F.G. 429th F.S.	6491
B-17 (42-31648)	379th B.G. 526th B.S.	5988
B-17 (42-97473)	390th B.G. 571st B.S.	5481

Table E.2. *continued*

Name	Buchenwald #	Date Shot Down
1st Lt. Daniel G. McLaughlin	78338	May 27, 1944
S/Sgt. Frederick C. Martini	78299	June 13, 1944
Sgt. Lovell O'Masters	78290	May 27, 1944
Sgt. William Emanuel Mauk Jr.	78298	June 25, 1944
S/Sgt. George L. Mikel Jr.	78266	Aug. 17, 1943
2nd Lt. Gerald Earnest Mitchell	78307	July 4, 1944
1st Lt. Joseph F. Moser	78369	Aug. 13, 1944
T/Sgt. Arthur M. Pacha	78288	Jan. 29, 1944
S/Sgt. Stanley Keith Paxton	78320	June 22, 1944
Sgt. Steve Pecus	78315	June 25, 1944
2nd Lt. Joseph W. Pederson	78351	June 17, 1944
T/Sgt. Arthur J. Pelletier	78335	May 11, 1944
S/Sgt. Sam A. Pennell	78289	June 12, 1944
1st Lt. Michael R. Petrich	78325	July 5, 1944
1st Lt. Byron F. Phelps Jr.	78331	June 14, 1944
1st Lt. William Powell	78296	Jan. 29, 1944
S/Sgt. Leo J. Reynolds	78292	Jan. 29, 1944
S/Sgt. G. Thomas Richey	78317	June 4, 1944
S/Sgt. Edwin W. Ritter	78311	Aug. 1, 1944
Sgt. Charles Robertson	78327	April 24, 1944
1st Lt. William Henry Ryherd	78358	Aug. 4, 1944
S/Sgt. Laurie August Salo	78270	July 4, 1944
Sgt. Bernard F. Scharf	78353	July 8, 1944
Sgt. George W. Scott	78330	June 3, 1944
T/Sgt. Donald R. Shearer	78332	July 5, 1944
2nd Lt. James H. Smith	78323	June 22, 1944
S/Sgt. Paul Anthony Stralka Jr.	78268	July 4, 1944
T/Sgt. Dwight E. Suddock	78273	May 27, 1944
1st Lt. Leroy Henry Sypher	78276	July 9, 1944
2nd Lt. Warren Archie Thompson	78329	May 27, 1944
S/Sgt. Edward J. Vallee	78293	June 12, 1944
1st Lt. Ira E. Vance	78360	Aug. 4, 1944
Edwin H. Vincent	78310	
1st Lt. Frank Vratny	78328	May 11, 1944
2nd Lt. Robert W. Ward	78355	July 8, 1944
S/Sgt. John Pershing Watson	78333	May 11, 1944
Sgt. William J. Williams	78294	Jan. 29, 1944
Sgt. Paul J. Wilson	78297	May 27, 1944
1st Lt. Raymond Wojnicz	78367	July 13, 1944
1st Lt. Arthur E. Zander	78368	June 10, 1944
Sgt. James F. Zeiser	78322	July 8, 1944

Aircraft	Unit	MACR #
B-17 (42-31594)	457th B.G. 751st B.S.	5299
B-17 (42-31762)	385th B.G. 551st B.S.	5628
B-17 (42-31594)	457th B.G. 751st B.S.	5299
B-24 (42-95249)	8th B.G. 489th B.S.	6987
B-17 (42-3435)	92nd B.G. 327th B.S.	654
B-24 (42-95317)	801st B.G. 850th B.S.	6989
P-38 (43-28378)	474th F.G. 429th F.S.	7642
B-17 (42-30354)	585th B.G. 549th B.S.	2268
B-24 (42-52759)	493rd B.G. 862nd B.S.	5937
B-24 (42-95249)	8th B.G. 489th B.S.	6987
B-17 (42-38163)	306th B.G. 367th B.S.	5896
B-24 (41-29468)	487th B.G. 838th B.S.	4750
B-17 (42-31762)	385th B.G. 551st B.S.	5628
B-26 (42-107811)	391st B.G. 575th B.S.	6360
P-38 (42-104211)	367th F.G. 393rd F.S.	6496
B-17 (42-30354)	585th B.G. 549th B.S.	2268
B-17 (42-30354)	585th B.G. 549th B.S.	2268
B-17 (42-97473)	390th B.G. 571st B.S.	5481
B-24 (42-95043)	93rd B.G. 328th B.S.	8234
B-17 (42-31346)	384th B.G. 544th B.S.	9355
B-26 (43-34118)	397th B.G. 598th B.S.	7874
B-24 (42-95170)	801st B.G. 850th B.S.	6774
B-17 (42-97173)	91st B.G. 323rd B.S.	8323
A-20 (43-9360)	416th B.G. 668th B.S.	6049
B-26 (42-107834)	391st B.G. 573rd B.S.	6359
B-24 (42-52759)	493rd B.G. 862nd B.S.	5937
B-24 (42-95170)	801st B.G. 850th B.S.	6774
B-17 (42-31975)	351st B.G. 510th B.S.	5331
P-51 (44-13576)	361st F.G. 375th F.S.	6790
A-20 (43-10218)	410th B.G. 647th B.S.	5037
B-17 (42-107048)	303rd B.G. 360th B.S.	5626
B-26 (43-34118)	397th B.G. 598th B.S.	7874
B-24 (41-29468)	487th B.G. 838th B.S.	4750
B-17 (42-97173)	91st B.G. 323rd B.S.	8323
B-24 (41-29468)	487th B.G. 838th B.S.	4750
B-17 (42-30354)	585th B.G. 549th B.S.	2268
B-26 (42-95827)	391st B.G. 574th B.S.	5131
B-17 (43-37788)	447th B.G. 709th B.S.	6938
B-24 (44-40107)	448th B.G. 718th B.S.	5630
B-17 (42-97173)	91st B.G. 323rd B.S.	8323

Table E.3. List of Known British Airmen Held at Fresnes Prison in Paris, France and Sent to Buchenwald Concentration Camp (August 20, 1944–October 19, 1944)

Name	Buchenwald #	Service
Harold Atkin	78440	RCAF
Harry Bastable	78378	RCAF
Ed Carter-Edwards	78361	RCAF
Don Clarke	78364	RCAF
Edwin Compton	78434	RCAF
John Crawford	78406	RCAF
Frederick Fulsher	78418	RCAF
William R. Gibson	78394	RCAF
Leon T. Grenon	78438	RCAF
John D. Harvie	78412	RCAF
Leslie Head	78430	RCAF
Stanley Hetherington	78436	RCAF
David High	78422	RCAF
Thomas R. Hodgson	78424	RCAF
Charles Richard Hoffman	78429	RCAF
Arthur G. Kinnis	78391	RCAF
Donald Eugen Leslie	78404	RCAF
Ralph J. McClenaghan	78373	RCAF
James E. Prudham	78374	RCAF
Patrick Scullion	78395	RCAF
Ernest G. Shepard	78372	RCAF
James Allen Smith	78428	RCAF
Joseph Sonshine	78343	RCAF
Willie Arthur Walderam	78402	RCAF
Earl Carruthers Watson	78431	RCAF
Calvin E. Willis	78342	RCAF
Mervyn James Fairclough	78427	RAAF
James Percival Gwilliam	78423	RAAF
Eric Lyle Johnston	78421	RAAF
Kevin William Light	78381	RAAF
Thomas Alexander Malcolm	78379	RAAF
Keith Cyril Mills	78405	RAAF
Robert Neil Mills	78426	RAAF
Raymond Walter Perry	78356	RAAF
Lesley Keith Whellum	78442	RAAF
Malcolm Ford Cullen	78388	RNZAF
Phillip John Lamason	78407	RNZAF
Jack Wilson Angus	78390	RAF
Leonard P. Barham	78432	RAF
Stuart Baxter	78384	RAF
Geoffery Bennett	78344	RAF
Thomas Henry Blackham	78380	RAF
Stanley Albert Booker	78370	RAF

Name	Buchenwald #	Service
Robert Bryden	78365	RAF
Kenneth Chapman	78409	RAF
Albert J. Chinn	78433	RAF
John Clark	78385	RAF
Eric James Davis	78346	RAF
Philip Dowdeswell	78410	RAF
Arthur Douglas Eagle	78403	RAF
Juan Fernandez	78352	RAF
Terrance Gould	78386	RAF
Michael Alexander Guilfoyle	78393	RAF
Robert Harper	78414	RAF
Patrick Heggarty	78420	RAF
Philip Derek Hemmens	78383	RAF
Ronald R. Hughes	78347	RAF
Edgar Jackson	78392	RAF
Douglas F. Jordin	78341	RAF
Reginald William Joyce	78401	RAF
William Kay	78400	RAF
Ronald L. Leverington	78382	RAF
Leslie John Lucas	78389	RAF
Wilfred Marshall	78417	RAF
Alexander J. MacPherson	78435	RAF
Derek K. Measures	78413	RAF
Neville E.S. Mutter	78375	RAF
Cyril Worsley Nuttall	78366	RAF
John N. Osselton	78371	RAF
Douglas Charles Percy	78411	RAF
Frank Peirson	78362	RAF
Edward K. Phelps	78419	RAF
John David Reid	78387	RAF
Ian Alexander Ross	78415	RAF
Andrew Rowe	78408	RAF
Frank Salt	78345	RAF
William Sharrate	78397	RAF
Splinter Adolph Spierenburg	78443	RAF
James A. Stewart	78416	RAF
Peter D. Taylor	78425	RAF
Ralph John Taylor	78376	RAF
Frederick Vincombe	78377	RAF
John Duncan Ward	78396	RAF
George Frank Watmough	78439	RAF
Laurie Wesley	78399	RAF
Llewelyn Williams	78437	RAF

Appendix F
List of Known Stolpersteine for Allied Airmen

Table F.1. List of Known Stolpersteine for Allied Airmen Who Were Murdered in Germany

Name	Date Killed	Perpetrator	Location	Dedicated
Sgt. Cyril William Sibley	February 21, 1945	party officials and security forces	Dirmstein	March 27, 2009
James Vinal	March 18, 1945	SA and HJ	Pforzheim	September 6, 2013
Harold Frost	March 17, 1945	SA and HJ	Huchenfeld (Pforzheim)	September 6, 2013
Gordon Hall	March 17, 1945	SA and HJ	Huchenfeld (Pforzheim)	September 6, 2013
Lt. Sidney Mathews	March 17, 1945	SA and HJ	Huchenfeld (Pforzheim)	September 6, 2013
Sgt. Edward Percival	March 17, 1945	SA and HJ	Huchenfeld (Pforzheim)	September 6, 2013

Bibliography

Archival Documents

United States

National Archives and Records Administration (NARA)

Army Intelligence Project Decimal File 1941–1945, NARA, RG 319, E47C, Portugal Box 964.

Brown, Major Robert, Assistant Military Attaché for Air in Turkey, to Military Attaché in Turkey, "Force landed Aircraft," dated November 23, 1943, MID 383.01, Top Secret Incoming and Outgoing Cables 1942–1945, Switzerland, RG 319, E58, Turkey Box 41, National Archives at College Park, College Park, MD.

Confidential and Secret Incoming and Outgoing Messages 1942–1945, RG 319, E57, Spain Box 594–601, Turkey Box 635, 636, RG 319, E58, Turkey Box 41, and RG 319, E47C, G2 Project Decimal File 1941–1945, Turkey Box 964, 1032, 1600, Spain Box 1008, National Archives at College Park, College Park, MD.

Deputy Theater Judge Advocate's Office, War Crimes Branch, January 16, 1946. Records of the Office of the Judge Advocate General (Army). RG 153, Entry 143, Boxes 147–510. National Archives at College Park, College Park, MD.

Escape and Evasion Reports, RG 498, Entry 133–34, Boxes 516–573, National Archives at College Park, College Park, MD.

Letter to Lieutenant Colonel I. Davidson, AAG Liaison (British), War Crimes Branch, USFET, March 20, 1946, RG 153, Entry 143, Box 512, National Archives at College Park, College Park, MD.

Office of Strategic Services (OSS) Research & Analysis Report (R & A) No. 1113.65, June 24, 1944, Page 3, RG 153, Entry 143, Box 235, Case 12-239-4. National Archives at College Park, College Park, MD.

Records of US Army Europe, War Crimes Branch, General Administration, and War Crimes Case Files, 1947-1958, RG 549, Entry 290, Boxes 1–13, 121–187, National Archives at College Park, College Park, MD.

Air Force Historical Research Agency (Maxwell AFB)

Escape Intelligence Bulletin. November 22, 1944. Fifteenth Air Force Headquarters. Maxwell AFB, Montgomery, AL.

Escape Intelligence Bulletin Number 4. November 13, 1944. From the Fifteenth Air Force Headquarters. Maxwell AFB, Montgomery, AL.

Escape Intelligence Report—Escape Information Series A-13. "Late Information on Dulag Luft." June 21, 1944. Maxwell AFB, Montgomery, AL.

Special Escape Bulletin No. 16a. Fifteenth Air Force Headquarters. Maxwell AFB, Montgomery, AL.

Online Sources

"Amerika als Zerrbild europäischr Lebensordnung." Schulungs-Unterlage Nr. 19. Der Reichsorganisationsleitung der NSDAP, Hauptschulungsamt, 1942. http://research.calvin.edu/german-propaganda-archive/hsa01.htm.

Army Air Forces Statistical Digest, World War II. Washington, DC: Office of Statistical Control—December 1945. http://www.dtic.mil/dtic/tr/fulltext/u2/a542518.pdf.

Army Battle Casualties and Nonbattle Deaths in World War II—Final Report: December 7, 1941–December 31, 1946. Statistical and Accounting Branch Office of the Adjutant General, 1950. https://archive.org/details/ArmyBattleCasualtiesAndNonbattleDeathsInWorldWarIiPt1Of4.

Control Council Law No. 10. Punishment of Persons Guilty of War Crimes, Crimes against Peace, and Crimes against Humanity. December 20, 1945. Reprinted in *XV Trials of War Criminals before the Nuremberg Military Tribunals under Control Council Law No. 10*. Washington, DC: Government Printing Office, 1950. https://www.loc.gov/rr/frd/Military_Law/pdf/NT_war-criminals_Vol-XV.pdf

"Datei:2009-Dirmstein-Sibley.jpg," Wikipedia, March 20, 2011. https://de.wikipedia.org/wiki/ Datei:2009-Dirmstein-Sibley.jpg#filelinks.

"Datei:Gedenktafel B -17 Borkum.JPG," Wikipedia, July 19, 2012. https://de.wikipedia.org/wiki/Datei: Gedenktafel_B_-17_Borkum.JPG.

DPAA, Service Personnel Not Recovered Following WWII for the United States Army Air Forces. July 26, 2019. https://www.dpaa.mil/Portals/85/Documents/WWIIAccounting/united_states_army_air_forces.html.

"Europe and Amerika: Fehlerquellen im Aufbau des amerikanischen Volkstums." Schulungs-Unterlage Nr. 18. Der Reichsorganisationsleitung der NSDAP, Hauptschulungsamt, 1942. http://research.calvin.edu/german-propaganda-archive/hsa02.htm.

"Evasion in Europe," Military Intelligence Service (MIS-X) Manual on Escape, Evasion, and Survival. Washington, DC: War Department, February 1944. https://wwiinetherlandsescapelines.files.wordpress.com/2012/08/evasion-in-europe-part-of-mis-x-manual.pdf.

Human Rights after Hitler. "United Nations War Crimes Commission Archives." http://www.unwcc.org/unwcc-archives/, accessed March 6, 2018.

International Committee of the Red Cross, "Treaties, States Parties and Commentaries: Convention (IV) Relative to the Protection of Civilian Persons in Time of War. Geneva, 12 August 1949," https://ihl-databases.icrc.org/ihl/385ec082b509e76c41256739003e636d/6756482d86146898c125641e004aa3c5.

International Committee of the Red Cross, "Treaties, States Parties and Commentaries: Protocol Additional to the Geneva Conventions on 12 August 1949, and Relating to the Protection of Victims of International Armed Conflicts (Protocol I), 8 June 1977," https://ihl-databases.icrc.org/ihl/INTRO/470.

Joseph Goebbels diary entry. June 30, 1943. In Nationalsozialismus, Holocaust, Widerstand, und Exil 1933–1945. Online-Datenbank, De Gruyter. http://db.saur.de/DGO/basicFullCitationView.jsf?documentId=TJG-5807.

Judgement of the International Military Tribunal for the Far East, Chapter VIII. 1948. http://www.loc.gov/rr/frd/Military_Law/pdf/Judgment-IMTFE-Vol-II-PartB-Chapter-VIII.pdf.

Köbler, Gerhard. "Deutsches Etymologisches Wörterbuch." *Deutsches Etymologisches Wörterbuch*, 1995. http://www.koeblergerhard.de/der/DERL.pdf.

Law-Reports of Trials of War Criminals, The United Nations War Crimes Commission, Volume III, London. HMSO, 1948. http://www.phdn.org/archives/www.ess.uwe.ac.uk/WCC/killinger.htm.

Missing Air Crew Reports (MACRs), 1942–1947, NARA, Record Group 92, Records of the Office of the Quartermaster General, https://catalog.archives.gov/id/305256.

"Recognizing and Commending American Airmen Held as Political Prisoners at the Buchenwald Concentration Camp during World War II for Their Service, Bravery, and Fortitude." H. Con. Res. 95. 105th Congress (1997–1998). https://www.congress.gov/bill/105th-congress/house-concurrent-resolution/95/text.

Records of the US Army, Europe, 1942–1991, RG 549, Entry A1 2238, Microfilm T1021, Reel 10 and 13, National Archives at College Park, College Park, MD. https://catalog.archives.gov/id/40957462.

"Special Operations: AAF Aid to European Resistance Movements, 1943–1945." U.S. Air Force Historical Study No. 121. Air Historical Office Headquarters, Army Air Forces, June 1947, 133–34.

"Straffreiheitsgesetz 1954." Bundestageblatt, Bonn. July 17, 1954. http://www.bgbl.de/xaver/bgbl/start.xav?startbk=Bundesanzeiger_BGBl&jumpTo=bgbl154021.pdf.

Trial of the Major War Criminals before the International Military Tribunal: Nuremberg, 14 November 1945–1 October 1946, Volume XX. Nuremberg, 1948, https://www.loc.gov/rr/frd/Military_Law/NT_major-war-criminals.html.

Trials of War Criminals before the Nurmberg Military Tribunals under Control Council Law No. 10. Vol. 11. Washington, DC: United States Government Printing Office, 1960. https://www.loc.gov/rr/frd/Military_Law/pdf/NT_war-criminals_Vol-II.pdf.

Vento, Carol Schultz. "The Missing in Action (MIA) of World War II." Defense Military Network. May 28, 2012. https://www.defensemedianetwork.com/stories/the-missing-in-action-mia-of-world-war-ii/.

Veterans History Project, The American Folklife Center of the Library of Congress, http://www.loc.gov/vets/, accessed February 24, 2016.

Germany

Bundesarchiv Berlin-Lichterfelde: Allgemeines (Tötung von Feindflieger)—R 001/24003.

Bundesarchiv Berlin-Lichterfelde: Anweisung an die RPÄ, über Fälle von Lynchjustiz zu berichten—RW 55/645.

Bundesarchiv Berlin-Lichterfelde: Aussagen Kriegsgefangener (Flieger)—R 55/560.

Bundesarchiv Berlin-Lichterfelde: Auswärtiges Amt—R 901/73270.

Bundesarchiv Berlin-Lichterfelde: Behandlung abgesprungener Feindflieger—R 58/9044.

Bundesarchiv Berlin-Lichterfelde: Behandlung des Luftkrieges im Propaganda—NS 18/772.

Bundesarchiv Berlin-Lichterfelde: Behandlung von Kriegsgefangenen (Sammlung von Rundlassen)—R 58/397.
Bundesarchiv Berlin-Lichterfelde: Flughafenbereichskommandos der Luftwaffe—RL 20/199.
Bundesarchiv Berlin-Lichterfelde: Generalstab der Luftwaffe/Luftwaffenführungsstab—RL 2-II/434; 435; 438; 510; 514; 522; 586; 989.
Bundesarchiv Berlin-Lichterfelde: Inner Dienst des Amtes Stabführung (feindlicher Kriegsverbrecher)—NS 19/3525; 3549.
Bundesarchiv Berlin-Lichterfelde: Letter from Günther Wieland to Prof. Dr. Olaf Groehler (Zentralinstitut für Geschichte der Akademie der Wissenschaften der DDR), March 30, 1984—DP 3/2223.
Bundesarchiv Berlin-Lichterfelde: Lynchjustiz an Angehörigen der US-Air Force—DP 3/2223, Bd. 35.
Bundesarchiv Berlin-Lichterfelde: Lynchjustiz in den USA—R 55/20935, 24823.
Bundesarchiv Berlin-Lichterfelde: Meldungen aus dem Reich (Lage und Stimmungsberichte des SD)—R 58/151; 152; 154; 155; 157; 159; 163; 183; 1143.
Bundesarchiv Berlin-Lichterfelde: Presse-Nachrichtenabteilung, Auswärtiges Amt—R 901/59692.
Bundesarchiv Berlin-Lichterfelde: Propaganda Ministry—R 55/24843.
Bundesarchiv Berlin-Lichterfelde: Prozesse gegen Kriegsverbrecher—R 1501/113532.
Bundesarchiv Berlin-Lichterfelde: Rassenfragen in Australian—R 4902/3859.
Bundesarchiv Berlin-Lichterfelde: Volksjustiz gegen anglo-amerikanische Mörder—NS 6/350.
Bundesarchiv Freiburg: Anordnungen und Befehle (Darmstadt)—RL 21/6.
Bundesarchiv Freiburg: Auswertestelle West Oberursel—RL 2-II/968, 987, 1017, 1018.
Bundesarchiv Freiburg: Bautruppen und Pioniere (Landesschützen und Kriegsgefangenenlager) der Luftwaffe—Kriegstagebuch—RL 23/97.
Bundesarchiv Freiburg: Behandlung feindlicher Terrorflieger—RW 4/700.
Bundesarchiv Freiburg: Disziplinarangelegenheiten: Tieffliegerbekämpfung—RH 38/286.
Bundesarchiv Freiburg: Dokumentenbuch: "Terrorflieger"—N 431/1508, 1511.
Bundesarchiv Freiburg: Einführung des Tieffliegervernichtungsabzeichens (aus dem *Völkischer Beobachter*)—RM 7/98, Folder 94.
Bundesarchiv Freiburg: Feindtätigkeiten (Oberursel)—RL 11/35.
Bundesarchiv Freiburg: Flugzeugabstürze—RL 21/5.
Bundesarchiv Freiburg: Frontstalag 194 (Abgesprungene Feindflieger)—RH 49/65.
Bundesarchiv Freiburg: IC Unterlagen—Allgemeines (Tarnung Feindflieger)—RS 21/29; 38.
Bundesarchiv Freiburg: Kommandantur und Sonderbefehle (Gütersloh)—RL 21/38.
Bundesarchiv Freiburg: Luftschutzwesen (Feindflieger)—RW 17/67.
Bundesarchiv Freiburg: Luftschutzwesen (Feindflieger)—RW 17/90.
Bundesarchiv Freiburg: Militärbefehlshaber Frankreich und nachgeordnete Dienststellen—RW 35/213.
Bundesarchiv Freiburg: 1939–1941 Bekämpfung von Fallschirmjägern/Luftlandtruppen—RW 4/145, Bd. 3.

Bundesarchiv Freiburg: 1933–1945 Tieffliegerbekämpfung—RW 59/36, Bd. 36.
Bundesarchiv Freiburg: OKW/Allgemeines Wehrmachtamt (Chef Kriegsgefangenenwesen)—RW 6/270; 273; 603; 274.
Bundesarchiv Freiburg: Richtlinien zur Untersuchung—RL 21/26.
Bundesarchiv Freiburg: Sammlung von Flugbefehlen (Fritzlar)—RL 21/25.
Bundesarchiv Freiburg: Tagesbefehle des Oberbefehlshabers Bezirk Nordfrankreich (Tarnung Feindflieger)—RH 33/30.
Bundesarchiv Freiburg: Tarnung Feindflieger—RH 26–353/6.
Bundesarchiv Freiburg: Wehrkreiskommandos (Mai—Dez. 1942 Jagdkommandos)—RH 53–17/120, Bd. 5.
Bundesarchiv Freiburg: Wehrmachtführungsstab—RW 4/765.
Bundesarchiv Freiburg: "Wie können wir mit der feindlichen Tieffliegerpest fertig warden?"—RH 11-III/50, Folders 1–19.
Bundesarchiv Koblenz: Terrorflieger—N 1583/ 53; 86; 87.
Bundesarchiv Ludwigsburg: NSG-Verfahren an bundesdeutschen Staatsanwaltschaften und Gerichten aus der Zeit vor dem 01.12.1958—B162/1489; 8026; 8705; 9966; 14358; 15171; 16543; 19752; 21044; 21266; 25092; 27884; 27885; 41417.
International Tracing Service Archive, Bad Arolsen, Germany.
Landesarchiv Nordrhein-Westfalen, Duisburg, Generalstaatsanwaltschaft Köln: Gerichte Rep. 334 Nr. 219.
Landesarchiv Nordrhein-Westfalen, Duisburg, Oberlandesgericht Düsseldrof: Gerichte Rep. 86 Nr. 1677.
Landesarchiv Nordrhein-Westfalen, Duisburg, Oberlandesgericht Köln: Gerichte Rep. 314 Nr. 3–4.
Landesarchiv Nordrhein-Westfalen, Duisburg: RW 0018 Nr. 20; 34, pages 214–216; 227–228; 237–251.
Landesarchiv Nordrhein-Westfalen, Duisburg: RW 0036 Nr. 38; 48, pages 109–126.
Landesarchiv Nordrhein-Westfalen, Duisburg: RW 0037 Nr. 20, pages 100–144.
Landesarchiv Nordrhein-Westfalen, Duisburg, Staatsanwaltschaft Aachen: Gerichte Rep. 87 Nr. 175–179, 11Ks 1/53.
Landesarchiv Nordrhein-Westfalen, Duisburg, Staatsanwaltschaft Aachen: Gerichte Rep. 270 Nr. 16, 3 Js 211/47; 3 Js 403/49; 4 Js 643/51; 9 Js 22/48.
Landesarchiv Nordrhein-Westfalen, Duisburg, Staatsanwaltschaft Aachen: Gerichte Rep. 0382 Nr. 1585–1586, 8 Js 789/69.
Landesarchiv Nordrhein-Westfalen, Duisburg, Staatsanwaltschaft Wuppertal: Gerichte Rep. 0747 Nr. 14.

Secondary Literature

Abrahams, Ray. *Vigilant Citizens: Vigilantism and the State*. Malden: Polity Press, 1998.
Ambrose, Stephan. *The Wild Blue: The Men and Boys Who Flew the B-24s over Germany, 1944–45*. New York: Simon and Schuster, 2001.
Anderson, Gary. "Lynchjustiz gegen alliierte Piloten: Drei Faelle aus dem Bodenseeraum 1944/45." In *Opfer des Unrechts: Stigmatisierung, Verfolgung und Vernichtung von Gegnern durch die NS-Gewaltherrschaft an Fallbeispielen aus Oberschwaben*, edited by Edwin Ernst Weber, 269–290. Stuttgart: Jan Thorbecke, 2009.

Ardery, Philip. *Bomber Pilot: A Memoir of World War II*. Lexington: University Press of Kentucky, 1996.

Arendt, Hannah. *Eichmann in Jerusalem: A Report on the Banality of Evil*. New York: Penguin Books, 2006.

———. *The Origins of Totalitarianism*. New York: Harcourt, 1973.

Ault, Brian, and William Brustein. "Joining the Nazi Party: Explaining the Political Geography of NSDAP Membership, 1925–1933." *American Behavioral Scientist* 41, no. 9 (1998): 1304–23.

Bachrach, Susan, and Steven Luckert. *State of Deception: The Power of Nazi Propaganda*. Washington, DC: United States Holocaust Memorial Museum, 2009.

Bajohr, Frank, and Michael Weldt, eds. *Volksgemeinschaft: Neue Forschungen zur Gesellschaft des Nationalsozialismus*. Frankfurt: Fischer, 2009.

Baldoli, Claudia, and Andrew Knapp. *Forgotten Blitzes: France and Italy under Allied Air Attack, 1940–1945*. New York: Continuum, 2012.

Baldoli, Claudia, Andrew Knapp, and Richard Overy, eds. *Bombing, States and Peoples in Western Europe, 1940–1945*. London: Continuum, 2011.

Bandura, Albert. "Moral Disengagement in the Perpetration of Inhumanities." *Personality and Social Psychology Review* 3, no. 3 (1999): 193–209.

———. "Selective Activation and Disengagement of Moral Control." *Journal of Social Values*, no. 46.1 (1990): 27–46.

———. "Social Cognitive Theory of Moral Though and Action." In *Handbook of Moral Behavior and Development*, vol. 1, edited by W. M. Kurtines and J. L. Gewirtz, 45–104. Hillsdale, NJ: Erlbaum, 1991.

Barber, Melanie. "Tales of the Unexpected: Glimpses of Friends in the Archives of Lambeth Palace." *Journal of the Friends Historical Society* 61, no. 2 (2007): 87–123.

Barclary, David E., and Elisabeth Glaser-Schmidt, eds. *Transantlantic Images and Perceptions: Germany and America since 1776*. New York: Cambridge University Press, 1997.

Bard, Mitchell G. *Forgotten Victims: The Abandonment of Americans in Hitler's Camps*. Oxford: Westview Press, 1994.

Barnett, Victoria J. *Bystanders: Conscience and Complicity during the Holocaust*. London: Praeger, 1999.

Bartov, Omer. *Germany's War and the Holocaust: Disputed Histories*. Ithaca: Cornell University Press, 2003.

———. *The Holocaust: Origins, Implementation, Aftermath*. New York: Routledge, 2000.

Beck, Levitt Clinton, Jr. *Fighter Pilot*. Los Angeles: Wetzel Publishing, 1946.

Becker, P. *Dem Täter auf der Spur. Eine Geschichte der Kriminalistik*. Darmstadt: Wissenschaftliche Buchgesellschaft, 2005.

Beer, Edith H., and Susan Dworkin. *The Nazi Officer's Wife: How One Jewish Woman Survived the Holocaust*. New York: William Morrow, 2015.

Benz, Wolfgang, and Walter H. Pehle, eds. *Encyclopedia of German Resistance to the Nazi Movement*. New York: Continuum, 1997.

Berg, Manfred, and Simon Wendt, eds. *Globalizing Lynching History: Vigilantism and Extralegal Punishment from an International Perspective*. New York: Palgrove Macmillan, 2011.

Bergerson, Andrew Stuart. *Ordinary Germans in Extraordinary Times: The Nazi Revolution in Hildesheim*. Bloomington: Indiana University Press, 2004.

Bernstein, David. *Rehabilitating Lochner: Defending Individual Rights against Progressive Reform*. Chicago: University of Chicago Press, 2011.

Bialas, Wolfgang. *Moralische Ordnungen des Nationalsozialismus*. Göttingen, Germany: Vandenhoeck and Ruprecht, 2014.

Bialas, Wolfgang, and Lothar Fritze, eds. *Ideologie und Moral im Nationalsozialismus*. Göttingen: Vandenhoeck and Ruprecht, 2014.

Bird, Tom. *American POWs in World War II: Forgotten Men Tell Their Stories*. Westport, CT: Praeger, 1992.

Blank, Ralf. "Wartime Daily Life and the Air War on the Home Front." In *Germany and the Second World War*, edited by Jörg Echternkamp, 371–478. Oxford: Oxford Univesity Press, 2008. This was first published in German as *Das Deutsche Reich und der Zweite Weltkrieg*. Munich: Deutsche Verlags-Anstalt, 2004.

Bloxham, Donald. "British War Crimes Trial Policy in Germany, 1945–1957: Implementation and Collapse." *Journal of British Studies* 42, no. 1 (2003): 91–118.

Boberach, Heinz, ed. *Meldungen aus dem Reich. Die geheimen Lageberichte des sicherheitsdienstes der SS 1938–1945*, vol. 15. Herrsching: Pawlak, 1984.

Bodson, Herman. *Agent for the Resistance: A Belgian Saboteur in World War II*. College Station: Texas A&M University Press, 1994.

———. *Downed Allied Airmen and Evasion of Capture: The Role of Local Resistance Networks in World War II*. London: McFarland and Company, 2005.

Böhler, Jochen. "Die Wehrmacht im Vernichtungskrieg." In *Naziverbrechen: Täter, Taten, Bewältigungsversuche*, edited by Martin Cüppers, Jürgen Matthäus, and Andrej Angrick, 89–102. Darmstadt: WBG, 2013.

Bower, Tom. *Blind Eye to Murder: Britain, America, and the Purging of Nazi Germany—A Pledge Betrayed*. New York: Harper Collins, 1981.

Brode, Patrick. *Casual Slaughters and Accidental Judgments: Canadian War Crimes Prosecutions, 1944–1948*. Toronto: University of Toronto Press, 1997.

Broszat, Martin. *The Hitler State*. New York: Routledge, 2013.

———. "Zur Struktur der NS-Massenbewegung." *Vierteljahrshefte für Zeitgeschichte*, no. 1 (1983): 52–76.

Brown, Courtney. "The Nazi Vote: A National Ecological Stud." *American Political Science Review* 76, no. 2 (1982): 285–302.

Brown, Harold H., and Marsha S. Bordner. *Keep Your Airspeed Up: The Story of a Tuskegee Airman*. Tuscaloosa: University of Alabama Press, 2017.

Browning, Christopher. *Ordinary Men: Reserve Police Battalion 101 and the Final Solution in Poland*. New York: Harper Perennial, 1992.

Brundage, W. Fitzhugh. *Lynching in the New South: Georgia and Virginia, 1880–1930*. Chicago: University of Illinois Press, 1993.

Bunyak, Dawn Trimble. *The Last Mission: A World War II Prisoner in Germany*. Norman: University of Oklahoma Press, 2003.

Burgress, Colin. *Destination: Buchenwald*. Australia: Kangaroo Press, 1995.

Buscher, Frank M. *The U.S. War Crimes Trial Program in Germany, 1946–1955*. New York: Greenwood Press, 1989.

Bytwerk, Randall L. *Bending Spines: The Propagandas of Nazi Germany and the German Democratic Republic*. East Lansing: Michigan State University Press, 2004.

Caine, Philip D. *Aircraft Down: Evading Capture in WWII Europe*. Washington, DC: Brassey's, 1997.

———. *Eagles of The RAF: The World War II Eagle Squadrons*. Washington, DC: National Defense University Press, 1991.

Carrigan, William D., and Christopher Waldrep, eds. *Swift to Wrath: Lynching in Global Historical Perspective*. Charlottesville: University of Virginia Press, 2013.

Casey, Donald E. *To Fight for My Country, Sir: Memoirs of a 19-Year-Old B-17 Navigator Shot Down in Nazi Germany and Imprisoned in the WWII "Great Escape" Prison Camp*. Chicago: Sterling Cooper, 2009.

Charlesworth, Lorie. "Forgotten Justice: Forgetting Law's History and Victims' Justice in British 'Minor' War Crime Trials in Germany 1945–8." *Amicus Curiae*, no. 74 (2008): 2–10.

Chickering, Roger, and Stig Förster. "Are We There Yet? World War II and the Theory of Total War." In *A World at Total War: Global Conflict and the Politics of Destruction, 1937–1945*, edited by Roger Chickering, Stig Förster, and Bernd Greiner, 1–16. Cambridge: Cambridge University Press, 2005.

Childers, Thomas, ed. *The Formation of the Nazi Constituency, 1919–1933*. New York: Routledge, 1986.

———. *Wings of Morning*. New York: Addison-Wesley Publishing, 1995.

Chorbajian, L., and G. Shirinian, eds. *Studies in Comparative Genocide*. New York: St. Martin's Press, 1999.

Clutton-Brock, Oliver. *Footprints on the Sands of Time: RAF Bomber Command Prisoners of War in Germany, 1939–1945*. London: Grub Street, 2003.

———. *RAF Evaders: The Comprehensive Story of Thousands of Escapers and Their Escape Lines, Western Europe, 1940–1945*. London: Grub Street, 2009.

Cohen, David. "Transnational Justice in Divided Germany After 1945." In *Retribution and Reparation in the Transition to Democracy*, edited by Jon Elster, 59–88. Cambridge: Cambridge University Press, 2006.

Counts, Major Laura C. "Were They Prepared? Escape and Evasion in Western Europe, 1942–1944." Thesis, Air Command and Staff College, Montgomery, AL, 1986.

Crane, Conrad C. *Bombs, Cities, and Civilians: American Airpower Strategy in World War II*. Lawrence: University Press of Kansas, 1993.

Crawley, Aidan. *Escape from Germany, 1939–1945: Methods of Escape Used by RAF Airmen during World War II*. London: Stationery Office, 2001.

Creydt, Detlef. *Luftkrieg im Weserbergland*. Holzminden: Jörg Mitzkat, 2007.

Culberson, William C. *Vigilantism: Political History of Private Power in America*. New York: Greenwood Press, 1990.

Dams, Carsten. *Staatsschutz in der Weimarer Republik, Die Überwachung und Bekämpfung der NSDAP durch die preußische politische Polizei von 1928–1932*. Marburg: Tectum Verlag, 2002.

Darling, Ian. *Amazing Airmen: Canadian Flyers in the Second World War*. Toronto: Dundurn Press, 2009.

Darlow, Steve. *Flightpath to Murder: Death of a Pilot Officer*. Somerset, UK: Haynes Publishing, 2009.

de Grazia, Victoria. *Irresistible Empire: America's Advance through Twentieth-Century Europe*. Cambridge, MA: Harvard University Press, 2005.

de Mildt, Dick. *In the Name of the People: Perpetrators of Genocide in the Reflection of their Post-War Prosecution in West Germany: The "Euthanasia" and "Aktion Reinhard" Trial Cases*. The Hague: Martinus Nijhoff, 1996.

Deutsch, Morton. "Psychological Roots of Moral Exclusion." *Journal of Social Issues* 46, no. 1 (1990): 21–25.

de Zayas, Alfred M. *The Wehrmacht Warcrimes Bureau, 1939–1945*. Rockport: Picton Press, 1989.
Diggins, John P. *Mussolini and Fascism: The View from America*. Princeton, NJ: Princeton University Press, 1972.
Dittmann, Fred. *Mitteldeutschland im Luftkrieg 1944 und 1945*. Lutherstadt Eisleben: Henke, 2001.
Dorr, Robert F., and Thomas D. Jones. *Hell Hawks!: The Untold Story of the American Fliers Who Savaged Hitler's Wehrmacht*. Minneapolis: Zenith Press, 2008.
Dower, John W. *War without Mercy*. New York: Pantheon Books, 1997.
Drooz, Daniel B. *American Prisoners of War in German Death, Concentration, and Slave Labor Camps*. Toronto: Edwin Mellen Press, 2004.
Dryden, Charles W. *A-Train: Memoirs of a Tuskegee Airman*. Tuscaloosa: University of Alabama Press, 1997.
Dwyer, T. Ryle. *Guests of the State: The Story of Allied and Axis Servicemen Interned in Ireland during World War II*. Dingle: Brandon Book Publishers, 1994.
Eher, Franz, ed. *Englands Alleinschuld am Bombenterror*. Volksausgabe des 8. Amtlichen Deutschen Weissbuches. Berlin: Zentralverlag der NSDAP, 1943.
Eiber, Ludwig, and Robert Sigel. *Dachauer Prozesse: NS-Verbrechen vor amerikanischen Militärgerichten in Dachau 1945–48*. Göttingen, Germany: Wallstein, 2007.
Eisner, Peter. *The Freedom Line*. New York: Harper Collins, 2004.
Ellwood, David. *The Shock of American: Europe and the Challenge of the Century*. New York: Oxford University Press, 2012.
Emsley, Clive. *Soldier, Sailor, Beggerman, Thief: Crime and the British Armed Services since 1914*. Oxford: Oxford University Press, 2013.
Evans, Richard J. *Rituals of Retribution: Capital Punishment in Germany 1600–1987*. Oxford: Oxford University Press, 1996.
———. *The Third Reich at War*. New York: Penguin Press, 2009.
Fahrenwald, Ted. *Bailout over Normandy: A Flyboy's Adventures with the French Resistance and Other Escapades in Occupied France*. Philadelphia: Casemate Publishers, 2012.
Falter, Jürgen W. "'Anfälligkeit' der Angestellten—'Immunität' der Arbeiter? Mythen über die Wähler der NSDAP." *Historical Social Research/Historische Sozialforschung*. Supplement, No. 25, Zur Soziographie des Nationalsozialismus: Studien zu den Wählern und Mitgliedern der NSDAP (2013): 90–110.
———. "Die 'Märzgefallenen' von 1933: Neue Forschungsergebnisse zum sozialen Wandel innerhalb der NSDAP-Mitgliedschaft während der Machtergreifungsphase." *Historical Social Research/Historische Sozialforschung*. Supplement, No. 25, Zur Soziographie des Nationalsozialismus: Studien zu den Wählern und Mitgliedern der NSDAP (2013): 280–302.
———. "Wählerbewegungen zur NSDAP 1924–1933. Methodische Probleme—Empirisch abgesicherte Erkenntnisse—Offene Fragen." *Historical Social Research/Historische Sozialforschung*. Supplement, No. 25, Zur Soziographie des Nationalsozialismus: Studien zu den Wählern und Mitgliedern der NSDAP (2013): 49–89.
———. "The Young Membership of the NSDAP between 1925 and 1933: A Demographic and Social Profile." *Historical Social Research/Historische Sozialforschung*. Supplement, No. 25, Zur Soziographie des Nationalsozialismus: Studien zu den Wählern und Mitgliedern der NSDAP (2013): 260–79.
Fangemann, H., U. Reifner, and N. Steinborn. *Parteisoldaten: Die Hamburger Polizei im 3. Reich*. Hamburg: VSA, 1987.

Fatz, M. *Vom Staatsschutz zum Gestapo-Terror. Politische Polizei in Bayern in der Endphase der Weimarer Republik und der Anfangsphase der nationalsozialistischen Diktatur*. Würzburg, Germany: Echter, 1995.

Feast, Sean, and Marc Hall. *Missing—Presumed Murdered: One Raid, Two Trials, Three Lost Airmen*. Hitchin, UK: Fighting High, 2018.

Ferguson, Niall. *The Pity of War: Explaining World War I*. New York: Basic Books, 1998.

Fischer, Klaus P. *Hitler and America*. Philadelphia: University of Pennsylvania Press, 2011.

Fitzgerald, David Scott, and David Cook-Martin. *Culling the Masses: The Democratic Origins of Racist Immigration Policy in the Americas*. Cambridge, MA: Harvard University Press, 2014.

Flammer, Philip M. "Dulag Luft: The Third Reich's Prison Camp for Airmen." *Aerospace Historian* 19, no. 2 (1972): 58–65.

Fleisher, Michael L. "'Sungusungu': State-Sponsored Village Vigilante Groups among the Kuria of Tanzania." *Journal of the Institutional African Institute* 70, no. 2 (2000): 209–28.

Fleming, Nicholas. *August 1939: The Last Days of Peace*. London: Davies, 1979.

Flint, Colin. "Electoral Geography and the Social Construction of Space: The Example of the Nazi Party in Baden, 1924–1932." *GeoJournal* 51, no. 3 (2000): 145–56.

———. "Forming Electorates, Forging Spaces: The Nazi Party Vote and the Social Construction of Space." *American Behavioral Scientist* 41, no. 9 (1998): 1282–300.

———. "A Timespace for Electoral Geography: Economic Restructuring, Political Agency and the Rise of the Nazi Party." *Political Geography* vol. 20, no. 3 (2001): 301–29.

Förster, Stig. "From 'Blitzkrieg' to 'Total War': Germany's War in Europe." In *World at Total War: Global Conflict and the Politics of Destruction, 1937–1945*, edited by Roger Chickering, Stig Förster, and Bernd Greiner, 89–108. Cambridge: Cambridge University Press, 2005.

Förster, Stig, and Jörg Nagler, eds. *On the Road to Total War: The American Civil War and the German Wars of Unification, 1861–1871*. Cambridge: Cambridge University Press, 1997.

Foot, Michael R. D., and J. M. Langley. *MI-9: Escape and Evasion, 1939–1945*. Boston: Little, Brown and Company, 1979.

Foy, David A. *For You the War Is Over: American Prisoners of War in Nazi Germany*. New York: Stein and Day, 1984.

Fredrickson, George. *Racism: A Short History*. Princeton, NJ: Princeton University Press, 2002.

Freeman, Gregory A. *The Forgotten 500: The Untold Story of the Men Who Risked All for the Greatest Rescue Mission in World War II*. New York: NAL Caliber, 2007.

———. *The Last Mission of the Wham Bam Boys: Courage, Tragedy, and Justice in World War II*. New York: Palgrave MacMillan, 2011.

Frei, Norbert. *Adenauer's Germany and the Nazi Past: The Politics of Amnesty and Integration*. New York: Columbia University Press, 2002.

———. *Vergangenheitspolitik*. Munich: Verlag C.H. Beck, 1997.

Friedhoff, Herman. *Requiem for the Resistance: The Civilian Struggle against Nazism in Holland and Germany*. London: Bloomsbury, 1988.

Friedlander, Henry. *The Origins of Nazi Genocide: From Euthanasia to the Final Solution*. Chapel Hill: University of North Carolina Press, 1995.
Friedrich, Jörg. *The Fire: The Bombing of Germany, 1940–1945*. Translated by Allison Brown. New York: Columbia University Press, 2006.
Funk, Albert. *Polizei und Rechtsstaat: Die Entwicklung des staatlichen Gewaltmonopols in Preußen 1848–1914*. Frankfurt/Main: Campus, 1986.
Galbreath D. L., and Léon Jéquier. *Lehrbuch der Heraldik*. Frankfurt am Main: Krüger, 1977.
Garraty, John. "The New Deal, National Socialism, and the Great Depression." *American Historical Review* 78, no. 4 (1973): 907–44.
Garrett, Stephen. *Ethics and Airpower in World War II: The British Bombing of German Cities*. Palgrave Macmillan, 1993.
Gatewood, Betty, and Jean Belkham. *Kriegie 7956: A World War II Bombardier's Pursuit of Freedom*. Shippensburg, PA: Burd Street Press, 2001.
Gazit, Nir. "State-Sponsored Vigilantism: Jewish Settlers' Violence in the Occupied Palestinian Territories." *Sociology* 49, no. 3 (2015): 438–54.
Geary, Dick. "Who Voted for the Nazis?" *History Today* 48, no. 10 (1998). https://www.historytoday.com/archive/who-voted-nazis.
Geck, Stefan. *Dulag Luft/Auswertestelle West: Vernehmungslager der Luftwaffe für westalliierte Kriegsgefangene im Zweiten Weltkrieg*. Frankfurt am Main: Peter Lang, 2008.
Geinitz, Christian. "The First Air War against Noncombatants: Strategic Bombing of German Cities in World War I." In *Great War, Total War: Combat and Mobilization on the Western Front*, edited by Roger Chickering and Stig Förster, 207–26. Cambridge: Cambridge University Press, 2000.
Gellately, Robert. *Backing Hitler: Consent and Coercion in Nazi Germany*. Oxford: Oxford University Press, 2002.
———. *The Gestapo and German Society: Enforcing Racial Policy, 1933–1945*. Oxford: Clarendon Press, 1990.
Gilbert, G. M. *Nuremberg Diary*. Boston: De Capo Press, 1961.
Goedde, Petra. *GIs and Germans: Culture, Gender, and Foreign Relations, 1945–1949*. New Haven, CT: Yale University Press, 2003.
Goldhagen, Daniel. *Hitler's Willing Executioners: Ordinary Germans and the Holocaust*. New York: Vintage Books, 1997.
Goldstein, Daniel M. "Flexible Justice: Neoliberal Violence and 'Self-Help' Security in Bolivia." In *Global Vigilantes*, edited by D. Pratten and A. Sen, 239–66. London: Hurst, 2005.
Goll, Nicole-Melanie, and Georg Hoffmann. "'Terrorflieger': Deutungen und Wahrnehmungen des strategischen Luftkrieges der Alliierten in der nationalsozialistischen Propaganda am Beispiel der sogenannten Fliegerlynchjustiz." *Journal for Intelligence, Propaganda, and Security Studies* 5, no. 1 (2011): 71–86.
Gotterbarm, Otmar. *Die Abgestürzten: Der Luftkrieg am 25. und 26. Februar 1944 über Augsburg und der Schwäbischen Alb*. Bad Schussenried: Gerhard Hess, 2013.
Graf, Christoph. *Politische Polizei zwischen Demokratie und Diktatur: Die Entwicklung der preußischen Politischen Polizei vom Staatsschutzorgan der Weimarer Republik zum Geheimen Staatspolizeiamt des Dritten Reiches*. Berlin: Colloquium, 1983.
Greene, Joshua M. *Justice at Dachau: The Trials of an American Prosecutor*. New York: Broadway Books, 2003.

Grill, Johnpeter Horst, and Robert L. Jenkins. "The Nazis and the American South in the 1930s: A Mirror Image?" *Journal of Southern History* 58, no. 4 (1992): 667–94.

Grimm, Barbara. "Lynchmorde an alliierten Fliegern im Zweiten Weltkrieg." In *Deutschland im Luftkrieg: Geschichte und Erinnerung*, edited by Dietmar Süß, 71–84. Munich: R. Oldenbourg, 2007.

Gross, Leonard. *The Last Jews in Berlin*. New York: Caroll and Graf: 1999.

Guettel, Jens-Uwe. *German Expansionism, Imperial Liberalism, and the United States, 1776–1945*. Cambridge: Cambridge University Press, 2012.

Guillemin, Jeanne. *Hidden Atrocities: Japanese Germ Warfare and American Obstruction of Justice at the Tokyo Trial*. New York: Columbia University Press, 2017.

Günther, Lothar. *Missionen und Schicksale im Luftkrieg über Südwest-Thüringen 1944/45*. Untermaßfeld: Wehry, 2015.

Hälbig, Eberhard, and Rainer Lämmerhirt. *Luftkrieg im Raum Eisenach, Gotha, Hainich, Werratal, Thüringer Wald: 1943–1945*. Bad Langensalza: Rockstuhl, 2012.

Halbrainer, Heimo, and Martin F. Polaschek. *Kriegsverbrecherprozesse in Österreich: Eine Bestandsaufnahme*. Graz: Clio Verlag, 2003.

Hall, Kevin T. "The Flyer Trials: Seeking Justice for Lynchjustiz Committed against American Airmen during the Second World War." *War in History*, Vol. 27(3) (2020): 486–516.

———. "*Luftgangster* over Germany: The Lynching of American Airmen in the Shadow of the Air War." *Jouranl Historische Sozialforschung/Historical Social Research* 32, no. 2 (2018): 277–312.

Hampe, Erich. *Der Zivile Luftschutz im Zweiten Weltkrieg*. Frankfurt am Main: Bernard and Gräfe, 1963.

Haney, Craig, Curtis Banks, and Philip Zimbardo. "Interpersonal Dynamics in a Simulated Prison." *International Journal of Criminology and Penology* 1, no. 1 (1973): 69–97.

Hassel, Katrin. *Kriegsverbrechen vor Gericht: Die Kriegsverbrecherprozesse vor Militärgerichten in der britischen Besatzungszone unter dem Royal Warrant vom 18. Juni 1945*. Baden Baden: Nomos, 2009.

Heberer, Patricia, and Jürgen Matthäus, eds. *Atrocities on Trial: Historical Perspectives on the Politics of Prosecuting War Crimes*. Lincoln: University of Nebraska Press, 2008.

Heiber, Helmut, ed. *Goebbels Reden 1932–1945*. Bindlach: Grondom, 1991.

Herf, Jeffrey. *The Jewish Enemy: Nazi Propaganda during World War II and the Holocaust*. Cambridge, MA: Harvard University Press, 2006.

———. *Nazi Propaganda for the Arab World*. New Haven, CT: Yale University Press, 2010.

Hessel, Peter. *The Mystery of Frankenberg's Canadian Airman*. Toronto: James Lorimer & Company, 2005.

Hilberg Raul. *The Destruction of the European Jew*. New York: Holmes and Meier, 1985.

Hilton, Fern Overbey. *The Dachau Defendants: Life Stories from Testimony and Documents of the War Crimes Prosecutions*. Jefferson, NC: McFarland, 2004.

Hingston, Michael. *Into Enemy Arms: The Remarkable True Story of a German Girl's Struggle against Nazism, and Her Daring Escape with the Man She Loved*. London: Grub Street, 2006.

Hodges, Andrew Gerow, Jr., and Denise George. *Behind Nazi Lines: My Father's Heroic Quest to Save 149 World War II POWs*. New York: Penguin, 2015.

Hoffmann, Georg. *Fliegerlynchjustiz: Gewalt gegen abgeschossene alliierte Flugzeugbesatzungen 1943–1945*. Paderborn: Ferdinand Schöningh: 2015.

———. "The Lynching of Airmen at Graz 1945: War Crimes Committed against Allied Airmen in the Context of Violence Control and Post-War-Trials." In *From the Industrial Revolution to World War II in Easter Central Europe*, edited by Marija Wakounig and Karl Ruzicic-Kessler, 207–25. Münster: LIT, 2011.

Horne, John, and Alan Kramer. *German Atrocities, 1914: A History of Denial*. New Haven, CT: Yale University Press, 2001.

Hurt, John J., and Steven E. Sidebotham, eds. *Odyssey of a Bombardier: The POW Log of Richard M. Mason*. Newark: University of Delaware Press, 2014.

Jefferson, Alexander, and Lewis H. Carlson. *Red Tail Captured, Red Tail Free: The Memoirs of a Tuskegee Airman and POW*. New York: Fordham University Press, 2005.

Johann, A. E. *Das Land ohne Herz: Eine Rise ins unbekannte Amerika*. Berlin: Deutscher, 1942.

Johnson, Eric A. *Nazi Terror: The Gestapo, Jews, and Ordinary Germans*. New York: Basic Books, 2000.

———. *Urbanization and Crime: Germany 1871–1914*. Cambridge: Cambridge University Press, 1995.

Johnson, Eric A., and Eric H. Monkkonen, eds. *The Civilization of Crime: Violence in Town and Country since the Middle Ages*. Urbana: University of Illinois Press, 1996.

Johnson, Eric A., and Karl-Heinz Reuband. *What We Knew: Terror, Mass Murder, and Everyday Life in Nazi Germany*. New York: Basic Books, 2005.

Johnston, Les. "What Is vigilantism?" *British Journal of Criminology* 36, no. 2 (1996): 220–36.

Jones, Heather. *Violence against Prisoners of War in the First World War*. Cambridge: Cambridge University Press, 2011.

Jost, Armin, and Stefan Reuter, eds. *Dillingen im Zweiten Weltkrieg: Eine Dokumentation der Dillinger Geschichtswerkstatt*. Dillingen, Germany: Geschichtswerkstatt, 2002.

Kakel, Carroll P. *The American West and the Nazi East: A Comparative and Interpretive Perspective*. New York: Palgrave Macmillan, 2011.

Kallis, Aristotle A. *Nazi Propaganda and the Second World War*. New York: Palgrave Macmillan, 2005.

Kater, Michael H. *The Nazi Party: A Social Profile of Members and Leaders, 1919–1945*. Cambridge, MA: Harvard University Press, 1983.

Katznelson, Ira. *When Affirmative Action Was White: An Untold History of Racial Inequality in Twentieth-Century America*. New York: Norton, 2005.

Kershaw, Ian. *The End: The Defiance and Destruction of Hitler's Germany*, 1944–1945. New York: Penguin Books, 2012.

———. *Hitler: A Biography*. New York: W. W. Norton, 2010.

———. *Hitler, the Germans, and the Final Solution*. New Haven, CT: Yale University Press, 2009.

———. *The "Hitler Myth": Image and Reality in the Third Reich*. Oxford: Oxford University Press, 2001.

———. *The Nazi Dictatorship: Problems & Perspectives of Interpretation*. Oxford: Oxford University Press, 2000.

———. "Working Towards the Führer' Reflections on the Nature of the Hitler Dictatorship." In *The Third Reich*, edited by Christian Leitz, 229–52. London: Blackwill, 1999.

Kirsch, Thomas G., and Tilo Grätz, eds. *Domesticating Vigilantism in Africa*. Rochester: James Currey, 2010.

Klee, Ernst, Willi Dressen, and Volker Riess. *"The Good Old Days:" The Holocaust as Seen by Its Perpetrators and Bystanders*. Translated by Deborah Burnstone. New York: Konecky & Konecky, 1991.
Klemp, Stefan. *Freispruch für das "Mordbataillon": Die NS-Ordnungspolizei und die Nachkriegsjustiz*. Münster: Lit, 1998.
Knell, Hermann. *To Destroy a City: Strategic Bombing and Its Human Consequences in World War II*. Cambridge, MA: De Capo Press, 2003.
Kochavi, Arieh J. *Prelude to Nuremberg: Allied War Crimes Policy and the Question of Punishment*. Chapel Hill: University of North Carolina Press, 1998.
Koller, Hans-Peter. *Der Fliegermord von Freienseen: Eine Dokumentation*. Giessen, Germany: Anabas, 1995.
Koonz, Claudia. *Mothers in the Fatherland: Women, the Family, and Nazi Politics*. New York: St. Martin's Press, 1987.
———. *The Nazi Conscience*. Cambridge, MA: Harvard University Press, 2003.
Kramer, Alan. *Dynamic of Destruction: Culture and Mass Killings in the First World War*. Oxford: Oxford University Press, 2007.
Krieger, Heinrich. *Dass Rassenrecht in den Vereinigten Staaten*. Berlin: Juncker and Dünnhaupt, 1936.
Krueger, Lloyd O. *Come Fly with Me: Experiences of an Airman in World War II*. San Jose: toExcel, 2000.
Krug-Richter, B., and H. Reinke, eds. *Von rechten und unrechten Taten: Zur Kriminalitätsgeschichte Westfalens von der frühen Neuzeit bis zum 20. Jahrhundert*. Westfälische Forschungen, vol. 54. Münster: Aschendorffsche Verlagsbuchhandlung, 2004.
Kühl, Stefan. *The Nazi Connection: Eugenics, American Racism, and German National Socialism*. New York: Oxford University Press, 1994.
LaGrandeur, Philip. *We Flew, We Fell, We Lived: Stories from RCAF Prisoners of War and Evaders, 1939–1945*. St. Catharines: Vanwell, 2006.
Leary, William M. *Fueling the Fires of Resistance: Army Air Forces Special Operations in the Balkans during World War II*. Washington, DC: US Air Force History and Museums Program, 1995.
Leonard, Thomas C. *Illiberal Reformers: Race, Eugenics, and American Economics in the Progressive Era*. Princeton, NJ: Princeton University Press, 2016.
Lichtenstein, Heiner. *Himmlers grüne Helfer: Die Schutz- und Ordnungspolizei im Dritten Reich*. Köln: Bund, 1990.
Linck, Stefan. *Der Ordnung verpflichtet: Deutsche Polizei 1933–1949; Der Fall Flensburg*. Paderborn, Germany: Ferdinand Schöningh, 2000.
Lipset, Seymour Martin. *Political Man: The Social Bases of Politics*. New York: Anchor, 1963.
Longden, Sean. *To the Victor the Spoils: Soldiers' Lives From D-Day to VE-Day*. Gloucestershire: Arris Books, 2004.
Longerich, Peter. *"Davon haben wir nichts gewusst!: Die Deutschen und die Judenverfolgung 1933–1945."* Munich: Siedler, 2006.
Lovenheim, Barbara. *Survival in the Shadows: Seven Hidden Jews in Hitler's Berlin*. New York: Open Road, 2002.
Lower, Wendy. *Hitler's Furies: German Women in the Nazi Killing Fields*. New York: Houghton Mifflin Harcourt, 2013.
Lulushi, Albert. *Donovan's Devils: OSS Commandos behind Enemy Lines—Europe, World War II*. New York: Arcade Publishing, 2016.

Macintyre, Ben. *Rogue Heroes: The History of the SAS, Britain's Secret Special Forces Unit That Sabotaged the Nazis and Changed the Nature of War*. New York: Crown, 2016.

Makepeace, Clare. *Captives of War: British Prisoners of War in Europe in the Second World War*. Cambridge: Cambridge University Press, 2017.

Mallmann, Klaus-Michael. "Nationalsozialistische Gewaltverbrechen Im Deutschen Reich." In *NS-Gewaltherrschaft: Beiträge Zur Historischen Forschung Und Juristischen Aufarbeitung*, vol. 11, edited by Alfred Gottwaldt, Norbert Kampe, and Peter Klein, 211–12. Berlin: Hentrich, 2005.

——. "'Volksjustiz gegen anglo-amerikanischen Mörder': Die Massaker an westalliierten Fliegern und Fallschirmspringern 1944/45." In *NS-Gewaltherrschaft: Beiträge Zur Historischen Forschung Und Juristischen Aufarbeitung*, vol. 11, edited by Alfred Gottwaldt, Norbert Kampe, and Peter Klein, 211–12. Berlin: Hentrich, 2005.

Matteson, Thomas T. (Commander, USCG). *An Analysis of the Circumstances Surrounding the Rescue and Evacuation of Allied Aircrew men from Yugoslavia, 1941–1945*. Air University Report No. 128. Air War College-Maxwell Air Force Base, Alabama, 1977.

McFarland, Stephan L. and Wesley Phillips Newton. *To Command the Sky: Battle for Air Superiority over Germany, 1942–1944*. Washington, D.C.: Smithsonian Institution Press, 1991.

McLaughlin, J. Kemp. *The Mighty Eighth in WWII: A Memoir*. Lexington: University Press of Kentucky, 2006.

McManus, John C. *Deadly Sky: The American Combat Airmen in World War II*. New York: Nal Caliber, 2016.

Mears, Dwight S. "Interned or Imprisoned?: The Successes and Failures of International Law In The Treatment of American Internees in Switzerland, 1943–45." Dissertation, University of North Carolina–Chapel Hill, 2012.

Merritt, Richard L. *Democracy Imposed: U.S. Occupation Policy and the German Public 1945–1949*. New Haven: Yale University Press, 1995.

Milgram, Stanley. *Obedience to Authority: An Experimental View*. London: Tavistock Publications, 1974.

Miller, Donald L. *Masters of the Air: America's Bomber Boys Who Fought the Air War against Nazi Germany*. New York: Simon & Schuster, 2006.

Miller, Scott. *Agent 110: An American Spymaster and the German Resistance in WWII*. New York: Simon and Schuster, 2017.

Mommsen, Hans. "Der Nationalsozialismus: Kumulative Radikalisierung und Selbstzerstörung des Regimes." In *Meyers Enzyklopädisches Lexikon*, vol. 16, 785–90. Mannheim: Inter Alia, 1976.

Morgan, Robert, and Ron Powers. *The Man Who Flew the Memphis Belle: Memoir of a WWII Bomber Pilot*. New York: Penguin Books, 2001.

Morris, Rob. *Untold Valor: Forgotten Stories of American Bomber Crews over Europe in World War II*. Washington, D.C.: Potomac Books, 2006.

Morrow, James D. *Order within Anarchy: The Laws of War as an International Institution*. Cambridge: Cambridge University Press, 2014.

Moser, Joseph F. *A Fighter Pilot in Buchenwald*. Bellingham: Edens Veil Media, 2009.

Mosse, George L. *Toward a Final Solution: A History of European Racism*. New York: Howard Fertig, 1997.

Moye, J. Todd. *Freedom Flyers: The Tuskegee Airmen of World War II*. Oxford: Oxford University Press, 2010.

Mrazek, Robert J. *To Kingdom Come: An Epic Saga of Survival in the Air War over Germany*. New York: Penguin Books, 2010.

Narayanaswami, Karthik. "Analysis of Nazi Propaganda: A Behavioral Study." https://blogs.harvard.edu/karthik/files/2011/04/HIST-1572-Analysis-of-Nazi-Propaganda-KNarayanaswami.pdf, accessed August 23, 2016.

Neave, Airey. *Little Cyclone*. London: Bitback Publishing, 1954.

Neitzel, Sönke, and Harald Welzer. *Soldaten: Protokolle vom Kämpfen, Töten und Sterben*. Frankfurt am Main: Fischer, 2011.

Neliba, Günter. *Lynchjustiz an amerikanischen Kriegsgefangenen in der Opelstadt Rüsselsheim (1944): Rekonstruktion einer der ersten Kriegsverbrecher-Prozesse in Deutschland nach Prozessakten (1945–1947)*. Frankfurt: Brandes and Apsel, 2000.

Nielsen, Major General Andreas L. "The Collection and Evaluation of Intelligence for the German Air Force High Command: Karlsruhe Study." Montgomery, AL: Maxwell Air Force Base, 1955. K113.107-17168.

Niethammer Lutz. *Die Mitlaüferfabrik: Die Entnazifizierung am Beispiel Bayerns*. Berlin: J. H. W. Dietz, 1982.

Nigro, Augusto. *Wolfsangel: A German City on Trial 1945–48*. Washington, DC: Brassey's, 2000.

Noakes, Jeremy, ed. *Nazism, 1919–1945*. Vol. 4, *The German Home Front in World War II*. Exeter: University of Exeter Press, 1998.

Noggle, Anne. *A Dance with Death: Soviet Airwomen in World War II*. College Station: Texas A&M University Press, 1994.

Nolzen, Armin. "The NSDAP, the War, and German Society." In *Germany and the Second World War*, vol. IX/I, edited by Jörg Echternkamp, 111–206. New York: Oxford University Press, 2008.

Norwood, Stephan H. *The Third Reich in the Ivory Tower*. New York: Cambridge University Press, 2009.

Nourse, Victoria. *In Reckless Hands*: Skinner v. Oklahoma *and the Near Triumph of American Eugenics*. New York: Norton, 2008.

O'Donnell, Patrick K. *Operatives, Spies, and Saboteurs: The Unknown Story of the Men and Women of World War II's OSS*. New York: Free Press, 2004.

O'Loughlin, John. "The Electoral Geography of Weimar Germany: Explanatory Spatial Data Analysis (ESPDA) of Protestant Support for the Nazi Party." *Society for Political Methodology* 10, no. 3 (2002): 217–43.

O'Loughlin, John, Colin Flint, and Luc Anselin. "The Geography of the Nazi Vote: Context, Confession, and Class in the Reichstag Election of 1930." *Annals of the Association of American Geographers* 84, no. 3 (1994): 351–80.

Olsen, Lynne, and Stanley Cloud. *A Question of Honor: The Kosciuszko Squadron; Forgotten Heroes of World War II*. New York: Vintage, 2003.

Ottis, Sherri Greene. *Silent Heroes: Downed Airmen and the French Underground*. Lexington: University of Kentucky Press, 2001.

Overy, Richard. *The Air War: 1939–1945*. Washington, DC: Potomac Books, 2005.

———. *The Bombing and the Bombed: Allied Air War over Europe, 1940–1945*. New York: Viking, 2013.

Pardo, Italo. *Morals of Legitimacy: Between Agency and the System*. New York: Berghahn, 2000.

Paris, John. *Pappy's War: A B-17 Gunner's World War II Memoir*. Bennington, VT: Merriam Press, 2005.

Paul, Gerhard, and Klaus-Michael Mallmann, eds. *Die Gestapo im Zweiten Weltkrieg: Heimatfront und "besetztes" Europa*. Darmstadt: Wissenschaftliche Buchgesellschaft, 2000.

———, eds. *Die Gestapo: Mythos und Realität*. Darmstadt: Wissenschaftliche Buchgesellschaft, 1995.

Pennington, Reina. *Wings, Women, and War: Soviet Airwomen in World War II Combat*. Lawrence: University Press of Kansas, 2001.

Peukert, Detlev J. K. *Inside Nazi Germany: Conformity, Opposition, and Racism in Everyday Life*. New Haven, CT: Yale University Press, 1987.

Piccigallo, Philip R. *The Japanese on Trial: Allied War Crimes Operations in the East, 1945–1951*. Austin: University of Texas Press, 1979.

Pitchfork, Graham. *Shot Down and on the Run: The RCAF and Commonwealth Aircrews Who Got Home from behind Enemy Lines 1940–1945*. Toronto: Dundurn Group, 2003.

Pratten, David, and Atreyee Sen, eds. *Global Vigilantes: Anthropological Perspectives on Justice and Violence*. London: Hurst, 2007.

Proctor, Tammy M. *Civilians in a World at War, 1914–1918*. New York: New York University Press, 2010.

Redding, Tony. *Bombing Germany: The Final Phase; The Destruction of Pforzheim and the Closing Months of Bomber Command's War*. South Yorkshire, UK: Pen & Sword Books, 2015.

Reifner, U., and B.-R. Sonnen, eds. *Strafjustiz und Polizei im Dritten Reich*. Frankfurt am Main: Campus, 1984.

Remarque, Erich. *All Quiet on the Western Front*. New York: Fawcett Books, 1987.

Reuter, Stefan. "'Operation No. 351'—Der 11. Mai 1944: Die Fliegende Festung des amerikanischen Piloten Marion Holbrook." In *Dillingen im Zweiten Weltkrieg: Eine Dokumentation der Dillinger Geschichtswerkstatt*, edited by Armin Jost and Stefan Reuter, 1–18. Dillingen, Germany: Geschichtswerkstatt, 2002.

Richard III, Oscar G. *Kriegie: An American POW in Germany*. Baton Rouge: Louisiana State University Press, 2000.

Richey, Robert J. *My Brother Glenn: A Prisoner of the Gestapo during World War II*. Bloomington, IN: Author House, 2011.

Riedel, Durwood. "The U.S. War Crimes Tribunals at the Former Dachau Concentration Camp: Lessons for Today." *Berkeley Journal of International Law* 24, no. 2 (2006): 554–609.

Rochlitz, Imre, and Joseph Rochlitz. *Accident of Fate: A Personal Account, 1938–1945*. Waterloo: Wilfrid Laurier University Press, 2011.

Rodger, Daniel. *Atlantic Crossings: Social Politics in a Progressive Age*. Cambridge: Harvard University Press, 1998.

Rollings, Charles. *After the Battle: Dulag Luft*. No. 106. London: Battle of Britain International Ltd, 1999.

Rückerl, Adalbert. *The Investigation of Nazi Crimes 1945–1978*. Translated by Derek Rutter. New York: Archon Books, 1980.

———. *NS-Verbrechen vor Gericht: Versuch einer Vergangenheitsbewältigung*. Heidelberg, Germany: C. F. Müller Juritischer, 1984.

Rüter, C. F. and D. W. de Mildt, eds. *DDR-Justiz und NS-Verbrechen: Sammlung Ostdeutsche Strafurteile wegen Nationalsozialistische Tötungsverbrechen, 1945–1999, Bd. 1–14*. Rüter: Amsterdam University Press, 1968–2012.

———. *Justiz und NS-Verbrechen: Sammlung Deutscher Strafurteile wegen Nationalsozialistische Tötungsverbrechen, 1945–1999, Bd. 1–49*. Rüter: Amsterdam University Press, 1968–2012.

Rumpf, Hans. *The Bombing of Germany*. Translated by Edward Fitzgerald. New York: Holt, Rinehart and Winston, 1962.

Saarpfalz-Blätter für Geschichte und Volkskunde, vol. 3, 1999.

Sagan, Günther. *Ostthüringen im Bombenkrieg 1939–1945*. Fulda: Michael Imhof, 2013.

Sakashita, Fumiko. "Lynching across the Pacific." In *Swift to Wrath: Lynching in Global Historical Perspective*, edited by William D. Carrigan and Christopher Waldrep, 181–214. Charlottesville: University of Virginia Press, 2013.

Samuel, Wolfgang W. E. *The War of Our Childhood: Memories of World War II*. Jackson: University Press of Mississippi, 2002.

Schaffer, Ronald. *Wings of Judgement: American Bombing in World War II*. Oxford: Oxford University Press, 1985.

Schivelbach, Wolfgang. *Three New Deals: Reflections on Roosevelt's America, Mussolini's Italy, and Hitler's Germany, 1933–1939*. Translated by Jefferson Chase. New York: Metropolitan, 2006.

Schmidt-Lux, Thomas. "Vigilantismus als politische Gewalt. Eine Typologie." *BEHEMOTH: A Journal of Civilization* 6, no. 1 (2013): 99–117.

Schmiechen-Ackermann, Detlef. *"Volksgemeinschaft": Mythos, wirkungsmächtige soziale Verheißung oder soziale Realität im 'Dritten Reich'?* Paderborn, Germany: Ferdinand Schöningh, 2012.

Schnatz, Helmut. "Lynchmorde an Fliegern." In *Kriegsverbrechen in Europa und im Nahen Osten im 20. Jahrhundert*, edited by Franz W. Seidlerand and Alfred M. de Zayas, 118–21. Hamburg: E. S. Mittler & Sohn GmbH, 2002.

Sebald, W. G. *On the Natural History of Destruction*. Translated by Anthea Bell. New York: Random House, 1999.

Seidler, Franz W. *Deutscher Volkssturm: Das letzte Aufgebot 1944/45*. Munich: Herbig, 1989.

Šelhaus, Edi. *Evasion and Repatriation: Slovene Partisans and Rescued American Airmen in World War II*. Manhattan: Sunflower University Press, 1993.

Sheridan, Jerome W. *Airmen in the Belgian Resistance: Gerald E. Sorensen and the Transatlantic Alliance*. Jefferson, NC: McFarland, 2014.

Shirer, William L. *Berlin Diary: The Journal of a Foreign Correspondent, 1934–1941*. New York: Rosetta Books, 1968.

Siebenborn, Kerstin. *Der Volkssturm im Süden Hamburgs 1944/45*. Hamburg: Verein für Hamburgische Geschichte, 1988.

Siemens, Daniel. *Stormtroopers: A New History of Hitler's Brownshirts*. New Haven, CT: Yale University Press, 2017.

Sigel, Robert. *Im Interesse der Gerechtigkeit: Die Dachauer Kriegsverbrecherprozesse 1945–1948*. Frankfurt: Campus, 1992.

Simmons, Kenneth W. *Kriegie*. New York: Thomas Nelson & Sons, 1960.

Simon, Marie Jalowicz. *Underground in Berlin: A Young Woman's Extraordinary Tale of Survival in the Heart of Nazi Germany*. New York: Bay Back Books, 2016.

Sirianni, Ralph E., and Patricia I. Brown. *POW #3959: Memoir of a World War II Airman Shot Down over Germany*. Jefferson, NC: McFarland, 2006.

Sollbach, Gerhard E. *Sie wollten die Heimat schützen*. Bochum: Project, 2010.

Sommers, Stan. *The European Story*. Marshfield, WI: American Ex-Prisoners of War, 1980.

Snyder, Timothy. *Bloodlands: Europe between Hitler and Stalin*. New York: Basic Books, 2012.

Spencer, Elaine Glovka. *Police and the Social Order in German Cities: The Düsseldorf District, 1848–1914*. DeKalb: Northern Illinois University Press, 1992.
Stahl, Hans-Günther. *Der Luftkreig über dem Raum Hanau: 1939–1945*. Hanau: VDS Verlagsdruckerei Schmidt, 2015.
Stargardt, Nicholas. *The German War: A Nation under Arms, 1939–1945*. New York: Basic Books, 2015.
———. "Legitimacy through War?" In *Beyond the Racial State: Rethinking Nazi Germany*, edited by Devin O. Pendas, Mark Roseman, and Richard F. Wetzell, 402–30. Cambridge: Cambridge University Press, 2017.
Staub, Ervin. "Genocide and Mass Killings: Origins, Preventions, Healing and Reconciliation." *Political Psychology* 12, no. 2 (2000): 367–83.
———. *The Roots of Evil: The Origins of Genocide and Other Group Violence*. New York: Cambridge University Press, 1989.
Steber, Martina, and Bernhard Gotto, eds. *Visions of Community in Nazi Germany: Social Engineering and Private Lives*. Oxford: Oxford University Press, 2014.
Stelbrink, Wolfgang. *Die Kreisleiter der NSDAP in Westfalen und Lippe Versuch einer Kollektivbiographie*. Münster: Nordrhein-Westfälischen Staatsarchiv Münster, 2003.
Stephenson, Jill. "The Home Front in 'Total War': Women in Germany and Britain in the Second World War." In *A World at Total War: Global Conflict and the Politics of Destruction, 1937–1945*, edited by Roger Chickering, Stig Förster, and Bernd Greiner, 207–32. Cambridge: Cambridge University Press, 2004.
Strachen, Hew. "Total War: The Conduct of War, 1939–1945." In *World at Total War: Global Conflict and the Politics of Destruction, 1937–1945*, edited by Roger Chickering, Stig Förster, and Bernd Greiner, 33–52. Cambridge: Cambridge University Press, 2005.
Strobl, Gerwin. *Bomben auf Oberdonau: Luftkrieg und Lynchmorde an alliierten Fliegern im "Heimatgau des Führers."* Linz, Austria: Oberösterreichisches Landesarchiv, 2014.
———. *The Germanic Isle: Nazi Perceptions of Britain*. Cambridge: Cambridge University Press, 2000.
Süß, Dietmar. *Tod aus der Luft*. München: Siedler, 2011.
Süß, Dietmar, and Winfried Süß. *Das "Dritte Reich": Eine Einführung*. Munich: Pantheon, 2008.
Tanner, Stephan. *Refuge from the Reich: American Airmen and Switzerland during World War II*. New York: Sarpedon, 2000.
Thurner, Paul W., Andre Klima, and Helmut Küchenhoff. "Agricultural Structure and the Rise of the Nazi Party Reconsidered." *Political Geography* 44 (2015): 50–63.
Thurston, Robert W. *Lynching: American Mob Murder in Global Perspective*. Farnham: Ashgate, 2011.
———. "Lynching and Legitimacy: Toward a Global Description of Mob Murder." In *Globalizing Lynching History: Vigilantism and Extralegal Punishment from an International Perspective*, edited by Manfred Berg and Simon Wendt, 69–86. New York: Palgrave Macmillan, 2011.
Toliver, Raymond F. *The Interrogator: The Story of Hanns Joachim Scharff, Master Interrogator of the Luftwaffe*. New York: Schiffer Publishing, 1997.
Tooze, Adam. *The Deluge: The Great War, American, and the Remaking of the Global Order*. New York: Penguin, 2014.
Tremble, Lee, and Jeremy Dronfield. *Beyond the Call: The True Story of One World War II Pilot's Covert Mission to Rescue POWs on the Eastern Front*. New York: Penguin, 2015.

Tsang, Jo-Ann. "Moral Rationalization and the Integration of Situational Factors and Psychological Processes in Immoral Behavior." *Review of General Psychology* 6, no. 1 (2002): 34–35.

Tyas, Stephan. *SS-Major Horst Kopkow: From the Gestapo to British Intelligence*. London: Fonthill, 2017.

Tzvetan Todorov. *Facing the Extreme: Moral Life in the Concentration Camp*. New York: Henry Holt, 1996.

Ueberschär, Gerd R. *Der Nationalsozialismus vor Gericht*. Frankfurt am Main: Fischerverlag, 1999.

Ute, Stiepani. "Die Dachauer Prozesse und ihre Bedeutung jm Rahmen der Alliierten Strafverfolgung von NS-Verbrechen." In *Der Nationalsozialismus Vor Gericht: Die Alliierten Prozesse Gegen Kriegsverbrecher Und Soldaten 1943–1952*, edited by Gerd R. Ueberschaer, 227–35. Frankfurt am Main: Fischer, 1999.

von Benda-Beckmann, Bas. *A German Catastrophe? German Historians and the Allied Bombings, 1945–2010*. Amsterdam: Amsterdam University Press, 2010.

Vordermayer, Margaretha Franziska. *Justice for the Enemy? Die Verteidigung deustcher Kriegsverbrecher durch britische Offiziere in Militärgerichtsprozessen nach dem Zweiten Weltkrieg (1945–1949)*. Baden Baden: Nomos, 2019.

Vourkoutiotis, Vasilis. *Prisoners of War and the German High Command: The British and American Experience*. New York: Palgrave Macmillan, 2003.

Wachsmann, Nichlaus. *Hitler's Prisons: Legal Terror in Nazi Germany*. New Haven, CT: Yale University Press, 2004.

Wagner, Patrick. *Hitlers Kriminalisten: Die deutsche Kriminalpolizei und der Nationalsozialismus*. Munich: C. H. Beck, 2002.

———. *Volksgemeinschaft ohne Verbrecher: Konzeptionen und Praxis der Kriminalpolizei in der Zeit der Weimarer Republik und des Nationalsozialismus*. Hamburg: Hans Christians, 1996.

Walzer, Michael, *Just and Unjust Wars*. New York: Basic Books, 1977.

Watt, George. *Escape from Hitler's Europe: An American Airman behind Enemy Lines*. Lexington: University Press of Kentucky, 1990.

Weber, Edwin Ernst, ed. *Opfer des Unrechts: Stigmatisierung, Verfolgung und Vernichtung von Gegnern durch die NS-Gewaltherrschaft an Fallbeispielen aus Oberschwaben*. Stuttgart: Jan Thorbeck, 2009.

Webster, Charles and Noble Frankland. *The Strategic Air Offensive against Germany*, vol. 4. London: Naval and Military Press, 2006.

Weinberg, Gerhard. *Hitler's Foreign Policy, 1933–1939: The Road to World War II*. New York: Enigma Books, 2010.

———. *A World at Arms: A Global History of World War II*. Cambridge: Cambridge University Press, 2005.

Weingartner, James J. "Americans, Germans, and War Crimes: Converging Narratives from 'the Good War.'" *Journal of American History* 94, no. 4 (2008): 1164–83.

———. *Americans, Germans and War Crimes Justice: Law, Memory, and "The Good War."* Santa Barbara: Praeger, 2011.

Welch, David. "Nazi Propaganda and the *Volksgemeinschaft*: Constructing a People's Community." *Journal of Contemporary History* 39, no. 2 (2004): 213–38.

———, ed. *Nazi Propaganda: The Power and the Limitations*. London: Routledge, 2014.

———. *The Third Reich: Politics and Propaganda*. New York: Routledge, 1993.

———. *World War II Propaganda: Analyzing the Art of Persuasion during Wartime*. Santa Barbara: ABC-CLIO, 2017.

Welzer, Harald. *Täter: Wie aus ganz normalen Menschen Massenmörder warden*. Frankfurt am Main: S. Fischer, 2005.

Werle, Gerhard. *Justiz-Strafrecht und polizeiliche Verbrechensbekämpfung im Dritten Reich*. Berlin: de Gruyter, 1989.

Wernette, Dee R. "Explaining the Nazi Vote: The Findings and Limits of Ecological Analysis." Working Paper #134. Kean College of New Jersey, 1976. Copies available from Center for Research on Social Organizations, University of Michigan, https://deepblue.lib.umich.edu/bitstream/handle/2027.42/50909/134.pdf?sequence=1.

Westricher Heimatblaetter Kusel, vol. 4, 1995.

Wette, Wolfram, ed. *Zivilcourage. Empörte: Helfer und Retter aus Wehrmacht, Polizei und SS*. Frankfurt am Main: Fischer Taschenbuch, 2004.

Wetzell, Richard. *Inventing the Criminal: A History of German Criminology, 1880–1945*. Chapel Hill: University of North Carolina Press, 2000.

Whitlock Flint. *Given Up for Dead*. New York: Basic Books, 2009.

Whitman, James Q. *Hitler's American Model: The United States and the Making of Nazi Race Law*. Princeton, NJ: Princeton University Press, 2017.

———. "Of Corporation, Fascism, and the First New Deal." *American Journal of Comparative Law*, no. 39 (1991): 747–78.

Widfeldt, Bo, and Rolph Wegmann. *Making for Sweden: The United States Army Air Force; The Story of Allied Airmen Who Took Sanctuary in Neutral Sweden*. Walton-on-Thames, UK: Air Research Publications, 1998.

Wiesen, S. Johnathan. "American Lynching in the Nazi Imagination: Race and Extra-Legal Violence in 1930s Germany." *German History* 36, no. 1 (2017): 38–59.

Wildt, Michael. "'Volksgemeinschaft': Eine Antwort auf Ian Kershaw." *Zeithistorische Forschungen/Studies in Contemporary History*, online edition, 8 (2011). www.zeithistorische-forschungen.de/16126041-Wildt-2011.

Wilhelm, Friedrich. *Die Polizei im NS-Staat: Die Geschichte ihrer Organisation im Überblick*. Paderborn, Germany: Ferdinand Schöningh, 1997.

Williams, Kenneth Daniel. "The Saga of Murder Inc." World War II—Prisoners of War—Stalag Luft I. http://www.merkki.com/murderinc.htm.

Wilson, Kevin. *Men of Air: The Doomed Youth of Bomber Command*. London: Phoenix Ebook, 2008.

Wingham, Tom. *Halifax Down!: On the Run from the Gestapo, 1944*. London: Grub Street, 2009.

Wittmann, Rebecca. "Tainted Law: The West German Judiciary and the Prosecution of Nazi War Criminals." In *Atrocities on Trial: Historical Perspectives on the Politics of Prosecuting War Crimes*, edited by Patricia Heberer and Jürgen Matthäus, 211–30. Lincoln: University of Nebraska Press, 2008.

Wolk, Bruce H. *Jewish Aviators in World War II: Personal Narratives of American Men and Women*. Jefferson, NC: McFarland, 2016.

Wood, Amy Louise. *Lynching and Spectacle: Witnessing Racial Violence in America, 1890–1940*. Chapel Hill: University of North Carolina Press, 2009.

Wyden, Peter. *Stella: One Woman's True Tale of Evil, Betrayal, and Survival in Hitler's Germany*. New York: Anchor Book, 1992.

Wylie, Neville. *Barbed Wire Diplomacy: Britain, Germany, and the Politics of Prisoners of War 1939–1945*. Oxford: Oxford University Press, 2010.

Yavnai, Elisabeth M. "Military Justice: The U.S. Army War Crimes Trials in Germany, 1944–47." PhD dissertation, University of London, 2007.

———. "Military Justice: The U.S. Army War Crimes Trials in Germany, 1944–47." In *Atrocities on Trial: Historical Perspectives on the Politics of Prosecuting War Crimes*, edited by Patricia Heberer and Jürgen Matthäus, 49–75. Lincoln: University of Nebraska Press, 2008.

Zimbardo, Philip G. "The Psychology of Evil: A Situationist Perspective on Recruiting Good People to Engage in Anti-Social Acts." *Japanese Journal of Social Psychology* 11, no. 2 (1995): 125–33.

Zimmer, Klaus. "Die Fliegende Festung 'Solid Sender' des amerikanischen Piloten Merlin Chardi abgestuerzt am 25. Februar 1944 bei Alschbach." In *Saarpfalz: Blaetter fuer Geschichte und Volkskunde*, vol. 3, 1999.

Zimmer, Klaus, and Edward D. McKenzie. "Die Fliegende Festung bei Bubach im Ostertal abgestuerzt am 24. April 1944." In *Westricher Heimatblaetter Kusel*, vol. 4, 1995.

Zink, Harold. *The United States in Germany, 1944–55*. Princeton, NJ: D. Van Nostrand, 1957.

Newspapers (Chronological Order)

New York Times. "Color Line in Berlin." October 4, 1908.

Los Angeles Harold. "Probe Lynching of Illinois German." April 18, 1918.

New York Times. "Germany Protests Prager Lynching." June 13, 1918.

New York Times. "Bitter at Attacks on Germans Here." June 17, 1918.

New York Times. "President Demands That Lynchings End." July 27, 1918.

New York Times. "Germans Magnify Lynchings Here." September 9, 1918.

New York Times. "Lynchings Shock People of Berlin." January 20, 1919.

New York Times. "Germans Threaten Rhine Lynchings." February 8, 1923.

New York Times. "Fight for Doomed Negroes." June 1, 1931.

New York Times. "Ask Pardon for 8 Negroes." March 27, 1932.

New York Times. "Appeals in Germany in Scottsboro Case." May 11, 1932.

New York Times. "Hitlerism Likened to Lynch Law Here." October 31, 1933.

New York Times. "British Gratified at Verdict on Fire." December 24, 1933.

New York Times. "All of Rebels Prisoners." July 26, 1934.

New York Times. "German Press Cites Race Hatred in U.S." August 30, 1935.

New York Times. "Methodists Find Liberty Ebbing." January 20, 1936.

Völkischer Beobachter. "Verfeinerte Demokratie = Lynchjustiz?" January 12, 1938.

Goebbels, Joseph. "Was will eigentlich Amerika." *Völkischer Beobachter*, January 21, 1939.

New York Times. "Nazi Guards 'Lynch' Two for Attempting to Escape." December 11, 1939.

San Bernardino Sun. "Revenge Pledged for Executed Fliers: Barbaric Japs Murder Captive Tokyo Raiders." April 22, 1943.

Army News (Darwin, Australia). "Jap Murders of U.S. Airmen Horrifies United Nations; Americans Angry." April 23, 1943.

Breckenridge (TX) American. "Believed Executed by Japs." April 23, 1943.

Daily Illini (Urbana-Champaign). "Nation's Anger Rises at Jap Murders." April 23, 1943.

Madera (TX) Tribune. "Bombers to Blast Japan Near Future." April 23, 1943.

Daily Illini. "World News at a Glance." April 23, 1943.
San Bernardino Sun. "Churchill Vows R.A.F. to Help Avenge Murder." April 24, 1943.
San Bernardino Sun. "German, Italy May Follow Jap Precedent in Executing Fliers." April 25, 1943.
Advocate (Burnie, Australia). "R.A.F. Will Help to Avenge Murdered U.S. Pilots." April 26, 1943.
Examiner (Launceston, Australia). "Axis Barbarity May Extend." April 27, 1943.
New York Times. "Flyers' Execution Urged: Rome Newspapers Call for Death Penalty for Our Bombers." April 30, 1943.
Queensland Times (Ipswich, Australia). "Japanese Appeal to America to Stop Tokio Raids." April 30, 1943.
New York Times. "Axis Reprisals on Flyers Are Demanded by Gayda." May 4, 1943.
Western Mail (Perth, Australia). "Allied Airmen Attacked Civilians in Italy." May 6, 1943.
Virginia Monocle. "U.S. Flyers Executed." May 14, 1943.
San Bernardino Sun. "Natives Betray Allied Airmen, Nurses to Japs." May 16, 1943.
Völkischer Beobachter (Berlin). "Jüdische Weltherrschaft auf den Spitzen der USA-Bajonette." August 10, 1943.
Brooklyn Daily Eagle. "Mobs Enraged Nazis Threatened Yank Airmen." October 21, 1943.
Daily Sun (San Bernardino). "Angry Germans Lynch American Bombing Fliers." October 22, 1943.
Mexia (TX) Weekly Herold. "Flier Tells How Yanks Lynched." October 22, 1943.
New York Times. "Citizens Menaced Hamburg Bombers." October 22, 1943.
Madera Tribune. "Germans Stone Yanks." October 28, 1943.
Völkischer Beobachter (Berlin). "USA—Luftgangster nennen sich selbst 'Mordverein.'" December 20, 1943.
New York Times. "Nazis Threaten Reprisal Trials on American and British Flyers." December 23, 1943.
Daily Banner (Greencastle, IN). "Death Facing Allied Airmen in Nazi Hands." December 24, 1943.
Jewish Criterion (Pittsburgh). "Jews Head List of U.S. Fliers Facing Nazi Trials." January 7, 1944.
Das Schwarze Korps (Germany). "Die Gefahr des Amerikanismus." March 14, 1944.
Fürholzer, Edmund. "Was ist englisch am Amerikanismus?" *Völkischer Beobachter* (Berlin), April 14–16, 1944.
Böttiger, Th."Die Spinnen Roosevelts." *Völkischer Beobachter* (Berlin), May 12–13, 1944.
Völkischer Beobachter (Berlin). "Von Washington bis Roosevelt: Geschichte der USA im Spiegel ihrer Briefmarken." May 19, 1944.
Brighamb, Daniel T. "Goebbels Invites Attacks on Fliers." *New York Times*. May 28, 1944.
Jewish Criterion. "Goebbels Invites Attacks on Flyers." May 28, 1944
The Times (London). "Goebbels on 'Murder' by Allied Airmen." May 28, 1944.
Goebbels, Joseph. "Ein Wort zum feindlichen Luftterror." *Völkischer Beobachter (Munich)*, May 28, 1944.
Palestine Post (Jerusalem). "Dr. Goebbels Incites to Murder." May 29, 1944.
Breckenridge American. "Five Yank Airmen Lynched by Nazis." May 30, 1944.

New York Times. "Flyers Reported Lynched in Reich." May 31, 1944.
Madera Tribune. "Huns Lynch Yank Airman." May 31, 1944.
New York Times. "Germany Admits Fliers' Lynchings." June 1, 1944.
New York Times. "Stimson Is Silent on Nazi 'Lynchings.'" June 2, 1944.
Army News (Darwin, Australia). "Nazis Wild Outburst on Airmen." June 4, 1944.
Jewish Criterion. "Urge Lynchings of Jewish Flyers." June 6, 1944.
Chicago Defender. "People and Places." June 10, 1944.
Völkischer Beobachter (Berlin). "Roosevelts Tiefflieger gegen Frauen und Kinder." June 14, 1944.
The Mercury (Hobart, Australia). "Reprisals Urged Against Japs: Murder of Airmen Angers American Public." July 17, 1944.
New York Times. "Reprisal on Enemy Sought." July 20, 1944.
New York Times. "Nazis Rebuff Eden on Slain Captives." July 23, 1944.
New York Times. "Prussian Killings Pressed by Nazis: Himmler Also Reported to Have Ordered Slaying of Allied Flyers Downed in Reich." July 27, 1944.
Westdeutscher Beobachter (Eupen). "Feindlicher Luftterror schon seit 1914." August 24, 1944.
San Antonio Register. "Lynchers at Work in Tennessee and Japan." December 1, 1944.
New York Times. "Nazi Leader Corps Splits Crime Court." December 18, 1945.
Killinger, Steffan. "Der Fliegermord von Weisenbach und ObertsroT." *Badisches Tagblatt*, August 9, 2011.
Army News. "WWII Army Aircrew Laid to Rest." October 26, 2011. https://www.army.mil/article/68064/wwii_army_aircrew_laid_to_rest.
Thüringer Allgemeine (Erfurt, Germany). "Lost Airmen und Ex-Häftling des KZ Buchenwald erinnert sich." April 16, 2012.
The Telegraph. "The Women Who Stole Downed German Airman's Silk Parachute to Make Knickerbockers." January 10, 2013.
Thüringer Allgemeine. "Ums Überleben gekämpft: Buchenwald gedenkt alliierter Flieger." April 4, 2014.
Thüringer Allgemeine. "KZ-Gedenken in Weimar: Vier ehemalige Flieger mit dabei." April 10, 2014.
Thüringer Allgemeine. "69. Buchenwald-Gedenkfeier: Vier lebensbejahende Zeugnisse." April 14, 2014.
Kessen, Hermann. "In 45 Tagen Gestapo-Haft den Freund nicht verraten." *Lingener Tagespost* (Lingen, Germany), November 2, 2015.

Magazines

Das Schwarze Korps. http://research.calvin.edu/german-propaganda-archive/index.htm, accessed March 6, 2015.
Kladderadatsch, Berlin, January 1942–May 1944. http://digi.ub.uni-heidelberg.de/diglit/kla.
Lustige Blätter. http://research.calvin.edu/german-propaganda-archive/index.htm, accessed March 6, 2015.

Websites

"Stalag Luft I—Prison Camp Graphics." http://www.b24.net/powStoriesLuft1toons.htm, accessed November 12, 2015.

"Capt. Chester E. Coggeshall Jr." http://www.station131.co.uk/55th/Pilots/343rd%20Pilots/Coggeshall%20Chester%20E.%20Jr.%20Capt.htm, accessed January 6, 2018.

"Cleveland WWII Airman Receives Funeral in Willoughby." *News-Herald*, May 2, 2015. https://www.news-herald.com/news/ohio/cleveland-wwii-airman-receives-funeral-in-willoughby/article_68982449-1428-5329-8ba7-577a98993fab.html.

"Ghost Train." World War Two Escape and Evasion. http://www.conscript-heroes.com/escapelines/EEIE-Articles/Art-17-Ghost-Train.htm, accessed August 26, 2017.

"Das Netz der Gestapo." Haus der Geschichte, Baden-Württemberg. http://www.geschichtsort-hotel-silber.de/das-netz-der-gestapo/europa/bds-fuer-die-operationszonen-alpenvorland-und-adriatisches-kuestenland-in-triest/, accessed September 12, 2017.

"Major Cyrus E. Manierre." World War II—Prisoners of War—Stalag Luft I. http://www.merkki.com/manierrecyrus.htm, accessed March 6, 2015.

"Remains of Fallen WWII Airman Returned to Family for Burial." Stars and Stripes, August 23, 2012, https://www.stripes.com/news/europe/germany/remains-of-fallen-wwii-airman-returned-to-family-for-burial-1.186673.

"Remains of Pilot Shot Down during WWII to be Buried in N.Y." CBS News, November 28, 2017. https://www.cbsnews.com/news/robert-mains-pilot-shot-down-wwii-remains-n-y-burial/.

Index

Page locators in italics indicate figures and tables.

KEVIN T HALL is a postdoctoral researcher at the Ruhr-Universtiät Bochum, Germany. He was a Fulbright grantee in Cologne in 2013–2014 and obtained his PhD from Central Michigan University in 2018. In 2019, he was a postdoctoral research historian at the Defense Prisoner of War/Missing in Action Accounting Agency (DPAA) in Honolulu, where he assisted the agency in accounting for US servicemen missing from past conflicts.

www.ingramcontent.com/pod-product-compliance
Lightning Source LLC
Chambersburg PA
CBHW051218150426
42812CB00053BA/2507